FINANCING EDUCATION IN A CLIMATE OF CHANGE

FINANCING EDUCATION IN A CLIMATE OF CHANGE

Fifth Edition

Percy E. Burrup
Brigham Young University

Vern Brimley, Jr.
Adjunct, Brigham Young University

Rulon R. Garfield
Brigham Young University

Allyn and Bacon, Inc.
Boston   London   Toronto   Sydney   Tokyo   Singapore

Library of Congress Cataloging-in-Publication Data

Burrup, Percy E., 1910–1986
    Financing education in a climate of change / Percy E. Burrup, Vern
Brimley, Jr., Rulon R. Garfield.—5th ed.
      p. cm.
    Includes bibliographical references and index.
    ISBN 0-205-14624-4
    1. Education—United States—Finance.   I. Brimley, Vern.
II. Garfield, Rulon R.   III. Title.
LB2825.B86   1993
379.1'21'0973—dc20   92-26847
                                                CIP

Printed in the United States of America
10 9 8 7 6 5 4 3 2 1   96 95 94 93 92 91

To Ora, Dawn, and Shirley

Preface

As in the previous edition of *Financing Education in a Climate of Change*, the fifth edition reflects the dynamic nature of school finance. The fourth edition was influenced greatly by "A Nation at Risk" and other national reports that resulted in a surge of support for education reform. As costs were determined, however, a retrenchment in funding followed and the road to reform was hampered. The fifth edition reflects the change from reform to *restructuring* as the governors of the states continue to be more actively involved in the education movement, coupled with the federal government promulgating national level goals detailed in *AMERICA 2000*. The courts have continued to be active with the equity issue, forcing states to analyze the structure of education finance. The challenges in Montana, Kentucky, Texas, and New Jersey have required change and served as a warning to other states to study their finance program in relation to their state constitutions. Business and industry have emerged as partners in education, with leaders emphasizing that education is too valuable to leave to educators. Administrators are entering partnerships with caution, analyzing what account-ability might be required if this resource is utilized. With greater state funding being the trend, the traditional role of the local board of education is being challenged. The call for choice is broadening the parameters of public money being expended in the private domain, including church-sponsored schools. The implications from demographic and social factors are having an impact on school districts throughout the country. The national economy, including debt, deficit financing, and the "peace bonus," will greatly influence school finance.

This edition maintains the philosophy of its predecessors: that education is an investment in human capital. Reform in school finance systems is still overdue in many states, even though progress continues to be made. Greater state participation in financing education—in the form of district power equalization or even full-state funding—is to be anticipated in future school finance formulas.

The development of school finance theory and practice is traced from the early period of complete local school funding, through various other plans, to present-day alternatives that involve greater equality of educational opportunity for students and greater equity for taxpayers. The concept of providing equal funds per weighted pupil unit is emphasized, taking into consideration the relative costs of educating individual students and providing variable-cost programs.

The principle of equalization of educational opportunity stands out as a dominant characteristic of American education. This ideal has not in any sense been totally achieved on a nationwide scale, but increasing clarification of the principle and increasing emphasis have recently carried it to the point of actual practice in a number of states. Democracy is best served by extending to all children an equal minimum opportunity to attend schools adequate for the achievement of self-realization, economic efficiency, civic responsibility, and effectiveness in human relationships.

Some of the unsolved problems of financing public education include providing high-quality education that is equitable to all students regardless of individual differences, place of residence, or the degree of parental affluence, and providing adequate funds with maximum fairness to all taxpayers. The text explores areas such as adequate financing of urban school districts, legal ways to keep public (as well as nonpublic) schools operating in the face of rapidly accelerating costs, and the condemnation leveled at the property tax by many people—in spite of its fundamental role in providing local school revenue.

The volume is intended as a text for a beginning course in school finance. However, practicing school administrators, teachers, school board members, and others interested in school finance will find information in the volume that will stimulate their thinking on how to finance education adequately and equitably. Since the chief school administrator is responsible for the overall school program and the financial reporting of the school district, some elementary aspects of school business administration are included.

The posture is static in some areas of education. In a brief five-year span, since the printing of the fourth edition, there have been many changes in school finance issues that have been covered in this new volume. The authors recognize and regret the fact that the problems involved in collecting, summarizing, and publishing school finance data at all levels make it impossible for any textbook to be completely up-to-date.

The authors take this opportunity to thank readers, instructors, and students who have made comments for the improvement of the previous editions and those who have graciously allowed the use of some of their materials. Special thanks is given to the late Percy Burrup, who is deeply missed in school finance circles and who made this work possible.

Vern Brimley, Jr.
Rulon R. Garfield

Contents

CHAPTER 3   FINANCING EDUCATION EQUITABLY

CHAPTER 4   SOURCES OF REVENUE

CHAPTER 5   ERODING LOCAL CONTROL

CHAPTER 6   EDUCATION: A STATE FUNCTION

CHAPTER 7   FEDERAL INTEREST IN EDUCATION

CHAPTER 8   THE INFLUENCE AND CLIMATE OF THE COURTS

CHAPTER 9   PATTERNS FOR DEVELOPING SCHOOL FINANCE SYSTEMS

CHAPTER 10   PUBLIC FUNDS AND NONPUBLIC SCHOOLS

CHAPTER 11   FINANCING SCHOOL FACILITIES

CHAPTER 12   ADMINISTERING THE SCHOOL BUDGET

CHAPTER 13   ACCOUNTING AND AUDITING

CHAPTER 14   PROPERTY, RISK MANAGEMENT, AND INSURANCE

CHAPTER 15   PERSONNEL ADMINISTRATION AND SCHOOL FINANCE

CHAPTER 16   THE ROAD AHEAD IN SCHOOL FINANCE

Chapter *1*

THE ECONOMICS OF EDUCATION

We must recognize the economic consequences of our educational policies. We have no choice but to make a significant investment in the human capital required to keep us competitive. —WALLACE G. WILKENSON, 1990

Many taxpayers view public education as an unnecessarily large industry whose high costs result in excessive tax burdens on many people and too large a drain on the public treasury. In their haste to condemn the system, many of them have forgotten that education has had much to do with the great progress and remarkable economic development of this country over the two centuries of its existence. Some have not yet become convinced that education is not really a cost but is, more accurately, an investment in human capital.

Educators and economists have not always recognized the close relationship between their disciplines. Recognition and understanding of the relationship between public education and the field of economics become more crucial as spiraling expenditures for education continue. That being true, educational leaders at all levels cannot continue to give mere fleeting glances and incidental references to fundamental economic theories and principles if they are to be effective in helping solve, or in reducing, the complex and persistent problems involved in financing education adequately and equitably. Some knowledge of economics and its partnership role with education is therefore deemed to be important for school finance students as well as practitioners. For that reason, this book begins with a brief discussion of some of the fundamental principles and concepts of economics that have practical application to the broad field of school finance. Numerous excellent references are cited at the end of the chapter for those who may desire to go into the subject more deeply.

ECONOMICS: ITS MAJOR CONCERNS

In simple terms, economics is the study of the production, allocation, and consumption of goods and services for the satisfaction of human wants. It is concerned with economic goods: material as well as nonmaterial (service) goods, consumer as well as producer goods, durable and nondurable goods, and single-use as well as multiple-use goods. Economics involves and relates the often unlimited human desires to obtaining and using the limited goods and resources available. Rogers and Ruchlin describe the issues involved in economics in the following:

> Economics is concerned with two primary phenomena, desires and resources. Because desires are psychological and physical, economics deals with man; because resources are constructed from matter, economics deals with nature. Economic issues involve a basic confrontation between opposing forces: desires and resources, or man and environment. The confrontation is brought into being primarily because desires are infinite, whereas resources are finite. The history of civilization is a continuous illustration of man's wants exceeding his means; and it appears safe to predict that as affluent as our society may yet become there will always be unfulfilled wants.[1]

Some aspects of the relation of education to economics are shown in Figure 1-1. Education can be seen to be an economic (not free), nonmaterial good (service), durable (if in regular use), multiple-use, and a producer as well as a consumer good (service).

Since primary interest here is with financing public education, the present treatment of economics will deal largely with its relation to the allocation of scarce resources to competitive consumers in the public sector. What will be the effect on the economy if the rapidly increasing demands for greater spending in the public sector are met? Is education to be considered an expensive luxury that has reached such proportions that it threatens the foundation of the nation's economic structure? Or is it, as most educators declare, an investment in human capital that stimulates rather than retards economic growth? These and many other questions relating to education and economics must be answered if education is to continue to serve its purpose. Some of the "answers" of past years that pointed the finger of blame at education for stifling the economy and overburdening the tax-paying public will need to be reanswered in terms of the needs of the future.

The major concern of economics is related to the proper and satisfactory allocation of scarce resources—goods and services—to the individuals, households, and institutions that desire and need them. Since there is no infallible law or formula for this distribution, the economist must become concerned with the anticipated results of resource allocation with the many alternative choices for such distribution. Goods or services allocated to one segment of the economy

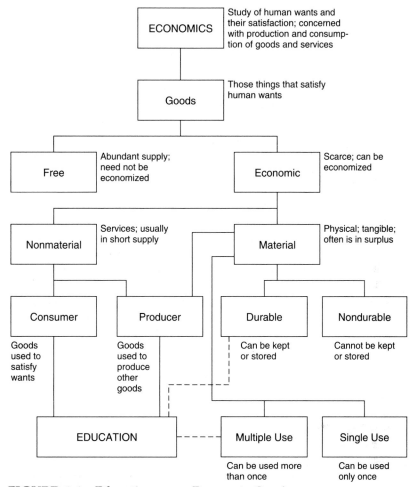

FIGURE 1-1 Education as an Economic Good

are, of course, being denied to another. The economist must determine the proper mix of such distribution that will bring maximum satisfaction to the various segments of society.

ECONOMICS AND SOCIAL PROGRESS

There are diverse ways of measuring or rating the degree of advancement or upward progress of a society. One way is to apply the economic dimension that attempts to determine the degree or percentage of total human effort that is being diverted to production and allocation of the material goods required for survival, such as food, clothing, and shelter. This measure of human efforts is then compared with that devoted to producing nonmaterial goods that make life more comfortable but are not required for survival. Societies at the low end of the social-progress continuum devote all or nearly all their efforts to producing essential material goods. As societies move up the scale of civilization, the percentage of human effort expended to produce services and goods not required for subsistence increases.

There is no valid reason or rationale that defends unlimited or surplus production and consumption of primary material goods beyond those required for survival or subsistence in any society. Most culturally advancing societies soon reach the limit in the production of material goods that are required for the absolute necessities for existence. Surpluses of durable goods for emergency purposes are often necessary, and production of these is justified before the forces of production are directed to those goods and services that are classified as luxuries. At this point, further human effort in producing necessities becomes indefensible. Consequently, effort is directed toward the production of educational, cultural, and other socially acceptable goods and services.

Thus it appears that the greater the degree of advancement of a society, the greater its potential for producing luxury goods and services, including education. Those countries that, by their lack of resources or lack of people with technical ability, must spend most of their time and effort in producing goods for subsistence and survival will have commensurately little time and ability to produce a good educational system. A report from the World Bank states:

> Although exceptions are made, in general the emphasis in low-income countries is on the development of low-cost basic education to lay the requisite foundation of science, language, mathematics, and other cognitive skills. In middle-income countries, where first-level education is already widely available, educational quality is emphasized, and with it the expansion of facilities to meet the needs of an increasingly sophisticated economy. As the absorptive capacity of an economy grows, the priority tends to shift toward providing higher level technical skills, as well as developing skills in science, technology, information processing, and research.[2]

A country that strives to produce educational services is constantly increasing the range of economic productivity and affluence for itself. Countries that make only a minor effort in education usually produce only the material goods necessary for subsistence. The educational system thus becomes a very important result, as well as a determinant, of the social and economic progress of a nation.

EDUCATION: AN IMPORTANT INDUSTRY

A common and certainly defensible description of education is that it is an industry in the sense that it utilizes money and other valuable resources to develop its product. Although it is this country's largest industry, it produces only intangibles in the form of nonmaterial goods or services that are valuable but difficult to measure. It is an industry where objective data are readily available to determine its financial input but where no research or empirical study has yet found a satisfactory way to measure, or even to approximate, its total output. It is devoid of a profit motive; it is usually operated by government but dependent on private enterprise for its financial support. The United States is a world leader in education, with about 25 percent of its population involved in one way or another. With regard to expenditures, statistics from the U.S. Department of Education show that 6.9 percent of the gross national product goes toward all educational institutions.[3] This percentage has been fairly consistent during the past decade.

Produces Nonfree Services

Any college student can attest to the fact that education is not a free commodity in the economic sense. When consideration is given to the indirect costs (the income lost while attending school) as well as the direct costs (living expenses and tuition), there is no need for an additional reminder that education is far from free.

As a purchaser of educational services, the student recognizes education as a consumer good, paying money for the avowed purpose of consuming as much education as possible under particular circumstances. On the other hand, because the instructor's salary has been augmented by the accumulation of some amount of education, education is simultaneously a producer good, for it provides the economic ability (money) to satisfy wants for other goods and services.

As the college graduate receives an academic degree and moves into the world of work, no stock of accumulated material goods is evident from educational experiences. The investment has been made in nontangible goods and services that, it is hoped, will be passed on to others in the necessary process of earning a living. These services may be used and reused almost without limit and are therefore described as multiple-use goods or services. In contrast with machines, equipment, and other physical goods that depreciate with use, the durability or utility of educational services normally increases with use.

While some learning is sought and obtained for its intrinsic and cultural value, much of the purpose of education is to increase the ability of the recipient to engage in some useful occupation or profession and thus to produce other goods and services. This process is an economic one, since it provides the means to satisfy wants as a consumer as well as to produce goods and services for other consumers. An education adds to the richness of life for its recipients and widens their scope in choices of consumer goods such as books, magazines, works of art, and musical compositions. Thus, education is literally a consumer's good as well as a producer's good.

Stimulates Economic Growth

Although interest in the economics of education is said to date back to the time of Plato, its close relation to the financing of education went almost unnoticed in this country until about the middle of the twentieth century. Since that time numerous economists and educators have given in-depth consideration to this relationship. They have established and documented the fact that increases in education bring increases in productivity and gains in social, political, and economic life. They have come to support the idea that the costs of education are in reality necessary and real investments in human capital.

Since educational institutions collectively are one of this country's biggest disbursers of public money, and since education is the greatest contributor to the production and consumption of many kinds of essential services, the positive relation of education to economic growth is real and obvious. This close and interdependent relationship has been understood by educators and economists for some time, but its inferential meaning has been ignored or misunderstood by American citizens generally. The American Association of School Administrators noted long ago that educational expenditures contribute greatly to the nation's economic growth and development:

> Finally, there must be no misunderstanding on the point that expenditures for education are economically productive. The schools are not economic parasites, draining off national income into some nonproductive enterprise. On the contrary, education (a) provides the intelligence and skill essential to modern industry; (b) contributes to health and safety; (c) results in better conservation of natural resources; (d) leads to personal thrift and the development of capital resources; (e) is the basis of efficiency in business management; (f) increases the volume and lifts the level of consumer demands; (g) improves the earning power and spending power of the people; and (h) thru the purchase of buildings, equipment, materials, and thru the salaries of its employees, turns its expenditures quite directly back into the economic life-stream of the nation.[4]

The governor of Kentucky, Wallace G. Wilkenson, stated in 1990:

> Economic growth in the past was fueled primarily by significant investment in capital goods. Industrialization required heavy investment in manufacturing plants, energy production and distribution facilities, necessary public services and an extensive transportation system, but required little investment in the work force. Workers for these industries were generally in sufficient supply, and the cost to make them productive was small and relatively insignificant compared to the investment in capital goods.
>
> However, as we have moved toward an information- and technology-driven economy, the nature of work has significantly changed. Automated machines now are the "workers," and employees are supervisors of machines that do the work they formerly did. Clearly, different skills are required in this new work environment.
>
> And therein lies the strategic role that our education systems must play in the future economic well-being of the state and nation. . . . [F]or at least

the next quarter century, the economic competitive edge will belong to those nations that succeed in developing a cost-effective system for education and training its population to be productive workers in a technology- and information-driven economy. Education and economic advantage are now interdependent variables.[5]

The first modern-day school finance writer to give emphasis to the economics of education was Charles S. Benson. His book received popular acceptance and established a relation between education and economics that has been recognized by most school finance writers since that time. His point of view is summarized in the following statement:

> Throughout the world, both philosophers and men of affairs appear to have reached consensus on this point: education is a major force for human betterment. Quality of education is intimately related to its financing. How much resources are made available, and how effectively these resources are used stand as crucial questions in determining the degree to which education meets the aspirations that people hold for it. . . . [6]

That expending adequate funds for education will provide economic dividends to society is now an established fact that is seldom disputed by students of economics. Quality education is expensive, but it brings commensurate benefits to individuals, families, business and professional people, and social agencies and institutions. Although direct and objective facts are difficult if not impossible to obtain, economists are generally agreed that adequate expenditures for education lead to increases in markets for goods and services, increases in business and industrial sales, and increases in the buying power of individuals and households. Such expenditures also tend to reduce the production costs of goods and services, to increase and hasten the adoption of technological changes, and to improve the performance skills and efficiency of the working force.

A Public Sector Responsibility

Education can be produced in the private sector of the economy as well as in the public. The educational system is largely produced by government at public expense, but many schools are sponsored by private individuals, companies, or churches. In certain other countries, education is largely a product of the private sector.

Schools in the private sector operate under a different set of theories and rules than those in the public sector. The organizations and institutions in the private sector, by the nature of their relations to their clientele, are controlled and changed more readily than those in the public sector. Consumer requirements, and the ability of the private school to meet them, largely determine how much financial support is available for future operation. The desires and even the whims of potential purchasers are soon met in the private sector, for to ignore such would mean a curtailment of sales and a loss of profits. Inefficiency, incompetence, or other internal deficiencies soon make themselves known and usually bring changes in schools in the competitive marketplace. No such rules apply to public schools. Government institutions, including public schools, are not required to react as quickly or as obediently to external pressure and public criticism as their counterparts in the competitive world. Compulsory school attendance laws, taxation laws, and social pressures combine to erode the effect of dissatisfaction and clamor for improvement of government-sponsored schools. Right or wrong, public institutions usually move more slowly to reduce the criticisms or implement the recommendations for improvement that their patrons make. Unfortunately, this fact has too often resulted in a high degree of resistance or practical indifference to change and innovation in public education.

EQUITY VERSUS EQUALITY

Public education systems are designed to produce equity (fairness) in the treatment of their students, but they do not, cannot, and should not aspire to produce complete equality. In the difficult process of allocating resources for education, some recipients must necessarily receive advantages over others, while some suffer disadvantages. This is inevitable in a process where there are innate and fundamental differences in student ability, interest, and desire to learn—as well as differences in the many factors that make up the school milieu.

Although the terms are sometimes used interchangeably, *equity* and *equality* are not synonyms. The public school system is dedicated to developing equity among its students, it often promotes some degree of inequality. In 1991 the Policy Committee of the Council for Economic Development (CED) expressed this thought in the following statement:

> Almost all local education revenues are still produced by property taxes. Although poorer districts tax property at a higher rate, the lower tax base usually yields fewer dollars overall and per pupil allocations that can be several thousand dollars lower than in wealthier districts . . . disparities in local funding are fueling a growing nationwide movement to revamp state education funding mechanisms in order to guarantee more equitable funding of rich and poor school districts. . . .
>
> We applaud this movement toward more equitable allocation of resources among school districts. *Nevertheless,* we do not believe that wealthier districts should be constrained from contributing what they believe to be an appropriate level of resources to educate their children.[7]

While some degree of inequality will exist, it should be minimized. There still needs to be caution as to the extent a local district is allowed to provide greater revenue for its students. Equality is lost as the chasm between expenditures per student in two districts grows larger. The disparity issue remains a dilemma.

RESOURCE ALLOCATION TO EDUCATION

Although the affluence of the people and the abundance of resources of the United States are well beyond those of most other countries, they have limits. The spiraling costs of the services of government and its institutions have sharpened competition for the tax dollar more than ever before. As an important economic service with increasing responsibility to the people of the nation, education would seem to have established itself as a strong and deserving competitor for the economic resources of each state responsible for its support.

As the twenty-first century approaches, the nation's governors, the Carnegie Forum, and the Holmes group, made up of deans of education from some universities, have issued three reports calling upon the states to seize the initiative in providing for education reform. The reports were entitled respectively, *Time for Results: The Governors' 1991 Report on Education, A Nation Prepared: Teachers for the 21st Century,* and *Tomorrow's Teachers.*

These reports had significant impact throughout the country. In 1990 Booth Gardner, governor of the state of Washington, said that their reform movement would include "restructuring our state's school finance system to increase the share of state support to about three-quarters of the total . . . and providing a state subsidy to equalize the tax rates for districts with low property values."[8]

This renewed focus on education may temporarily draw attention from other areas, but educators will have to provide a continued impetus to obtain a slice of the available economic resources. Since the nonprofit public sector has no way to obtain funds directly for establishing and operating the social, cultural, and governmental institutions (including schools) that it sponsors, money must be diverted from the private sector to the public sector by some process of taxation. The academic disciplines of education, economics, and political science are all vitally concerned with the process and the results of such diversion. One of the chief problems of government is to determine how much of private-sector income can and should be diverted to the public sector. Gardner emphasized: "[A]s we move into the twenty-first century . . . our states *will accept* responsibility for adequate and equitable distribution of financial resources. . . ."[9]

A Political Responsibility

Allocating economic resources to education is one of the primary responsibilities of local, state, and federal lawmaking bodies. According to Garvue, the procedures and guidelines they have used to determine such allocations in the past have been ambiguous and nonscientific.[10] In the absence of objective guidelines for determining the proper balance of resource needs of public sector institutions and agencies, government agencies usually base allocation decisions on factors such as organizational objectives and needs, the potential contribution and overall influence of each institution, and ordinary political expediency. Education tends to suffer comparatively in such allocations, because it is unable to show and measure in objective terms the increased output provided with additional units of input.

Of the several methods of allocating funds to education, perhaps the most common is trying to maintain an average practice model—a *leveling up* to provide all weaker units with the same proportional resources as the average unit. Occasionally, the antithesis is practiced to a limited extent, with more affluent units being leveled down or required to "mark time" until the weaker ones reach a comparable plateau.

Resource-allocating bodies may also use some presumed measurement of educational outcomes as the determinant for education's share of limited resources. Such measurements are often more imaginary than real, for many of the results of a good educational program cannot be measured objectively. One of the basic problems education faces in its request for greater resource input is the common belief that it is so complex that members of lawmaking organizations cannot understand its purposes, needs, and contributions to society. Then, too, economy-minded legislators often are quick to minimize or eliminate allocations of scarce resources to high-cost programs, for they do not understand their contribution to the overall educational program.

The reluctance of educators to communicate with the politicians in lawmaking bodies and tell them their problems has added to the allocation puzzle. Fortunately, the educational establishment now recognizes that decisions concerning resource allocation are made in the political arena.

Political leaders in the various legislatures often find themselves under pressure from economic and educational advocates as they attempt to make decisions to establish and support public educational institutions. They understand only too well that education as an industry does not and cannot operate in a vacuum without reference to economics, politics, or related disciplines.

To become effective, educators must be cognizant of the philosophy of individual politicians. Educators must understand that politicians are their clients as much as students are. Whether it be a school board member making programmatic or salary decisions, a legislator determining the level of school support, a member of Congress, or the president of the United States, each is influential in determining fiscal matters that affect the educational program. If placed on a continuum, a politician with liberal views will probably have a greater affinity for governmental involvement at the central level. On the other hand, a conservative would believe in more private involvement, and prefer government action to be at the state or local level.

Economic Philosophies

A cursory look at the political and economic philosophies of Karl Marx, Adam Smith, John Maynard Keynes, John Kenneth Galbraith, and Milton Friedman shows that the recommended role of governments in economics varies from the central government having absolute control (Marx), to government assisting in cases of economic depression (Keynes), to more support of the public sector and more government resources being derived from the affluent private sector (Galbraith), to government intervention generally hampering progress (Friedman), to the government having little, if any, involvement (Smith) (Table 1-1). Each of the philosophers feels that education is important; the differences involve the *how* and the *what*. According to Marx, education should be free, state-controlled, and financed by centralized government. It exists to train citizens in the value system of the government. Keynes and those who espouse his philosophy believe it a governmental duty to provide complete education. Galbraith maintains that education is vital for technical and human advancement and must be supported to a more significant level by the resources that are abundant in the affluent private economy. Friedman sees government as overgoverning education; he believes the solution is the individual's freedom to choose what education is most suitable, using a voucher to shop for that education. Smith sees education as one of the essential services of government.

The five philosophers all see the need for and the power of education. When seeking financial support for the schools, educators must understand the diverse philosophies in politics and communicate across the political spectrum by using concepts that resonate within the particular politician's philosophy.

Economics, Politics, and Education

Educational leaders, too, now seem to understand that all major social forces must not only recognize each other's objectives and alternatives but also work cooperatively to solve each other's problems. Until recent years, educators and political leaders have been largely indifferent to each other's needs and problems.

According to CED, important progress is being made at national, state, and local levels to better define what the results of education should be. The President and the nation's governors have provided critically needed national leadership by developing and mutually endorsing a broad-based set of six national goals for education outlined in the document *AMERICA 2000.*

- All children will start school ready to learn.
- The high school graduation rate will be at least 90 percent.
- Students will leave grades four, eight, and twelve having demonstrated competency in challenging subject matter, and all students will be prepared for responsible citizenship, future learning, and productive employment.
- U.S. students will be first in the world in math and science.
- All American adults will be literate, able to compete in a global economy, and able to exercise responsible citizenship.
- Every school will have an environment conducive to learning and free of drugs and violence.

TABLE 1-1 Political and Economic Continuum

	Marx	Keynes	Galbraith	Friedman	Smith
Government or economy	Communist	Government intervention	Liberal	Conservative	Capitalist
Role of government	Central government has total control; sets policy and goals in all aspects of society; strong bureaucracy.	Government will help the economy in depression or recession by public works projects, etc. Deficits accumulated thereby will be repaid during good economic times.	Government is a dominant factor in society. Limit overproduction by private sector. Control wages, prices. Provide affluence for all citizens.	Government interventions have hampered programs. Should reduce bureaucracy because people are free to choose without bureaucratic influence create a better quality of life.	The invisible hand of competition will run the economy in a natural way. Government should govern only—no government interference in business or trade, just preserve law and order, defend the nation, enforce justice. Least government best.
Educational perspective	Free public education, controlled and financed by centralized government. Trains in value system of the government.	There is an inequitable distribution of wealth and income.	Education is vital for technical advances and growth. Education must be encouraged for future research and development in technology.	Government over-governs education. Voucher system for education. It is essential in maintaining free enterprise, political freedom, and open economy.	Education is one of the essential government services to make capitalism work; competition between schools. Local education control, compulsory education at elementary level.

(Continued)

	Marx	Keynes	Galbraith	Friedman	Smith
Taxes	Highly graduated progressive tax on income.	Progressive tax to redistribute wealth so the poor can spend more and the wealthy save less. Deficit financing in times of depression.	Public economy starved, private economy bloated. Tax the affluent society (private sector) more to provide needed public services, education, etc.	The private economy is starved, public economy bloated. Tax reform to encourage investment in private sector. Negative income tax should replace welfare.	Taxes should reflect ability to pay, not be arbitrary; convenient and efficient. Need to provide for essential government services.
Property	No private ownership of property—owned by the centralized government.	Private property essential; however, government most important element of the economy.	Private ownership has been oversold through advertising; the affluence of private sector has cheated public needs. Fiscal policy is essential.	People must be free to own and exchange goods. Monetary policy, not fiscal policy, is essential in shaping economic events.	Private property is essential to freedom; if state owns, freedom vanishes.
Vantage point in history	Reaction to exploitation of workers in the Industrial Revolution. History is determined by economic conditions.	Predicted ruin of Europe's economy because of harsh economic conditions imposed on Germany by the Treaty of Versailles. Capitalism usually better than alternatives. Ideas included in F.D.R.'s New Deal in 1930s. U.S. was to spend its way back to prosperity.	Conventional wisdom always in danger of becoming obsolete. Rejects orthodox views of economics. Holds that quality of life, not gross national product, should be the measure of economic achievement.	Freedom is more important than prosperity. However, freedom is the best environment for economic prosperity. Friedman rejects keynesian fiscal policy; monetary policy leads to stability.	Wrote *The Wealth of Nations* in 1776, but its major impact came in early 1800s. Reaction to British mercantilism; tariffs and limited "free" trade.

The national goals initiative provides important national leadership for ensuring that all children are educated well; yet, it is only a first step. Colorado has initiated a program entitled *COLORADO 2000* and "Maine and at least eight other states have scheduled their own *STATE 2000* kickoff for the fall [1991]."[11] The larger task remains ahead. Public education is still primarily a state and local responsibility, and there is considerable variation from community to community in the quality of the schools, the needs of students, and the resources available. The states should provide guidance and resources to help local districts and schools meet their goals.[12]

The Scope of Educational Services

In the competitive market, consumers of economic goods and services generally determine, by their ability and willingness to purchase, just what a particular industry will make available for sale—within the limits of the supply of resources. Demands for goods and services are determined by those who consume such products directly. Public and individual demands for education, however, are unlike the demands for most other goods and services. In education, these must originate from those who pay for its services, but who do not usually receive its benefits directly. The quality and quantity of educational services are determined in large measure by the pleasant or unpleasant experiences adults have had with education in their own lives as well as by how such demands will affect their share of the tax cost. The degree of satisfaction of the direct recipients of education is too often secondary to the degree of tax burden sustained by those who determine the extent of such services available. Thus, educational expenditures are often determined in a right-to-left direction—in much the same way as a customer who is short of cash might approach the menu in a luxurious restaurant.

The individuals who determine the supply of education to be made available often have no family or other direct relationship with any of the individuals who are its potential consumers. For that reason board members and others responsible for educational supply may approach school finance with a neutral or even a negative attitude, for their decisions may be made in terms of their own real or imaginary financial tax burden to the exclusion of more relevant and necessary educational needs. This often results in exaggerated criticism of increases in educational expenditures, especially in areas where there is little objective evidence of commensurate results. Regular and substantial increases in input are necessary, however; teachers and others who spend their time in educational activities must be protected against the ravages of inflation and increasing living costs, even though only small increases in their productivity are possible.

The Marginal Dollar Principle

How does a free society determine the amount of resources it will spend for such an important service of government as education? Theoretically, it would be done in the same way an individual decides how much money will be spent for a particular good or service in a free market—by considering the marginal utility of that good or service. The utility is determined in large measure by the value prospective consumers place on the goods or services to be purchased and by the number of such goods or services already in their possession or available to them.

The usefulness and utility of additional units of a particular item usually decrease as they are added; a third car usually has less real value to a purchaser than a second one, and the second car has less value than the first. Similarly, the public may place high value on the purchase of elementary education for all its children at public expense and give high priority to this undertaking, but it would put less emphasis on education for four years of high school and still less emphasis on providing funds for higher education. The public may feel, too, that an expenditure of $3000 per pupil per year is highly desirable, that an additional $1000 might be less desirable, and that a further addition of $1000 might be undesirable or unwise—for it might require taking funds away from some other, seemingly more important, goods or services.

Marginal utility thus becomes a measure of desire for additional units of a good or service. The marginal dollar is the dollar that would be better spent for some other good or service. Thus, allocating funds for education becomes a problem of determining at what point an additional amount proposed as an expenditure for education would bring greater satisfaction or worth if it were spent for other goods or services.

Allocating resources by this method is difficult, as McLure noted:

> The theory of marginal utility cannot be applied as clearly in education as in some other operations. It is difficult, for example, to determine when the addition of one more staff member may or may not produce results which would be equal to or less than the value of the money paid the person. In industry, however, the addition of one worker would be at the margin if the increased income would be equal to the cost of the worker.[13]

The Point of Diminishing Returns

Undoubtedly, there is a point of diminishing returns in the expenditure of funds for education: a point beyond which additional expenditures will yield very little or no additional educational returns. Where this point is—in terms of expenditures per pupil—has not yet been determined. Most of the schools of this country have been forced to operate on a financial level far below such a theoretical point.

Determining the relation of the per-pupil expenditures for education to the quality of the product has proved to be a popular, but elusive, research subject for many years. Cubberley was concerned with it in the early years of this century, and it has been an important topic of study for many school finance scholars since that time.

It is normal for people, especially overburdened taxpayers, to compare the costs and apparent productivity of various public institutions or industries—particularly those in direct competition with each other for scarce tax dollars. Such comparisons may reflect unfavorably upon education for reasons not under the control of those involved. Advocates of the sciences, agriculture, medicine, and industry point with understandable pride to the fact that increased expenditures for upgrading their operations and increasing their research effort have greatly increased their annual production of goods and services over a period of time. This has been particularly noticeable in agriculture and in medicine. Such results are, of course, applauded by people everywhere.

The problem of producing spectacular improvements in education with the allocation of additional funds is another matter. Greatly increased expenditures for education have not, cannot, and will not produce such large or fantastic increases or improvements in its products. The nature of the learning process being what it is, increases in learning effectiveness can be anticipated only in small percentages, regardless of the magnitude of the financial increments applied to the improvement process. It is unlikely that the field of education, even with the application of almost limitless resources, will ever have available ways of multiplying the quantity or the quality of learning that human beings can achieve in a predetermined amount of time. Such a fact may cause some to believe that public education has already reached the marginal dollar and a point of diminishing returns and that available funds should be diverted from it to other industries that have the potential for higher percentage increases in productivity. This would be folly of the highest order, for whatever improvements can be made to make education more effective, more extensive, and more applicable to the lives of United States citizens should be made, regardless of what spectacular results could be produced elsewhere with similar dollars.

EDUCATION AS HUMAN CAPITAL

The importance of education to the growth of the national economy is no longer challenged. Historically, education has been the largest public function—and the country's biggest business, when viewed in terms of the numbers of people and dollars of income involved in its operation. The expansion of educational services and the greatly increasing costs of education year after year have had a tremendous beneficial effect on the nation's economy. It is not likely that this condition will change.

Most economists now recognize the importance of investment in education for developing the nation's large reservoir of human capital. The economists of an earlier era emphasized the roles of land, labor, and capital in achieving economic growth, and they gave only passing attention to the economic importance of education.

The economist paid little attention to this point of view until after World War II. Since that time, most of them have emphasized the value of education as a factor in stimulating economic growth. Education is now popularly referred to as investment in human capital. Such leaders in the field as John Kenneth Galbraith, Harold Groves, Milton Friedman, Theodore Schultz, and Charles Benson have documented the relation between education and economic growth. They have deplored the waste of manpower and human resources that automatically accompanies inadequate education, regardless of its causes.

The apparent paradox that some economists have attached to the concept that human beings are a form of capital goods is pointed out by Schultz in the following:

> The mere thought of investment in human beings is offensive to some among us. Our values and beliefs inhibit us from looking upon human beings as capital goods, except in slavery, and this we abhor. We are not unaffected by the long struggle to rid society of indentured service and to evolve political and legal institutions to keep men free from bondage. These are achievements that we prize highly. Hence, to treat human beings as wealth that can be augmented by investment runs counter to deeply held values.[14]

Thus far, I have been using the term "human capital" as if it were obvious what it means. Although by implication the meaning of the concept has been at least in part revealed, it calls for further definition. Consistent with what has already been noted, human capital has the fundamental attributes of the basic economic concept of *capital*; namely, it is a source of future satisfactions, or of future earnings, or both of them. What makes it *human* capital is the fact that it becomes an integral part of a person. But we were taught that land, capital, and labor are the basic factors of production. Thus we find it hard to think of the useful skills and knowledge that each of us has acquired as forms of capital.[15]

Education in a Worldwide Perspective

The point of view that prevailed until the late 1950s—that financial investments in physical assets such as ports, roads, irrigation dams, factories, and machines would generate higher output than investments in education—was initially reflected in the allocations of the World Bank, an organization that provides funds to countries for reconstruction and development. This trend changed in 1963, and in the next 30-year period loans for education were awarded to developing countries. At the request of member governments, the bank has moved from "manpower" development and now assists in financing such needs as textbooks, curriculum development, computer centers, and many other educational areas that the organization recognizes as critical to economic growth. In *Education and Development, Views from the World Bank,* Aklilu reviews the experience of the World Bank in lending money for education and training,

demonstrating the broadening of priorities in this area over time. Psacharopou-
los reports on the productivity of education investments in terms of the monetary and nonmonetary benefits that flow to individuals and to society as a whole.
Heyneman examines the reasons why education is so productive in developing
countries, stressing that the pressure for increasing school enrollments in all
nations may be widening the gap in school quality between developing and
industrialized countries, which may result in an inability to maintain even the
minimal standards necessary for productivity outcomes in developing nations.
The authors agree that "Education and training benefit the society at large in a
profound way; and although the path to development (however defined) con-
tains many other important variables, the education of the population—up to a
reasonable standard of quality—is one of the very few that has proved to be
essential."[16]

Human capital has the fundamental characteristics of any form of economic
capital. It is a source of future satisfaction or of future earnings, or both. It is
human capital because it is a part of the person possessing it. Such capital
deteriorates with inactivity, but it does not disappear completely until the death
or complete incapacity of the person possessing it. It often needs to be reacti-
vated and updated to lessen its degree of obsoleteness or the extent of its
inadequateness.

Economic Benefits of Education

Right or wrong, the main thrust of expenditures for public education is toward
transmitting known information to individual consumers. Since the generally
accepted philosophy of education requires that all citizens have a high-quality
education through most of their preadult life, the costs of a formal education
program must of necessity be proportionately higher for the United States than
for countries that are disposed to release their youth at an earlier age. But what
of the benefits of education to individuals under a system that requires participation for such an extended period?

Many studies have been conducted and estimates made to determine the
economic benefits that accrue to the average person with varying amounts of
formal education. Universally, these reports indicate the high pecuniary benefits
of education (Table 1-2).

The educated person enjoys a broader range of job opportunities than his or
her less well-educated counterpart. Since unemployment is usually closely
related to lack of education and adequate work skills, education provides some
security against joblessness in periods of change or a slackening of business and
industrial activity. However, no figures can be quoted to indicate the economic
benefits of education to individuals in such matters as increases in vocational
alternatives, increases in vocational and avocational interests, and greater appreciation for cultural and intellectual pursuits.

Many people view education strictly in terms of costs, legislative allocations,
and percentage of taxes. If education is considered as an investment in human

TABLE 1-2   A Good Reason for Going to School

Educational Attainment	Total Lifetime Earnings*	Earnings Increase For Education	Additional Days of School	
			Number	Value of Each Day
MALES				
5+ Years College	$2,252,000	$166,000	360 a/	$461
4 Years College	$2,086,000	$355,000	360	$986
1–3 Years College	$1,731,000	$171,000	360 b/	$475
High School Graduate	$1,560,000	$295,000	360	$819
High School Dropout	$1,265,000	————	— c/	—
Summary for Males	————	$987,000	1,440	$685
FEMALES				
5+ Years College	$1,431,000	$164,000	360 a/	$456
4 Years College	$1,267,000	$194,000	360	$539
1–3 Years College	$1,073,000	$123,000	360 b/	$342
High School Graduate	$ 950,000	$201,000	360	$558
High School Dropout	$ 749,000	————	— c/	—
Summary for Females	————	$682,000	1,440	$474

Source: Utah Department of Employment Security, LMI Services, February 1992, utilizing data published by the US Census Bureau in Current Population Reports, Series P-60, Number 139, February 1983.
* For an 18-year-old person who will work year-round full-time. Earnings amounts are in 1991 dollars.
a/ Two years of graduate work is assumed for this illustration.
b/ Two years of college is assumed.
c/ Dropping out after completing tenth grade is assumed.

capital, the problem becomes one of extracting sufficient resources from the present economy to provide educational opportunities to the populace now that will be adequate to pay dividends to society in the future. As the CED points out:

- Every "class" of dropouts earns about $237 billion less than an equivalent class of high school graduates during their lifetimes. As a result, the government receives about $70 billion less in tax revenues.
- Each year, taxpayers spend $16.6 billion to support the children of teenage parents.
- About 82 percent of all Americans in prison are high school dropouts, and it costs an average of $20,000 to maintain each prisoner annually. In comparison, a year of high-quality preschool costs about $4,800 and has been shown to decrease the rate of arrest in the teenage years by 40 percent.[17]

Opponents to revenue increases for schools need to consider the high cost to society when education is not provided. There are data comparing the average educational level of the United States population (12.3 years) to the average

TABLE 1-3 High School Dropout Rates in Relation to Prisoner Levels

Lowest dropout rates (and lowest prisoner levels)		Highest dropout rates (and highest prisoner levels)	
1. Minnesota	9.4	50. Florida	41.2
2. Wyoming	10.7	49. Louisiana	39.9
3. North Dakota	11.6	48. Michigan	37.6
4. Nebraska	13.3	47. Georgia	37.5
5. Montana	13.8	46. New York	37.1
6. Iowa	13.8	45. Arizona	35.6
7. Wisconsin	15.6	44. Mississippi	35.2
8. Ohio	17.2	43. Texas	34.9
9. Kansas	17.9	42. California	33.9
10. Utah	19.4	41. Alaska	33.3
11. Connecticut	19.5	40. South Carolina	33.1
12. South Dakota	20.3	39. Kentucky	32.6
13. Pennsylvania	21.3	38. North Carolina	32.2
		Tennessee	32.2

Source: H. Hodgkinson, *Beyond the Schools* (Washington, D.C.: American Association of School Administrators and National School Boards Association, 1991), p. 14.
States with the lowest dropout rates also have the lowest prisoner levels. Those with high dropout rates have correspondingly high prisoner levels. Rates are given per 100,000 residents.

educational level of prison inmates (10.2 years). The average amount of money spent on those who receive welfare aid, or participate in other costly social programs, has been compared to the amount it costs per year to educate a child in school. The assumption is that if more money were spent on education, less would have to be spent on social problems such as crime, poverty, juvenile delinquency, child abuse, drug abuse, and other such ills.

Table 1-3 lists those states with the highest and lowest rates of high school dropouts. It is significant that with one exception the states with the lowest dropout rates are the states with the lowest rate of prisoners per 100,000 people, while with two exceptions those states with the highest dropout rates have the highest levels of prisoners per 100,000 population.

The issue becomes: Should money be invested in education, or on prisons, rehabilitation centers, welfare payments, court systems, and law enforcement needs?

CREATION OF WEALTH AND EDUCATION

The creation of wealth is essential to the continuing growth of a nation. Five important elements in the creation of wealth are labor, capital, technology, resources, and management. All five are enhanced through education, increasing individual wealth, and improving the quality of life for society.

Concerning labor, educated workers are more skilled, take more pride in their work, and are able to do a better job, faster and more creatively than less educated workers. Education moves workers to more production and better fulfillment of organizational and personal needs.

Capital begets capital. Those who have a college education generally earn nearly twice as much as high school dropouts and consequently have more to invest. Investment in organizations—public or private—generally benefits society through the production of goods and services for all. The more education, the more wealth is developed for investment purposes, which creates more capital, in an endless cycle.

The wonders of modern technology have been made possible largely because of education. The position the United States holds in technical improvements is the result of an educational system that encourages research, creativity, and practical application. Much of today's wealth is tied to technology, and technology is advanced through education.

Every area of resources—human, physical, and financial—is improved and refined through education. Even the environment is better appreciated and preserved through education. Methods of mining, lumbering, and other forms of natural resource production and use have been improved through the development of skills and training, and more wealth is produced through better use of resources.

Management enhances wealth. As managers and leaders learn about personnel skills, they are better able to make decisions leading to more production, less dissatisfaction among workers, and more efficient accomplishment of the organization's goals. Effective management of the other four elements of wealth—labor, capital, technology, and resources—promotes wealth.

INCREASING EXPENDITURES AND THE ECONOMY

It has been established that there is a close and positive relationship between investment in education and the productivity of a nation. Educational development is more important than the extent of natural resources in determining the productivity and individual income level of nations. Fortunate indeed is a nation that has extensive natural resources and also highly developed human resources. A nation with high educational development may overcome to a great degree any lack of natural resources, but no nation having a poor educational system, even with tremendous stores of natural wealth, has been able to approach high individual economic productivity. A deficiency in both these areas automatically relegates a nation to low productivity and inferior economic status.

Expenditures Benefit Individuals and Society

There is proof that education helps the individual, and those who point to the costs of education often consider only individual benefits. It is true that an individual gains social mobility, a better paying, higher status job, more appreciation for arts and culture, and the ability to participate more fully in the democratic process. In addition, benefits accrue to the individual's family, neighborhood, business, society, and culture. Children of college graduates are more likely to attend college and be successful in college, creating a family education cycle. The whole of society benefits from scientific inventions. Business organizations benefit from higher skilled and motivated workers. Individuals learn to appreciate and to patronize the arts, benefiting all. Education also preserves a nation's culture and a people's sense of identity. Only through education can the history and traditions of a people be preserved and the standard of living (as measured by quantity of money and quality of life) be enhanced.

Generally, the more education a person attains, the better job he or she will have. As income rises, so do taxes, which benefit society's programs. Then more services can be provided without increasing the tax burden on individuals.

Expenditures Return Quickly to Private Sector

Expenditures for school purposes, particularly those for salaries (75 to 80 percent of the total for current expenditures), quickly find their way back into the private economy through normal flow in the economic system. Thus, their withdrawal from the private sector in the form of taxes paid, their passage into and through the public sector via the payroll, and their return to the sector of their beginning usually form a cycle that is operative in such a short period of time that the original withdrawal effect on the economy is minimal. "In a sense, education merely borrows funds for use until the resources flow system returns them with interest to the people."[18]

Burton Weisbrod listed seven broad economic benefits that are attributed to education:

1. Direct financial returns. Although partly due to ability, ambition, and a host of socioeconomic variables, no researcher has denied the positive role played by education.
2. Financial options. Each level of education prior to the highest achievable level provides the opportunity (option) of acquiring yet additional education and reaping the extra benefits of that education.
3. Hedging options. Increasing the probability that an individual will be able to adapt to the effects of technological change.
4. Non-market returns. Result from all the do-it-yourself types of work that a person can perform as a result of his education, such as filing one's own income tax.
5. Residence-related benefits (external to the individual). Those benefits accruable to the family of the individual, his neighbors, and taxpayers at large.

6. Employment-related benefits. The effects of the educated individual on the overall productivity of his colleagues.
7. Societal benefits. Literacy is a requisite for an intelligent citizenry, for economic activity, and for economic growth; education minimizes welfare services.[19]

The economic benefits of education to those obtaining it are many. "People who have a good education produce more goods, earn more money, buy and consume more goods, read more magazines and newspapers, are more active in civic and national affairs, enjoy a higher standard of living, and in general, contribute more to the economy than those who are not as well educated."[20]

NONECONOMIC BENEFITS OF EDUCATION

The positive economic effects of good education are extremely important. Much is said and written about "education as an investment in people." Sometimes, however, in an effort to show its economic investment characteristics, people may inadvertently overlook one of its social benefits that may outweigh all the others. As Lee DuBridge has expressed it, education does much to preserve a free, highly productive, and democratic society:

> A technologically advanced nation requires an educated body of citizens. When every man on the street is concerned about nuclear war or fallout, about automation, or space; when every family has possession of dozens of the products of modern technology, ranging from an automobile to a television set, automatic toaster, and electric clock; when every citizen must vote for candidates for public office, who in turn must make decisions on matters of national defense, atomic power, space exploration, the regulation of industry, communication, and transport, it is clear that an educated citizenry is an essential national requirement.[21]

Norton argues that when education is thought of for reasons other than its economic benefits, it loses the necessary amount of financial support to keep it in operation:

> Education for intellectual development and for informed and perceptive minds was never needed more than it is today. The danger is that when education is thought of solely in these lofty and noble terms it is likely to suffer financial limitations which will prevent full achievement of both its intellectual and its economic goals. The latter cannot be ignored in a nation such as the United States, in which world leadership and even survival depends upon economic power.[22]

Some of the noneconomic benefits of education that come to an individual also come to society. Perhaps this point is obvious, but Marshall's statement in this regard is significant:

> We may then conclude that the wisdom of expending public and private funds on education is not to be measured by its direct fruits alone. It will be profitable as a mere investment, to give the masses of the people much greater opportunities than they can generally avail themselves of. . . . And the economic value of one great industrial genius is sufficient to cover the expenses of the education of a whole town; for one new idea, such as Bessemer's chief invention, adds as much to England's productive power as the labour of a hundred thousand men. Less direct, but not less in importance, is the aid given to production by medical discoveries such as those of Jenner or Pasteur, which increase our health and working power; and again by scientific work such as that of mathematics or biology, even though many generations may pass away before it bears visible fruit in greater material well-being. All this is spent during many years in opening the means of higher education to the masses would be well paid for if it called out one more Newton or Darwin, Shakespeare or Beethoven.[23]

EDUCATION PRODUCES EXTERNAL BENEFITS

Education, just as other public services, produces and extends benefits beyond the internal values obtained by its recipients. It is therefore said to possess *externalities*—values and benefits for people outside or beyond those who are its direct consumers. This fact is used to justify financing it by a process of taxation rather than by fee collecting, rate bills, or tuition charges. Education's externalities are such that society does not permit individuals to purchase it, or even determine the minimum amount of it to be purchased, on the basis of desire or felt need alone, for some would purchase little or none of it if allowed to exercise their individual option. As a result, society has deemed it advisable to require the consumption of a minimum amount of education by all its citizens. Such service is supported financially by some form of tax, the amount based on some measure of ability to pay. This system presumes no direct relation between the amount of taxes paid and the amount of direct or internal value received by the taxpayer. To a great degree it denies the individual the right of choice of the kind or amount of educational services he or she is required to assume.

It is evident that individuals are not only aware of, and concerned with, the amount of education they consume; they are also concerned with the extent of education others consume. Standards of living are raised and economic growth enhanced by the externalities that are generated by the education of the members of a social group. Individuals tend to gain more personally with the education of many in a society than they will gain if only a few purchase education's services.

Externalities and the Benefit Principle

The private sector is much better qualified than the public sector to produce and distribute goods and services that can be purchased at the option of individuals and households. Such purchases of goods and services ordinarily create no automatic or residual benefits to society but bring such benefits only to the purchaser. This is commonly referred to as the *exclusion* principle. As an example, the private sector can provide gasoline and other service station products to any and all individuals and organizations that need and can pay for such goods and services. The purchaser receives personal benefits directly related to the quantity of such products he or she buys.

Education does not follow the exclusion principle. Everyone benefits from education when the results are lower social costs, increased wealth, greater income and sales tax revenue, and development of the five elements that expand the economy: resources, labor, capital, technology, and management. It is thereby impossible to assess costs in terms of potential benefits to purchasers and at the same time exclude nonpurchasers from similar benefits.

Externalities Justify the Ability Principle

The problem of financing education is different from that of marketing most other goods and services. The existence of externalities and the nonexistence of the exclusion principle changed the method of financing education from the *benefit* principle to the *ability* principle. The lessons learned in the prepublic school era in this matter should not be forgotten. Unfortunately, some individuals in every society would not be partakers of education if it were purchasable only on a voluntary basis. Not only do they not demand the service, but they must be required by government to obtain it in some minimum quantity by compulsory school attendance laws. A second important factor is that education not only benefits individuals in proportion to their purchase or consumption of it; it also pervades society and indirectly affects all citizens. These effects lead to higher standards of living and allow greater consumption of cultural goods and services.

It is impossible to measure the benefits that come to the individual or to society from individual purchases of educational services. That being true, the most defensible approach is to assume that all individuals in society benefit to about the same degree or extent. On that basis, the costs of education should be paid by all members of society in terms of their ability to pay. Under this *ability* principle, the wealthy pay more for the services of government, but their comparative burden is no greater than that borne by the less affluent.

Taxation and Education

To tax individuals in direct relation to the benefits they receive from the service or commodity that is provided by that tax would seem to be defensible, provided that the benefit is observable and to a high degree measurable, and provided further that they alone benefit from the tax they pay. Proponents of the benefit system of taxation argue that taxation by the ability principle penalizes the affluent and financially successful person. Such a process, they contend, stifles and curtails further activities of an economic nature and tends to create an indolent society. They point to the extremely high rate of the upper level of income tax of a few years ago and its negative effect on business and industrial expansion.

Education and certain other services of government do not lend themselves to the benefit principle of taxation. A weakness of the benefit principle of taxation is included in the following statement by Salisbury: "If everyone paid only for benefits received, there could be no surplus to support other functions. Modern governmental services must go far beyond such a limited view and extend to many functions which simply cannot be measured by so restricted a base."[24] Every state has had or now has a compulsory school attendance law that requires all children of certain ages to spend a predetermined amount of time in formal education. What about those required to attend who do not have the financial ability to pay for such required services of government? Are the parents of six children to pay six times as much as the parents of one child? Is the adult without children to be exempt from school taxation altogether? Such questions have faced the states through the years; even today the relative importance of this form of taxation varies considerably among the states.

COST-QUALITY RELATIONSHIP IN EDUCATION

Economic, political, and educational leaders are concerned with the question of how the amount of money spent for education relates to the quality of the educational product. Various reform movements have sought more productivity from instructional staff, lower administration costs, better utilization of buildings, and other cost-saving remedies, with the anticipation that the quality of services would not be affected. It is difficult to obtain data and other available evidence in relation to such cost-quality relationships.

The difficulty of solving the cost-quality problem in education is increased by the fact that the term *high quality* has not been defined in terms that are measurable and acceptable to all concerned. Is high-quality education something that can be measured by scores on achievement and other tests? What relation does it have to vocational training or to the kinds of attitudes and habits developed by students? Is a student's score of 95 on an examination compared with a score of 80 by another student a measure of a difference in quality or in quantity of education? Does extending the school year provide for potentially greater quality of education, or is quantity the variable? These and many other similar questions make the resolution of this important problem difficult, if not impossible.

The goals of education have been under almost continuous critical evaluation, resulting in frequent restatements. The quality of education should be a measurement of the extent to which the recipients of the educational offering of the schools have attained the established goals. But therein lies the difficulty—the "goals" of education vary from place to place and from time to time; even if they are agreed on, there is no way to measure all of the changes in human behavior that are the products of formal education. While advances in scholarship and academic achievement can be measured objectively, there have always been other goals of varying importance, for which there are only the crudest methods of determining their degree of inculcation in the lives of the school's clientele.

The cost-quality relation, in reality a matter of the efficiency with which the schools reach their objectives with the smallest outlay of money, is not unique to education. All institutions that are financed with public funds are, to some degree at least, concerned with maintaining maximum efficiency—if such can be attained. This must always be true with the institutions and agencies of government that are responsible for wise and defensible expenditures of the limited tax dollar. A lack of concern for efficiency tends to destroy public confidence in social and governmental institutions.

Research Limitations

Educational research does not have a particularly successful history in the United States. Public education has been notoriously indifferent to its existence. Funds for this potentially important aspect of education have been lacking; public school personnel, for the most part, have been ill-equipped by training and experience to initiate and conduct research on a satisfactory level. Traditionally, the research function has been reserved for higher education, and little has been done to alter the pattern. Future expenditures for education should include more adequate allotments for educational research. Colleges, universities, private institutions, and state departments of education, often using federal funds, have initiated much research; some progress is under way, and public school teachers, especially those who have revolted against past routines, are becoming more research-oriented.

Research studies of cost-quality relations in education have been numerous, but their results have not been conclusive. They have been centered around the measurement of *input* (time, money, and human capital that has been used to create a product or provide a service) and *output* (quality of the product that has been produced). Input measurement offers no particular problems, but measurement of the output of educational institutions is at best a highly subjective procedure.

Cost-quality research studies had their real emphasis under the late Paul Mort. He summarized his studies with the statement: "Every empirical study of the relationship between expenditure level and quality of education adds its bit to the presumption that the relationship is strong."[25] This relation, he reported, appeared to hold through all levels of expenditures experienced up to the date of his studies.

Mort and Reusser summarized the results of numerous studies of cost-quality relations in education as follows:

> Expenditure level is one of the highly important factors in achieving good education. Communities spending more for education get more in the way of results generally desired by people.
>
> The early studies showed that those communities which spend more get more in the way of services: longer terms, better trained teachers, more special services, etc.
>
> Later studies show that communities which spend more tend to be more adaptable, tend to utilize improved methods more quickly. In addition, higher expenditure schools get a different behavior pattern in the schools; the skills and knowledges are taught more in line with the best understanding of how human beings learn; more attention is given to the discovery and development of special aptitudes; more attention is given to the positive unfolding in individual boys and girls of stronger patterns of behavior—citizenship, personality, character.[26]

The relation of cost and quality in education has been questioned more critically as a result of studies by Coleman [27] and Jencks. [28] The results of these studies seem to indicate that costs (as evidenced in such things as salaries and facilities) have only a minor effect upon achievement of students when compared with the much larger effect of their intelligence and family background. The net effect of these studies has been to raise doubts and controversy concerning input-output relations in education. Perhaps the debate was best summarized by Coons, Clune, and Sugarman in the following:

> There are similar studies suggesting stronger positive consequences from dollar increments, and there are others suggesting only trivial consequences, but the basic lesson to be drawn from the experts at this point is the current inadequacy of social science to delineate with any clarity the relation between cost and quality. We are unwilling to postpone reform while we await the hoped-for refinements in methodology which will settle the issue. We regard the fierce resistance by rich districts to reform as adequate testimonial to the relevance of money. Whatever it is that money may be thought to contribute to the education of children, that commodity is something highly prized by those who enjoy the greatest measure of it. If money is inadequate to improve education, the residents of poor districts should at least have an equal opportunity to be disappointed by its failure.[29]

Salary Policies Create Problems

The organization and operation of schools create some difficult problems that tend to prevent realistic studies of cost-quality relations. Teacher organizations have consistently resisted the use of devices and mechanisms to determine the degree of success or failure of individual teachers. Salary schedules with automatic increments are almost universally accepted to the almost complete exclusion of merit or achievement provisions. Some of the severe indictments made against education in this regard are stated by Levin:

> Finally, incentives for maximizing educational outcomes for a given budget do not seem to be important characteristics of schools as organizations. Financial rewards and promotion for school personnel are handed out in a mindless fashion according to the years of service and accumulation of college credits. Individual schools, teachers, or administrators who are successful in achieving important educational goals are treated similarly to those who are unsuccessful, mediocre, or downright incompetent. In lockstep fashion the schools reward all equally. It is no wonder, then, that schools can fail persistently to teach children to read, or to foster the formation of healthy attitudes, for there are no direct incentives to change the situation. That is, success is not compensated, or formally recognized, and the reward structure is systematically divorced from educational effectiveness. In contrast, commercial enterprises tend to compensate their personnel on the basis of their contributions to the effectiveness of the organization. Commissions for sales personnel, bonuses, promotions, profits, and salary increases all represent rewards for individual or organizational proficiencies.[30]

Critics of the single-salary schedule are legion, but suggestions for its replacement have been conspicuous by their absence. Although few people seriously defend a system where the mere passage of time and/or accumulation of college credits automatically brings equal salary increases to the competent and the incompetent alike, a system or systems guaranteed to solve the problem of determining teacher salaries on the basis of success or merit has not yet been supported by the teaching profession. This unfortunate fact indicates that for the time being little can be done to make effective comparisons of cost-quality relations, until some process is found to determine the degree of success of individual teachers.

Economists refer to education as a labor-intensive activity. Since approximately three-fourths of the costs of education are required to pay the salaries of personnel, and since these salaries are not related to the degree of success achieved by the individuals receiving them, additional funds for education may be merely increases in salaries. This is particularly true in areas where teacher organizations have become powerful and effective in their bargaining with local boards of education.

Some of the operations of the schools seem to recognize that there is a positive relationship between cost and quality in education. Coons, Clune, and Sugarman state a practical and reasonable rationale concerning that point of view:

> The statutes creating district authority to tax and spend are the legal embodiment of the principle that money is quality in education. The power to raise dollars by taxation is the very source of education as far as the state is concerned. By regulating the rates of taxation, typically from a minimum to

a maximum, the state is in effect stating that dollars count (at least within this range) and that the district has some freedom to choose better or worse education. If dollars are not assumed to buy education, whence the justification for the tax?[31]

SUMMARY

Funding the rapidly increasing costs of public elementary and secondary education will be a severe challenge to the people of the nation into the twenty-first century. The problem is complicated by the fact that commensurate gains in output cannot be shown for increases in dollar input in education.

Education has become the largest industry in the United States and is recognized as an important stimulator of economic growth. Its sponsorship and financing is a public-sector responsibility. Its services should be provided equitably, but they cannot be provided with equality to all.

Economists have come to regard education as an investment in human capital. Resource allocations to education are a responsibility of government at all levels. The scope of services provided is determined by the value of those services as compared to the value of other services at the same cost, but the point of diminishing returns for investment in education has yet to be reached.

Economists and politicians ranging over the ideological spectrum value education. Not only does the individual benefit from an investment in an organization, but society as a whole benefits when goods and services are produced for all. When seeking financial support for the schools, educators need the insight to relate to these various philosophies and understand their political implications.

Although expenditures for education continue to increase annually, the burden is eased by the fact that most school costs involve money, particularly in salaries, that is returned quickly to the private sector. It is not money that is removed from the marketplace.

Education provides many benefits to individuals and households—economic as well as social and political. Since it provides external benefits beyond those provided to its consumers, it must be financed by the ability principle rather than by the benefit principle. The relationship between cost and quality in education is high, but there is little definitive research proving this fact. Defining and measuring quality in education is one of the difficult problems in conducting needed research in this important area.

ASSIGNMENT PROJECTS

1. Trace the development of the economic theory that education is an investment in human capital.
2. Show, by application of concrete data or information, that education is one of this country's most important industries.

3. Prepare a paper to be presented to a state legislature to aid it in determining the extent of state resources that should be allocated to public education in comparison with those allocated to other services of state government.

4. Prepare a feature article for a local newspaper in support of an upcoming school election for an increase in the local tax levy. Show that education is an investment in, not a drain on, the local economy.

5. Choose a prominent economist and study his or her economic theories. Relate those theories to education and the role of government in education.

6. Choose a social statistic (such as number of welfare recipients in a state) and relate it to educational attainment of the target group, cost to society, and potential savings to society were the educational level of the target group increased.

SELECTED READINGS

Becker, H. S. *Human Capital*. New York: Columbia University Press, 1964.

Benson, Charles S. *The Economics of Public Education*. 3rd ed. Boston: Houghton Mifflin, 1978.

Bottlieb, Manuel. *Comparative Economic Systems*. Iowa City: Iowa State University Press, 1988.

Carnegie Forum on Education and the Economy. *A Nation Preparing Teachers for the 21st Century*. Washington, D.C.: Carnegie Forum on Education and the Economy, 1990.

Chubb, J. E., and T. M. Moe. *Politics, Markets, and America's Schools*. Washington, D.C.: Brookings Institution, 1990.

DeYoung, Alan J. *Economics and American Education*. New York: Longman, 1989.

Friedman, Milton, and Rose Friedman. *Free to Choose, A Personal Statement*. New York: Harcourt Brace Jovanovich, 1980.

Galbraith, John Kenneth. *The Affluent Society*. 4th ed. Boston: Houghton Mifflin, 1984.

Guthrie, James W., Walter I. Garms, and Lawrence C. Pierce. *School Finance and Education Policy: Enhancing Educational Efficiency, Equality, and Choice*. 2nd ed. Englewood Cliffs, N.J.: Prentice Hall, 1988.

Johns, Roe L., Edgar L. Morphet, and Kern Alexander. *The Economics and Financing of Education*. 4th ed. Englewood Cliffs, N.J.: Prentice Hall, 1983.

Keynes, John Maynard. *The Collected Writings of John Maynard Keynes*. 24 vols. New York: Macmillan, 1971.

Marcus, Laurence R., and Benjamin D. Stickney (with 16 other contributors). *Politics and Policy in the Age of Education*. Springfield, Ill.: Charles C Thomas, 1990.

Marx, Karl. *Das Kapital*, ed. Frederick Engels. Chicago: Encyclopedia Britannica, Inc., 1952.

Marx, Karl, and Frederick Engels. *The Communist Manifesto*, Trans. Samuel Moore. Chicago: Regnery, 1963.

Mill, John Stuart. *On Liberty*. London: Longmans, Green, 1913.

Mort, Paul R., Walter C. Reusser, and John W. Polley. *Public School Finance*. New York: McGraw-Hill, 1960.

Odden, Allan R., and Lawrence O. Picus. *School Finance: A Policy Perspective*. New York: McGraw-Hill, 1992.

Perkinson, Henry J. *The Imperfect Panacea: American Faith in Education, 1865–1990*. New York: McGraw-Hill, 1991.

Sirotnik, K. A. "The School as the Center of Change," In *Schooling for Tomorrow: Directing Reform to Issues That Count*, eds. T. J. Sergiovanni and J. H. Moore. Newton, Mass.: Allyn and Bacon, 1989.

Smith, Adam. *An Inquiry into the Nature and Causes of the Wealth of Nations*, general eds. R. H. Campbell and A. S. Skinner, textual ed. W. B. Todd. New York: Oxford University Press, 1976.

———. *The Theory of Moral Sentiments*. London: Oxford Clarendon Press, 1976.

Sowell, Thomas. *Race and Economics*. New York: David McKay, 1975.

Stevens, Edward, Jr., and George H. Wood. *Justice, Ideology, and Education*. 2nd ed. New York: McGraw-Hill, 1992.

Thomas, J. Alan, and R. K. Wimpelberg, eds. *Dilemmas in School Finance*. Chicago: Midwest Administration Center, University of Chicago, 1978.

Underwood, Julie K., and Deborah A. Verstegen, eds. *The Impact of Litigation and Legislation on Public School Finance: Adequacy, Equity and Excellence*. New York: Harper & Row, 1990.

Webb, L. D., Martha M. McCarthy, and Stephen B. Thomas. *Financing Elementary and Secondary Education*. Columbus, Ohio: Merrill, 1988.

Werbane, Patricia H. *Adam Smith and His Legacy for Modern Capitalism*. New York: Oxford University Press, 1991.

ENDNOTES

1. Daniel C. Rogers and Hirsch S. Ruchlin, *Economics and Education* (New York: The Free Press, 1971), p. 5.

2. Habte Aklilu, *Education and Development—Views from the World Bank* (Washington, D.C.: World Bank, 1983), p. 8.

3. *Statistics of State and School Systems: Revenues and Expenditures for Public Elementary and Secondary Education; Financial Statistics of Higher Education* (Washington, D.C.: National Center for Education Statistics, U.S. Department of Education, 1990).

4. *The Expanding Role of Education* (Washington, D.C.: American Association of School Administrators, 1948), pp. 281–82.

5. Wallace G. Wilkenson, "Education Reform and Economic Competition: Critical Issues," *Journal of Education Finance*, Vol. 15, No. 4, Spring 1990, p. 604.

6. Charles S. Benson, *The Economics of Public Education* (Boston: Houghton Mifflin, 1961), p. vii.

7. *The Unfinished Agenda: A New Vision for Child Development and Education* (New York:

Research and Policy Committee, Council for Economic Development, 1991), p. 61 (emphasis added).

8. Booth Gardner, "Directions for Education in America," *Journal of Education Finance, Ibid.*, Vol. 15, No. 4, Spring 1990, p. 599.

9. Ibid., p. 602 (emphasis added).

10. Robert J. Garvue, *Modern Public School Finance* (London: Macmillan, 1969), p. 67.

11. *Education Reports*, National Center for Education Information, Vol. 12, No. 33, August 26, 1991, p. 3.

12. *The Unfinished Agenda*, pp. 43–44.

13. William P. McLure, "Allocation of Resources," in Warren E. Gauerke and Jack R. Childress, eds., *The Theory and Practice of School Finance* (Chicago: Rand McNally, 1967), p. 78.

14. Theodore W. Schultz, "Investment in Human Capital," in Charles S. Benson, ed., *Perspectives on the Economics of Education* (Boston: Houghton Mifflin, 1963), pp. 13–14.

15. Theodore W. Schultz, "The Human Capital Approach to Education," in Roe L. Johns, et al., eds., *Economic Factors Affecting the Financing of*

Education (Gainesville, Fla.: National Educational Finance Project, 1970), p. 31.

16. Aklilu, *Education and Development*, p. 6.

17. *The Unfinished Agenda*, p. 11.

18. C. R. Carpenter, "Society, Education and Technology," in Edgar L. Morphet and David L. Jesser, eds., *Planning for Effective Utilization of Technology in Education* (Denver: Designing Education for the Future, August 1968), p. 25.

19. As quoted by Rogers and Ruchlin, *Economics and Education*, pp. 3–4.

20. *Education: An Investment in People* (Washington, D.C.: Chamber of Commerce of the United States, Education Department, 1955), Introduction.

21. *Education Is Good Business* (Washington, D.C.: American Association of School Administrators, 1966), p. 12.

22. John K. Norton, *Education and Economic Well-Being in American Democracy* (Washington, D.C.: Educational Policies Commission, 1940), p. 2.

23. Alfred Marshall, "Education and Invention," in Benson, *Perspectives on the Economics of Education*, p. 83.

24. C. Jackson Salisbury, "The Theory of Taxation as Related to School Finance," in Gauerke and Childress, *Theory and Practice of School Finance*, p. 46.

25. *Problems and Issues in Public School Finance* (Washington, D.C.: National Conference on Professors of Educational Administration, 1952), p. 9.

26. Paul R. Mort and Walter C. Reusser, *Public School Finance*, 2nd ed. (New York: McGraw-Hill, 1951), pp. 140–41.

27. James S. Coleman et al., *Equality of Educational Opportunity* (Washington, D.C.: U.S. Government Printing Office, 1966).

28. Christopher Jencks et al., *Inequality: A Reassessment of the Effect of Family and Schooling in America* (New York: Basic Books, 1972).

29. John E. Coons et al., *Private Wealth and Public Education* (Cambridge: Belknap Press of Harvard University Press, 1970), p. 36.

30. Henry M. Levin, "The Effect of Different Levels of Expenditure on Educational Output," in Roe L. Johns et al., *Economic Factors Affecting the Financing of Education*, p. 181.

31. Coons et al., *Private Wealth and Public Education*, p. 26.

Chapter 2

Financing Education Adequately

Adequacy has taken on a new dimension for the 1990s and beyond . . .
Newly defined, adequacy means access to high-quality education for all
children.   —JAMES GORDON WARD, 1991

No adequate substitutes have been coined to replace the clichés, "education in the United States is big business," and "education is a major user of the nation's economic resources." Although the meanings of the statements are obvious, they fail to communicate their real significance, and relatively few people realize the enormity of educational operations in this country. As "big business," the field of formal education employs more people than any other industry in the United States. It has an annual budget of nearly $400 billion 1989–90 adjusted dollars[1] (inflation-adjusted figures now used by the Department of Education in making comparisons), with an estimated additional $200 billion spent on education and training in private industry. The clientele served in 1990 included 59,750,000 students (kindergarten through graduate school[2]) and about 4,300,000 teachers, 5,200,000 professionals, administrators and support staff, all of which makes education the primary activity for more than 69 million Americans.[3] About one of every four Americans is involved in some aspect of education as student, teacher, administrator, counselor, aide, or service worker.

Constantly increasing school expenditures, inequities in the amounts of revenue available per person to be educated, and heavy property tax burdens on individual citizens were some of the principal reasons for numerous court decisions in the 1970s. "A Nation at Risk" and other blue-ribbon reports in the 1980s provided motivation for school finance reform in nearly every state. Spiraling increases in spending were related to several factors: (1) increasing and changing enrollments of students; (2) increases in programs and services provided, including the areas of computer literacy and other technological fields; (3) inflation; and (4) inequities in the quantity and quality of services provided in the country's thousands of school districts.

Schools of the 1990s have found little relief from those problems experienced during the previous decade. The states' share of funding education has grown to 50 percent, and local tax dollars are eroding. States are struggling with the equity issue, revising their finance systems for a better distribution between poor and wealthy districts. Student enrollments have reached a plateau and are actually decreasing in many states and school districts. This phenomenon is reflected in the changing patterns of population growth shown in Table 2-1. Projections are for populations to grow in the Southwest and Far West by 20 percent and in New England by 7 percent, with the Mideast, Plains, and Great Lakes populations remaining about the same or decreasing by the year 2010. Costs continue to rise as a result of the great influx of handicapped, gifted, bilingual, compensatory, and minority students being brought into the formal school program. The costs for educating students have risen about 5 times in a 20-year period (Table 2-2).

Inflation rates, which reached double digits at the beginning of the 1980s, were reduced to a moderate rate into the 1990s, giving some relief to school budgets. Economists differ in their projections of inflation trends, making it difficult for educators to shape long-range plans.

In spite of widespread and persistent public resistance to taxes, especially on property, the demand for more and better educational services continues. Even in some of the states where drastic curtailments of public school revenues were effected in recent years (due to court decisions, legislative actions, or referenda), the demands on the schools continue to mount. Thus, it appears as if the unsolved problems of financing education in the 1990s will continue to plague school boards and state legislatures into the twenty-first century.

EDUCATION DESERVES HIGHER PRIORITY

Unfortunately, many of the citizens of this country have never given education the high priority it deserves, requires, and must have if the schools are to accomplish their objectives. Comparatively few people realize the contribution that formal education has made to the social, political, and economic achievement of the United States. In general, the citizens of the nation are not yet giving the educational programs of the schools the effort and dedication they require.

In 1983, "A Nation at Risk" stated, "We recommend that citizens across the nation hold educators and elected officials responsible for providing the leadership necessary to achieve these reforms and that citizens provide the support and stability required to bring about the reforms we propose."[4]

There is little evidence that citizens of the United States have reacted positively to giving education the higher priority that it requires and that school finance authorities have been requesting for a long time. Indeed, the events of the 1980s and early 1990s seem to indicate that the number one state and national priority is to reduce the capability of school boards and legislatures to obtain the necessary funds with which to operate their educational programs—including

TABLE 2-1   Resident Population, by Region and State, Selected Years, 1965–2010

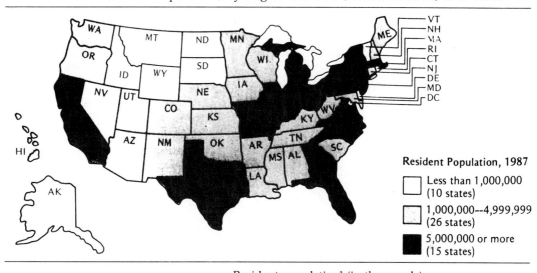

Resident Population, 1987

☐ Less than 1,000,000 (10 states)

☐ 1,000,000–4,999,999 (26 states)

■ 5,000,000 or more (15 states)

Region and state	Resident population[a] (in thousands)						
	1965	1970	1980	1987[b]	1990[c]	2000[c]	2010[c]
50 States and D.C.	193,460	203,302	226,546	243,400	249,891	267,747	282,055
New England	11,329	11,847	11,402	12,844	13,077	13,776	14,243
Connecticut	2,857	3,032	3,108	3,211	3,279	3,445	3,532
Maine	997	994	1,125	1,187	1,212	1,271	1,308
Massachusetts	5,502	5,689	5,737	5,855	5,880	6,087	6,255
New Hampshire	676	738	921	1,057	1,142	1,333	1,455
Rhode Island	893	950	947	986	1,002	1,049	1,085
Vermont	404	445	511	548	562	591	608
Mideast	41,025	42,442	42,236	43,234	43,508	44,677	45,403
Delaware	507	548	594	644	666	734	790
D.C.	797	757	638	622	614	634	672
Maryland	3,600	3,924	4,217	4,535	4,729	5,274	5,688
New Jersey	6,767	7,171	7,365	7,672	7,899	8,546	8,980
New York	17,734	18,241	17,558	17,825	17,773	17,986	18,139
Pennsylvania	11,620	11,801	11,864	11,936	11,827	11,503	11,134
Southeast	41,857	43,825	52,659	58,023	60,270	66,691	71,977
Alabama	3,443	3,444	3,894	4,083	4,181	4,410	4,609
Arkansas	1,894	1,923	2,286	2,388	2,427	2,529	2,624
Florida	5,954	6,791	9,746	12,023	12,818	15,415	17,530
Georgia	4,332	4,588	5,463	6,222	6,663	7,957	9,045
Kentucky	3,140	3,221	3,661	3,727	3,745	3,733	3,710
Louisiana	3,496	3,645	4,206	4,461	4,513	4,516	4,545
Mississippi	2,246	2,217	2,521	2,625	2,699	2,877	3,028
North Carolina	4,863	5,084	5,882	6,413	6,690	7,483	8,154
South Carolina	2,494	2,591	3,122	3,425	3,549	3,906	4,205
Tennessee	3,798	3,926	4,591	4,855	4,972	5,266	5,500

(Continued)

37

TABLE 2-1 *(Continued)*

Region and state	Resident population[a] (in thousands)						
	1965	1970	1980	1987[b]	1990[c]	2000[c]	2010[c]
Virginia	4,411	4,651	5,347	5,904	6,157	6,877	7,410
West Virginia	1,860	1,744	1,940	1,897	1,856	1,722	1,617
Great Lakes	36,225	41,795	41,684	41,904	42,054	41,745	41,111
Illinois	10,081	11,110	11,427	11,582	11,612	11,580	11,495
Indiana	4,662	5,195	5,490	5,531	5,550	5,502	5,409
Michigan	7,823	8,882	9,262	9,200	9,293	9,250	9,097
Ohio	9,706	10,657	10,799	10,784	10,791	10,629	10,397
Wisconsin	3,952	4,418	4,706	4,807	4,808	4,784	4,713
Plains	15,395	16,237	17,185	17,634	17,722	17,850	17,907
Iowa	2,758	2,825	2,914	2,834	2,758	2,549	2,382
Kansas	2,179	2,249	2,364	2,476	2,492	2,529	2,564
Minnesota	3,414	3,806	4,076	4,246	4,324	4,490	4,578
Missouri	4,320	4,678	4,917	5,103	5,192	5,383	5,521
Nebraska	1,411	1,485	1,570	1,594	1,588	1,556	1,529
North Dakota	632	618	653	672	660	629	611
South Dakota	681	666	691	709	708	714	722
Southwest	14,161	16,550	21,275	24,947	26,381	30,173	33,359
Arizona	1,302	1,775	2,718	3,386	3,752	4,618	5,319
New Mexico	951	1,017	1,303	1,500	1,632	1,968	2,248
Oklahoma	2,328	2,559	3,025	3,272	3,285	3,376	3,511
Texas	9,580	11,199	14,229	16,789	17,712	20,211	22,281
Rocky Mountains	4,317	5,008	5,249	7,273	7,534	8,134	8,629
Colorado	1,754	2,210	2,890	3,296	3,434	3,813	4,098
Idaho	667	713	944	998	1,017	1,047	1,079
Montana	675	694	787	809	805	794	794
Utah	891	1,059	158	1,680	1,776	1,991	2,171
Wyoming	330	332	470	490	502	489	487
Far West	21,483	27,038	32,600	37,540	39,342	44,703	49,428
Alaska	226	303	402	525	576	687	765
California	15,717	19,971	23,668	27,663	29,126	33,500	37,347
Hawaii	633	770	965	1,083	1,141	1,345	1,559
Nevada	285	489	800	1,007	1,076	1,303	1,484
Oregon	1,769	2,092	2,633	2,724	2,766	2,877	2,991
Washington	2,853	3,413	4,132	4,538	4,657	4,991	5,282

Sources: *Current Population Reports,* Series P-25, U.S. Bureau of the Census (Washington, D.C.: GPO), No. 460, June 1971, table 1; No. 727, July 1978, table 3; No. 876, February 1980, table 1; No. 937, August 1983, table 1; News Release, CB87-205, December 30, 1987; 1988, forthcoming report.
From: 1989–90 Fact Book on Higher Education, American Council on Education. New York, Macmillan Publishing Company, pp. 10–11.
[a]The U.S. totals shown here will not agree with total U.S. population shown elsewhere because the latter includes estimates for U.S. armed forces overseas. Details may not add to totals because of rounding. Data for 1970 and 1980 are as of April 1; data for other years are estimates and projections as of July 1.
[b]Provisional estimates.
[c]Census projections, middle series.

TABLE 2-2 Average Cost per Pupil in Average Daily Attendance (in Current Dollars) for Each Year Since 1980–81 and Percent Increases in Cost per Pupil in ADA

School year	Expenditure per pupil in ADA	Percent change From 1980–81	From previous year
1980–81	$2,489		
1981–82	2,753	10.6	10.6
1982–83	2,960	18.9	7.5
1983–84	3,185	28.0	7.6
1984–85	3,483	39.9	9.4
1985–86	3,764	51.2	8.1
1986–87	3,994	60.5	6.1
1987–88	4,278	71.9	7.1
1988–89	4,617	85.5	7.9
1989–90	4,952	99.0	7.3
1990–91	5,208	109.2	5.2

Source: *Estimates of School Statistics 1990–91,* National Education Association, Research Division, 1991, p. 25.

some of those that have been in operation long enough to prove their worth. The movement that was generated by groups against the payment of property taxes for financing public education and other institutions of government has become widespread. Although some taxpayer relief may be necessary and overdue in some states and school districts, the field of education in particular stands to lose much—and the nation stands to lose more—if taxpayer revolts continue without serious and knowledgeable consideration of the harmful effect they will have on the future of the public school system. In 1991 the Committee for Economic Development indicated that "Educationally, the United States remains a nation at risk"[5] and stated:

> We believe that education is an investment, not an expense. If we can ensure that all children are born healthy and develop the skills and knowledge they need to be productive, self-supporting adults, whatever is spent on their development and education will be returned many times over in higher productivity, incomes, and taxes and in lower costs for welfare, health care, crime, and a myriad of other economic and social problems.[6]

THE INCREASING COSTS OF EDUCATION

Education is most meaningful when it is fashioned in terms of goals or objectives, whether they are implied or formally stated in the literature. Education without purpose or philosophical commitment would have little value and would stimulate little if any support or dedication.

The purposes of education have much to do with the cost of the program that is established and operated to achieve those objectives. To compare the problems of financing a three Rs curriculum with those of financing a program constructed to achieve the far-reaching and comprehensive goals of present-day education is a futile exercise, guaranteed to result in frustration. As the schools reach out to supply new curricula and provide new methods of attaining increasingly complex and comprehensive goals for their clientele, the costs multiply, and taxpayers are forced to reach deeper and deeper into depleted treasuries. The end is not near, for the public adds additional goals and responsibilities to the school program year after year and seldom, if ever, relieves it of any purposes or programs that might be offered at lower cost or with greater effectiveness elsewhere.

The revenues made available for financing public elementary and secondary schools from local, state, and federal sources increased from $100 billion in 1960 to over $350 billion in 1989–90 (Figure 2-1), while the number of enrollees increased less than 30 percent. This cost increase reflects not only curriculum changes but is a mirror of society. Education problems do not belong to educators alone. Institutions and the family must share in preparing children for the future. When deciding how much should be spent for education, educators and

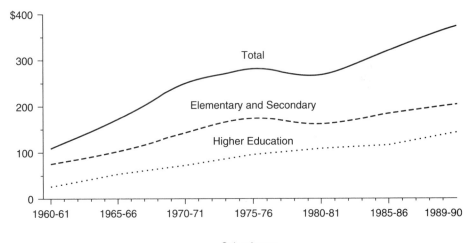

School year

FIGURE 2-1   Expenditures, in billions of constant 1989–90 dollars. (Source: *Statistics of State School Systems; Statistics of Public Elementary and Secondary School Systems; Statistics of Nonpublic Secondary School Systems; Statistics of Nonpublic Elementary and Secondary Schools; Revenues and Expenditures for Public Elementary and Secondary Education; Fall Enrollment in Institutions of Higher Education; Financial Statistics of Institutions of Higher Education;* and Common Core of Data surveys, U.S. Department of Education, National Center for Education Statistics.)

legislators must agree on what the schools are expected to do. As the goals and objectives of education become more inclusive and more difficult to achieve, the taxpayer must face the stark fact that the costs will likewise increase.

Goals Have Increased

The persistent but irregular march of change and innovation in the public schools is shown by the many successive changes in the goals and objectives of education in the last half-century. Such redefinitions have usually come after serious study, based on changing needs. Not all resultant statements have made an indelible imprint on education in the United States, but a few have.

Early statements of the objectives of education were very limited, relatively easy to achieve in a limited way, and correspondingly inexpensive. But the goals of the school became more comprehensive and costly as the schools improved and as public confidence in them increased. The Seven Cardinal Principles of Secondary Education, the Four Objectives of the Educational Policies Commission, and the Ten Imperative Needs of Youth are examples of some of the important statements of what Americans have at different times viewed as the important goals of education.

As far back as 1966, a study of the needs and problems of education appeared. The statement of this study, published by the American Association of School Administrators, expressed the thinking of a commission on the goals or "imperatives" of education in the years ahead. The commission had been appointed by the AASA and was charged "with responsibility for identifying and stating in clear and concise fashion major educational imperatives that must be at the forefront as curriculums are modified, instructional methods revised, and organizational patterns reshaped to meet the educational needs of this country in one of its dynamic periods."[7]

The nine imperatives of education formulated by the commission are evidence of the changing and increasing needs of education. The general themes of development of the individual and need for social betterment pervades the statement. The nine imperatives are:

1. To make urban life rewarding and satisfying
2. To prepare people for the world of work
3. To discover and nurture creative talent
4. To strengthen the moral fabric of society
5. To deal constructively with psychological tensions
6. To keep democracy working
7. To make intelligent use of natural resources
8. To make the best use of leisure time
9. To work with other peoples of the world for human betterment

Although these imperatives were not intended to be "educational goals" nor to encompass the entire educational program, "they are points at which the educational program must be revised and reshaped to meet the needs of the times." The imperatives strike tellingly at some of the main problems of education today. They indicate the areas of greatest concern, the areas of greatest failure with regard to the needs of the day, and the areas where improvements must be made if education is ever to be efficacious for all. In that sense they are the goals, the objectives, the "cardinal principles" of today and of the immediate future.

The inclusiveness of this set of imperatives for education seems to signal financial trouble for the already overburdened taxpayers who must assume the gargantuan costs of such an ambitious but necessary program. That these high costs, if properly and efficiently applied to meet these imperatives, will actually become large investments that will bring great economic benefits to all our citizens cannot be denied. However, that does not help much in determining how to raise such large sums of money from the private sector of the economy to give the system a chance to provide the quality of education necessary to meet these challenges.

Just as the costs of education have increased almost geometrically, so have the demands placed upon schools. Each level of government, each important social organization, and almost every individual continues to increase the expectations with which the school is confronted and upon which its achievements are evaluated.

Richard Miller, Executive Director of the American Association of School Administrators, states:

> We depend on the schools to help solve some of the most important problems and deal with some of the most important challenges in our society. (1) In the 1950s, when Sputnik was launched, we looked to the schools to produce scientists and mathematicians who have helped to develop our technological leadership among the nations of the world. Our scientists also took us successfully to the moon and have expanded our frontiers in space. (2) When our society called for social integration, people looked to the schools for a remedy. The schools organized to meet the social challenge. Now our nation faces an economic emergency. We are concerned about the productivity of the Japanese and Germans. (3) We have also looked to the schools to deal with the needs of the handicapped, to make students employable and to provide them with a multitude of other skills.[8]

People Want Better Education

George Gallup's 1990 poll of public attitudes toward schools revealed that in a period of seven years there was no statistical change in the ratings people gave their local public schools. The low point in the decade was in 1983, which may have been a reflection of the "A Nation at Risk" report. People gave higher grades to their local public schools than they gave schools nationally. Parents who had children currently attending schools gave the grade of A or B to their local schools 72 percent of the time, but those same parents gave an A or B to the nation's public schools only 21 percent of the time—a striking contrast.[9]

Citizens of the United States continue to make large investments in the educational enterprise in spite of its alleged inadequacy in many states and school districts. The reasons for these perennial increases are often beyond the power of school boards or administrators to change. However justified these increasing costs become when viewed in proper perspective and in comparison with the alternatives, they tend to irritate the overburdened taxpayer, whose resistance tends to become a cumulative matter and often one of deep personal concern.

For what reason or reasons do people continually approve high taxation rates to provide revenue for financing education? According to the Phi Delta Kappa Commission on Alternative Designs for Funding Education, there are three fundamental reasons for continuing to improve the nation's educational system:

> This vast commitment of funds by the government can realistically be justified on grounds that the people want it. After all, the expenditure of government funds should reflect the needs, wants, and demands of the people. But the justification for expenditure of public funds for education goes much deeper than a mere common desire to possess knowledge. Mass public education can be justified on the more basic grounds that it creates and perpetuates the culture, promotes social equality, and enhances economic development.
>
> Each of these alone may be ample reason for government to finance education, but to view them in combination leaves little doubt as to the importance of education. Of the three, the most significant is undoubtedly to gain and advance the accumulated culture and knowledge of man, create a respect for humanity, promote the attributes of citizenship, and inculcate ethical and moral character. Education not only preserves the cultural heritage but also exalts the status of man and provides at least a minimum level of citizenship. In this regard the advantages of education cannot be quantified. The benefits of reading a book, appreciating a painting, playing a violin, speaking a foreign language, and understanding a theorem are priceless, even though they may not be of any substantial economic importance.[10]

Demographic Changes

The history of public education in the United States has been one of generally rapid growth and expansion. Most of the serious problems of financing it have been concerned with rapidly increasing enrollments, shortages of buildings and classrooms, inadequate facilities, and the need to employ greater numbers of teachers and other staff members. With such causal factors, taxpayers were generally able to understand the reasons for annual increases in their investment in education.

But the general pattern has changed. Many states and school districts now face problems centered around the effects of declining enrollments, decreased building needs, and, ironically, rapidly increasing costs. It is easier to convince the tax-paying public of the need to increase school budgets when student enrollment increases and buildings need to be built, but it is a different matter when enrollments are constant. School finance problems have not lessened, and the public often offers stern resistance to increases in school budgets year after year. Public elementary school enrollment has been relatively constant and this trend is projected to continue (Figure 2-2).

The enrollment data reaffirm the complexity of funding education in an atmosphere of change. When enrollment was declining, the public in general, and school boards and legislatures in particular, seemed to indicate that it was an unimportant phenomenon that would pass away quickly and quietly. Consequently, very little planning was done to cope with this turn of events. Some educators even view a decline with a degree of enthusiasm in anticipation of having fewer students in classrooms, more opportunity for quality instruction, and more money for enrichment of the curriculum. These seemed to be obvious results to many who had struggled for years with overcrowded classrooms and inadequate facilities. Relatively few of those who were responsible for financing education seemed to realize that inflation and its resulting problems would keep costs rising, regardless of the number of students in attendance. They ignored the obvious fact that it costs just as much to heat, light, and maintain a school building that houses only a few students as it does if the building is over-

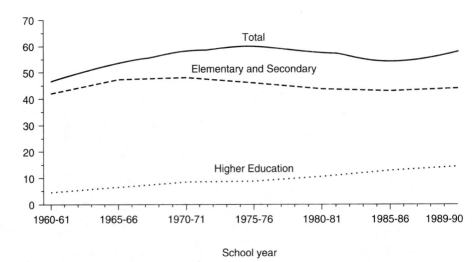

Enrollment, in millions

FIGURE 2-2 Enrollment by level of education: 1960-61 to 1989–90. Source: *All Levels of Education,* U.S. Department of Education, National Center for Education Statistics, 1991.

crowded, and that declining enrollments do not necessarily reduce the number of teachers or other staff members required. They did not anticipate the expanding numbers of high-cost disadvantaged, handicapped, compensatory, and minority group students that were beginning to be brought into the schools, thereby increasing the cost of education per student. Neither did they anticipate that more effective bargaining for higher salaries for all employees, the cost of new and expensive federal programs for exceptional and bilingual students, and the high cost of implementing desegregation programs in some schools would keep the total cost of education on a steep incline in spite of fluctuating enrollments. Of course, demographic changes vary from place to place and from school district to school district.

In the 1980s the average daily attendance in public elementary and secondary schools remained relatively constant, with 37,837,375 attending at the beginning of the decade and 38,099,634 attending in 1990–91 (Table 2-3). However, in two states, West Virginia and Michigan, there was a decrease of 5 percent or more. In eighteen states there was no increase or a decrease of less than 5 percent: Massachusetts, Connecticut, New York, Pennsylvania, New Jersey, North Carolina, Kentucky, Ohio, Indiana, Illinois, Minnesota, Iowa, Oklahoma, Louisiana, North Dakota, Montana, Wyoming, Colorado. In Alaska, Hawaii, Idaho, New Mexico, South Dakota, Nebraska, Missouri, Arkansas, Alabama, Tennessee, Wisconsin, South Carolina, Virginia, Maryland, Rhode Island, and the District of Columbia (sixteen entities), the enrollment figures have increased less than 5 percent. The dramatic demographics are those in eleven states, mostly in the West and South where there has been an increase of 5 percent or more (Figure 2-3).

TABLE 2-3 Average Daily Attendance of Elementary and Secondary Students in the United States: 1980–1991

School year	Average daily attendance	Percent change	
		From 1980–91	From previous year
1980–81	37,857,375		
1981–82	37,071,838	−2.1	−2.1
1982–83	36,752,323	−2.9	−0.9
1983–84	36,508,384	−3.6	−0.7
1984–85	36,530,477	−3.5	0.1
1985–86	36,681,428	−3.1	0.4
1986–87	36,902,568	−2.5	0.6
1987–88	37,058,875	−2.1	0.4
1988–89	37,173,858	−1.8	0.3
1989–90	37,442,063	−1.1	0.7
1990–91	38,099,634	0.6	1.8

Source: *Estimates of School Statistics 1990–91*, National Education Association, Research Division, 1991.

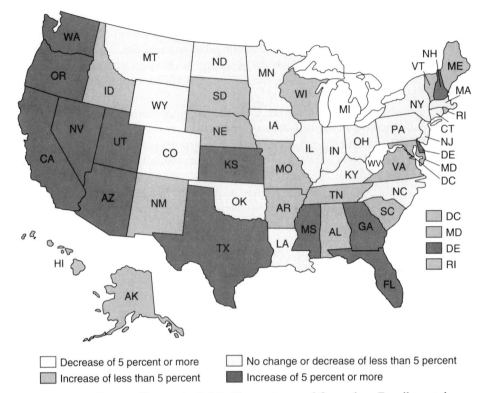

Decrease of 5 percent or more   No change or decrease of less than 5 percent
Increase of less than 5 percent   Increase of 5 percent or more

FIGURE 2-3   Percent Change in Public Elementary and Secondary Enrollment, by
State: Fall 1984 to Fall 1989. (Source: Common Core of Data
Surveys, U.S. Department of Education, National Center for
Education Statistics.)

Despite the constant enrollment in the 1980s, the National Education Association reports that:

> Research literature and media accounts have been advising educators, poli-
> cymakers, and the public that enrollment increases are on their way, and
> indeed, state education agency figures for 1985–86 signaled the end of an era
> of enrollment decline and the beginning of an upward trend in public school
> enrollment for most states. Implications for the demand for public school
> teachers and other education personnel are obvious, and education expendi-
> ture decisions by state-local government will need to accommodate expand-
> ing resource demands associated with enrollment growth.[11]

More children were born in 1990 than in any year since 1961,[12] which has
created an echo baby boom. Four million, two hundred thousand babies were
born in 1990, which makes it the second year in a row in which more than four

million babies were born. These children being born are a surprise to forecasters. In fact, the number is 12 percent higher than the Census Bureau projected. The boom is confounding forecasters for two reasons: "First, the total fertility rate edged up from 1.8 to 1.9 births per woman between 1987 and 1988. Second, age-specific fertility rates are increasing fastest among women in their 30s."[13]

Echo baby boom women are still in their late 20s and early 30s—prime years for postponed child-bearing as well as having additional children. Projection assumptions are varied, but if the trend of 1989 and 1990 continues, the number of preschoolers will be 20.2 million, about the same as at the peak of the baby boom in 1960, which had 20.3 preschoolers.

Enrollment in preprimary education has increased significantly. The number of three- to five-year-old children attending school rose 19 percent from 1970 to 1980 and an additional 24 percent in the 1980s. Enrollment in full-day preschool programs rose even more sharply—in 1980, 32 percent of preschool-age children attended preschool, while in 1989, 37 percent did so.[14] With this prekindergarten surge, the public school enrollment in 1990–91 was 41 million students. An additional 5.2 million enrolled in private schools.[15]

In the period from 1990 to 2010, it is estimated that the total population will increase from 250 million to 282.5 million—an increase of 7.1 percent from 1990 to 2000 and 5.3 percent from 2000 to 2010. The school-age group of 5 to 17 years remains constant. However, that group will make up 18.2 percent of the population in 1990, but only 16.2 percent of the population in 2010. The numbers range from 45.2 million to 45.7 million—a change of only 500,000 (Table 2-4).

Another indication of the population shift is graphically demonstrated in the official U.S. Census. In 1991 the Census Bureau announced the redistribution of seats in the U.S. House of Representatives based on the change in population—New York lost three seats; Michigan, Ohio, Pennsylvania, and Illinois each lost two seats; and Iowa, Kansas, Kentucky, Louisiana, Massachusetts, Montana, New Jersey, and West Virginia each lost one seat. California picked up seven; Florida, four; Texas, three; and Arizona, Georgia, North Carolina, Washington, and Virginia each picked up one seat.

In addition to the change from state to state there has been significant growth in urban areas. From 1950 to 1990 the percent of the U.S. population living in metropolitan areas of 1 million or more rose from 29.7 to 50.2. The number of metropolitan areas with a population of 1 million or more increased from 14 to 39 percent. When metropolitan areas of less than 1 million are included, the figures are significantly greater, with 77.5 percent of the U.S. total living in urban areas. The 10 largest metropolitan areas are, in millions; (1) New York, 18.1; (2) Los Angeles, 14.5; (3) Chicago, 8.1; (4) San Francisco-Oakland-San Jose, 6.3; (5) Philadelphia, 5.9; (6) Detroit, 4.7; (7) Boston, 4.2; (8) Washington D.C., 3.9; (9) Dallas-Fort Worth, 3.9; and (10) Houston, 3.7. Four areas entered the million plus category in 1990: Charlotte, Salt Lake City, Orlando, and Rochester, N.Y.[16] (Table 2-5).

TABLE 2-4 Projections of the Total Population by Age, Sex, and Race: 1980 to 2010

Age, sex, and race	Percent change		
	1980–1990	1990–2000	2000–2010
Total	9.9	7.1	5.3
Under 5 years old	11.8	−8.2	0
5–17 years old	−3.4	7.0	−6.3
18–24 years old	−13.9	−3.5	7.6
25–34 years old	16.7	−15.4	1.1
35–44 years old	46.5	15.9	−15.3
45–54 years old	12.0	46.0	16.1
55–64 years old	−1.8	13.1	46.7
65–74 years old	17.4	−.7	15.3
75 years old and over	31.2	26.2	10.1
16 years old and over	11.9	8.9	8.2
Male, total	10.2	7.3	5.4
Under 5 years old	12.0	−8.1	.1
5–17 years old	−3.2	7.1	−6.2
18–24 years old	−13.8	−3.4	7.7
25–34 years old	17.8	−15.5	1.2
35–44 years old	47.7	16.8	−15.3
45–54 years old	12.8	47.5	17.1
55–64 years old	−.8	14.4	48.6
65–74 years old	20.3	.9	17.6
75 years old and over	30.9	28.9	10.8
16 years old and over	12.4	9.2	8.5
Female, total	9.7	7.0	5.2
Under 5 years old	11.7	−8.3	−.1
5–17 years old	−3.7	6.9	−6.4
18–24 years old	−14.0	−3.6	7.6
25–34 years old	15.7	−15.4	1.1
35–44 years old	45.4	14.9	−15.3
45–54 years old	11.3	44.7	15.0
55–64 years old	−2.8	11.9	44.9
65–74 years old	15.1	−2.0	13.5
75 years old and over	31.3	24.7	9.8
16 years old and over	11.5	8.6	7.9
White, total	7.7	5.2	3.4
Under 5 years old	10.4	−10.5	−1.8
5–17 years old	−6.3	5.6	−8.6
18–24 years old	−16.7	−6.2	6.5
25–34 years old	13.6	−18.1	−1.3
35–44 years old	44.1	13.2	−18.0
45–54 years old	9.8	44.0	13.4
55–64 years old	−4.5	10.9	44.7
65–74 years old	16.1	−3.5	13.1
75 years old and over	30.2	25.1	7.6
16 years old and over	9.6	6.8	6.2

(Continued)

TABLE 2-4   (*Continued*)

Age, sex, and race	Percent change		
	1980–1990	1990–2000	2000–2010
Male	8.0	5.4	3.5
Female	7.4	4.9	3.2
Black, total	15.8	12.8	10.6
Under 5 years old	13.7	−2.3	2.6
5–17 years old	2.5	10.1	−1.1
18–24 years old	−5.4	2.9	9.9
25–34 years old	31.2	−7.4	6.2
35–44 years old	52.9	30.2	−7.4
45–54 years old	17.4	52.9	30.8
55–64 years old	12.1	19.6	55.0
65–74 years old	19.0	14.9	23.2
75 years old and over	33.1	27.7	23.5
16 years old and over	19.2	15.7	14.6
Male	16.2	13.2	10.8
Female	15.4	12.4	10.3
Other races, total	67.2	34.5	27.0
Under 5 years old	47.7	17.8	20.4
5–17 years old	58.2	22.2	14.1
18–24 years old	41.9	31.1	17.9
25–34 years old	57.3	17.1	26.3
35–44 years old	103.8	34.5	14.7
45–54 years old	84.5	76.2	32.0
55–64 years old	81.1	59.9	67.1
65–74 years old	101.2	51.9	51.8
75 years old and over	109.6	79.3	61.8
16 years old and over	71.5	40.5	30.1
Male	66.5	33.3	26.5
Female	67.8	35.6	27.5

Source: *Current Population Reports*, Series P–25, No. 1018, U.S. Bureau of the Census.

The population's increasing mobility results in increased school costs, particularly for new school facilities. As families move, they leave behind partially occupied school buildings and reduced pupil-teacher ratios. They frequently find that the places to which they move have overcrowded classrooms and high pupil-teacher ratios. Such imbalances naturally increase the total cost of

TABLE 2-5   Growth of Metropolitan Areas[a]

Year	Number	Population (millions)	Percent of U.S. population
1950	14	44.9	29.7
1960	22	63.9	35.6
1970	31	83.9	41.0
1980	35	104.0	45.9
1990	39	124.8	50.2

Source: U.S. Bureau of the Census.
[a]Population of one million or more.

education and change the responsibility of the various states and the nation for financing education.

The effect upon budgets has been greatest in some of the large urban districts. They have been forced to react with decreases in staff, reductions in pupil services, early closing of schools, elimination of some school attendance areas, and various other methods of reducing the costs of education—all of which reduce the quantity and quality of education being offered.

Occupancy of School Facilities

The typical school year is nine months. A few states and many school districts have established year-round schools, extended the length of the school day, or extended the school year. It is a sad commentary on education in the United States that the time actually spent in formal education by typical students continues to be far less than that of their counterparts in most other countries. The waste, not only in human time and development, but also in depreciation of empty school buildings and unused facilities for such an extended period of time every year, is a human capital and financial loss that this country can ill afford to sustain. The traditional three-month summer vacation compounds the problem of teacher unemployment; at the same time, releasing students of all ages to long periods of unsupervised activity often creates home and neighborhood problems. Plans for varying the school year and utilizing school buildings to a much greater extent need to be explored, developed, and evaluated.

Additional Services Require Additional Funds

Year after year student and community services offered by the public schools have continued to increase in spite of the rising costs of education. The school constantly receives added responsibilities for teaching new programs, techniques, and processes. Seldom, if ever, are successful school services taken away and given to other social agencies or institutions.

Society recognizes that few institutions are better prepared than the schools to render certain emerging social services. For example, the schools are more or less ideal institutions for offering new vocational programs, preschool services, counseling programs, special services for exceptional students, extension of adult education, and many other community and individual services. The point, however, is that such additional services require additional funds, and the taxpaying public must accept financial responsibility for the added costs. Comparisons of the annual costs of public education should be interpreted in the light of the additional services that are provided year after year in the name of public education.

Effects of Inflation

Although the problem of procuring sufficient funds for educating millions of public elementary and secondary school students has always been a difficult one, the inflation rates of the last half of the twentieth century greatly increased the difficulty. The erosive effect of high and continuous inflation of the dollar on school budgets needs few illustrations and little documentation, for it is an undesirable phenomenon that affects every citizen and every school in the nation. The problem of financing education, once considered the responsibility of only a few specialists with vested interests in the schools—boards of education, school administrators, state departments of education, and state legislatures—developed into a priority item for virtually all citizens.

Uncontrolled inflation causes the dollar cost of education to rise rapidly. Inflation not only reduces the real income of the individuals but also increases their tax obligations under a progressive income tax system. For example, doubling one's income because of inflation—even though the relative purchasing power may not have changed—could put an individual in a higher income tax bracket and, in some cases, more than double the tax obligation. Inflation causes people to cut back on the purchase of goods and services in an attempt to maintain their economic position. The result is disastrous for schools. At the same time as taxpayers press to reduce their tax burden, the costs of operating an educational program usually continue to increase. Predicting inflation is difficult, for it is very changeable as Figure 2-4 shows. It is nevertheless an important factor to consider when determining costs of education.

Scarcity and High Cost of Energy

The cost of energy is a crucial factor in the increasing costs of education and conservation is the key to survival when reviewed in the tumultuous world scene influenced by oil-producing countries. School programs are affected as the cost of gasoline and oil products necessary for the transportation of millions of students to and from school increase, as was evidenced during the 1991 "Desert Storm" conflict.

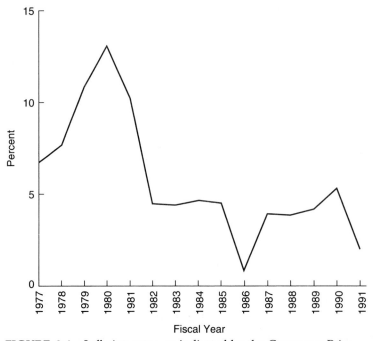

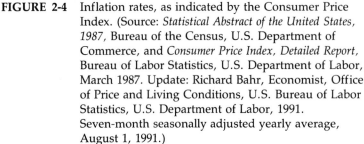

FIGURE 2-4   Inflation rates, as indicated by the Consumer Price
Index. (Source: *Statistical Abstract of the United States,
1987,* Bureau of the Census, U.S. Department of
Commerce, and *Consumer Price Index, Detailed Report,*
Bureau of Labor Statistics, U.S. Department of Labor,
March 1987. Update: Richard Bahr, Economist, Office
of Price and Living Conditions, U.S. Bureau of Labor
Statistics, U.S. Department of Labor, 1991.
Seven-month seasonally adjusted yearly average,
August 1, 1991.)

Schools in general should be well equipped to initiate and carry out their
own conservation measures. Some of the lessons this nation has generally
ignored about the wise use of limited energy resources can be practiced effectively in school operations. More energy-efficient construction and maintenance procedures decrease energy expenditures without seriously diluting the
overall school program. School officials need to be alert to the volatile nature of
the oil industry, and the international political and economic forces that control
energy sources.

Social Indicators

The United States is undergoing significant social changes, including dramatic
alterations in the nature of the typical family. The traditional family—two

parents with children—continues to decline. Only 26 percent of U.S. families in 1990 met this definition, compared to 40 percent in 1970. The decline is fueled by the rise in single-parent families which, between 1980 and 1990, showed a 41 percent growth—half of the 82 percent increase between 1970 and 1980. Nearly all single parents are women. Black single parents outnumber whites by three to one, which represents more than one-half of black homes. Nearly one in every three Hispanic homes is headed by a single man or woman. In a White, Asian or Pacific Islander home, there is a single head of household in nearly one in every five homes[17] (Figure 2-5).

The problem of single families is further exacerbated by the change in family income when parents separate. According to a study by the U.S. Bureau of the Census, within four months of separation the percentage of children living in poverty increased from 19 percent to 36 percent. At the four-month mark after separation, 18 percent were recipients of Aid to Families with Dependent Children. That figure increased to 22 percent at one year. The percentage of families receiving food stamps was 27 percent at the four-month mark and remained at that level at one year.[18]

The long-run impact of poverty prevails, according to another study by the Census Bureau with children in single-parent homes more likely to live in poverty. In the United States, 51 percent of children in single-parent homes were poor.[19]

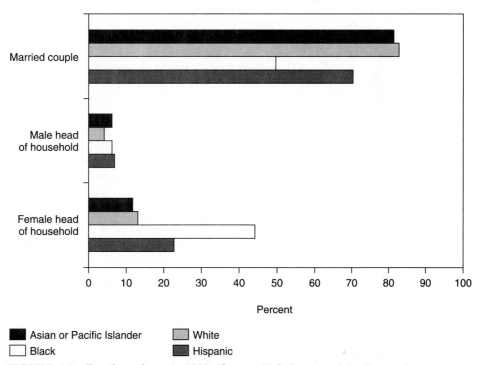

FIGURE 2-5 Family makeup in 1990. (Source: U.S. Bureau of the Census.)

In a recent study 14 percent of 8th graders surveyed were home after school without adult supervision for more than three hours. According to the survey, 13 percent were home alone two to three hours, 28 percent were home one to two hours, 32 percent were home less than one hour—totaling 87 percent of 8th graders coming home to an unsupervised environment. Only 13 percent usually had an adult to greet them as they returned from school.[20] The "latchkey" child influences the social structure of this country.

Since 1973 the percent of children 0 to 18 years old living in poverty increased by 33$\frac{1}{3}$ percent.[21] Data show that one of four children under the age of 6 lives in poverty.[22] It is estimated that 375,000 infants born in 1990 were exposed to drugs and that it will cost in excess of $15 billion annually to get them ready for school, not even considering the enormous costs when they are enrolled.[23] "Mounting societal pressures . . . have forced public schools to assume responsibilities for the welfare of children that go well beyond their traditional educational mission. As a result many public schools . . . are increasingly pursuing a broad social agenda and are providing a wide range of social services . . . to fully address the increasing social-support needs of their students. With resources stretched thin, it is not surprising that in many schools neither the academic nor the social agenda is being fully realized."[24]

Coleman and his associates note that higher educational achievement is attained by children from higher-income families, by children whose parents complete more years of school, by children who have fewer siblings, and by children whose parents have higher education expectations for them. In contrast, children from single-parent homes and from homes where both parents work achieve lower levels of education.[25] Another study noted that, of 100 children born in 1986, 18 were illegitimate, 37 of their parents will be divorced, 9 of their parents will be separated, 2 will have one parent die before the child is 18, and only 4 will be in the "typical" nuclear family—working father, homemaker mother, two school-age children.[26] These research studies indicate the importance of social statistics in planning for America's schools.

Each of these problems, taken alone, would probably not cost school districts much in comparison with the enormous total cost of education, but collectively they represent a burden that districts can ill afford. Present socioeconomic conditions represent an ominous threat to the social welfare as well as to the already tight budgets of many urban school districts. Significant changes are in progress, but too many educators have ignored the social changes and refused to recognize their impact on individual students, classrooms, and schools.

THE CONSEQUENCES OF NOT EDUCATING PEOPLE

Perhaps all people think of the high costs of educating the nation's citizens, but comparatively few give much thought to the higher cost of *not* educating them. Crime rates and costs related to public welfare or private charity are much greater among those who have an inadequate education to allow them to succeed in today's society than for those with an adequate education. The direct costs to taxpayers of keeping a person incarcerated are many times the per-pupil cost of educating a student. Additional costs are incurred by the victims, and often by the prisoner's family. In the future the costs of dealing with failing to educate the populace will undoubtedly be exponentially greater than would be the provision of additional finances for a quality education for all the people.

Failure to apply the theory of equality of educational opportunity results in some penalties to the students involved and is a costly injustice to society in general.

Illiteracy

Notwithstanding compulsory attendance laws, illiteracy is more common in this country than is generally believed. In the United Nations there are 158 members; 48 countries reported having higher literacy levels than the United States in 1983.

In 1986, *Time* quoted Robert Barnes, an official of the U.S. Department of Education, who stated, "we are creating a new generation of illiterates." Barnes stated, "17 million to 21 million adults in the U.S. cannot read. And this is only some of the bad news. . . . The new study shows that the majority of nonreaders are under 50."[27] Even if one questions the accuracy of these statistics, the socio-economic results of illiteracy represent a financial and social loss that this country cannot afford. Certainly, this condition of inadequate schooling, with attendant unemployment and the problems that accompany low incomes, contributes significantly to the problems of America's poor.

Time continued, "The total cost of illiteracy to the U.S. economy cannot be accurately measured. But critics insist the nation is paying dearly in lost productivity and in human misery."[28]

In 1989 the U.S. Department of Education developed three scales to test literacy skills: prose, document, and quantitative. Using a numerical factor of 200 or more, 250 or more, 300 or more, and 350 or more, Table 2-6 explains the varied abilities in total, ethnic, and educational attainment factors. Generalizations from the data reveal that individuals from all races who are not high school graduates, and black non-Hispanics in general, have serious literacy problems.

Unemployment

Unemployment is closely related to lack of adequate education. Figures show that it is much more of a problem to school dropouts and to those with a minimum education than to those who have attended schools and succeeded academically. Unemployment is further complicated by the need to retrain and reequip countless workers in business and industry every few years. Those with adequate education are usually able to adjust to new jobs and new occupations more easily and with less frustration than those with limited schooling.

TABLE 2-6 Literacy Skills and Reading Scores of Young Adults,[a] by Race/Ethnicity and Level of Education: 1985

Young adult characteristic	Prose literacy scale[b] percent with score of				Document literacy[c] percent with score of				Quantitative literacy[d] percent with score of			
1	2	3	4	5	6	7	8	9	10	11	12	13
	200 or more	250 or more	300 or more	350 or more	200 or more	250 or more	300 or more	350 or more	200 or more	250 or more	300 or more	350 or more
Total	96.1	82.7	56.4	21.1	95.5	83.8	57.2	20.2	96.4	84.7	56.0	22.5
Race/ethnicity												
White, non-Hispanic	98.1	89.7	63.0	24.3	98.2	89.5	64.1	24.9	98.1	89.4	62.9	24.8
Black, non-Hispanic	86.3	57.2	21.3	3.5	84.4	56.5	20.1	2.2	87.8	58.0	21.4	3.3
Hispanic	93.5	73.6	40.9	13.5	92.0	69.8	35.9	9.4	92.8	72.5	35.2	9.2
Educational attainment												
Not high school graduate	85.4	57.9	24.1	3.4	83.4	53.6	18.8	1.5	86.1	57.7	20.6	3.5
High school graduate	99.6	81.6	45.1	10.5	96.5	81.8	46.2	9.0	96.9	80.5	45.2	10.1
Some postsecondary	98.8	92.0	67.0	26.8	99.0	92.1	68.0	27.2	99.3	92.7	66.8	27.0
College graduate	99.9	97.7	84.3	44.8	99.9	98.0	85.6	48.8	99.9	97.8	84.1	45.3

Source: *Young Adult Literacy and Schooling*, U.S.Department of Education, National Center for Education Statistics. (This table was prepared May 1989.)

[a] Includes persons 21 to 25 years old. Excludes persons not living in households and those who were unable to speak English.

[b] Prose comprehension test measures the knowledge and skills needed to gain understanding and use information from texts such as editorials, news stories, and poems. A score of 200 indicates an ability to write a simple description of the type of job one would like to have. A score of 300 indicates an ability to locate information in a news article or an almanac. A score of 350 indicates an ability to synthesize the main argument from a lengthy newspaper editorial.

[c] Document literacy test measures the knowledge and skills required to locate and use information from documents such as indexes, tables, paycheck stubs, and order forms. A score of 200 indicates ability to match money-saving coupons to a shopping list of several items. A score of 300 indicates an ability to follow directions to travel from one location to another using a map. A score of 350 indicates an ability to use a bus schedule to select the appropriate bus for given departures and arrivals.

[d] Quantitative literacy test measures the knowledge and skills needed to apply the arithmetic operations of addition, subtraction, multiplication, and division, either alone or sequentially. A score of 200 indicates an ability to total two entries on a bank deposit slip. A score of 300 indicates an ability to enter deposits and checks and balance a checkbook. A score of 350 indicates an ability to determine the amount of a tip in a restaurant using a given percentage.

According to the National Committee for Support of the Public Schools, the great financial and social losses from unemployment can never be recovered:

> Economic losses from unemployment are never regained. The social costs of unemployment are even greater than the economic losses. The discouragement and frustration of able-bodied men and women, eager to work but unable to find employment, cannot be measured in dollars any more than can the distress of their families. Prolonged unemployment contributes to further unemployment, since human capital deteriorates when it is idle. Unemployment impairs the skills that workers have acquired. It also contributes to family disintegration, crime, and other social ills.[29]

Military Service Incapability

Those who think that the current level of investment in education is adequate and that schools are satisfactory should look at the disgraceful record of educational preparation of youth that was brought to light by World War II and verified by data from the Korean and Viet Nam conflicts. It was a record that shocked the nation—a nation that had believed with firm conviction that its educational system was adequate if not superior. The rejection of large numbers of young men from induction into military service was a severe indictment against the effectiveness of prewar education in this country.

"In World War II, some 400,000 illiterates were accepted for military service. The Armed Forces provided these men with the educational fundamentals necessary for useful service. Another 300,000 illiterates—equal to 20 army divisions—were rejected completely."[30]

> Despite the pressing demand for military manpower, nearly thirty percent of all men examined by Selective Service in World War II were rejected as mentally, physically, or morally unfit to serve their country. This is all the more shocking in view of the fact that the incidence of unfitness could have been greatly reduced. Rejection rates cannot be attributed to lack of schooling alone, but they correlate highly with lack of education and with low expenditures. . . . Rejection rates ranged from fifty to fifty-five percent for the entire period. More recent statistics show that this tragic inadequacy has continued to plague the states where education is poorly financed and where large numbers attend school for only a few years. In short, under-education saps the nation's defense potential and places a disproportionate share of Selective Service demands on the states which provide better education.[31]

In 1991, in a speech to the U.S. Chamber of Commerce, Secretary of Defense Richard Cheney indicated that the United States was not interested in soldiers without high school diplomas. He indicated that modern warfare, in the era of Patriot missiles, Stealth airplanes, and other sophisticated weapons, could not endure a poor or inadequate education.[32]

Inadequate Occupational Preparation

The media is replete with reports that applicants seeking occupational positions in business and industry lack adequate educational preparations. Business and industry have implemented basic education and retraining programs to overcome these inadequacies. This condition results in an obvious waste in time and cost for American industry.

Education is an investment in human skills, involving both a cost and a return. In summarizing statistics on the employment benefits of education, the U.S. Department of Education notes that:

> Among the returns related to the labor market are better employment opportunities, jobs that are less sensitive to general economic conditions, better opportunities to participate in employer-provided training, and higher earnings. . . . [T]he immediate difficulty of making the transition from full-time school attendance to full-time work appears much greater for those who leave school before finishing high school. In October 1989, of young people who had left high school during the previous year without finishing only 47 percent were employed. In contrast, of those who had graduated from high school in 1989 and did not enroll in college 72 percent were employed. (Figure 2-6.)[33]

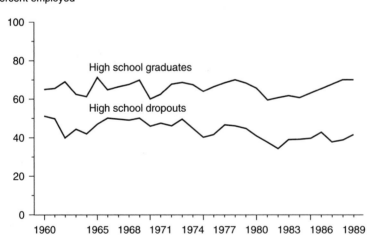

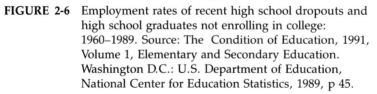

FIGURE 2-6 Employment rates of recent high school dropouts and
high school graduates not enrolling in college:
1960–1989. Source: The Condition of Education, 1991,
Volume 1, Elementary and Secondary Education.
Washington D.C.: U.S. Department of Education,
National Center for Education Statistics, 1989, p 45.

Speaking to this issue, Gardner said: "Education is the key to improving the quality of life for individuals, for improving the climate of economic development in our state, and for maintaining and improving our national democracy and economic competitiveness."[34]

Although accurate figures are not available, the mass rejections of unqualified applicants seeking occupational positions in business and industry indicate a high percentage of people with inadequate educational qualifications. This condition results in an obvious waste of much of the time and cost of maintaining employment offices. Unsuccessful job hunting represents a big loss to employers as well as to those applying for positions. The problem becomes more acute as technology replaces common labor and the qualifications and skills required in most occupations continue to increase.

Dependence on Public Relief

There appears to be a high positive relation between inadequate education and an individual's need for financial assistance. A number of recent studies have shown that recipients of public assistance are likely to be individuals of low educational attainment.

A Chicago study of relief recipients showed that 50.7 percent of the sample studied could not pass reading and vocabulary tests at the fifth grade achievement level. "The conclusion was that the problems of public welfare stem from unemployment and economic and technological displacement and, most important, from relief recipients' lack of basic educational skills which are essential to compete in our modern society."[35]

A high positive relationship between inadequate education and an individual's need for financial Aid for Dependent Children (AFDC) has been shown in several recent studies. Recipients of public assistance are likely to have less education than nonparticipants. Levitan stated: " 'AFDC' mothers have substantially lower educational attainment than adult women in general. Only three out of seven completed high school, compared to five out of seven of the entire adult population."[36] Nineteen percent of families headed by a female householder who have no husband present and are below the poverty level have had eight years or less of education.[37] Only four-tenths of one percent have graduated from college.[38]

Studies have been conducted to try to determine the characteristics of long-term recipients of welfare in order to "target employment and social services toward them in an effort to reduce their dependency, both for fiscal and humanitarian purposes."[39] Ellwood indicated that the length of time or duration for welfare dependence would be affected by three factors, two of which were related to education. He stated, "The single most powerful predictor of duration, when all else is not held constant, is marital status. . . . Race and education also show powerful effects. . . . The group least at risk is older women with strong education and work experience."[40] Ellwood continues: "If years of schooling were the only factor that differed among AFDC recipients, we would predict that those with fewer than 9 years of education would tend to have longer first spells of AFDC (5.6 years) than would those with more than 11 years (3.7 years)."[41]

There are many reasons why families may need public assistance. Lack of education shows up as a significant factor. Compounding the problem, those with less education need assistance for a longer period of time.

Society Suffers the Effects of Poor Education

The individual who suffers the consequences of poor or inadequate education is not confined to a particular ghetto area, town, city, or state. The frustrations that unemployment, inadequate income, and substandard living conditions bring often produce high mobility rates among those who suffer them. The problems related to poor education in one locality then become the welfare or reeducation problems of another community. High mobility rates of people may quickly move the problems of the disadvantaged (higher welfare and law-enforcement costs, for example) from the source of their creation to a state or locality whose educational system is adequate or even superior. Thus, the effects of poor education cannot be localized. The problems of providing adequate and high-quality education are not only local but also statewide and national in scope. No longer can states and districts have concern for their own citizens only.

EDUCATION AND ACCOUNTABILITY

The spiraling costs of education and the changing social climate of the country have combined to raise serious questions concerning public education. Have the increased costs resulted in proportionately increased productivity? Why has the public lost confidence in the schools? Why does the public not accept the arguments for increased costs of education as explained by the professionals? These are a few of the unanswered questions that have resulted in taxpayer revolts, student militancy, racial unrest in the schools, and a general deterioration in the traditional confidence that citizens have usually shown in their schools.

The Public Demands Improvement

The public demands improvement and increased efficiency in the operation of public schools. Their cry is couched under the broad umbrella of *accountability*. The accountability movement has gathered momentum; critics and also friends of public education hold the schools firmly accountable for making output commensurate with input. Public sentiment virtually demands that the educational establishment produces objective information and proof that the schools are achieving their intended objectives and that in the process they are using tax revenues efficiently.

Although actions toward accountability are desirable and should be encouraged, some potential dangers are inherent in rushing too quickly into the process. One danger is that taxpayers may expect the schools to be accountable, at the same time ignoring their own responsibility for providing adequate funds for achieving the comprehensive goals of education. Closely related is the possibility that some lawmaking bodies may, without fully understanding the ramifications, legislate school accountability laws; these could involve such questionable notions as requiring all pupils to take certain academic examinations to determine the degree of success or failure of the schools to achieve their purposes.

Equality Not Yet Attained

Equality of educational opportunity is sound philosophy. Lawsuits in some states demonstrate the changing attitudes of people toward this concept of opportunity in education. In *San Antonio Independent School District v. Rodriguez* (1973)[42] the Supreme Court ruled that education is not a *fundamental right* under the federal Constitution; the state may provide merely a minimum foundation educational program. Yet states should deal fairly and objectively with social injustices and base their decisions for change on educational premises, for some state courts question their own response to equity.

One of the primary problems in this regard—dealing fairly and objectively with social and racial injustices—must base its chances for solution on education. The hordes of disadvantaged people that congest urban areas must be given the educational opportunity and the motivation to bring them into the mainstream of society and social progress. No other agency or institution has greater hope and greater responsibility than education for eradicating the hazards that prevent such a cultural and economic improvement. Just as the schools have justified national faith in them in their responsibility for dissolving the great problems created by differences in national origin of students, so are they now challenged by the tremendous problem of providing equality of educational opportunity. The price of such a worthy goal will be high in dollars and human effort, but it is a price that all thinking citizens will be willing to pay. If education fails in this, its most challenging charge, future generations may never receive the same chance or responsibility.

UNDERINVESTMENT IS POOR ECONOMY

The determination of the optimum amount of money the nation should invest in education is a difficult problem. Although there are numerous schools without financial problems, there are also many that operate with inadequate laboratories, limited libraries, overcrowded classrooms, and poorly trained teachers. Of course, not all the limitations of poor schools are the result of insufficient financing. Adequate revenues provide the possibility of producing a good educational program but do not guarantee it. Inadequate revenues, however, will almost certainly guarantee a poor educational program. No prudent person would invest large sums of money in an enterprise and then forget it or refuse to use all possible means of protecting that investment. Sometimes adequate protection may involve spending additional funds. Such is the case with investment in education, for inadequate future expenditures may result in loss of all or a major part of the original investment. John Ruskin expressed the point when he said, "It is not wise to pay too much, but worse to pay too little. When you pay too little, you sometimes lose all—because the thing you bought is not capable of doing that which you bought it to do."

Every economist and most intelligent citizens readily recognize the fallacy of assuming that economy requires spending the smallest amount of money possible in purchasing a good or service. Certainly, examples of underspending that have resulted in lack of protection of original investment are easy to discern in any area of business, industry, or education. For example, the school board that employs an unqualified or incompetent teacher at low salary, or refuses to keep its buildings and equipment in good repair with the excuse of saving money, will sooner or later recognize such actions as poor business and a violation of true economy. The educational system that provides only a small part of an optimum program for its students will at some time come to realize that the taxpayers' investment in human capital has not been protected adequately. This country must protect the value of its investment in the education of its citizens; this cannot be fully measured in standard dollars and cents. It must also protect the individual's indirect and intangible benefits that are a part of the educational process.

Education, or the lack of it, has serious social consequences. Hodgkinson stated:

> In a state that retains a high percentage of its youth to high school graduation, almost every young person becomes a "net gain" to the state—with a high school diploma, there is a high probability of that person getting a job and repaying the state for the cost of his education. However in a state with a poor record of retention to high school graduation, many youth are a "net loss" to the state, in that without a high school diploma, the chances of that student getting work and thus repaying the state for that person's education, are very small indeed.[43]

A Question of Priorities

In the past, educators and economists have done remarkably well in convincing large numbers of taxpayers that education is an investment in people. But they have done less well in showing the investors how much they have earned on the added investments that education has required each year. In our current frenzy to try to place a dollar value on the student who submits to the educational process, it must be understood that benefit-cost studies have not been producing conclusive results concerning this complex problem and cannot be expected to do so.

All groups of people that are concerned with education appear to be demanding their own version of accountability—often with little regard for their own responsibility. But the principle of accountability applies to all segments of the school complex: administrators, students, teachers, boards of education, parents, and the legislative bodies. The public schools cannot prosper or achieve their intended place in the lives of their students if any one of these groups is not held accountable to play its part in the educational process. However, the important point as far as school finance is concerned is that the educational fraternity—administrators, teachers, and other staff members—should note that the taxpaying community needs and demands more comprehensive and objective ways to measure output of education compared with input. Without such accountability, the economic theories and principles that are generally followed in financing education may be counterbalanced by the actions of skeptical taxpayers. Education will suffer irreparable damage if the public decreases its support because of insufficient evidence that schools are doing what they purport to do.

Many people believe that education is receiving its equitable share of the wealth of this country and that even in its state of affluence additional funds are not available. Others insist that the nation's priorities are inconsistent with its values and that there is little, if any, defense for the fact that more is spent on cosmetics, liquor, and tobacco than on education.

Education's Share of the Gross National Product

Of all the available measures of the nation's productivity and the state of its economy, gross national product (GNP) is the most meaningful, the best understood, and the most often used. Its refers to the market value of all final goods and services produced within a specified period—in practice, one year. "It measures the output in terms of the expenditures by which these goods are acquired. These expenditures are the sum of four major items: (1) personal consumption expenditures, (2) gross private domestic investment, (3) net exports of goods and services, and (4) government purchases of goods and services."[44]

The GNP is usually shown in current dollars as well as in constant dollars. It has increased yearly in both current and 1982 constant dollars. Between 1970 and 1980, the GNP increased from $1,015 billion to $2,732 billion in current dollars; in 1982 constant dollars, it increased from $2,416 to $3,187 billion—a more modest increase. From 1980 to 1987 the growth in current dollars was to $4,488 billion, but in constant dollars, $3,821 billion (Table 2-7).

The gross national product is often used to determine potential expenditure levels for education as well as for other public services. A comparison of

TABLE 2-7   A Comparison of Gross National Product in Current and 1982 Dollars: 1930–1987

Year	GNP[a] (in billions of dollars)		Year	GNP[a] (in billions of dollars)	
	Current dollars	1982 dollars		Current dollars	1982 dollars
1930	91.1	642.8	1965	705.1	2,087.6
1935	72.8	580.2			
1940	100.4	772.9	1966	772.0	2,208.3
1945	213.4	1,354.8	1967	816.4	2,271.4
			1968	892.7	2,365.6
1946	212.4	1,096.9	1969	963.9	2,423.3
1947	235.2	1,066.7	1970	1,015.5	2,416.2
1948	261.6	1,108.7			
1949	260.4	1,109.0	1971	1,102.7	2,484.8
1950	288.3	1,203.7	1972	1,212.8	2,608.5
			1973	1,359.3	2,744.1
1951	333.4	1,328.2	1974	1,472.8	2,729.3
1952	351.6	1,380.0	1975	1,598.4	2,695.0
1953	371.6	1,435.3			
1954	372.5	1,416.2	1976	1,782.8	2,826.7
1955	405.9	1,494.9	1977	1,990.5	2,958.6
			1978	2,249.7	3,115.2
1956	428.2	1,525.6	1979	2,508.2	3,192.4
1957	451.0	1,551.1	1980	2,732.0	3,187.1
1958	456.8	1,539.2			
1959	495.8	1,629.1	1981	3,052.6	3,248.8
1960	515.3	1,655.3	1982	3,166.0	3,166.0
			1983	3,405.7	3,279.1
1961	533.8	1,708.7	1984	3,772.2	3,501.4
1962	574.6	1,799.4	1985	4,010.3	3,607.5
1963	606.9	1,873.3			
1964	649.8	1,973.3	1986	4,235.0	3,713.3
			1987	4,488.5	3,821.0

Sources: *Survey of Current Business*, Vol. 67, No. 7, U.S. Department of Commerce, Bureau of Economic Analysis (Washington, D.C.: GPO, July 1987), pp. 1, 2, 6, 7; *Economic Indicators*, Joint Economic Committee of the U.S. Congress (Washington, D.C.: GPO, March 1988), pp. 1–2.

[a]"Gross National Product . . . represents the total national output of goods and services at current market prices. It measures this output in terms of the expenditures by which these goods are acquired. These expenditures are the sum of four major items: (1) personal consumption expenditures, (2) gross private domestic investment, (3) net exports of goods and services, and (4) government purchases of goods and services."

educational expenses as a percentage of the GNP from 1959 to 1989 is shown in Table 2-8. What percentage of the GNP should be invested in education? To achieve education goals estimates range from 8 to 12 percent. The amount provided in current dollars has remained nearly constant, hovering at about 7 percent of the GNP.

TABLE 2-8 Total Expenditures of Educational Institutions as a Percentage of the Gross National Product: 1959–1960 to 1989–1990

| | | | Total expenditures for education (amounts in millions) | | | | | |
| | | | All educational institutions | | All elementary and secondary schools | | All colleges and universities | |
Year	Gross national product (in billions)	School year	Amount	As a percent of gross national product	Amount	As a percent of gross national product	Amount	As a percent of gross national product
1	2	3	4	5	6	7	8	9
1959	$ 495.8	1959–60	$ 23,860	4.8	$ 16,713	3.4	$ 7,147	1.4
1961	533.8	1961–62	28,503	5.3	19,673	3.7	8,830	1.7
1963	606.9	1963–64	34,440	5.7	22,825	3.8	11,615	1.9
1965	705.1	1965–66	43,682	6.2	28,048	4.0	15,634	2.2
1967	816.4	1967–68	55,652	6.8	35,077	4.3	20,575	2.5
1969	963.9	1969–70	68,459	7.1	43,183	4.5	25,276	2.6
1970	1,015.5	1970–71	75,741	7.5	48,200	4.7	27,541	2.7
1971	1,102.7	1971–72	80,672	7.3	50,950	4.6	29,722	2.7
1972	1,212.8	1972–73	86,875	7.2	54,952	4.5	31,923	2.6
1973	1,359.3	1973–74	95,396	7.0	60,370	4.4	35,026	2.6
1974	1,472.8	1974–75	108,664	7.4	68,846	4.7	39,818	2.7
1975	1,598.4	1975–76	118,706	7.4	75,101	4.7	43,605	2.7
1976	1,782.8	1976–77	126,417	7.1	79,194	4.4	47,223	2.6
1977	1,990.5	1977–78	137,042	6.9	86,544	4.3	50,498	2.5
1978	2,249.7	1978–79	148,308	6.6	93,012	4.1	55,296	2.5
1979	2,508.2	1979–80	165,627	6.6	103,162	4.1	62,465	2.5
1980	2,732.0	1980–81	182,849	6.7	112,325	4.1	70,524	2.6
1981	3,052.6	1981–82	197,801	6.5	120,486	3.9	77,315	2.5
1982	3,166.0	1982–83	212,081	6.7	128,725	4.1	83,356	2.6
1983	3,405.7	1983–84	228,597	6.7	139,000	4.1	89,597	2.6

(*Continued*)

TABLE 2-8 (Continued)

			All educational institutions		All elementary and secondary schools		All colleges and universities	
Year	Gross national product (in billions)	School year	Amount	As a percent of gross national product	Amount	As a percent of gross national product	Amount	As a percent of gross national product
1	2	3	4	5	6	7	8	9
1984	$3,772.2	1984–85	$247,657	6.6	$149,400	4.0	$ 98,257	2.6
1985	4,014.9	1985–86	269,485	6.7	161,800	4.0	107,685	2.7
1986	4,231.6	1986–87	291,823	6.9	175,200	4.1	116,623	2.8
1987	4,524.3	[1] 1987–88	313,600	6.9	187,900	4.2	125,700	2.8
1988	4,880.6	[2] 1988–89	337,000	6.9	201,100	4.1	135,900	2.8
1989	5,234.0	[2] 1989–90	358,700	6.9	215,500	4.1	143,200	2.7

Source: *Statistics of State School Systems; Revenues and Expenditures for Public Elementary and Secondary Education; Financial Statistics of Institutions of Higher Education*, Common Core Data survey, and "Financial Statistics of Institutions of Higher Education" survey, and unpublished data U.S. Department of Education, National Center for Education Statistics; and *Economic Indicators*, Council of Economic Advisers. (This table was prepared in July 1990.)
Note—Total expenditures for public elementary and secondary schools include current expenditures, interest on school debt, and capital outlay. Data for private elementary and secondary schools are estimated. Total expenditures for colleges and universities include current fund expenditures and additions to plant value and exclude expenditures of noncollegiate postsecondary institutions. Some data have been revised from previously published figures. Because of rounding, details may not add to totals.
[1] Preliminary.
[2] Estimated.

SUMMARY

Most citizens of the United States recognize education as "big business." The taxpayers of America often do not give it high enough priority so that it can receive the resources it requires.

During the decade of the 1970s taxpayers in many areas of the country demonstrated their displeasure with the public schools by voting against tax increases and bond issues. In some places, tax reduction became more important than providing funds for a good school program.

There are numerous reasons for the greatly increasing costs of education year after year. These include: (1) the nation's educational goals and objectives continue to increase; (2) communities are constantly demanding more and better services from the schools; (3) more programs and professional services are being provided for high-cost students such as the handicapped; (4) double-digit inflation increased costs in the 1970s; (5) the cost of treating deviant behavior of students has accelerated; (6) the high cost of energy increased costs; and (7) changing social and demographic influences affect expenditures.

As expensive as public education may be, the cost to society of not educating people is much higher. The detrimental effect of illiteracy on employment, on military capability, and on the size of welfare and relief rolls is strong evidence of the costliness of permitting people to remain uneducated.

Financing education at less than an adequate level is poor economy. With such a large investment in buildings and facilities, the fifty states must provide enough revenue to protect that investment and to achieve the best possible education for all their youth, regardless of their place of residence, the wealth of their parents, or the wealth of their school district.

ASSIGNMENT PROJECTS

1. Present information to show the great increases in public school expenditures in the last several years and the major causes for such increases.
2. Show by a review of some school districts that have experimented with an extension of their school year what the problems and the advantages of such extensions are.
3. What evidences can you find that increasing social problems are causing large increases in the annual costs of public elementary and secondary education?
4. Show how projected demographic and economic changes in a local area will affect the revenue and expenditures of the school district. Determine what school officials should do to prepare for such changes.
5. Determine what research and innovation is being done in a local school district. What are the direct and indirect costs? Who will benefit? What research is needed? What technological changes are needed?
6. Study the shift in population within a state and report on the impact it has had on the finances of various local districts within the state.

SELECTED READINGS

Benson, Charles S. *The Economics of Public Education.* 3rd ed. Boston: Houghton Mifflin, 1978.

Break, George F. *Financing Government in a Federal System.* Washington, D.C.: Brookings Institution, 1980.

Browning, Edgar K., and Jacqueline M. Browning. *Public Finance and the Price System.* New York: Macmillan, 1983.

Carnegie Forum on Education and the Economy. *A Nation Preparing Teachers for the 21st Century.* Washington, D.C.: Carnegie Forum on Education and the Economy, 1990.

Coons, John E., and Stephen D. Sugarman. *Education by Choice: The Case for Family Control.* Berkeley, Calif.: University of California Press, 1978.

Digest of Education Statistics, 1990. Washington, D.C.: National Center for Education Statistics, U.S. Department of Education, 1990.

Estimates of School Statistics, 1990–91. Washington, D.C.: National Education Association Datasearch, 1991.

Guthrie, James W., Walter I. Garms, and Lawrence C. Pierce. *School Finance and Education Policy: Enhancing Educational Efficiency, Equality, and Choice.* 2nd ed. Englewood Cliffs, N.J.: Prentice Hall, 1988.

Jordan, K. Forbis, and Nelda Cambron-McCabe. *Perspectives in State School Support Programs. Second Annual Yearbook of the American Education Finance Association.* Cambridge, Mass.: Ballinger, 1981.

Kronick, Robert F., and Charles H. Hargis. *Dropouts: Who Drops Out and Why, and the Recommended Action.* Springfield, Ill.: Charles C Thomas, 1990.

Monk, David H. *Educational Finance: An Economic Approach.* New York: McGraw-Hill, 1990.

Mueller, Van D., and Mary P. McKeown. *The Fiscal, Legal and Political Aspects of Elementary and Secondary Education. Sixth Annual Yearbook of the American Education Finance Association.* Cambridge, Mass.: Ballinger, 1985.

Odden, Allan R., and Lawrence O. Picus. *School Finance: A Policy Perspective.* New York: McGraw-Hill, 1992.

Ogle, Laurence, Nabeel Alsalam, and Gayle Thompson Rogers. *The Condition of Education, 1991: Elementary and Secondary Education.* Washington, D.C.: National Center for Educational Statistics, U.S. Department of Education, 1991.

Verstegan, D. A. *School Finance at a Glance.* Denver, Colo.: Education Commission of the States, 1990.

Webb, L. D., Martha M. McCarthy, and Stephen B. Thomas. *Financing Elementary and Secondary Education.* Columbus, Ohio: Merrill, 1988.

ENDNOTES

1. *All Levels of Education* (Washington, D.C.: U.S. Department of Education, National Center for Education Statistics, 1991), p. 8.

2. Ibid.

3. Ibid.

4. The National Commission on Excellence in Education, "A Nation at Risk: The Imperative for Educational Reform" (Washington, D.C., April 1983), p. 32.

5. *The Unfinished Agenda: A New Vision for Child Development and Education* (New York:

Committee for Research and Policy, Committee for Economic Development, 1991), p. 2.

6. Ibid., p. 15.

7. *Imperatives in Education* (Washington, D.C.: American Association of School Administrators, 1966).

8. Richard Miller, as quoted by Patricia McCormack, UPI Education Editor, "What's Right About American Education," United Press International, New York, 1986.

9. Stanley M. Elam, "The 22nd Annual Gallup Poll of the Public's Attitudes Toward the Public School," *Phi Delta Kappan,* September 1990, p. 42.

10. *Financing the Public Schools* (Bloomington, Ind.: Phi Delta Kappa Commission on Alternative Designs for Funding Education, 1973), p. 6.

11. *Estimates of School Statistics 1990–91* (Washington, D.C.: National Education Association, Research Division, 1991).

12. "And Baby Makes 20 Million." *American Demographics,* July 1991, p. 55.

13. Ibid.

14. "Preprimary Enrollment," *Education Week,* April 3, 1991, p. 3.

15. "1990–91 Enrollment," *Education Week,* April 10, 1991, p. 3.

16. "The Urbanization of America," *Education Week,* February 27, 1991, p. 3.

17. "Changing Family Makeup," *Education Week, Dimensions,* February 10, 1991, p. 3. (Primary Source: "Household and Family Characteristics: March 1990 and 1989," Stack No. 803-005-00046-0).

18. "Slipping into Poverty," *Education Week, Dimensions,* March 13, 1991, p. 3. (Primary Source: "Family Disruption and Economic Hardship: The Short-Run Picture for Children," Washington, D.C.: U.S. Government Printing Office).

19. "The Growth of Single-Parent Families," *Education Week,* January 16, 1991, p. 3.

20. "Home Alone," *Education Week,* March 6, 1991, p. 3. (Primary Source: Nels: 1988 study "A Profile of the American 8th Graders," Washington, D.C.: U.S. Government Printing Office.)

21. Kay Floyd, ed., *American Education Association Newsletter,* Summer Edition, 1991.

22. Ibid.

23. "Demographics for Education," *Center for Demographic Policy Newsletter,* June 1991, p. 2.

24. *The Unfinished Agenda,* p. 5.

25. Coleman et al., *Public and Private Schools and High School Achievement* (1981), provided by the United States Department of Education, 1986.

26. Harold Hodgkinson, *All One System: Demographics of Education, Kindergarten through Graduate School* (Washington, D.C.: Institute for Educational Leadership, Inc., 1985), p. 3.

27. Robert Barnes, as quoted in Ezra Bowen, "Losing the War of Letters," *Time,* May 6, 1986, Vol. 127, No. 18, p. 68.

28. Ibid.

29. *Changing Demands on Education and Their Fiscal Implications* (Washington, D.C.: National Committee for Support of the Public Schools), p. 11.

30. Wilbur J. Cohen, *Adult Basic Education Act of 1962* (Washington, D.C.: U.S. Government Printing Office, 1962), p. 12.

31. *National Policy and the Financing of the Public Schools* (Washington, D.C.: Educational Policies Commission, 1969), pp. 10–11.

32. Speech given by Richard Cheney to U.S. Chamber of Commerce Convention, Washington, D.C., April 29, 1991.

33. *The Condition of Education, 1991: Volume 1, Elementary and Secondary Education.* (Washington, D.C.: U.S. Department of Education, National Center for Education Statistics, 1991), p. 42.

34. Booth Gardner, "Directions for Education in America," *Journal of Education Finance,* Vol. 15, No. 4, Spring 1990, p. 602.

35. *Changing Demands on Education and Their Fiscal Implications,* pp. 49–50.

36. Sar A. Levitan, *Programs in Aid of the Poor,* 5th ed. (Baltimore, Md.: Johns Hopkins University Press, 1985), p. 38.

37. *Characteristics of the Population Below the Poverty Level, 1984* (United States Department of Commerce, Bureau of the Census), p. 21.

38. United States Department of Health and Human Services, *Aid to Families with*

Dependent Children—1979 Recipient Characteristics Study (Baltimore, Md.: Social Security Administration, 1982), p. 51.

39. David T. Ellwood, *Targeting "Would Be" Long Term Recipients of AFDC* (Princeton, N.J.: Mathematics Policy Research, Inc., 1986), p. ix.

40. Ibid., p. xiii.

41. Ibid.

42. *San Antonio Independent School District v. Rodriguez*, 411 U.S. 1, 93 S.Ct. 1278 (1973), *rehearing denied*.

43. Hodgkinson, *All One System: Demographics of Education, Kindergarten through Graduate School*, p. 11.

44. *1989–90 Fact Book on Higher Education*, (American Council on Education New York, Macmillan Publishing Company) p. 49.

Chapter 3

Financing Education Equitably

Although it is rooted in numbers and complicated school financing formulas, equalization is an emotional issue that evokes powerful images of disparity between educational haves and have-nots. At the heart of the controversy—often portrayed as a struggle between classes—is the issue of equal educational opportunity for all.   —JO ANNA NATALE, 1990

Equally difficult and important as financing education adequately is the challenge of distributing and expending available revenues with fairness to schools and to students, regardless of their location within a state. This is the principle of *equity* or fairness. Equity should not be considered synonymous with equality in this context.

Equality as it relates to educational opportunity is a fundamental principle in American education. Democracy is best served by extending to all children an equal opportunity to attend schools that are adequate for the achievement of self-realization, economic sufficiency, civic responsibility, and satisfactory human relationships. Equality in this sense does not mean an identical education for all children, but rather the provision of certain minimum essentials, with no ceiling on opportunity. Spending the same number of dollars on each student is evidence of *equality*, but it may not be equitable—some students, such as the handicapped, require greater expenditures for their education than do other students.

The problem of equity as it applies to financing public education is often discussed in the literature. The following statements illustrate the concern with which writers discuss equity as it applies to the various school finance systems of the nation. "Equity in school finance systems is a complex concept. . . ." "Equity is difficult to define." "Taxpayer 'equity' and 'social justice' are terms often used but seldom defined." "Equalization and equity in school finance have different meanings for different people. . . ."

In common and accepted usage, equity means providing for equal treatment of equals—its horizontal component—and fair and reasonable, but unequal treatment of unequals—its vertical dimension. Such definitions are easy to state, but they are of little worth unless they are more specifically defined and applied.

INEQUALITIES IN FINANCING EDUCATION

As previously stated, education should be financed and operated equitably, but this cannot and should not be done with complete equality, because of the many differences in the abilities and needs of students. Charles S. Benson and associates emphasized this point in the following:

> Obviously, providing equal dollar inputs for unequal students produces unequal results. Equal spending does not make education the "great equalizer of the conditions of men" as Horace Mann suggested in the last century. If education is to facilitate the movement of the poor and disadvantaged into the mainstream of American social and economic life, if it is to afford everyone equal probability of success (however one defines it), then equal facilities, teaching skills, and curriculums are not the answers. Additional resources must be made available to students who enter and pass through the educational system with handicaps such as language barriers for which they are not responsible. We do not know how much more should be spent to make these additional resources available. . . . [1]

This apparent dilemma has received considerable treatment by writers in the field, as well as in the formulas for financing education adopted by various states since the court ruling in *Serrano* v. *Priest* (1971)[2] and subsequent legal cases in the 1970s. A few of these rulings have been misinterpreted or overstated in their application. For example, in *Serrano,* the principle of fiscal neutrality was established—a child's education must not be affected by wealth, except the wealth of the state. This principle, made applicable as a standard for California by the court and applied in practice to other states as well, did not mandate equal dollar expenditures per child in any state. It did not rule out expending more money for children with higher educational costs— handicapped, bilingual, minority, or compensatory students—the *weighted-pupil* approach to equity in school finance. It did not exclude property taxes as a basis for local financial support of education. In short, it did not legislate equality in financing education.

Equality in the support of the educational program does not always produce equal learning. Many factors other than money affect educational achievement. These include, but are not limited to: the quality of the family, the intelligence of the student, school leadership, time on task, school climate and culture, community attitudes, parental support, high expectations by the teacher, curriculum, and instructional strategies. Some districts, because of location, may attract and retain good teachers and administrators. Individual students may take better advantage of opportunities.

EQUITY ISSUE REVISITED

The equity issue which fomented a revolution in state spending on public schools during the 1970s resurfaced with greater impact during the late 1980s and into the 1990s. Litigation in several states stimulated vigorous debate in nearly half of the states. In 1989 six states had active school finance suits, and twenty-one had reviewed school-funding formulas to make them more equitable.[3]

Court cases in states such as Kentucky (*Rose* v. *Council for Better Education*,[4] decided by the Kentucky Supreme Court June 8, 1989) and Texas (*Edgewood* v. *Kirby*,[5] decided by the Texas Supreme Court October 2, 1989) reemphasized the need for legislators to analyze the equity question in relation to their school finance funding. As the 1990s began, court cases and legislative actions in several states such as Alabama, Connecticut, North Carolina, Ohio, and New York addressed the issue of those states' school finance inequalities. Solving the dilemma is not an easy task; researchers have used various criteria to determine equity, but find it elusive. Some suggest that if per pupil funding or expenditures are within 10 percent limits, then equity is attained. Table 3-1 demonstrates how a specific program, in this case a local voted leeway, can shift the delicate balance of equity. Note that 1 mill (.001) raises $125.00 per student in District A while in District F it raises only $10.26 because of the low assessed value of property in relation to the number of students. If the average per pupil expenditure in the state is $3,000, then District A is able to provide over 40 percent additional revenue per pupil when voters approve a 10 mill local voted leeway. This example also demonstrates the inequity between districts if one is able to pass a local leeway while voters in another district may not be willing to do so, as in District G.

TABLE 3-1   Revenue Raised in Local Districts with a Voted Leeway and No State Support

District	Revenue per mill	Number of students	Revenue per mill per student	Mills approved by voters	Total revenue per student
A	$ 200,000	1,600	$125.00	10	$1250.00
B	$3,000,000	35,000	$ 85.71	4	$ 342.84
C	$ 375,000	7,500	$ 50.00	3	$ 150.00
D	$ 480,000	16,000	$ 30.00	7	$ 210.00
E	$1,600,000	82,000	$ 19.51	9	$ 175.59
F	$ 400,000	39,000	$ 10.26	10	$ 102.60
G	$ 600,000	20,000	$ 30.00	0	$ 0

States vary in their assessing practices and in the ways they levy taxes on property. A tax levy may be based on a *rate,* a *percent of market value, mills* (.001) or *dollars per $100* ($/per $100 assessed valuation[AV]), or *dollars per $1000* ($/per $1000 assessed valuation). The tables and text of this volume are shown in mills. The reader can easily convert mills by studying the following:

Assessed value of property	Tax levy	Revenue generated
$ 100,000	60 mills (.060)	$600.00
$ 100,000	$6/per $100 AV	$600.00
$ 100,000	$60/per $1000 AV	$600.00

QUALITY VERSUS FISCAL EQUITY

As a result of the emphasis on excellence by the several blue-ribbon reports of the 1980s, further differences of opinion have developed about equity. Some believe that larger resources will be necessary to attain quality. Those who espouse excellence as a priority see the main goals of financing education to be the attainment of quality. Others feel that states have yet to reach fiscal equity and that the priority still rests there. Those who promote equity based on quality emphasize that districts that do better on prescribed standards should be rewarded monetarily, that the use of dollars should be refocused from attendance to competence. Grants should be given to those schools and districts that demonstrate excellence; state support should be differentiated according to the quality of instruction. Rewards should be given to districts that show improvement. Advocates of fiscal equity would rely on formula grants, cost reimbursement, general aid, and special support for poor students, handicapped students, and low achievers.

In regard to this dilemma, Odden stated:

> Some people worry that the concern for excellence will submerge the concern for fiscal equalization, that students from poor and minority backgrounds will be forgotten in the push for excellence (with its attendant emphasis on mathematics and science), and that the focus of the excellence movement on the process of schooling will erode the legal base for improving education for the poor (since the courts are reluctant to interfere with the educational process).
>
> Other people claim that the extra dollars now spent on fiscal equalization could be better spent on promoting excellence, that the fragmentation that equity necessitates is in conflict with the integration that school improvement demands, and that competitive grants are more likely than formula grants to stimulate efficiency.[6]

Although the above points of view are now in conflict, the advocates of excellence and equity may come to realize that their goals are more similar than dissimilar.

EQUITY: AN OBJECTIVE OF SCHOOL FINANCE REFORM

The main thrust of the decisions in *Serrano* and more recent cases is toward equity or fairness in public school finance systems. The school finance reforms in most of the fifty states seem to echo the words "sameness," "standardization," "fairness," and "equity." The new formulas generally emphasize two aspects of equity: fairness for the children who are being educated and fairness for the taxpayers who defray the costs of education.

Equity for Children

Equity for children concerns fairness in the amount of revenue and the services provided for children—the actual expenditures per child. To be completely fair, such equity would involve all funds expended, but common practice in comparing such expenditures usually includes only local and state revenues, disregarding federal finance programs. Such comparisons also usually include only current expenditures, ignoring the area of capital outlays.

Equity for children should be more concerned with equality of output than with equality of input in the educational process. Since the input is only a means to an end, equity should involve evenness of attainment of school objectives. There must be some accurate measurement of achievement, competencies developed, degree of fulfillment of requirements for graduation or grade advancement, attainment of positive attitudes and habits, and similar goals of an educational program.

At present, equity for children can best be measured in terms of comparing the expenditures per child, although the more important comparisons are those of outputs and eventual outcomes of education, which cannot be measured with any high degree of confidence in the results. Horizontal equity (equal treatment of equals) is relatively easy to attain, for it implies only equal dollars spent per student. Vertical equity (unequal treatment of unequals) is more difficult to determine, since no one can define fairness with complete assurance when treating children with physical or mental handicaps or other unequal characteristics.

The Weighted-Pupil Approach

One of the most common and suitable methods used to improve the equity of school finance formulas in allocating funds to local districts is the use of pupil weightings. These are nothing more than cost differentials injected in the formula to compensate or allow for the additional cost of education of some students because of their innate characteristics, the types of educational programs they pursue, or other pertinent cost factors. Weightings (additional funds) for handicapped, bilingual, compensatory, or minority group students are often used in recognition of the disadvantages they suffer and the higher cost of their education. For several years some states have provided cost differentials for pupils in small and more costly schools—usually in sparsely populated and isolated areas. A few states provide density weighting or correction factors for pupils in large cities where the higher cost of educational and other government services is such that financial relief is required, in the interest of fairness to the pupils being educated as well as to the taxpayers bearing the cost. A number of other weightings are sometimes found in state formulas, such as those for secondary school students over those in elementary grades, although this practice is becoming less justified as the costs of elementary education move closer to those of secondary education. Some states also provide for weightings for teachers who have more academic preparation and experience (and who therefore are higher on the salary schedule), weightings for early education pupils (prekindergarten, kindergarten, and the first two or three years of elementary school), and weightings for higher-than-average-cost programs, such as vocational education and driver education.

The weighted-pupil approach adds objectivity and equity to the school finance system. Under this concept all programs suffer or prosper comparably when funds are reduced or increased. This is particularly beneficial to high-cost programs, which are often the first ones to be cut back or deleted when school revenues are reduced.

A number of states and finance authorities have favored the weighted-pupil approach to equity in school finance. Some support for this principle came with the *Serrano* requirement that substantially equal amounts of money per pupil be provided, taking into consideration the differences in costs of various school programs. Such an approach has several advantages over the use of the actual number of students attending school, including the following: (1) The costs of education are not the same for all students. (2) Many court decisions considered the unequal cost of education, as reflected in the cost per person being educated. (3) The principle tends to build fairness into a finance formula, for *all* classifications of pupils receive their proportionate share of revenue increases as well as decreases with changes in the school budget. (4) Several states, including Washington, Minnesota, and Utah, have used such an approach with remarkable success. (5) The principle tends to reduce the number of categorical grants that are required in the financing of educational programs, such as those for the handicapped. (6) Such an approach usually results in a simplification of the state's school finance formula. For these reasons, it seems likely that the weighted-pupil approach to equity will continue to gain popularity.

Equal Protection and School Finance

Traditionally, each state has enjoyed almost complete freedom in the way it has allocated funds to local school districts. Some states chose to leave the financing of education almost completely to each local district; others used grants of varying kinds to alleviate local overburden; still others used equalization programs of varying degrees of complexity.

Allocations of state money to local districts have usually been made on the basis of the number of pupils to be educated and in terms of the ability of the district to finance a minimum or foundation program. Equality of educational opportunity has been interpreted to mean providing the same amount of money for each pupil who is to be educated. Gradually, however, financing formulas have recognized that it costs more to educate some pupils than others. Among the earliest changes in this regard was providing more money per pupil for those who lived in rural areas where the unit cost of education was higher and where transportation was an important cost factor. Later, the provision of additional funds for educating exceptional children, especially the physically and mentally handicapped, became acceptable and desirable. Today, one of the great needs is for special financial consideration for large city and metropolitan districts, where deprivation, tax overburden, and racial and ghetto area problems have increased the unit costs of education well beyond those in average districts.

Implementation of programs with unequal amounts of money per pupil is fertile ground for confrontation and litigation. In one form or another, the issue of equal protection of all citizens as provided by the Fourteenth Amendment has often been a matter of litigation. In 1954 the Supreme Court required equal rights for the education of all citizens regardless of race. By 1962, geographic discrimination was eliminated in the legislative reapportionment decision. By 1965, the Court had determined that lack of financial resources could not be used to deny criminals equal protection of the law. By 1968, the courts faced the issue of unequal protection of students because of unequal expenditures of money for children attending different school districts.

Noting the wide disparities in expenditures of money per pupil in every state, school finance students had long anticipated legal action contesting such a system. As early as 1954, notice was taken of the terseness of the U.S. Supreme Court wherein it was stated: "In these days, it is doubtful that any child may reasonably be expected to succeed in life if he is denied the opportunity of an education. Such an opportunity, where the state has undertaken to provide it, is a right which must be made available to all on equal terms."[7]

Equity for Taxpayers

Equity for taxpayers is more difficult to achieve in a finance formula than is commonly believed. Theoretically, taxes should be paid according to the ability of taxpayers to pay, or according to the burden the tax imposes on them. The problem of providing equity is illustrated in the example on the next page.

Consider the question of taxpayer equity for the following mythical taxpayers under the conditions of ownership of real property, income, wealth, and taxpaying ability, as indicated.

This example illustrates some of the inequities that may exist in the taxation pattern in a typical school district, where local taxes for public education are determined by a fixed tax rate levied on the assessed value of real property. Assessed value is a percentage of the actual market value of property; in some states the assessed value is 20 percent of the actual market or cash value. Thus, a home and property with a market value of $100,000 would have an assessed valuation of $20,000. In the example, all five individuals would pay taxes on

Taxpayer	Annual income	Total wealth	Real property	Ownership (real property)	Tax (mills)	Total taxes
A	$80,000	$500,000	$100,000	$100,000	20	$2,000
B	50,000	400,000	100,000	80,000	20	2,000
C	25,000	200,000	100,000	60,000	20	2,000
D	20,000	100,000	100,000	40,000	20	2,000
E	16,000	40,000	100,000	20,000	20	2,000

Tax amount as percent of property value

	Property owned	Income	Wealth
A	2.0	2.5	.4
B	2.5	4.0	.5
C	3.3	8.0	1.0
D	5.0	10.0	2.0
E	10.0	12.5	5.0

$100,000 of real property at the rate of $2 per $100 of assessed valuation. Some would argue that there is complete taxpayer equity, since all five pay 2 percent of the total value of the property being taxed. However, it becomes obvious that equity is lacking when the amount of taxes paid is measured as a percentage of each individual's actual ownership in the property, or of annual income, or of the total wealth of each. Local taxes are usually not equitable on the basis that most states levy property taxes—without regard to the degree or amount of ownership the taxpayer has in the parcel of land being taxed. Robert Berne and Leanna Stiefel referred to the fallacy of equating equity with equal tax rates in the following:

> There are multiple formulations of taxpayer equity in school finance. . . . On the one hand, there are cases where taxpayer equity is equated with an ambiguous formulation such as 'equal tax rates,' a formulation that is equitable only by definition. On the other hand, less ambiguous formulations such as 'equal yield for equal effort' are utilized without reference to other equally plausible ones. A useful distinction that has been introduced into the school finance literature is between ex ante and ex post taxpayer equity. . . .
>
> Ex ante taxpayer equity is generally evaluated by examining the characteristics of a school finance plan, while ex post equity involves an assessment of the actual spending patterns that result from school districts' response to a school finance plan. . . . [8]

In the example, only A has complete ownership of the property being taxed; the other four owe varying amounts on loans or mortgages (usually at high rates of interest), which affect their ability to pay taxes. In terms of the value of the property being taxed, without regard to the extent of actual ownership of each, there appears to be fairness in the taxes to be collected from each of the five tax-payers. Considering the degree of ownership of each, the range of the percent of taxes to ownership goes from 2 percent to 10 percent. In terms of annual income, A pays 2.5 percent in property taxes, whereas E pays 12.5 percent; if wealth is used as the base of ability to pay, A is required to pay only 4 percent in taxes, whereas E must pay 5 percent.

Other practices in the process of taxing real property add to the unfairness of this method of obtaining local revenue for public schools. One of these is unequal rates of assessment of like parcels of property found in taxing jurisdictions. Such unfairness can be seen in the following example, which uses the same individuals as in the previous one. The only difference is that varying rates of assessment have been used to determine the assessed valuation of the property being taxed.

Taxpayer	Market value of property	Assessed valuation	Tax rate (in mills)	Taxes paid	Taxes as a percent of real value
A	$100,000	$100,000	20	$2,000	2.0
B	100,000	80,000	20	1,600	1.6
C	100,000	60,000	20	1,200	1.2
D	100,000	40,000	20	800	.8
E	100,000	20,000	20	400	.4

In the above example, A's property was assessed at 100 percent of its real or market value. At the other end of the scale, E's property was assessed at only 20 percent of its real value. Under this arrangement A paid 2 percent of the total value of the property in taxes, while E paid only .4 percent. This example shows extreme differences, but many states, particularly those that use local or politically appointed assessors, are not able to assess all similar parcels of property at the same rate, thus leading to unfairness in local taxation practices.

Assessing or reassessing the current value of property is not an easy task, though most states now use computers to assist in updating records more rapidly. Without current figures, if property values increase because of inflation or other economic factors and the assessments are not brought up to date over a three- to five-year period, the actual percentage of market value decreases, causing inequities. Those who have just purchased property, had property reassessed, or had a newly constructed home put on the tax rolls suffer; those who have owned property for a period of time benefit. For example, a taxpayer whose home was assessed four years ago at $100,000 (at 20 percent of actual market value) and who lives in an area where inflation is 4 percent per year, now has a home with a value of over $116,000. Without reassessment, the present assessed valuation is only 17 percent of market value instead of 20.

The following example compares three individuals who pay different tax amounts on their income, according to every measure of taxation commonly used. The table illustrates proportional, regressive, and prgressive taxation of income but does not show all the possibilities of regressive or progressive taxation.

Since taxation theory is based on the premise that taxes paid should be related to the burden each taxpayer bears, it is reasonable to argue that taxes should increase proportionately faster than income—assuming that income is the measure of fiscal capacity being used. In the following example, it is reasonable to expect A to pay a much higher tax than either B or C, since A's income is much greater. Although A has five times the income, he or she pays more than eight times the taxes paid by C. In terms of the burden caused by such progressivity of taxes, A "suffers" less than C because of the much larger amount of money at his or her disposal after taxes. The problem for tax authorities is not whether A, B, and C should pay the same tax rate; rather, it is how much greater the tax rate of A should be than that of B and C, and how much greater the tax rate of B should be than that of C. They must decide the degree of progressiveness that is most desirable and that produces the greatest equity in the burden borne by taxpayers with high incomes, wealth, or property ownership, whichever form is used to determine fiscal capacity in that taxing district. Here, the important question of values comes into operation. It must be determined what portion of taxes should be paid by each level of income or wealth, without partiality and without undue burden or hardship on any classification of tax-paying ability.

Taxpayer	Proportional taxation		
	Annual income	Taxes paid	Taxes as a percent of income
A	$100,000	$5,000	5.0
B	60,000	3,000	5.0
C	20,000	1,000	5.0
	Regressive taxation		
A	100,000	5,000	5.0
B	60,000	3,600	6.0
C	20,000	1,400	7.0
	Progressive taxation		
A	100,000	5,000	5.0
B	60,000	2,400	4.0
C	20,000	600	3.0

MEASURES OF SCHOOL DISTRICT WEALTH

There is currently quite general agreement that the valuation of real property, regardless of its percent of market value, is not the best possible measure of local fiscal capacity to support public education. Although such a measure has been standard for determining school district wealth in most state school finance programs, its appropriateness is now being questioned by many students of school finance. Some relatively new measures are being considered and tried as possible alternatives (singly or in combination) to property values in determining school district wealth or tax-paying ability. What, then, is the ideal measure of fiscal capacity as far as equity to children and equity to taxpayers are concerned? There is no easy answer to that question.

Assessed Valuation Per Pupil

The principal objection to using assessed valuation of real property per pupil in determining the comparative wealth of districts is that property is no longer a fair or accurate measure of the wealth of people or of school districts. Too many people have invested their wealth in assets that are not readily available for taxation. In spite of that fact, about 75 percent of the states still use that method of determining local fiscal capacity. That this method causes inequality in expenditures per child was noted by Walter W. McMahon:

> It is the theme of this paper that both the inequality in expenditure per child and tax inequity are aggravated by a common key factor—the narrow definition of wealth based only on property wealth that is still used in most states to measure both local ability-to-pay and local effort. . . . Wealth in Elizabethan times consisted almost exclusively of land and buildings, but in modern industrialized societies other forms of capital and the incomes they yield have become much more important. . . . [9]

It is argued, too, that since all taxes must be paid out of income—past, present, or future—taxes and measures of wealth should bear some relation to income. Assessed valuation of real property per pupil favors districts with greater educational needs and discriminates against those that have other needs not related to the number of school pupils to be educated. Increases in the book value of property do not increase the tax-paying ability of the owner of property unless it is sold. For example, the farmer whose property increases from $100,000 to $120,000 in one year does not have increased ability to increase products or crops on the land and thus to pay higher taxes, barring other improvements. However, with real property tax laws, the farm land now presumably (and legally) generates more taxes because of the increased value. The only practicable way in which that farmer can profit from the increased book value of a farm is to sell it at a higher price than could have been demanded before the increase in its value.

Assessed Valuation Per Capita

The assessed valuation of real property per capita indicates the ability of a district to raise funds for any or all purposes. Although not as common a measurement of fiscal capacity as assessed valuation per pupil, it is used in a number of states, particularly for noneducation purposes. See Figure 3-1 for a comparison of the wealth of ten districts based on the number of students and the population. Note that differences occur in the rankings.

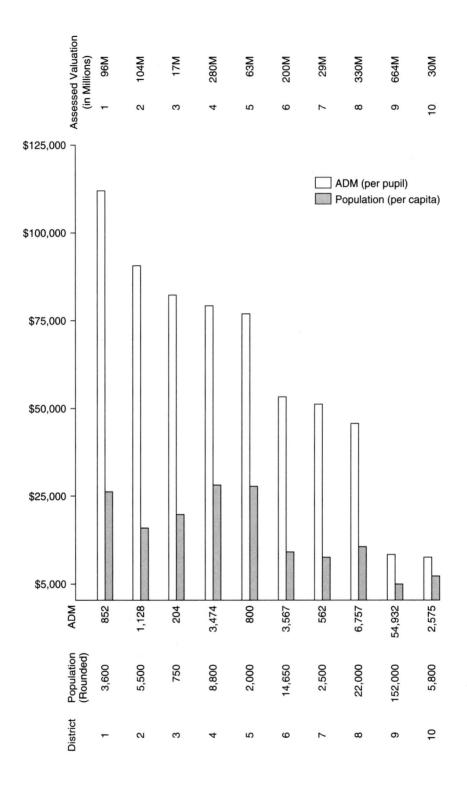

District	Population (Rounded)	ADM		Assessed Valuation (in Millions)
1	3,600	852	1	96M
2	5,500	1,128	2	104M
3	750	204	3	17M
4	8,800	3,474	4	280M
5	2,000	800	5	63M
6	14,650	3,567	6	200M
7	2,500	562	7	29M
8	22,000	6,757	8	330M
9	152,000	54,932	9	664M
10	5,800	2,575	10	30M

ADM (per pupil)
Population (per capita)

The following example compares the ability of three districts to raise funds under assessed valuation per pupil and under assessed valuation per capita. It illustrates how the state would help in supplying the funds necessary for a minimum school program where the state guarantees a stipulated amount of money per student, with the local district required to make the mandated levy for that program.

District	Assessed valuation	Total population	Total pupils	AV/pupil	AV/capita
1	$120,000,000	10,000	4,000	$30,000	$12,000
2	120,000,000	10,000	3,000	40,000	12,000
2	120,000,000	10,000	2,000	60,000	12,000

Under a state-guaranteed minimum school program

District	State-guaranteed ($1,000/pupil)	Required mill levy	Local revenue	State revenue	Percent of state revenue
1	$4,000,000	15	$1,800,000	$2,200,000	55.0
2	3,000,000	15	1,800,000	1,200,000	40.0
3	2,000,000	15	1,800,000	200,000	10.0

The illustration above shows that in three districts with equal populations of 10,000 people, equal property assessments of $120,000,000, but unequal numbers of pupils, District 1 with 4,000 pupils would receive 55 percent of its guaranteed school program from the state, District 2 would get only 40 percent, and District 3 would get 10 percent. Of course, state funds should be directly related to the number of pupils to be educated—the educational need. From the point of view of education, there is little argument against this method of measuring wealth to determine the flow of state funds to local districts in an equalization program—assuming that property values are accepted as reasonable measures of tax-paying ability. The advantage as well as the disadvantage of using assessed value of property per pupil as a measure of fiscal need was noted by Russell Harris:

> Although the measure of equalized market value per pupil is the variable used most often in school finance formulas many people consider it to be biased in favor of certain communities at the expense of others. It is argued that the measure is biased in favor of communities whose pupil population, relative to the total population is higher in number than the average. On the

FIGURE 3-1 A comparison of the wealth of 10 districts determined on a per-pupil basis and a per capita basis. ADM, average daily membership.

other hand, it is biased against those communities whose pupil population is lower in number than the average or those communities with a large number of children attending nonpublic schools. It is important to note, however, that where a large proportion of the school age children attend nonpublic schools, the total cost of education is significantly less expensive because fewer children need the service.[10]

In the example cited above, assume that fiscal ability is determined by the assessed valuation of real property per capita instead of per pupil to be educated. The state-local partnership pattern of providing funds for all purposes, including education, now becomes:

District	State-guarantee ($400/capita)	Required	Local revenue	State revenue	Percent of state revenue
1	$4,000,000	15	$1,800,000	$2,200,000	55.0
2	4,000,000	15	1,800,000	2,200,000	55.0
3	4,000,000	15	1,800,000	2,200,000	55.0

In this example, the unfairness of using assessed valuation per capita of education is immediately obvious. District 3, with exactly half as many pupils to be educated as District 1, would receive just as much state money—a gross violation of the principle of equity. On the other hand, if the plan is used to finance *all* state-local partnership programs (assuming that they are not a function of the number of pupils in each district) the plan is better than using assessed valuation per pupil. Thus, it can be said that the merits of these two plans of determining fiscal capacity depend upon the purposes to be attained.

Statistical Approaches to Equalization

Several states have considered moving to a per capita measure, and some states have used both in educational formulas. Various statistical approaches have been used to analyze fiscal equalization, including the Pearson coefficient of correlation and the Spearman rank order correlation, both of which can determine the relationship between per-pupil wealth and per-pupil expenditure. Also, the Lorenz curve, Gini coefficient, Theil index, McCloone index and Atkinson index have been used to measure the extent of fiscal equalization in a state. There are many examples in the literature of complicated plans that attempt to meet the need of being "fair and equitable" to both students and taxpayers. In many approaches, these two factors are given various weightings. Legislators have found most to be too complicated to incorporate into the system, even though some have great merit.

Income Tax

It does not seem reasonable to compare the abilities of districts or states to finance education by comparing their share of potential assets or taxes that are not available for use by the districts or states being compared. Income has therefore not been used as a measure of the fiscal capacity of school districts, because school districts by and large do not have access to local income taxes. Few people, however, deny its place as a determinant, in whole or in part, of ability to pay taxes for the financing of education. In recent years, local governments in a few states have introduced income tax capability to school districts.

Roe L. Johns summarized a point of view concerning the use of tax measures that are not available for local use:

> If the foundation program equalization model is used, the measure of local taxpaying ability should include only the local tax sources to which the school district has access. This is, if the only local tax revenue available to the district is the property tax, then the measure of local taxpaying ability should be based entirely on the equalized value of taxable property. However, if a local district can levy a local sales tax, or a local income tax, or some other local tax, then that local nonproperty tax source can equitably be included in the measure of local taxpaying ability.[11]

There is no general rule or standard correlation between the income of a person or school district and the property tax obligations or ability of the same person or district. For example, generally high values of large agricultural areas of land often do not translate into high incomes for the owners of that land.

The states of Kansas and Maryland utilize income taxes that are available to local school districts. They use taxable income in addition to assessed valuations in determining their state allocations to local districts. A few states, such as Rhode Island and Connecticut, use income figures along with property values in their school finance formulas. A number of other states are moving in the direction of utilizing income as an addition to their other measures of fiscal capacity.

According to Beck, Odden lists three reasons for using an income measure in determining school district wealth for the purpose of allocating state funds to local school districts:

> First, in states where school districts can levy income taxes—such as Maryland and Kansas—the relation of income to fiscal capacity is clear. Odden's second reason applies even to states where districts can only tax property; "income is the best single explanatory variable for government expenditures" and should, therefore, be used as a measure of "fiscal capacity." Property value per pupil is not a satisfactory proxy for income because the relation with district median family income is variable, with positive

correlations in some states and negative correlations in others. Odden's third reason is that "as an indicator of ability to pay, income links taxes raised to the burden the taxes place on the community and its citizens." Regardless of the base on which taxes are levied, all taxes are paid out of income. The ratio of local tax revenues to income is then an indicator of the tax burden on the local school district.[12]

Wealth Tax

Fairness of taxation is increased when more kinds of wealth are included. The use of a wealth tax as an alternative revenue source to the property tax has often been considered by tax authorities who recognize the unfairness and limitations of the traditional property tax in determining the fiscal capacity of school districts.

A wealth tax, as the term implies, is based on the net worth of an individual or a household. By definition, this means all assets minus all liabilities. In contrast, a property tax is a tax on the gross value of a particular kind of property, regardless of the equity the taxpayer has in the object being taxed or in other forms of wealth he or she owns.

A wealth tax would eliminate discrimination against the person who pays full property taxes but who has only limited or incomplete ownership in the property being taxed. It measures *total* ability to pay. It has the advantage over an income tax, in that the latter taxes only annual increases in ability to pay, without regard to accumulated ability. For example, under an income tax A and B may have the same income per year, but A may derive income from interest on property owned, whereas B may get income from personal services without the added property values that A has. In the event of total loss of income, A has assets in the form of property to rely on; B has nothing to replace loss of income. Thus, even though their incomes are identical, their ability to pay taxes is not the same.

There are certain disadvantages that would affect the use of a wealth tax. Some of the most obvious are the following: (1) It is administratively difficult to determine the total wealth of an individual or household; it is almost impossible for taxing authorities to learn of all the individual pieces and the value of all the items of wealth that are owned by an individual or a household, particularly if the people involved are uncooperative. (2) There is the question of privacy and people's dislike of having government representatives aware of their financial affairs—even among honest people. (3) The cost, timing, and actual process of assessment would undoubtedly create major problems. The difficulty that some states have had in past years in locating and taxing personal property equitably would seem to indicate that this would be a very difficult aspect of such a form of taxation. Although experience with a wealth tax is very limited in the United States, certain European countries have applied such a tax with considerable fairness and success.

HISTORICAL INFLUENCES ON EQUITY

In the early history of public education the states seemed content to accept responsibility for education but were reluctant to assume major responsibility for financing it. Local school districts—usually of small size and often with limited resources—bore the responsibility of financing education for many years without state assistance. It is true that the states generally provided ways of legalizing local school property taxes, but grants, equalization funds, and a general state-local "partnership" arrangement received little attention until the second quarter of this century.

This system of operating an educational program was generally satisfactory and workable in most school districts during the time when there was extreme local pride in the public schools and limited competition for the property tax dollar. This was true, perhaps, because of satisfaction with limited curricula, low costs, and little state control or interference. But its obvious weakness soon rose to the surface, and demands for change and for some form of state financial support began to be heard in the legislative halls. Even though citizens continued to hold fast to their historic conviction that public schools should function as locally controlled institutions, they began to advocate the idea of some form of state support for financing education in order to equalize educational opportunity and equalize the burden of paying for continuously expanding school programs.

Much of the early inequality and inequity in financing education was caused by the fact that school districts varied greatly in size and in wealth, from large city districts to ones that operated only one- or two-room schools. The taxable property base per person to be educated varied tremendously from one district to another, resulting in similarly large variations in property tax levies.

Reorganization of School Districts

Reduction of the number of school districts in a state gradually reduced the range of variation in ability of its districts to finance education. But school district reorganization and the elimination of many small and inefficient districts was a very slow process until the 1940s and 1950s. Such reorganization was hampered by three major conditions: (1) Permissive reorganization laws required the exercise of local initiative and voter approval—a requirement that by its nature was unpopular and resulted in few successes. (2) Voters in low-levy school districts bitterly resisted merging with districts that required higher millages for school operation. (3) Reorganization issues were usually settled on the basis of the emotional responses of citizens to their local school and community, with little consideration of the potential educational benefits of such reorganization.

Mandatory legislation reorganizing school districts has always been a possibility for quick action in such matters, but its implementation has been infrequent.

With a few exceptions, such as Utah in 1915, West Virginia in 1933, and Nevada in 1956, most state legislatures appeared to be content to wait until the people concerned made the first move under provisions of permissive legislation to reorganize schools.

The semipermissive legislation that was adopted in many states during the 1940s and 1950s did much to reduce the number of local school districts, but the process has not yet been completed. Some states still operate with large numbers of districts; these need to be combined with others in order to provide greater equality of educational opportunity.

LOCAL DISTRICT FUNDING

Full local district funding was the first of all school finance plans. Over the years it has proven to be the least desirable and the least effective in producing equality of educational opportunity among the districts within a state. Its operation as the sole producer of school revenue terminated near the turn of the twentieth century, with the beginning of state grants and other allocations to local districts. Its almost exclusive use in the years preceding the use of flat grants and foundation programs preceded any modern-day philosophy of equal educational opportunity or equal sharing of the burden of taxation. The place of a child's birth determined to a large degree the quality and the quantity of education he or she received. A person's place of residence and the extent to which he or she invested in real property were major factors in the calculation of his or her burden in financing education.

As the costs of education increased and as competition for the revenues generated by a local property tax became greater, it was logical and necessary for local districts to obtain some financial assistance from state government. This support emerged principally as flat grants and categorical aids until the theory of foundation programs and equalization was developed and implemented.

Although state financial support for education is largely a twentieth-century development, Mort reported that about one-fourth of public school revenue in 1890 came from state sources. He did not differentiate between the funds derived from federal land grants and those obtained from strictly state sources.

Flat Grants

In the early attempts of states to assist local districts in financing their schools, flat grants were used extensively. These grants were usually funds per pupil, funds per teacher, or percentage grants. They were provided as a form of relief to local taxpayers, with no real intent of providing equalization. Their effect on local districts was usually nonequalizing, except with the use of percentage grants, which do not change the ratio of tax effort among districts either toward or away from equalization of tax effort. To illustrate this, assume that Districts A and B have the following characteristics:

District	Assessed valuation	Paid by state	Budget needs	Mill levy	Number of pupils
A	$6,000,000	nil	$240,000	40	120
B	5,000,000	nil	100,000	20	80

Under local district funding, since District A is required to levy 40 mills for its program and District B needs a levy of only 20 mills, the effort ratio (ER) is expressed as 2:1. The purpose of equalization is to create an effort ratio of 1:1. All attempts to provide state aid should be directed toward reducing the ER to that value.

Suppose, in the above example, the state provides $500 per pupil as a flat grant. District A's requirements from local property taxes now become $180,000 and District B's become $60,000, requiring levies of 30 mills and 12 mills, respectively. The effort ratio now becomes 2.5:1. Thus, the flat grant is nonequalizing in its effect upon the two districts, for it has actually increased rather than decreased the ER.

As an example of state percentage grants, assume that the state pays 40 percent of the budget needs of each district. Under this arrangement, District A is now required to raise $144,000 by using a property tax levy of 24 mills, and District B $60,000 using a levy of 12 mills. Thus, the ER remains at 2:1; the percentage grant has been neither equalizing nor nonequalizing in its effect upon these two districts. This type of grant is seldom used in modern school finance programs. There is little to recommend it when compared to other models that have some degree of equalizing effect in their application.

Model 3-1 shows the effect of a flat grant of $400 per pupil upon the three districts.

District	State funds per pupil	Local funds per pupil	Total funds per pupil	Mills tax levy	Total funds per M/pupil
L	$400	$1,200	$1,600	60	$ 26.67
M	400	1,200	1,600	30	53.33
H	400	1,200	1,600	15	106.66

In Model 3-1 the flat grant of $400 per pupil leaves each district with the need to provide the additional $1,200 by a local property tax levy varying from 60 mills in District L to 15 mills in District H. Since the state is providing one-fourth of the

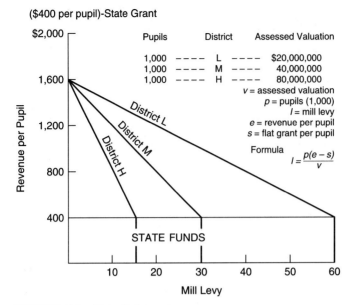

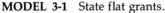

MODEL 3-1   State flat grants.

revenue of each district, the grant has the same effect as any percentage grant—the ratio of highest tax levy to lowest tax levy remains the same as without the grant (in this example 4:1), and no equalization is effected. If examples are used with varying numbers of weighted pupil (or other base on which the grant is made), the effect of the grant is usually nonequalizing.

Even though flat grants do not usually accomplish the purpose for which they are intended, they obviously reduce the burden on taxpayers in all districts and are therefore a first step in replacing the outmoded system of complete local financing. For example, in the model, District L has had its tax burden lessened by 20 mills, District M has had its tax burden lessened by 10 mills, and District H has been able to reduce its tax by 5 mills. In terms of percentage decrease, each has reduced its required mill levy by 25 percent.

Even though flat grants are generally not equalizing to local school districts, they are still being used in some state school finance formulas, usually in combination with other equalizing state allocations. Tradition continues to play an important role in financing education, even though there are far better methods of allocating state funds to local districts.

Flat grants were first provided by states to local districts on an incidental and haphazard basis. Gradually, however, the states developed theories and guidelines for such appropriations. Thurston and Roe noted the crudeness with which these funds were being allocated in the early part of this century:

A look at the state aid plans in effect in the various states shows that the great majority of the states have taken steps that are definitely designed to assure reasonably adequate educational opportunities for all children in properly organized school districts. Close investigation, however, shows that these plans are really a curious combination of refined methods of financing based upon logical principles, mixed with crude and awkward schemes of disbursement.[13]

As one takes a serious look at the various state systems of allocating funds to local districts, one may ask some pertinent questions concerning the processes used and the supporting rationale. What purpose is the state trying to serve with such allocations? What processes will best serve the purposes and objectives that are being sought? What guidelines are appropriate in making such allocations? These and many other questions need to be answered before value judgments can be made on any of the programs being considered.

Equalizing Grants

Most states now use the equalizing grant in allocating some or all of their state money to local districts. Such grants are made in terms of tax-raising ability of the local districts. Some states use combinations of grants—equalizing, percentage, flat, and variations of these—but the trend is toward allotting a higher percentage of all state funds on an equalization basis.

While the equalizing-grant method of allocating state funds has been used for a long time in some states, it is relatively new in others. Most of the state funds allotted to local districts take the form of nonrestrictive general-purpose grants. While some standards or guidelines are usually provided for the districts receiving these grants, it is intended that their use be determined by the local school boards, with little or no restriction by the state. States, for the most part, put the onus on the receiving districts for proper and wise use of such funds.

The states do not want to absorb all of the yearly school cost increases at the state level. Consequently they often devise ways short of mandated levies to keep local effort as high as possible, in order to keep state increases within bounds. Traditionally, this has been done by "reward for additional tax effort" or by "reward for performance." Cubberley's finance proposals included a kind of reward for effort; not only was this nonequalizing, but it actually increased the degree of inequality in many instances. His plan was to provide more funds for those districts with more teachers and for those with schools with enriched or extended school services. Since the more wealthy districts already had more of both, the incentive plan was a benefit to them but of little help to the poorer districts. As a result, the states have used various kinds of programs to aid districts that make the tax effort to go beyond the foundation program—supplementary or leeway programs that usually have some degree of equalization built into them. Most state school finance plans are not set up in pristine simplicity; they often combine several kinds of state aid in varying mixes.

Programs beyond the foundation must be supported solely by the local district. Utah requires the local overage of a required foundation program levy— if a district has such—to revert to the Uniform School Fund to be used to help finance the minimum program in other districts.

THE EQUALIZATION PRINCIPLE

The work of Strayer and Haig in introducing the foundation program principle of financing education was a major breakthrough in school finance theory. It now seems unfortunate that such a simple and defensible principle should not have been discovered and applied much earlier in school finance history. Its relatively late appearance, near the end of the first quarter of this century, was followed by an even slower rate of adoption by the states. For years knowledge-able people had observed and deplored the disparities, the inequities, and the injustices that existed in the United States in terms of unequal wealth, unequal incomes, and unequal opportunities. Similar inequities in educational opportunities and in sharing the costs of education seem to have been accepted with the same feelings of frustration and inability to change the existing situation.

The birth of the foundation program concept provided a means of removing some of the disparities in school revenues and expenditures. But changes come slowly, and some states were reluctant to apply the principle to their school finance program to any great degree. The principle is not perfect and has many limitations, but its application would have eliminated or at least reduced much of the unfairness of revenue distribution that still exists in many states. Improved finance formulas involving extensions and improvements of Strayer-Haig-Mort foundation programs have been visible and available; yet their utilization has been sporadic or nonexistent. Adoption of the foundation concept is a necessary first step to the even more effective program of power or open-end equalization now being advocated in the field of school finance theory.

IMPROVING STATE EQUALIZATION PRACTICES

The theory of the foundation program to achieve equalization of educational opportunity is relatively simple, but its practical application is often complex, usually unnecessarily so. The formula that each state uses involves three essential conditions:

1. Calculation of the "monetary need" of each school district necessary to obtain a state-guaranteed minimum program, measured objectively in terms of the number of weighted pupils (and other measures of need)—to be financed at the level of support that the state will guarantee.

2. Determination of the amount of local school revenue that can be expected with a state-established uniform tax rate levied against the equalized assessed valuation of all taxable property within the district.

3. Determination of the state allocation by finding the difference between the district's established need and the revenue obtainable from its required local tax effort.

Complications arise in applying the theory in practice, for a number of reasons:

1. Not all pupils require the same number of dollars of expenditure, even under a commitment to the principle of equality of opportunity. Handicapped children are more expensive to educate than non-handicapped ones, and children who attend very small schools and those who attend very large ones are more expensive than those in medium-sized ones.

2. Wide variations exist in the assessment practices in the districts of a state, even when all are presumed to be assessed at uniform rates.

3. The quality of the teaching staffs may vary considerably, as determined by educational preparation and experience, thus varying the costs of instruction among the districts.

4. The dollars provided do not purchase the same amount or quality of goods and services in all districts, thus favoring some districts and penalizing others.

5. Some states operate many different kinds of school districts with different taxing responsibilities and restrictions.

The net result of these and other differences among districts is that finance formulas usually include provisions to try to offset inequalities. Weightings for school size differentials, such as sparsity and density factors, special consideration for exceptional children, allowances for transportation costs, and provision for additional funds for better-qualified teachers, are among the most common adjustments in formulas. Such adjustments add to their complexity but also increase their validity and effectiveness.

FOUNDATION PROGRAM VARIATIONS

The foundation program concept can be applied with a number of variations: with or without local options to go above the state guaranteed minimum program, with or without state matching of local optional revenues, or in combination with flat grants and/or categorical allocations. Some of these possibilities are illustrated in the following simplified models.

Model 3-2 consists of two parts. The vertical columns marked "a" for each of the three districts illustrate a foundation program constructed with the mill levy necessary to produce the state program in the richest district, with no surplus being generated. The three columns marked "b" illustrate the same program with a required levy high enough to give the wealthiest district a surplus, which may or may not be recaptured by the state, depending on the philosophy of the particular state using the program.

This model is a mandatory foundation program comparing the three districts L, M, and H, which have assessed valuations of $20,000,000, $40,000,000, and $80,000,000, respectively; each district has 1,000 weighted pupil units. In the part "a" example, a required mill levy of 20 mills is applied, with no surplus above the foundation program. There is no provision in this model for board or voted options to go above the mandate program. Hence, it is an unequalized minimum as well as maximum program. It illustrates the application of a simple form of foundation program where equality of educational opportunity, as measured by equal dollars of total revenue per weighted pupil, is achieved; at the same time,

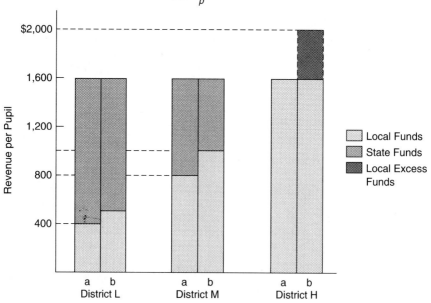

a – – – – Local Levy of 20 mills
b – – – – Local Levy of 25 mills (with surplus in wealthy district)

v = assessed value of taxable property
l = mandated tax levy
e = revenue per weighted-pupil unit
p = number of weighted-pupil units
s = state allocation per weighted pupil

$$s = \frac{ep - vl}{p}$$

MODEL 3-2 Foundation program (without local options).

local property taxpayers share the burden equitably. In its simplest form (without local capability of supplementing the program) it makes "perfect" equalization of a minimum-maximum program; it provides no opportunity for districts to enrich the state-mandated program. It is usually unsatisfactory unless accompanied by provisions for local extension of the program beyond the foundation level, unless it is equalized at a high enough level to provide adequate funds for all districts.

District	State funds per WPU	Required tax levy	Local funds	Total funds	
				per WPU	per mill per WPU
L	$1,200	20 M	$ 400	$1,600	$80
M	800	20 M	800	1,600	80
H	Nil	20 M	1,600	1,600	80

Columns "b" illustrate the use of the foundation program concept when the required local levy produces more revenue in some districts than the state-guaranteed level per weighted-pupil unit (WPU). The surplus may be left with the local district, or it can be used (recaptured) by the state to help equalize the costs in other districts. The argument in favor of its being kept where it is produced is that since it is coming from a so-called wealthy district, the taxpayers there are already providing proportionately higher percentages than in poorer districts to the state coffers through sales taxes, income taxes, and the like. On the other side of the argument is the observation that even with state recapture, the local district taxpayers are paying the same property tax rate as is being paid by those in all other districts. Model 3.2b illustrates a foundation program (without state recapture of surplus local funds raised by a 25-mill local levy).

District	State funds per WPU	Required tax levy	Local funds per WPU	Total funds	
				per WPU	per mill per WPU
L	$1,100	25 M	$ 500	$1,600	$64
M	600	25 M	1,000	1,600	64
H	Nil	25 M	2,000	2,000	80

Columns "b" with recapture become the same as Columns "a," except that equalization has been effected in all three districts—but with a 5-mill higher local levy being required.

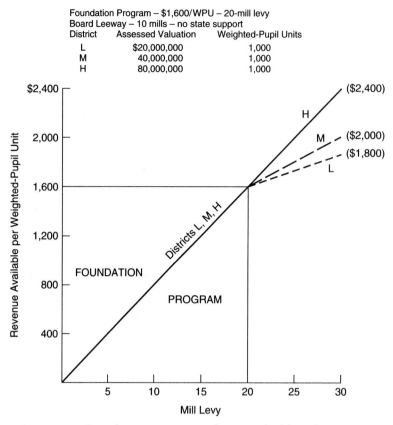

Foundation Program – $1,600/WPU – 20-mill levy
Board Leeway – 10 mills – no state support

District	Assessed Valuation	Weighted-Pupil Units
L	$20,000,000	1,000
M	40,000,000	1,000
H	80,000,000	1,000

MODEL 3-3   Foundation program with unmatched board
leeway.

Model 3-3 illustrates a foundation program with board leeway options not
supported with state funds. It assumes the same three districts as before, with
the following characteristics:

District	Assessed valuation	Required levy (mills)	Board leeway (mills)
L	$20,000,000	20	10
M	40,000,000	20	10
H	80,000,000	20	10

This model shows that the equalizing effect of a foundation program guaranteeing $1,600 per weighted-pupil unit with a required levy of 20 mills is eroded with
each district using a 10-mill (unsupported) tax levy beyond the foundation pro-

gram. Such a plan reduces the inequalities shown in the earlier models but falls far short of complete equalization. The lower the base of the foundation program and the greater the leeway above it, the greater are the inequalities that result from the use of this model.

District	Foundation program funds per WPU			Leeway program funds per WPU			Total program funds per WPU		
	State	Local	Total	State	Local	Total	State	Local	Total
L	$1,200	$ 400	$1,600	Nil	$200	$200	$1,200	$ 600	$1,800
M	800	800	1,600	Nil	400	400	800	1,200	2,000
H	Nil	1,600	1,600	Nil	800	800	Nil	2,400	2,400

Thus, District L has $60 available per weighted-pupil unit per mill levied, District M has 66.67, and District H has $80.

All the school finance models used in this text are shown in their simplest form. It should be noted that differences in the numbers of weighted-pupil units, differences in local levies to be made, differences in the amount of state funds to be provided, and the possibility of numerous combinations of these programs would increase the inequities shown in these models.

Models 3-4 and 3-5 show the effect of some combinations of flat grants and foundation programs, with or without school board and voted options. The various states have used varying methods and procedures to go above the state-guaranteed program. The kind and number of combinations of such programs is almost unlimited. Various states have used different combinations to suit their own school finance philosophy.

It should be emphasized that whatever system or process a state may use in financing education, the state should support the program to a greater extent in poor districts than in wealthy ones. It serves no useful purpose for a state to provide unsupported board options and taxpayer-voted options that go above the state program. Such a process simply widens the gap between the wealthy and poor districts and thus produces a nonequalizing effect in the finance program.

As the straight line in Models 3-4 and 3-5 that relates local tax effort and revenue per weighted pupil is flattened by a reduction of state support, the net effect becomes evident. For example, in Model 3.5, District H can obtain $2,800 per weighted pupil unit with a total levy of 40 mills, whereas District L obtains only $2,200 with the same levy. They each would receive $2,000/WPU for a 30-mill levy, so the unsupported voted leeway in this model has thereby added a nonequalizing factor. With the district power equalization principle now being emphasized (state support at the same rate at all tax-rate levels), there would be no such discrimination between districts that use leeway levies above the foundation program.

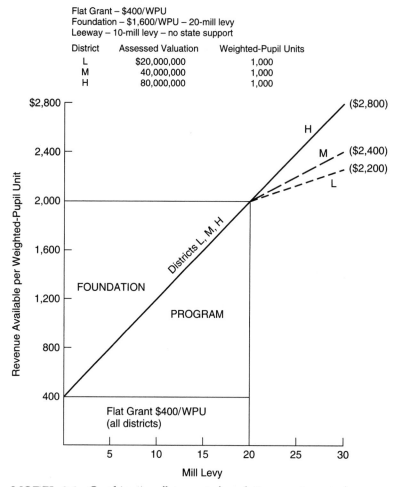

Flat Grant – $400/WPU
Foundation – $1,600/WPU – 20-mill levy
Leeway – 10-mill levy – no state support

District	Assessed Valuation	Weighted-Pupil Units
L	$20,000,000	1,000
M	40,000,000	1,000
H	80,000,000	1,000

MODEL 3-4 Combination flat grant, foundation program and unmatched board leeway

CONFUSION IN CURRENT SCHOOL FINANCE PRACTICES

Court cases have not solved the problem of providing equal financial opportunity for all children within a state; they have simply opened the door for debate and reform. Certainly they have raised more questions than they have answered. What direction should states now take in financing their educational programs in the light of limitations on property tax as a source of locally provided revenue for schools? How can other taxes be used to replace or reduce property taxes, with control of education skill kept at the local level? To what extent

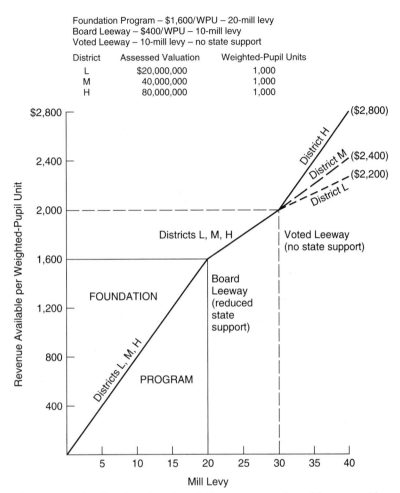

Foundation Program – $1,600/WPU – 20-mill levy
Board Leeway – $400/WPU – 10-mill levy
Voted Leeway – 10-mill levy – no state support

District	Assessed Valuation	Weighted-Pupil Units
L	$20,000,000	1,000
M	40,000,000	1,000
H	80,000,000	1,000

MODEL 3-5 Combination foundation program, board leeway with reduced support, and voted leeway with no state support.

do these court decisions mandate standardization and uniformity of school programs? What are the ramifications of the reshaping of the federal income tax law for local and state funding?

As a result of this confusion in school finance, some states and school districts continue to use educational finance practices that have been determined to be ineffective and obsolete:

1. Some states still require local school districts to rely almost completely on a local property tax as the source of funds for education in spite of the unfairness and regressiveness of such a means.

2. In spite of sound theories of equalization that have evolved during the last half-century from the thinking of numerous school finance specialists such as Strayer, Haig, Updegraff, and Mort, some of the fifty states have not yet incorporated these principles in their school finance programs.

3. Although it can be documented that education is really an investment in people, many legislative bodies give the impression that the cost of education threatens the economic capability of those who provide its funds.

4. It has been known for a long time that small schools are more expensive and less productive educationally than larger ones, but local pride and resistance to change are still effective in thwarting those who favor large and viable school organization patterns.

5. Many different groups of people are denied equity by the failure of state and local governments to provide sufficient funds to educate them. Students who are handicapped or gifted, aspire to vocational training, or are not of the dominant culture may not always have a reasonable chance to reach their potential as citizens.

6. Even though pride in "free education" seems to be a sincere expression on the part of nearly all citizens, in practice such a designation is almost a mockery in many places. Numerous fees and incidental charges in many schools discriminate against children of low-income families and relegate them to second-class citizenship.

SUMMARY

Equity in school finance refers to fairness in the expenditures per pupil and fairness in the treatment of taxpayers. In this context, equity and equality, although often used synonymously, do not mean the same. Fairness is more important in financing education than evenness or sameness, because students have wide differences in their abilities, needs, and educational desires. The school finance reforms of the 1970s emphasized equity of educational input; it is impossible to measure accurately equity of output.

Even though real property taxes are usually paid at the same tax rate in a given district, they are not always equitable, because of different rates of assessment as compared to market values, different degrees of ownership of the property being taxed, and differences in the income or the wealth of taxpayers— even though their property taxes may be relatively similar. Income and wealth have some advantages over property assessments in formulas for determining the fiscal capacity of school districts.

It is much easier to treat equals equally—the horizontal component of equity—than to treat unequals unequally—the vertical component of equity. No one has determined exactly how unequally those with unequal needs or abilities should be treated. Since the cost of education varies with the abilities and the needs of students, the use of weighing factors adds some measure of fairness to finance formulas. Although there are numerous weighting factors in use, those for disadvantaged children, small classes, vocational and other high-cost programs, and those for the early years of elementary education are the most widespread. The use of assessed valuation of property per pupil is more equitable than assessed valuation of property per capita for the operation of school finance programs. Wealth and income are gaining some support as bases for determining fiscal capacity.

In the early history of the United States, many of the individual states were slow in accepting responsibility for financing their public schools. Consequently, full local district funding was the first of all school finance systems. Because of the extreme differences in the size and wealth of local districts, local financing proved to be a very unfair and discriminatory method of financing education.

Early efforts of the states to aid local districts in financing education came principally in the form of flat grants. These, too, proved to be nonequalizing. Gradually, however, the states moved to equalizing grants and to the equalization principle in supporting local districts.

The Strayer-Haig equalization principle of distributing state funds to local districts began to be used in the second quarter of this century. Gradually, improvements were introduced—largely through the studies of Paul Mort and his students and colleagues.

School district reorganization began in earnest in the late 1940s. With great reductions in the number of local school districts, the range in size and comparative wealth decreased, and school finance formulas became simpler and fairer to students and to taxpayers alike.

Some states and school districts continue to use obsolete and unfair educational finance practices in spite of the relationship between equal protection and equalization in school finance. Such practices are being challenged in state courts in the 1990s.

ASSIGNMENT PROJECTS

1. Compare various definitions found in the literature of *equality* and *equity* in school finance programs or formulas.
2. Discuss the problems and ramifications involved in improving school finance formulas in order to provide greater equity for taxpayers.
3. According to the literature, what are the apparent trends in the measurement of school district wealth? What are the problems involved in applying these measures to school finance formulas?
4. Provide specific definitions for the following terms: assessed valuation, market value, weighted-pupil, wealth tax, minimum or equalization program.

5. Some states express their tax rates in mills; others express them in dollars per hundred dollars of assessed valuation. For example, in some states the tax rate for school purposes might be expressed as 50.5 mills; in others it would be expressed as $5.05 per $100 of assessed valuation (AV). It could also be expressed as $50.50 per $1,000 of assessed valuation. Express the following as indicated:

1. 156.25 mills as dollars
2. $0.375 as mills
3. $17.51 as mills
4. 57.3 mills as dollars per $100 (AV)
5. $3.60 per $150 (AV) as mills
6. $0.136 per $1 (AV) as dollars/$1,000 (AV)
7. .78 mills as dollars
8. .78 mills as dollars per $100 (AV)
9. .78 mills as dollars per $1,000 (AV)
10. 2,341.5 mills as dollars
11. $5,491.54 as mills
12. $48.54 per $1,000 (AV) as mills per $1 (AV)

6. Look up *Serrano* v. *Priest* and similar court rulings and determine how *equity* and *equality* in education were used by the courts.

7. Trace the assessed value and taxation rate of a piece of local property and determine the reasons for its changing value and tax rate.

State Allocation Plans

Flat Grants   8. With the help of the following information, answer the questions concerning the effect of flat grants upon the two districts.

District	Assessed valuation	Paid by state	Budget needs	Mill levy	Number of students
A	$6,000,000	nil	$240,000	_____ (1)	360
B	5,000,000	nil	100,000	_____ (2)	150

Effort ratio _____ : _____ (3)
Would a grant of $24,000 by the state to each district be equalizing in its effect upon the two districts? Yes _____ No _____ (4)
The new effort ratio would be _____ : _____ (5)
Would a state grant of $100 per student be equalizing in its effect upon the two districts? Yes _____ No _____ (6)
The new effort ratio would be _____ : _____ (7)

District	Assessed valuation	Paid by state	Budget needs	Mill levy	Number of teachers
C	$ 8,000,000	nil	$400,000	_____ (8)	50
D	10,000,000	nil	300,000	_____ (9)	40

Would a grant of $40,000 be equalizing in its effect upon the two districts?
Yes _____ No _____ (10)
The new effort ratio would be _____ : _____ (11)
Would a state grant of $500 per teacher be equalizing in its effect upon the two districts? Yes _____ No _____ (12)
The new effort ratio would be _____ : _____ (13)

Foundation Programs 9. Determine the state funds that would be paid in the following equalization program.
District A has an assessed valuation of $10,580,000. Its budget needs for this part of the program are $495,000. The required local levy is $1.56 per $100 of assessed valuation. Under an equalized program, the state would pay the district $_____ (14)

What are the three parts of any state foundation program?
(15) _____
(16) _____
(17) _____

Using Census, Average Daily Membership (ADM), and Average Daily Attendance (ADA) in Allocating State Funds

10. Assuming a certain state has a fixed dollar amount of money to allocate to the following three districts on a proportionate share basis, which district would probably prefer to have the state use each of the three methods of allocation?

	District A	District B	District C
Pupils on census list	2,000	2,500	3,000
Pupils in ADM	1,860	2,140	2,000
Pupils in ADA	1,548	2,052	1,820

(1) (Census)—District _____
(2) (ADM)—District _____
(3) (ADA)—District _____

(4) What is the advantage of using ADA in allocating state money to local school districts? _____

(5) What is the advantage of using ADM in allocating state money to local school districts? _____

(6) What would be the advantage of using aggregate days attendance in allocating state money to local school districts? _____

SELECTED READINGS

Berne, Robert, and Leanna Stiefel. "The Equity of School Finance Systems over Time: The Value Judgments Inherent in Evaluation," *Educational Administration Quarterly 15,* Spring 1979.

Carnegie Forum on Education and the Economy. *A Nation Preparing Teachers for the 21st Century.* Washington, D.C.: Carnegie Forum on Education and the Economy, 1990.

Coleman, J. S. *Equality of Educational Opportunity.* Washington, D.C.: U.S. Government Printing Office, 1966.

Cubberley, Ellwood P. *School Funds and Their Apportionment.* New York: Teachers College, Columbia University, 1905.

Ellwood, D. T. *Poor Support: Poverty in the American Family.* New York: Basic Books, 1988.

Garfinkel, I., and S. S. McLanakan. *Single Mothers and Their Children: A New American Dilemma.* Washington, D.C.: Urban Institute Press, 1986.

Guthrie, James W. *School Finance Policies and Practices, the 1980s: A Decade of Conflict. First Annual Yearbook of the American Education Finance Association.* Cambridge, Mass.: Ballinger, 1980.

Guthrie, James W., Walter I. Garms, and Lawrence C. Pierce. *School Finance and Education Policy: Enhancing Educational Efficiency, Equality, and Choice.* 2nd ed. Englewood Cliffs, N.J.: Prentice Hall, 1988.

Honeyman, D. S., D. C. Thompson, and R. C. Wood. *Financing Rural and Small Schools: Issues of Adequacy and Equity.* Gainesville: University of Florida Press, 1989.

Jencks, C., M. S. Smith, H. Acland, M. J. Bane, D. Cohen, H. Gintis, B. Heyna, and S. Michaelson. *Inequality: A Reassessment of the Effect of Family and Schooling in America.* New York: Harper & Row, 1972.

Kronick, Robert F., and Charles H. Hargis. *Dropouts: Who Drops Out and Why, and the Recommended Action.* Springfield, Ill.: Charles C. Thomas, 1990.

Leppert, Jack, and Dorothy Routh. *A Policy Guide to Weighted Pupil Education Finance Systems: Some Emerging Practical Advice.* Washington, D.C.: National Institute of Education, September, 1979.

Levitan, Sar A. *Programs in Aid of the Poor.* Baltimore, Md.: Johns Hopkins University Press, 1985.

Odden, Allan R., and Lawrence O. Picus. *School Finance: A Policy Perspective.* New York: McGraw-Hill, 1992.

Thomas, Gloria Jean, David J. Sperry, and F. Del Wasden. *The Law and Teacher Employment.* New York: West Publishing Company, 1991.

Toward High and Rigorous Standards for the Teaching Profession. 3rd ed. Washington, D. C.: National Board for Professional Teaching Standards, 1991.

The Unfinished Agenda: A New Vision for Child Development and Education. New York: Committee for Economic Development, 1991.

Verstegan, D. A. *School Finance at a Glance.* Denver, Colo.: Education Commission of the States, 1990.

Webb, L. D., Martha M. McCarthy, and Stephen B. Thomas. *Financing Elementary and Secondary Education.* Columbus, Ohio: Merrill, 1988.

ENDNOTES

1. Charles S. Benson, et al., *Planning for Educational Reform* (New York: Dodd, Mead, 1974), p. 8.

2. *Serrano* v. *Priest* (I), 96 Cal. Rptr. 601, 487 P.2d 1241 (Calif. 1971).

3. Nancy Mathis, "In Finance Arena, a New Activism Emerges," *Education Week,* April 26, 1989, pp. 1, 8, 10.

4. *Rose* v. *Council for Better Education,* 790 S.W.2d 186 (Ky. 1989).

5. *Edgewood Independent School District* v. *Kirby,* 777 S.W.2d 391 (Texas 1989).

6. Allan Odden, "Financing Education Excellence," *Phi Delta Kappan,* Vol. 65, No. 5, January 1984, p. 316.

7. *Brown* v. *Board of Education,* 347 U.S. 483, 74 S. Ct. 686 (1954).

8. Robert Berne and Leanna Stiefel, "Taxpayer Equity in School Finance Reform: The School Finance and the Public Finance Perspectives," *Journal of Education Finance,* Vol. 5, No. 1, Summer 1979, p. 37.

9. Walter W. McMahon, "A Broader Measure of Wealth and Effort for Educational Equality and Tax Equity," *Journal of Education Finance,* Vol. 4, No. 1, Summer 1978, pp. 65–66.

10. Russell Harris, "Act 59 and the Prospects for Reforming School Finance in Pennsylvania," *Journal of Education Finance,* Vol. 3, No. 4, Spring 1978, p. 497.

11. Roe L. Johns, "Improving the Equity of School Finance Programs," *Journal of Education Finance,* Vol. 1, No. 4, Spring 1976, p. 547.

12. Allan Odden, as quoted by John H. Beck, "The Effects of Power Equalizing School Aid Formulas with an Income Factor," *Journal of Education Finance,* Vol. 5, No. 1, Summer 1979, p. 57.

13. Lee M. Thurston and William H. Roe, *State School Administration* (New York: Harper & Row, 1957), p. 84.

Chapter *4*

Sources of Revenue

Education . . . must overcome formidable obstacles . . . if America is to remain preeminent, economically and politically, in our increasingly interdependent world. . . . School systems, faced with growing expectations, must receive enough funding to meet those expectations.   —AASA/NSBA, 1991

Profits are realized only in the private sector of the economy. Since the public sector requires financial resources to perform its various functions and provide necessary services for society, some satisfactory system of diverting funds from the competitive and profit-making sector to public institutions must be arranged. The most successful system yet devised for that purpose is taxation. By such a process, resources are transferred with relatively little difficulty from where they are produced to where they are needed. Although the United States tax system has its critics and its areas of unfairness, no country has yet devised a better system for the orderly transfer of private monies to public purposes.

Economists often refer to the affluence of the private economy, but similar references to the financial status of the public sector are seldom made. The latter is always dependent upon the former for its degree of affluence, and even its survival. Periodically, people in the private sector indicate their dissatisfaction with the performance or the products of public institutions and withdraw a portion or all of their financial support from the "offenders." Because of taxpayer revolts against taxes, court or legislative action, or even voter indifference, the financial well-being of public institutions is determined by the attitude of those who provide its financial support through a system of taxation.

THE TAXATION SYSTEM

The term *tax* serves as a firm reminder to people that they have been given personal and mandatory responsibility to divert a certain amount of their wealth—past, present, or future—to become part of the revenue required by institutions and units of government performing public services. A direct relation may or may not exist between the amount of tax paid and observable benefits to the individual taxpayer.

Taxes are a function of three variables: (1) the tax base (value of the objects or items to be taxed); (2) the assessment practices being followed (the percentage of market value applied to the object being taxed); and (3) the tax levy (the rate applied to the assessed value of an object or item to determine the amount of tax obligation). Tax rates mean little until they are related to assessment practices and values or compared with them. When comparing taxes and tax effort where there are differing assessment practices, one must convert assessed value into market or sale value of the property in question.

A county in Pennsylvania draws attention to the misleading practice of determining a true tax effort. The homes in Delaware County are assessed at about 3.5 percent of market value—as used here, this means the price that would be paid in a free market by a willing buyer to a willing seller. To raise needed revenue, districts have coped by imposing extremely high tax rates, such as $450 per $1000, which raises $2700 on a home with an assessed value of $6000. While this approach provides funding for the schools, it presents a distorted picture of the wealth of the district and an unusually high tax effort. "If the house were assessed at 85 percent of its sale price *of $200,000* . . . the same revenue could be produced by a rate of $15.90 per $1000. That would offer a totally different snapshot of the area: an affluent neighborhood with a reasonable tax effort."[1]

The tax system, even though it has existed and operated for a long time in each state, does not provide an easy answer to the question of how much or what percentage of government revenue should be alloted to each of the institutions or agencies it sponsors. What formula or what device should be used to allocate private funds to the publicly sponsored organizations in order to bring maximum benefits to society? No one claims to have found the answer to this question.

Although the public sector obtains most of the revenue it uses by taxation, several other minor sources are used to supplement tax funds. The sale of government services or products, the sale of government-owned property—including land and such other assets as surplus equipment—licenses, fines, forfeitures, incomes from investment, special fees, gifts, and transfer funds from other levels and agencies of government are among the other sources of such funds.

Education—Financed by Government

Education is a beneficial service (nonmaterial good) that should be made available to all eligible citizens of a country regardless of their degree of affluence. Under such a system it is necessary for education to be financed by government with its capability of collecting resources from the private sector and distributing them equitably among institutions in the public sector. In spite of the fact that education produces externalities and large-scale spillovers that benefit the larger society, it has generally been financed largely at the local school district level. In the opinion of many, this fact creates one of the most difficult problems with which educators must concern themselves—providing equitable school programs and creating equitable tax burdens with the almost exclusive use of a regressive and inadequate property tax system.

Rate Bills Are Obsolete

Early in its history, this country proved to the satisfaction of its citizens that rate bills (the requirement that each pupil pay a fee), tuition charges, fees, and the like would not provide universal and equal education for its children and youth. Discrimination against the poor and against large families destroyed the supporting philosophy for this method of financing education. The only defensible alternative was the development of a tax system with a supporting rationale. It was slow in its implementation; states gradually adopted their own unique systems of taxation. Although these were satisfactory for a long period of time, local dependence on property taxes to the almost complete omission of other forms of taxation has been widely criticized in recent years.

Taxes Are Often Unpopular

It has been said that the only good tax is the one paid by someone else. Dislike for paying taxes that increase year after year is a normal reaction for people for many reasons. (1) If the tax rate is high, paying taxes may seriously curtail other activities and reduce the quantity and quality of other economic goods and services then available to the taxpayer. (2) The complex society of interrelated institutions makes it increasingly more difficult for a taxpayer to see and understand the personal benefits resulting from tax dollars. (3) The increased services that are required as the population increases and social institutions become more complex are not understood or favored by many people. (4) When increased taxes are being considered, much misleading information concerning taxation is often issued by those who favor increased taxes as well as by those who oppose them. (5) The average taxpayer thinks of the "cost" of education rather than the "investment" in human capital that results from taxation for that purpose. (Unfortunately, there is little opportunity to provide the information necessary to develop this important concept for a majority of the adults in society.)

GENERAL CLASSIFICATION OF TAXES

Taxes may be classified as proportional, progressive, or regressive. The proportional tax requires that the same percentage of each person's total taxable income, regardless of income size, be paid in taxes. A tax is progressive if the percentage of the total taxable income required for taxes increases as the taxable income becomes higher. A regressive tax finds higher incomes paying lower percentages of the total taxable incomes for taxes than do lower incomes. For example, three households with incomes of $10,000, $20,000, and $40,000 that pay taxes of $1,000, $2,000, and $4,000 are paying a proportional tax, as each is paying 10 percent of income for taxes. If the three households pay $1,000, $3,000 and $10,000 in taxes, the tax is said to be progressive: the household with the smallest income pays 10 percent in taxes, the next larger one pays 15 percent, and the largest pays 25 percent. On the other hand, if the same three households pay $1,000, $1,500 (or anything less than $2,000), and $2,400 (or anything less than $4,000), the tax is regressive. In the last instance, the lowest income was taxed at 10 percent, the middle income at 7.5 percent, and the highest income at 6 percent.

CHARACTERISTICS OF A GOOD TAX SYSTEM

Most school finance and tax authorities agree on many of the most important guidelines that should be followed in establishing or evaluating a good tax system. It is extremely difficult to achieve complete or even satisfactory implementation of these general principles, however. Consequently, no taxing unit—local, state, or federal—has yet produced a taxation program that meets universal acceptance by all its tax-paying clientele. Nonetheless, certain basic principles and theories of taxation are generally accepted as appropriate characteristics of a viable tax system at any level of government.

Tax Systems Should Be Coordinated

Even though there is usually very little planned coordination in the tax programs of the three levels of government, none of the three can be evaluated realistically without simultaneous consideration of the other two. Individuals tend to measure their tax "burden" by the total taxes they are required to pay rather than those they are required to pay to any one level of government. It is important, then, that the total number of tax systems operable in any community or geographic unit be coordinated and interrelated in a defensible and balanced program. Any duplication of taxation structure should be minimal. Equity and balance should exist among the various forms of taxes that are an integral part of the total system.

All Citizens Owe Taxes

The benefits of government services are shared by all the nation's citizens in varying degrees, depending upon their needs. Protection from fire and acts of violence, and also many other aspects of the police power exercised by government, are the inherent right of all individuals, businesses, and other organizations. Financial support for these services is therefore required from all who receive the benefits or who stand to receive them.

A good tax system provides that every person and every business be required to pay some tax to government. It is a distinct violation of good taxation theory to use tax laws that have gaping loopholes whereby any citizens can escape paying their share of the tax burden. Such unfair exclusions make those who have average incomes pay more than their fair share of the costs of government services.

Justice and Economic Neutrality

As a matter of simple fairness, a good tax system distributes the burden it creates among all its citizens in an equitable manner. Admittedly, what is equitable is often a question of the frame of reference of the person or organization making the determination. Generally, however, it can be shown that a progressive income tax on businesses as well as on individuals is the most equitable single tax. Income is the best of all the measures of tax-paying ability; progressive tax rates make the tax fair, for even though higher incomes require much higher taxes, the burden to the taxpayer is not greater. In spite of the advantages of the income tax, no economist or tax authority would favor using it to the exclusion of all others. A single tax, regardless of its basic fairness, can never be fair for all citizens of a taxing unit. Taxation theory requires diversification as a base, so that an individual's "escape" from a particular kind of tax does not mean complete exemption from paying a tax of any kind.

While diversification of taxes is important, simplicity is equally necessary in any good tax system. Taxpayers cannot be expected to support intricate and complicated taxing laws they cannot understand. In theory, taxpayers should be able to calculate their own taxes with a minimum of help or instruction.

The maintenance of economic neutrality among taxpayers must not be disturbed by patterns of taxation. Citizens and business should be left in the same relative position to one another after paying taxes as they were before. Persons with greater income before taxes are paid should still have greater unspent income after taxes are deducted than their lower-income friends. It is important that special taxes that affect certain individuals or businesses be minimized in comparison with broadly based taxes.

Adequacy of Yield

Maintenance of the extensive services of government requires large amounts of tax revenue. It is therefore important that taxes be applied to productive sources. There is no point in complicating the system by the addition of taxes that have little individual potential for yielding revenue in substantial amounts. Nuisance taxes that provide only minimum revenue should be avoided as much as possible in the taxing system of any level of government.

Progressive Versus Regressive Taxes

The proportional, progressive, and regressive features of taxes should be considered in devising or improving a tax system. Taxes should involve at best the defensible characteristic of being progressive; at worst, they should be proportional. Ideally, they should never be regressive, but in practice they often contain regressive features. All taxing devices should be constructed to reduce their regressive features as much as possible. High incomes should never pay lower rates than lower incomes, if it is assumed that the taxing system should be based on the ability-to-pay principle.

Tax Erosion Should Be Minimized

Tax erosion possibilities and provisions should be minimized or eliminated for every tax. For example, the deserving veteran and the worthy widow or homesteader may well deserve pecuniary benefits from government, but they should be provided by government in some form other than exclusion from property-tax-paying obligations. Erosion of the tax base, regardless of the worthiness of the cause, entails more problems than it solves. Special pleadings and other avenues of escape from tax paying should be reduced to a more reasonable base by tighter laws and better enforcement practices. Estimates by some tax authorities of the amount of such tax base erosion have amounted to as high as one-fourth of the total real property value in the United States. The effect of such tax losses on schools and other government institutions that depend on tax revenues for their operation is obviously great.

A tax system should avoid or minimize preferential tax treatment sometimes offered to attract individuals or businesses to a state or community. Experience indicates that the differences in initial tax burden are usually relatively minor factors in influencing the locating of businesses and industries. More important, perhaps, is the quality and the quantity of public services—especially education—that are available for the employees of companies seeking a new location. On the other hand, the tax system should obviously not be oppressive to the point where it discourages new industry.

Taxpayer Convenience Is Important

It is generally believed that taxes should be direct rather than indirect. Taxpayers should know when they are paying a tax and should be able to do so as conveniently as possible. Paying hidden or indirect taxes, standing in long lines to pay taxes, and hearing about others who have escaped similar tax payments are examples of practices that demoralize many otherwise conscientious taxpayers. Fairness and courtesy in collecting taxes and in dealing with tax problems must characterize any successful taxation structure.

Collection Costs Should Be Low

To the extent possible, the taxes that are used should have a relatively low collection and administrative cost. Government institutions are interested in the amount of net revenue available to them rather than the gross amount of dollars collected. For example, the high cost of locating, assessing, and eventually collecting personal property taxes has been such that most of the states have either minimized or eliminated this potentially excellent source of tax revenue.

Taxes and Services Should Be Visible

A common complaint of taxpayers is that they cannot see what value they are receiving for the taxes they pay. Too often, they appear to take the services of government for granted. It is a proper function of government and its institutions to make taxpayers aware that their payments are contributing to the important services of government that they have demanded. Theoretically, this makes them demand fewer of such services and increases their demand for operational efficiency.

Tax Shifting Should Be Minimized

The tax system of any unit of government should be such that tax shifting possibilities are minimized. To the casual observer it would seem that taxes are paid by the person on whom they are imposed and that it would be an easy matter to add taxes on any group in society or drop them. This would mean that if property owners or wage earners were not being taxed to their fair share of the burdens of government services, the correction could be made by additional taxes on property in the first case or by increased income taxes for the wage earners. The impact of the tax would appear to be at the intended point. But this reasoning ignores the complex device of tax shifting—passing the tax burden to someone else. In the first example, the property owner shifts the increased tax to the renter in the form of increased rent; in the second example, the wage earner often demands higher wages, with the result that the increased tax is paid by the employer. In neither of these examples does the tax shifting stop at the point intended.

Shifting taxes to the point that the impact of a tax (point of tax imposition) is different from the incidence of that tax (person who finally pays the tax) makes taxation extremely delicate and difficult to regulate. In far too many instances, it may result in overtaxation of some groups and undertaxation of those groups who can successfully shift some or all of their tax burdens to others.

Earmarked Taxes Should Be Minimized

Dedicating tax revenues to a particular purpose should be avoided as much as possible. Such earmarking makes for too much rigidity in the budget practices of the receiving institution. Under such regulations, the minimum expenditure tends to become the maximum, thus depriving administrative boards of the flexibility so necessary in publicly controlled organizations. On the other hand, designating the use of some taxes based on the benefit principle is justifiable, as when a gasoline or motor fuels tax is earmarked for the maintenance of streets and highways.

Tax Structure Should Avoid Restrictions

Taxes sometimes have effects that may seriously change the economic practices of the individuals who pay them. The intent of taxation is to divert private funds into the public sector to produce necessary goods and services; it is not its purpose to alter the behavioral patterns of taxpayers.

Excessive taxes on certain commodities or services may destroy producers' competitive potential in the market or reduce their economic productivity. This violates a fundamental concept of taxation, for the tax on a desirable economic good should never be such that its more favored competitor has free access to a noncompetitive market.

The taxing pattern should not unduly restrict an individual in determining economic behavior in earning a living or in choosing the goods or services desired to satisfy needs or wants. Nor should the taxing system create a desire to restrict production of economic goods and services by individuals or organizations. In short, the taxing pattern should have the least possible negative effect on the living style of its contributors and the greatest possible positive effect in developing and achieving the goals of the agencies and institutions it is constructed to serve.

CRITERIA FOR EVALUATING TAX STRUCTURE

McCann and Delon emphasized certain criteria for evaluating a tax system and the governmental structure necessary to administer it.[2] The characteristics they rated important in any tax system include efficiency, equity, adequacy, and adaptability. By *efficiency*, they referred to the structure for fiscal administration, which is best when operated with the least economic and social costs and the highest order of services for the money spent. They used the term *equity* to mean that the structure should provide the highest degree of fairness in the treatment of the individual citizen. The criterion of *adequacy* indicates that the system ought to provide enough funds to support the level of public service that is adopted for the particular government agency in question. By *adaptability*, they meant that any system that provides for the administration of a program of school finance ought to be adaptable to (1) changing economic conditions, (2) modified social demands for education, and (3) significant changes in education.

Taxpayers themselves are constantly evaluating the tax system to which they are responsible. They do not usually formally rate all the individual segments of the structure, but they have a practical way of making their opinions known concerning the total tax pattern. School administrators know all too well what will happen to their appeals for increased taxes when the public feels that they are already high enough. Citizen evaluation of the taxes required for government services often results in lost elections for bond and even current expenditure levy questions. Taxation cannot be pushed to a point beyond the limit of taxpayer acceptance. Benson refers to the "normal" as well as the "absolute" limits of taxation in the following:

> During any period of relative stability in a society, certain "normal" levels of taxation are extremely difficult to breach. Such conventional levels of taxation should never be confused with absolute limits. For any major tax instrument an absolute limit to yield does not in the practical sense exist. In a major social upheaval, such as a war, the conventional limits of taxation are likely to be discarded. After the period of upheaval has passed, the volume of nonemergency public services is more likely to expand and absorb the revenue than are tax rates to fall to their former levels.[3]

TAXES FOR EDUCATION

Some of the principal taxes used to transfer funds to the public sector include property, personal income, corporation income, sales, and sumptuary taxes. Most of these are used to some degree in financing education in all of the fifty states. Others that are being considered but have not yet received general acceptance include site-value, value-added and severance taxes. In several states one popular revenue source that has the effect of transferring funds to the public sector is a lottery. Of course, there is continuing debate as to whether the concept is truly a tax or not. Many states still use the property tax as their most reliable and lucrative source of revenue, with only minor reliance on other forms of taxation.

THE PROPERTY TAX

A property (*ad valorem*) tax is levied against the owner of real or personal property. Real property is not readily movable; it includes land, buildings, and improvements. It is usually classified as residential, industrial, agricultural, commercial, or unused (vacant). Personal property is movable; it consists of tangibles, such as machinery, livestock, automobiles, and crops, or intangibles, such as money, stocks, and bonds.

Property taxes were the first kinds of school taxes, and they still constitute almost the complete local tax revenue for schools. Property tax rates are usually expressed in mills per dollar of assessed valuation or dollars per hundred dollars of assessed valuation, though some states use a *tax rate* on market value. Facility in changing or interpreting different ways of stating tax rates is a valuable skill for anyone interested in comparing district budgets and taxing procedures in different states.

Historical Use

The states have based their local school revenue systems on a property tax. This policy seems to have been justified in its early history, for property ownership was considered to be a good measure of the wealth of people—especially before the advent of industrialization. For a long time, the property tax seemed to be reasonably satisfactory, and severe critics of it were relatively few. During the nineteenth century and much of the twentieth, the property tax at the local level has proved to be a good and reliable source of revenue for operating schools and providing many other services of government.

The following characteristics are generally accepted as desirable traits of the property tax:

- Operated as a direct tax, with most people understanding its purpose.
- Easily collected by the regular machinery of state and county government.
- Regulated and controlled by local boards of education according to the provisions of state law.
- Avoidance of payment is almost impossible.
- Highly productive—mainstay of local governments for generations.
- Highly visible—provides direct linkage between services provided by local government and the cost of those services.
- Produced adequate revenue for most school districts (until recently).

Assessment Practices

Widespread unfairness exists in the assessment practices and in the adequacy of property tax administration in the various states. Unequal assessment practices are often found among the parcels of property within any one school district. It may be argued that such a condition simply means that a higher tax rate must be used to get the desired amount of revenue, but such an argument is of little value, because the general public resists increased tax levy rates, and state laws often prohibit them. Thus, a school board often finds itself powerless to overcome the revenue problems caused by underassessment.

The application of the *foundation program* concept of allocating state funds to local districts has created another problem involving underassessment. Fractional assessment was originally only a problem of inadequate revenue to the district concerned. Now, however, in financing the foundation program, underassessment becomes an advantage to that district, because the decreased revenue from its own property taxation will be offset by the addition of an equal increase in state funds. This places a premium on underassessment and certainly is not fair to other districts that are fully assessed.

Assessment practices vary widely, but few states actually assess at more than 60 percent of the market value of property. Many of them assess at less than 20 percent. Some states assess real property according to its classification or type, and some assess personal property at a different rate from real property.

Tax authorities argue for assessment of property at 100 percent of its market value. Such a practice would be desirable, but its impracticality under present taxing systems makes the argument meaningless. The main reason for fractional rather than full assessment of property has been that assessors have been unwilling and unable to keep assessment increases in line with changes in market value.

Present problems of property assessment are largely the result of the predominantly political system under which taxation laws have been made and administered. Elected county, town, or township assessors, often not particularly well qualified for their responsibilities, face the difficult problems of raising assessments because of inflation or actual improvements in the property, keeping assessments fair and equitable among all property owners, deciding on the relative worth of different kinds of property, and other equally difficult problems. Assessors, under this obsolete system of tax administration, have to weigh the value of fairness and equity against their desire to be reelected to their positions.

In addition to the problem of fractional assessment, determining whether or not to use classified property assessments still remains in question. Should property used for one purpose be assessed differently from property used for another purpose? If so, how should relative rates be determined? What should be the relative assessment value placed on residential property as compared with income property? What is the proper relation of assessment to be applied to a corner business lot as compared to a similar lot in the middle of the block? These and many other unresolved assessment problems make the property tax system less equitable than would be expected.

Unfairness of the Property Tax

Even though the property tax has served the schools well for many years, it has always been under some criticism. Its abuses and unfairness have become more apparent year after year. Some features that were generally accepted as advantages early in its existence now seem to have changed to disadvantages. It is not the fair or equitable measure of tax-paying ability that it was years ago. People are now inclined to invest their surplus earnings in personal property, much of which can escape taxation. The owner of land and buildings fares less well than a counterpart who puts wealth into more intangible assets that are less likely to be included in the normal taxation process. This makes the property tax regressive—a violation of the ability-to-pay principle on which sound tax systems for financing education are based. A few states are reducing regressivity by using tax credit plans that provide property tax relief to low-income families, particularly to elderly people.

The finance problems encountered by most urban centers illustrate some of the deficiencies of the property tax. The typical city's tax base is eroded to a serious degree by the departure of the middle-class central cities under federal court pressure for desegregation, by old industries leaving and new ones becoming reluctant to locate there, and by the high percentage of tax-exempt property—the property of government, churches, schools, and welfare organizations. To complicate the condition further, cities have higher percentages of high-cost students to educate—the handicapped, the disadvantaged, and minority students. They suffer, too, from pressures for higher salaries by strong unions, higher costs for building sites and construction, and higher costs for noneducational services, commonly referred to as *municipal overburden.*

The property tax is unfair to the person who must pay taxes on the full value of property of which he or she does not have complete ownership. This disparity is shown in a simple example. A and B both have tax responsibility for $50,000 worth of property, for which they each owe $2,000 in taxes. A owns the property; B is purchasing the property and has only $10,000 of equity in it. A pays only 4 percent of property wealth in taxes, whereas B pays 20 percent of equity in taxes. If wealth instead of property were the base of the tax, B would owe only $400 in taxes as compared to the $2,000 owed by A.

Other Criticisms of the Property Tax

Another serious defect of the property tax system arises from the limitations that states sometimes place on it. This has been achieved by state-imposed tax rate restrictions—legislated during depression years to protect beleaguered taxpayers. Although such restrictions have been liberalized to some degree since World War II, many school districts are still struggling to raise adequate local revenues with state limitations on tax levies. In some states (Utah, for example), the state legislature has imposed a tax rate limit, which can be increased to a higher limit only by a favorable vote of the people in the district. The practical effect is that few school districts are able to exceed the limit under which the school board is required to operate. Since all taxes are paid from income, the critics of the property tax and other taxes wonder why there should be any other tax than one on income. The local school board, however, is virtually powerless to control an income tax, but a property tax is comparatively easy for it to administer. Its use as a source of local revenue for schools has been alternately praised and condemned.

Walker discusses some of the most obvious limitations in property taxes:

> Today, all states have some form of tax limitations on local property taxes through assessment limits, tax rate limits, tax levy limits, or expenditure limits. These limitations generally are applied in conjunction with local tax "relief" devices such as homestead exemptions, circuit breakers, classification schemes, homestead credits, tax deferral plans, or tax freezes for selected citizens. The numerous limitation and relief devices, when juxtaposed against the fierce struggles of the nineteenth century to obtain and to utilize the tax, reflect current theories about the inefficacy of the local property tax.
>
> The same criticisms are heard today about the property tax as were heard in 1900. One reason for the continuing controversy is that in a nonagrarian

economy the property tax is a poor index of both public services received by households and businesses and the ability to pay of all taxpayers. Another objection is the supposed regressivity of the tax, although newer research shows that it is probably progressive, on the average. Still a third objection is that administration of the tax is poor and should be improved. These eternal objections, plus citizen response to local budgetary decisions, have created a "limitation" atmosphere manifested by such actions as Proposition 13 in California (1978) and "Proposition $2\frac{1}{2}$" in Massachusetts (1980).

It can be argued that tax limitations have had both beneficial and adverse effects on the property tax and local school district revenues. Among the positive effects are a reduction in taxes on real estate, a broadening of the tax base (especially at the state level), more realistic assessment levels, and increased state aid. Some of the negative effects have been a proliferation of overlapping local governments, shifts of responsibility away from the local level, reduction of freedom of the electorate, impairment of good budgeting procedures, conflicting pressures on assessors, and outmoded types of limitations.[4]

The condemnation of the property tax has reached new heights as a result of court decisions in some states, adverse opinions of the tax by many governmental leaders, and the negative vote of people in referenda in some states. The revolt has been directed particularly against the abuses and unfairness of the property tax. Described by many as the most oppressive and inequitable tax of all, it has lost much of its traditional popularity as a source of revenue for schools. Many segments of society—taxpayers, educators, and economists—have added their protests to its use and particularly to its extension.

Although the courts have not declared the property tax unconstitutional, they have said that disparities and inequalities exist. Thus, the structure of school finance laws is changing, and the years ahead may see other modifications in the use and administration of the property tax.

Circuit Breakers

A plan used to protect certain classes of individuals from excessive property tax burdens is the *circuit breaker*. It is designed to provide that the property taxes of people with low incomes will not exceed a stated portion or percent of their annual income, regardless of the value of their property or the tax in effect in their taxing unit.

As an illustration of the circuit breaker principle, a person with an annual taxable income of $6,000 who owns property assessed at $17,500 with a tax rate of 20 mills would ordinarily pay a property tax of $350. Under a circuit breaker provision requiring that not more than 4 percent of income be paid in property taxes, the calculated amount of taxes due ($350) would be reduced to $240. Although the person would be required to pay the $350 of property taxes (ostensibly to avoid erosion of the funds necessary to provide public services—including education), he or she would receive a tax refund from the state for $110. Under this arrangement, local property tax increases would not affect low-income tax-payers, for all such tax increases would be paid by the state in the manner outlined previously.

More complicated circuit breaker plans than the one described here are used by some states. There may be progressive percentage limits of income to be paid in property taxes with increases in annual income, or the state might be required to pay a certain percent of a person's property taxes. The main point, of course, is that the lower the income, the greater the percent of property tax relief.

Determination of "income" and how to apply the circuit breaker principle to welfare recipients and renters are some of the most difficult problems facing states that use this method of providing property tax relief.

Personal Property Taxes

While the real property tax with all its objectionable features remains the backbone of the local school finance structure, the personal property tax is an enigma in local tax theory and practice. On the surface, the personal property tax has many attractive characteristics, and it is used quite successfully in some states.

Today, much of the wealth of people is invested in personal property holdings such as stocks, bonds, mutual funds, and savings accounts. This vast pool of wealth is a potentially lucrative source of revenue to help defray the costs of government, but the problem of getting such property assessed and on the proper tax rolls has not been solved. Lack of information or evidence of ownership and almost complete reliance on owners to report the extent of their personal property assets have served to defeat this form of taxation. Unfortunately, this measure of the wealth and tax-paying ability of people is therefore minimized as a source of public school or other government revenue. Hence, local taxes continue to be almost exclusively taxes on real property.

INCOME TAXES

The personal income tax is usually a progressive tax levied on the income of a person received during the period of one year. It is the basis of the federal financial structure, but it is also used to a lesser degree by nearly all of the states. The relationship of income taxation and the ability-to-pay principle was pointed out by the National Education Association in the following:

> Long after Adam Smith's time, there developed in economics the principle that as more and more of any good is purchased, its utility to the consumer becomes less and less. The first pair of shoes, for example, is a necessity, the second very important, the third important, the fourth useful perhaps, and the fifth, sixth, and the like, successively less desirable. Application of this

theory proved useful in explaining the fact that as the supply of a commodity increases, the price at which it is sold decreases. Then, as often happens, this principle, formulated for use in one area of human thought, was extended to others. It came to be believed that the law of declining utility also applied to money. Once that was accepted, the extension to taxation was thought to be clear. The rate, it was said, should increase in some ratio to the declining utility of the dollars of increased income. Thus the theory of ability to pay was born.[5]

Income taxes should include taxes on personal and on corporation incomes. The rationale justifying taxes on corporations is that otherwise individuals and organizations would incorporate to avoid taxation. "Corporation income taxation has been justified on the ability to pay, privilege or benefit, cost of service, state partnership, and control theories."[6] It is used in nearly all the states. It is responsive to economic and income changes, but it is sometimes complex in form and difficult to administer.

The real value of the personal income tax (and by implication the corporate tax as well) was emphasized in the following:

A personal income tax is the essential added ingredient to erase the regressive effects of property and sales taxes. Moreover, the income tax is far more sensitive to economic growth than are property or sales taxes and therefore can help solve the state-local fiscal crisis. Once the initial political hurdle of enacting an income tax is overcome . . . future rate increases can be few and far between—economic growth takes over.[7]

The income tax is probably the fairest of all taxes, and it has the advantage of producing large amounts of revenue at proportionately low collection costs. In practice, archaic laws and unfair provisions make it less than ideal as a revenue-collecting measure.

There is a continual cry for a revamping and overhaul of income tax laws at both the national and state levels. Though the federal income tax code was changed drastically for 1987, basic questions about its equitability for taxpayers still remain. Labeled as revenue neutral, the tax codes still cause concerns about fairness to some groups in society. The law shifted $20 billion a year in federal taxation from individuals to corporations and expanded the federal tax base by more than $800 billion, mainly by altering tax shelters. Yet several billion dollars in special-interest shelters remained or were added in the code.

The impact of the 1987 revision was significant not only at the national level but it also had a dramatic effect on state finances as well. Without modifications in some state tax codes, taxpayers by April 1988 would have paid a substantial increase in income taxes at the state level as a result of the federal tax changes. States with the largest projected increases included Colorado (22 percent), Montana and New Mexico (20 percent), and Utah and Oregon (19 percent). A total of 27 states would increase their tax revenues if their legislatures failed to make changes in state codes, resulting in possible increases in resources allocated to education. In 18 states, because of no state income tax or because state tax rates are not based on federal income taxes, the effect of the new code resulted in no increase or an actual decrease in state tax revenue by April 1988. Those states with the biggest decline were Rhode Island (−11 percent), North Dakota (−10 percent), and Nebraska (−9 percent).

By 1993 most states had made corrections to compensate for the negative effects the federal income tax code had on revenue sources.

SALES TAXES

A sales tax is a levy imposed on the sale value of certain goods and services. It is generally imposed at the retail operation, rather than the wholesale. Sales tax rates are usually at the same level for all transactions, but if food and other necessities are subject to a sales tax, the tax becomes regressive. The sales tax is used most often at the state level of government, although it is sometimes used at the county and city levels. It produces large amounts of revenue, but its use without exclusion of necessary goods and services tends to overburden poor families.

The sales tax could become a fairer and more effective tax with certain improvements: (1) Auditors need to be sufficient in number and well-trained, since they have much to do with the honesty and the efficiency of administration of the tax. (2) There should be strict enforcement by the states of tax collections and reporting. (3) Exemptions should be restricted to items of food and medicine. (4) A service or use tax should be included. (5) Loopholes in taxes on goods purchased in other states and on casual sales between individuals (such as on used cars) should be eliminated, and tax collection simplified, in those states that provide for more than one agency of government to collect tax revenues.

The value of the sales tax as a source of state revenue is indicated in the following:

> The general sales tax is the largest single state tax source, accounting for almost one-third of all state tax revenue. It is a broad-based tax and fairly sensitive to economic growth. But in one respect it is too broad based, for in most states it taxes food. Since low-income families spend a larger proportion of their budget on food than do high-income families, the tax on food introduces a strong element of regressivity.[8]

SUMPTUARY TAXES

A sumptuary tax is sometimes imposed by government, with the primary purpose of helping to regulate or control a certain activity or practice not deemed to be in the public interest. In this kind of tax, the collection of revenue is only a secondary purpose of the tax. For that reason, this revenue is usually compara-tively small, and there is little room for expansion or extension of the tax. Such taxes provide a division of interest, as indicated by Corbally:

> In general, sumptuary taxation receives little support from tax theorists. The fact that sumptuary taxes do, in fact, produce revenue often leads to a situation in which a governmental unit in need of funds is tacitly encourag-ing an activity which tax legislation sought to discourage. Liquor taxes, for example, have the intent of "punishing" the user of an "immoral" commod-ity and yet the revenue from these taxes often becomes such an important source of funds that a government unit establishes attractive establishments for the retail sale of the heavily taxed product.[9]

Taxing goods and services that are generally held to be against the public interest is usually justifiable, but it can be overdone. Such sumptuary taxes should be used with caution and wisdom, to minimize the negative effects of taxing any particular segment of society for the benefit of another. Such contro-versial forms of taxation become highly discriminatory if used too extensively. Governmental control of socially unacceptable practices usually requires more than excessively high taxation to curb such activities.

SEVERANCE TAX

A severance tax is used in some states for financial support of education. Rev-enue is generated on the taking and using of natural resources through a tax imposed at the time the mineral or other product is extracted (severed) from the earth. Levies are made for the privilege of removing a given commodity from the ground or from water. These levies are sometimes called production, conserva-tion, or mine (or mining) occupation taxes. The concept originated as a way to collect revenues in lieu of property taxes, because it was difficult to determine an appropriate assessed valuation for mineral lands, water, and the commodities produced from them. The justification for assessing a severance tax is that the mineral or resource is irreplaceable, and through a severance tax the state can, to some degree, advance its human resources with the loss from the natural resources. Also, some believe that charging a tax to extract natural resources may deter exploitive use of them and therefore enhance conservation and rational resource development.

A number of states have severance taxes on coal, oil, gas, oil shale, refined petroleum, liquid hydrocarbons, and minerals. The use of severance tax is varied. In 1990 the Bureau of the Census reported that 34 states imposed the tax with a range from no revenue in 16 states to 49.5 percent of total state tax revenue collected in Alaska. Though a significant revenue source in several

TABLE 4-1 Severance Tax Revenue as a
              Percentage of State Tax
              Collections (1989)

State	Percentage
Alaska	49.6
Wyoming	39.8
New Mexico	13.6
North Dakota	12.0
Montana	11.7
Louisiana	10.4
Texas	8.4
West Virginia	7.1
Kentucky	4.9
Kansas	3.2
Utah	2.2
South Dakota	1.97
Mississippi	1.95
Alabama	1.7
All States	1.46

Source: *State Government Tax Collections: 1989*, U.S. Department of Commerce, Bureau of the Census, issued July 1990.
The table lists all states obtaining at least 1 percent of their
tax revenue from severance taxes in fiscal 1989. Tax revenue
is defined according to Census Bureau procedures, which
may not agree with those used by states.

states the overall impact is only 1.46 percent of total tax revenues reported in
all states[10] (Table 4-1).

Excessive reliance on severance taxes can cause serious fiscal problems in
certain states. With the fall of oil prices in 1986, Alaska, Oklahoma, Texas, and
Louisiana had serious tax shortfalls. It was expected that Texas would have a loss
of over $2 billion in taxes that year, about one-third of which would be directly
attributable to the decrease in severance taxes.

Significantly, the justification for the tax—advancement of human resources
when natural resources are lost—is being heralded as the answer to the tax
shortfall by Texans. As noted in *U.S. News and World Report:*

> Texans have been talking about the need for a broader economic base for
> years . . . Now, the oil crash has added a new sense of urgency—almost
> frantic in its intensity—to talk of diversification . . . there is agreement on
> one point: The best way out of the state's dilemma is to improve its educa-
> tional system, then use the expertise and knowledge at colleges and univer-
> sities to create new businesses.[11]

POTENTIAL NEW TAXES

The pressure that courts applied on the states to achieve equity in financing education will likely be followed by similar legal pressure to provide equity in other functions of government. With the accompanying acceleration of criticism of the property tax will come increased emphasis on attempts to discover and use other kinds of taxes. This will require revision and upgrading of the taxing pattern of the states and local school districts. As the state assumes more of the responsibility of financing education, the principal base for the taxing structure increases, and as limitations on property taxes are imposed, the importance of finding new revenue sources for financing education is going to become even more critical in the next decade.

Site-Value Tax

Recommendations for improving or replacing the present property tax system have taken many different forms. Some economists advocate a site-value, or land tax. This is a tax on the actual value of the land, whether improved or not. As the land appreciates in value from investments or changes of any nature, the value of the tax revenue produced increases proportionately. Some other countries are using such a tax, and the plan has gained some support in this country, where the idea of property tax reform is old but untried.

Value-Added Tax

Another tax proposal that has received considerable support is a national value-added tax—popularly referred to as VAT. In its simplest form, it is a tax on the value of goods at each transaction level from production to consumption. The price of an economic good rises at every stage of its production and development. The farmer tilling the soil, sowing the seeds, harvesting the crop, delivering it to the miller, and the baker converting the grain into bread to be marketed is a process that involves numerous steps. A tax could be levied on the value added to the good or service at each stage of its production. Thus, a value-added tax is in reality a multiple sales tax.

A value-added tax has been proposed in Congress a number of times in the last half-century, but no law has ever been passed to utilize such a tax in this country. Its proponents point to its wide acceptance in the industrialized nations of Europe and the fact that it would be a single-rate tax with few exemptions. They admit that passage of such a tax would require reductions in other taxes in order to reduce the burden on taxpayers. Opponents of such a tax say that it would be regressive and would create a tax burden on poorer people if necessities, especially food items, were to be included. They say that in order to make the tax less regressive there would need to be so many exemptions that the tax would be difficult to administer. To offset its alleged unfairness, proposals have been made to give tax rebates to the poor who would be adversely affected. Some economists believe that a VAT would decrease spending and thus release more money for savings and investments. Others say that it would result in serious inflationary trends and would probably result in higher wages in the labor market.

LOTTERIES

One system of raising funds for state governments that began in 1964 in New Hampshire is the lottery. In 1989 lotteries were being used in 33 states and the District of Columbia. Lottery revenues reached $20 billion in fiscal 1990 compared to $5.5 billion in 1983. The increase in revenue was partly due to the increased number of states with lotteries. The net income increased 28 percent from 1988 to 1989.[12] As interest in lotteries expands, so does the debate as to whether or not lotteries are an appropriate way for governments to raise revenue.

Thomas Jefferson called the lottery a "wonderful thing, it lays taxation only on the willing." Lotteries were used to support colonial soldiers and to build Harvard, Princeton, Yale, Dartmouth, Columbia, and William and Mary.[13] Lotteries have been used from time immemorial; the Bible describes property distributions made by the process. The term comes from the Germanic word *Hleut*, which describes a dish or pebble that was cast to divide property, settle uncertainties, or decide disputes.[14] The concept has grown in popularity because legislators are looking for tax alternatives, and lotteries are popular with the public. People like to participate because there is always a hope that they can strike it rich. Tickets are inexpensive and the poor feel happy about giving money to the government if they stand a chance of reaping a large reward. This attitude is one of the major problems of the lottery as a revenue source. Though the question remains as to whether or not a lottery is a tax, the end result is that it is regressive in nature—those who can afford it least are paying the most. Bayer reports: "Most studies indicate that the average lottery player is middle class and that the poor are no more likely to buy lottery tickets than others. However, lottery wagers do consumer a greater share of poor player's income . . . a Duke University study found that the poorest third of households bought more than half of all weekly lottery tickets sold."[15]

Basically, lotteries for schools are not as great a revenue source as publicity would suggest, generating only a small percentage of total state revenues. In most states the lottery contributed less than 2 percent to state treasuries, with no state generating more than 4 percent. Lotteries are inefficient in that it costs 10¢ to 40¢ to collect one dollar, as compared to 5 percent from conventional taxing procedures. It is also difficult to measure accurately what impact present lottery allocations have on education. Though earmarked for education, lotteries often become more of a political ploy than an actual benefit. When the general fund distributions are made, they are often reduced in proportion to increases that may come from the lottery, leaving education with no greater funding sources than before the lottery.[16] In California for instance, the lottery was to provide 34 cents of every dollar for education. A high-ranking state education official stated that the money has simply replaced school funding rather than augmenting it: "The public is now reluctant to pass education bond issues because they think we're floating in lottery money." In Florida critics say earmarked funds for education have ended up replacing general funds rather than providing new school revenues.[17]

Though teacher organizations will continue to negotiate for lottery money, school boards and administrative representatives need to be cautious about such uncertainties as projecting receipts from a lottery into a salary schedule.

Summing up the pros and cons of the lottery, Thomas and Webb offer the following:

> In each area where the lottery has been legalized, or is being considered, similar arguments pro and con have been proposed. The primary arguments supporting the lottery are: that it is a rather painless way to increase revenues; that the lottery is not a tax, or if it is a tax, it should be considered a "voluntary tax"; that the desire to gamble is inherent to man and that it is socially more desirable for gambling to be offered by the government than by organized crime. . . .
>
> Those who oppose the lottery contend that it is capable of increasing state revenues by only a small percent; that it is more costly to administer than other taxes; that it will not reduce the present level of taxation; that it is a regressive form of taxation; and that it does not substantially compete with illegal games. It also is argued that although people may have a strong desire to gamble, such activity undermines the moral fiber of society, and that government is obliged, at the very least, not to encourage gambling, either through sponsorship and solicitation, or by making it convenient.[18]

PRIVATE FOUNDATIONS

In an effort to meet the demands of tighter budgets, school districts are reaching out to the private sector to develop new revenue sources. Some districts have established private foundations for the purpose of raising funds for local schools. White and Morgan, board members of a local school district foundation in Pennsylvania, note that the foundation serves as a "catalyst that mixes corporate and community support—money, services and equipment—that might otherwise remain beyond the reach of hard-stretched school budgets."[19]

Only a few foundations existed prior to 1980. The Ford Foundation formerly had an interest in promoting the concept in several states but discontinued the support in 1987. By 1990 many foundations had been organized throughout the country with sixty-five grass-roots groups participating in the Public Education Fund Network based in Pittsburgh.[20] The predominant number of foundations are in California where school systems had budgets slashed after Proposition 13 was passed.

The California Consortium of Education Foundations indicates that the number of districts in the state with foundations has stabilized at around 140. The range of expected revenue for districts in California from this private source in 1990 was as follows:

Budget range	Number of districts
None reported	8
to $ 5,000	10
to $ 10,000	18
to $ 20,000	18
to $ 50,000	33
to $100,000	20
to $150,000	6
to $200,000	8
to $500,000	9
to $1 million	2
to $1.5 million	1
$2 million	1

The two districts in California reporting the collection of $1 million were Beverly Hills and San Marino. The San Francisco Foundation reported raising $1.5 million and Los Angeles Education Foundation raised $2 million.[21]

In Utah the state legislature has provided a minimal amount of matching money in its Incentive for Excellence program, which provides funds for districts that are able to match the revenue from the private sector. The program has motivated about one-half of the 40 school districts to establish foundations.

The foundation programs raise some school finance issues. (1) What role should school officials play in the foundation and in the determination of how money should be expended? (2) Will states reduce their aid to school systems that have successful foundations? (3) Since affluent school systems are more likely to have successful foundations, will private money damage efforts to make the quality of education more uniform among rich and poor communities?[22]

SCHOOL-BUSINESS PARTNERSHIPS

The thrust for school-business partnerships is closely related to the foundation movement. The natural evolvement of seeking revenues extended to asking business and industry leaders for contributions to assist schools in meeting budget needs and extending programs. However, simultaneously the business-education relationship was emerging on its own as business executives felt an urgency to coordinate efforts with educators to meet the needs of developing a work force that could compete in a global marketplace. The concept gained impetus with the Department of Education establishing the New American Schools Development Corporation in 1991.

Education-related partnerships are big business. From 1984 to 1988 there was an increase from 40,000 to 140,000 and by April 1991 the National Association of Partners in Education estimated the number to be over 200,000.[23] Partnerships can vary greatly in scope and are as diverse as the companies involved:

> There are two levels of involvement: short-term, local projects, such as adopt-a-school and volunteer programs, and long-term efforts that are broadly based and are likely to involve several businesses and community groups. These go under several names: coalitions, compacts, and alliances. Business roundtables are another effective means for companies to become involved in a public policy mode.[24]

Business and industry interests are not completely altruistic. They have an agenda. However, the concept that makes the partnership function is that educators are striving for the same goal—to produce students that are prepared for the twenty-first century. Hird expresses the dilemma facing companies noting, "If we don't systematically change our schools so that we're not only looking at what the needs are today, but at those in the future, in the year 2010 we'll be preparing students for the 1980s and 1990s. Schools have to deliver education in a fundamentally different way to stay in touch with the work force and societal needs."[25] The world of work is changing so drastically that there is great mismatch between the skills workers possess and the qualifications needed on the job. "Three-fourths of new work-force entrants will be qualified for only 40% of new jobs created between 1985 and 2000 . . . business will have to take more responsibility for preparing their future labor force by forming partnerships with schools."[26]

Louis V. Gerstner Jr., chairman of RJR Nabisco Inc., emphasized the business interest in schools in a *Fortune* magazine interview, stating that "Education is too important to be left to the educators." In 1991, The RJR Nabisco Company awarded $30 million to school projects aimed at rewarding innovation in the Next Century Schools program.[27] There are many examples in the literature of companies that have been generous with both money and in-kind contributions for schools. In 1989 businesses donated $2.35 billion to education. Though the largest share from major corporations has gone to support higher education, the trend is changing. Business leaders are recognizing the necessity to start in preschool and elementary schools if students are going to be prepared for college.[28]

A spokesperson for the National Association of Partners in Education states that solutions need to be locally based; there is not one solution that is going to be applicable to every community. Therefore, the partnerships need to be at the local district level where those who live in the community can work toward defining and solving the problems.[29] This raises some concerns. After reviewing various partnership studies, Pautler noted that many districts in the United States are in rural areas far from major businesses and such partnerships may be difficult to arrange.[30]

The collaboration of business with education has never been greater. As school administrators look to business and industry as an additional funding source to supplement the education budget, business and industrial leaders who support education with corporate dollars will be expecting educators to produce a student who is literate, prepared, and already employable when graduating from high school. Accountability and results are expected when business and industry "foot the bill."

SUMMARY

Taxation is a system of transferring money from the private sector to the public sector of the economy. The public institutions of the nation are almost completely dependent upon this method of obtaining funds for their operation. Taxation is fairer and more dependable for financing education than the previously used rate bills, tuition charges, and student fees.

Taxes are classified into three general types: proportional (the same percent of income spent for taxes for all levels of income), progressive (higher percent of income for taxes for higher levels of income), and regressive (lower percent of income for taxes for higher incomes). It is generally agreed that progressive taxes are the most equitable and regressive taxes the least equitable.

A good tax system should include the following features: (1) There should be coordination among all levels of government with little or no duplication of taxes. (2) All citizens should pay some tax. (3) Taxpayers should be left in the same relative financial position with each other after taxes are paid. (4) The tax should bring a reasonable yield, not be merely a nuisance tax. (5) Tax erosion should be minimal, regardless of the benefits government owes to deserving citizens. (6) Tax collection should be simple and convenient for taxpayers and of little cost to the collectors. (7) The tax should be levied on the person or household who pays it—the shifting of the tax should be minimized. (8) The payment of the tax should not cause a major change in the economic practice or vocation of the taxpayer.

The property tax is becoming less and less fair as people increasingly invest their surplus monies in other forms of wealth. The unfairness of a property tax is evident in many ways, such as unequal assessment practices, taxation without relationship to net ownership of the property being taxed, unequal tax bases per pupil to be educated in various kinds of school districts, and lack of a direct relationship between the taxes owed and the amount of wealth or income of the person or household being taxed. Taxpayer resistance to property taxes has increased greatly.

Circuit breakers were adopted by most states to relieve elderly and low-income people of part of their property tax burden. Legal steps were taken in a number of states to restrict the use of the property tax—the passing of Proposition 13 in California being the most extreme example. Some other states passed legislation restricting government expenditures.

Personal property taxes are difficult to collect, and their use has proven to be somewhat ineffective. Income taxes are probably the most equitable of all taxes, but their use at the local level is limited for two major reasons: (1) They are already used to a high degree by the federal government and to a limited degree by most states. (2) It is relatively easy for resisting taxpayers to find loopholes to avoid such taxes.

Sales taxes are effective at the state level but are not readily manageable at the local level, especially in small school districts. Sales taxes are regressive when food items and other necessities are taxed, since low-income families generally spend a higher percentage of their income on necessities than the more affluent do.

Potential new taxes include site-value and value-added taxes, which have a history of successful use in some foreign countries. Congress has attempted unsuccessfully to introduce the use of some new kinds of taxes several times in the last few years.

Though the concept is very old, lotteries have recently become popular in some states as a source of revenue for the schools. Since lotteries generate only a small percentage of total state allocations, school administrators need to be concerned about relying on this source because of the uncertainty of receipts. The debate will continue on whether or not a lottery is truly a tax. In any case, it is regressive in nature, since most buyers of tickets are among the members of society who can least afford them. The pros and cons will continue to be debated as more states consider the possibilities of instituting lotteries to raise money for state budgets.

Private foundations may be a new source of revenue for school districts. However, the collaborative effort of the private and public sectors working for education may have a greater impact than the actual funds raised through foundations.

School-business partnerships are gaining momentum as business and industry leaders are becoming more concerned with developing a work force that can compete in a global marketplace. Impetus has come from the New American Schools Development Corporation established by the Department of Education. The collaborative efforts will require revenues from business and industry and accountability from educators.

ASSIGNMENT PROJECTS

Property Assessments, Tax Rate, Rates, Revenue

For taxation purposes property is usually assessed at a fractional part of its sale (market) value. Revenues are determined by applying tax rates against these assessed values. Since states use different percentages of sale value in calculating assessed value, comparisons between states require the determination of sale values and true tax rates.

(assessed value) (tax rate) = (sale value) (true tax rate)
(AV) (tr) = (SV) (ttr)

Thus, if property valued at $50,000 and assessed at $20,000 has a tax rate (some-times called apparent tax rate) of 40 mills, it would have a true tax rate of 16 mills.

Problems

1. If the assessed value of a piece of property is 25 percent of its sale value, you know immediately that its true tax rate is what percent of its apparent tax rate?

1. _____ percent

2. If a piece of property is assessed at $12,675 under a fractional practice of 65 percent, what is the sale value of the property?

2. $_____

3. If a district requires revenue of $1,487,424 and the sale value of all tax-able property is $106,000,000 (to be assessed at 60 percent), what will the tax rate be in dollars per $100 of assessed valuation?

3. $_____/$100 (AV)

4. In problem 3 above, what is the true tax rate in mills?

4. _____ mills

Mr. Smith has a house assessed at $51,000 (60 percent of sale value). His tax is $3.50 per $100 of AV. Mr. Jones has a house assessed at $35,550 (45 percent of sale value). His tax rate is 36.2 mills. From this information, answer the following:

5. Who pays the greater tax?

5. _____

6. How much greater?

6. $_____

7. Using the tax rate and the assessment practices of Mr. Smith's district, how much tax would Mr. Jones pay?

7. $_____

Mr. Brown has a house assessed at $39,680 (62 percent of sale value). His tax rate is $3.25 per $100 of assessed valuation.

FMV ✓

64,000

Mr. Barnes has a house assessed at $30,250 (48 percent of sale value). His tax rate is $32.75 per $1,000 (AV). *990.69*

63,020

1289.6

39072

8. Who pays the greater tax?

8. _____

9. How much greater?

9. $ *298.91*

10. Using the tax rate and the assessment practices of Mr. Brown's district, how much tax would Mr. Barnes pay? *1269.87*

10. $_____

School District A has an assessed valuation of taxable property of $49,410,000. It has 5,400 public school pupils. School District B has an assessed valuation of taxable property of $86,260,000 and 9,500 public school pupils.

11. Which district has the greater ability to support its schools?

11. _____

12. In problem 11, how much greater?

12. $_____ / pupil

John Doe has a house assessed at $36,000 (45 percent of its sale value). His tax rate is $4.20 per $100 of AV. Tom Gale has a house assessed at $44,000 (50 percent of sale value). His tax rate is 35.25 mills.

13. Who pays the greater tax?

13. _____

14. How much greater?

14. $_____

15. If both houses were taxed on full sale value with a true tax rate of 23.3 mills, who would pay the greater tax?

15. _____

16. How much greater?

16. _____

SELECTED READINGS

Benson, Charles S. *The Economics of Public Education.* 3rd ed. Boston: Houghton Mifflin, 1978.

Cohn, Elchanan. *The Economics of Education.* rev. ed. Cambridge, Mass.: Ballinger, 1979.

Coons, John E., William H. Clune III, and Stephen D. Sugarman. *Private Wealth and Public Education*. Cambridge, Mass.: Belknap Press of Harvard University Press, 1970.

Guthrie, James W., Walter I. Garms, and Lawrence C. Pierce. *School Finance and Education Policy: Enhancing Educational Efficiency, Equality, and Choice.* 2nd ed. Englewood Cliffs, N.J.: Prentice Hall, 1988.

Odden, Allan R., and Lawrence O. Picus. *School Finance: A Policy Perspective.* New York: McGraw-Hill, 1992.

Peckman, Joseph A. *Tax Reform, the Rich and the Poor.* 2nd ed. Washington, D.C.: Brookings Institution, 1989.

Salmon, Richard G., and S. Kern Alexander. *The Historical Reliance of Public Education upon the Property Tax: Current Problems and Future Role.* Cambridge, Mass.: Lincoln Institute of Land Policy, 1983.

ENDNOTES

1. Lonnie Harp, "Property Assessments Loom as a Key Issue in Education Finance," *Education Week*, Vol. 10, No. 17, January 16, 1991, p. 21.

2. Lloyd E. McCann and Floyd G. Delon, "Governmental Structure for School Finance," in Warren E. Gauerke and Jack A. Childress, eds., *Theory and Practice of School Finance*, (Chicago: Rand McNally, 1967), pp. 90–93.

3. Charles S. Benson, *Perspectives on the Economics of Education; Readings in School Finance and Business Management* (Boston: Houghton Mifflin, 1963), p. 160.

4. Billy D. Walker, "The Local Property Tax for Public Schools: Some Historical Perspectives," *Journal of Education Finance*, Vol. 9, No. 3, Winter 1984, p. 265.

5. *Taxes Contribute to Progress* (Washington, D.C.: National Education Association Committee on Education Finance, 1960), p. 18.

6. Ibid., p. 19.

7. *Productivity in Education: Measuring and Financing* (Washington, D.C.: National Education Association Committee on Educational Finance, 1972), p. 146.

8. Ibid., pp. 145–46.

9. John E. Corbally, Jr., *School Finance* (Boston: Allyn and Bacon, 1962), p. 14.

10. *State Government Tax Collection: 1989* (Washington, D.C.: U.S. Department of Commerce, Bureau of the Census, July 1990).

11. "Texas Takes a Tumble," *U.S. News and World Report*, April 21, 1986, p. 23.

12. Richard L. Worsnop, "Lucrative Lure of Lotteries and Gambling," *Congressional Quarterly's Editorial Research Reports*, October 19, 1990, pp. 635, 641.

13. Ibid., p. 637.

14. Stephen B. Thomas and L. Dean Webb, "The Use and Abuse of Lotteries as a Revenue Source," *Journal of Education Finance*, Vol. 9, No. 3, Winter 1984, p. 289.

15. Amy Bayer, "Are Lotteries a Ripoff?" *Consumer's Research*, January 1990, p. 15.

16. Thomas and Webb, "The Use and Abuse of Lotteries as a Revenue Source," p. 303.

17. Erik Calonius, "The Big Payoff from Lotteries," *Fortune*, March 25, 1991, p. 109.

18. Thomas and Webb, "The Use and Abuse of Lotteries as a Revenue Source," pp. 297–98.

19. George P. White and Nicholas Morgan, "Education Foundations: The Catalyst That Mixes Corporations and Community to Support Schools," *The School Administrator*, April 1990, p. 22.

20. Ibid.

21. *California Consortium of Education Foundations Directory*, San Jose, Calif., December 1990.

22. Thomas Toch, "Time for Private Foundations for Public Schools," *Education Weekly*, Vol. II, No. 9, November 1982, p. 15.

23. Charlene Marmer Solomon, "New Partners in Business," *Personnel Journal*, April 1991, p. 59.

24. Ibid.

25. Janice Hird, as quoted by Solomon, "New Partners in Business," p. 59.

26. Marvin J. Cetron and Margaret Evans Gayle, "Educational Renaissance: 43 Trends for U.S. Schools," *The Futurist,* September/October 1990, pp. 34, 37.

27. Solomon, "New Partners in Business," p. 59.

28. Ibid.

29. Ibid.

30. Albert J. Pautler, reviewing "Three Books on Partnership in Practice," *Phi Delta Kappan,* June 1990, p. 818.

Chapter 5

Eroding Local Control

Tough-decision makers at the local level are pilloried as troglodytes resisting change. But school boards are gatekeepers of reality.
—THOMAS A. SHANNON, 1991

State responsibility for education and local control of the schools have operated with remarkable success throughout the history of the nation. The constantly increasing financial support of local school districts by the various states in recent years, with increases in state controls and standards, has resulted in a challenge to the traditional concept of local control of education.

DIMINISHING LOCAL CONTROL

Citizens of the United States typically view the gradual change from local to state control of the public schools with some degree of alarm, yet they know that such a change is inevitable. They look upon local control as a frontier where people in small towns and neighborhoods can make their voices heard in determining who shall be educated and by what process. They feel threatened by nationwide trends toward centralization and standardization. They value their importance as citizens in the selection of school board members, in voting for or against levies and bond issues, and in their right to evaluate the accomplishments of their schools.

At the same time, they feel a degree of helplessness and inability to influence state legislatures; they envision the federal government as being far beyond their horizon of influence. Consequently, they tend to hold firmly to their commitment to local control of education. They accept its accomplishments with pride when it excels and fault themselves and their community when it falls short or fails to compare favorably with schools elsewhere. In their pride for school and community, they often lose sight of the high price that must be paid for maintaining small districts and small attendance areas. In their minds it is a price worth paying. They tend to evaluate the schools' successes and failures in terms of what the situation was when they were in school and often have closed minds with regard to the potential virtues of school reorganization and consolidation.

As states are playing a greater role in financing public schools, they are assuming firmer control. The adage, "he who holds the purse strings holds the power" is apparent as state governments continue to provide the largest part of budgets for operating public schools. The present ratio is 49.3 percent at the state level and 44.5 percent at the district level.[1] The education and equal protection clauses of the various state constitutions have had an influence on how education is funded and have placed more responsibility on state legislators to provide additional financial aid to local education agencies. Courts have had an impact as they have instructed some state leaders to provide more equitable financing for local districts from state resources. These and other factors are reasons why state governments are generally considered to be the institutions in the 1990s that will be required to meet the expanding financial needs of the schools.

DECREASING RURAL INFLUENCE ON EDUCATION

Throughout the history of American legislative action, legislators representing rural areas have often controlled or dominated the lawmaking bodies of the states. Disproportionate representation in at least one branch of the legislature was usually given to small towns, counties, and sparsely populated areas, as compared with the representation given to large towns, cities, and metropolitan areas. Since property taxes bore a major portion of school costs, rural legislators and rural school board members tended to be reluctant to provide the funds necessary for optimum school programs. The reapportionment of the membership of state legislatures in the 1960s to meet court demands of "one man-one vote" reduced the relative legislative power of rural areas and increased that of cities.

Also, as the United States has become less of an agrarian society, and people have moved away from rural areas, the number of one-teacher schools and of local educational agencies governing schools is decreasing. One-teacher schools have nearly disappeared (Table 5-1).

DECREASING URBAN ECONOMIC ADVANTAGES

Although cities have gained in their representation in legislative bodies, they have lost their economic advantage in the operation of schools. When property taxes were the main source of school revenue and state allocations were minimal, city school districts usually enjoyed certain revenue advantages. City school

TABLE 5-1 Decrease in Number of One-Teacher Schools

School year	All schools	One-teacher schools	
		Number	Percent of all schools
1947–48	172,244	75,096	43.6
1953–54	136,512	42,865	31.4
1957–58	120,953	25,341	21.0
1963–64	104,015	9,895	9.5
1973–74	90,976	1,365	1.5
1982–83	84,740	798	0.9
1988–89	82,081	583	0.7

Source: *Digest of Education Statistics, 1990*, U.S. Department of Education, National Center for Education Statistics, Office of Educational Research and Improvement (NCES 91-660), February 1991.

boards tended to be less vocal in their opposition to property tax increases for education than their rural counterparts. As a consequence, city schools generally outdid their rural neighbors in providing good education. City schools became the leaders in administrative efficiency and in student achievement.

In recent years, however, the pattern has changed. Gradual changes in the socioeconomic makeup of larger cities, with consistent emigration of the more affluent to suburbia, have resulted in cities losing much of their previous financial advantage. Legislative bodies that once faced the formidable problem of financing small rural schools equitably now face a larger problem in providing adequate and equitable revenue for urban districts.

SCHOOL DISTRICTS: BASIC ADMINISTRATIVE UNITS

The local school district is the basic administrative unit for the operation of public schools in this country. Each district has a governing board, usually referred to as the school board, and a chief administrative officer, usually called the superintendent of schools. The size, characteristics, and authority of school districts vary greatly from state to state and even within the same state. In most of the states, school districts operate as independent governmental units. In about 40 percent of the states, however, school districts are dependent on some other unit of government for certain aspects of their operation—usually budgetary operations.

The number of school districts in the country reached the staggering total of 127,649 in 1932. Fortunately, much progress has been made in reducing the number since that time. As might be expected, reorganization of school districts proceeded at a snail's pace at first. However, improvements in the laws providing for such mergers did much to accelerate the process, especially during the 1940s and 1950s. Texas and California continue to have more than 1,000 independent school districts. Ten other states still have 500 or more (Figure 5-1).

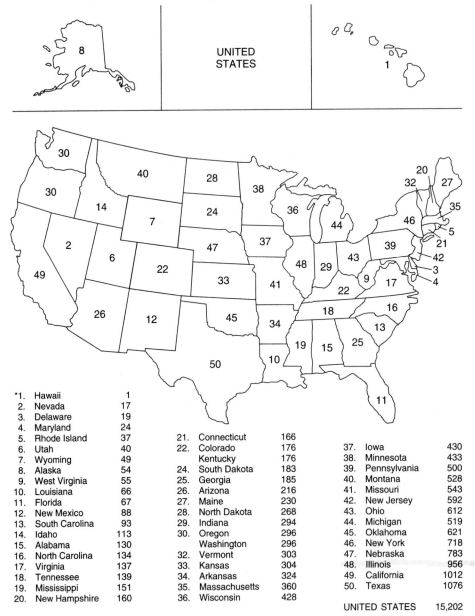

<table>
<tr><td>*1.</td><td>Hawaii</td><td>1</td></tr>
<tr><td>2.</td><td>Nevada</td><td>17</td></tr>
<tr><td>3.</td><td>Delaware</td><td>19</td></tr>
<tr><td>4.</td><td>Maryland</td><td>24</td></tr>
<tr><td>5.</td><td>Rhode Island</td><td>37</td></tr>
<tr><td>6.</td><td>Utah</td><td>40</td></tr>
<tr><td>7.</td><td>Wyoming</td><td>49</td></tr>
<tr><td>8.</td><td>Alaska</td><td>54</td></tr>
<tr><td>9.</td><td>West Virginia</td><td>55</td></tr>
<tr><td>10.</td><td>Louisiana</td><td>66</td></tr>
<tr><td>11.</td><td>Florida</td><td>67</td></tr>
<tr><td>12.</td><td>New Mexico</td><td>88</td></tr>
<tr><td>13.</td><td>South Carolina</td><td>93</td></tr>
<tr><td>14.</td><td>Idaho</td><td>113</td></tr>
<tr><td>15.</td><td>Alabama</td><td>130</td></tr>
<tr><td>16.</td><td>North Carolina</td><td>134</td></tr>
<tr><td>17.</td><td>Virginia</td><td>137</td></tr>
<tr><td>18.</td><td>Tennessee</td><td>139</td></tr>
<tr><td>19.</td><td>Mississippi</td><td>151</td></tr>
<tr><td>20.</td><td>New Hampshire</td><td>160</td></tr>
</table>

21.	Connecticut	166
22.	Colorado	176
	Kentucky	176
24.	South Dakota	183
25.	Georgia	185
26.	Arizona	216
27.	Maine	230
28.	North Dakota	268
29.	Indiana	294
30.	Oregon	296
	Washington	296
32.	Vermont	303
33.	Kansas	304
34.	Arkansas	324
35.	Massachusetts	360
36.	Wisconsin	428

37.	Iowa	430
38.	Minnesota	433
39.	Pennsylvania	500
40.	Montana	528
41.	Missouri	543
42.	New Jersey	592
43.	Ohio	612
44.	Michigan	519
45.	Oklahoma	621
46.	New York	718
47.	Nebraska	783
48.	Illinois	956
49.	California	1012
50.	Texas	1076
	UNITED STATES	15,202

*District of Columbia also has 1 school district
*Puerto Rico has 100 school districts

FIGURE 5-1 Estimated number of basic administrative units (regular school districts including supervisory union components), 1990–91. (Source: *Estimates of School Statistics 1990–91*, National Education Association, Research Division, 1991.)

In the past, most of the problems of school district reorganization were concerned with combining small districts into larger ones to improve the educational opportunities for children and at the same time provide a broad tax base, reduce variations in the tax-paying ability of districts, and provide some degree of stabilization, equity, and satisfactory management of funds. Recently, however, the problem of decreasing the sizes of some large metropolitan districts or reorganizing them by allowing other public-sector agencies, such as universities, to sponsor public schools has emerged. Such competition could bring diversity within urban schools and pressure ineffective schools to change. Olson outlines some changes taking place in urban districts:

> [One] solution is to drastically diminish the role of big-city school boards through the kind of radical decentralization now being tried in Chicago. There, the powers of the board of education have been cut back and supplemented by those of local school councils that operate at each school. Parents, who compose the majority of council members, have the authority to hire and fire the principal, set school goals, and oversee the school budget.
>
> Similar legislation introduced recently in the Ohio legislature would affect cities with populations over 175,000.[2]

The traditional argument that large school districts allow greater economy in the operation of schools can easily be overemphasized. Quite often the funds saved in some aspects of the programs are spent to enrich or extend educational services—one of the main reasons for combining the districts in the first place. The argument that reorganization will save educational dollars, which may appeal to some taxpayers as a possibility for tax relief or reduction, often falls of its own weight. Instead of saving school tax money, reorganization usually results in a better school program, with little if any reduction in cost. However, reduction in the number of school districts will usually result in some subtle, but important and relevant, improvements in financing education:

1. The range in local ability to pay for education in the wealthiest as compared with the poorest district (as measured by the assessed value of taxable property per pupil to be educated) will be reduced.

2. State support formulas can be simplified, and greater equality of educational opportunity for all school pupils can result as the number and kinds of administrative units are reduced.

3. Larger school districts make possible greater efficiency in the expenditure of funds (but do not guarantee it) in nearly all categories of the maintenance and operation of schools, but particularly in administration, instruction of pupils, and purchase of supplies and equipment.

Each state has been free to determine the kind and number of local school units or districts that can be operated within its own boundaries. The number of such districts within a state varies from 1,076 in Texas to 1 in Hawaii.

The arguments concerning relative costs and quality of education in large, medium, and small school districts are still being debated in some parts of this country. Most informed students of educational administration recognize some relation between the costs of education and the organizational pattern of schools and school districts the state operates. The following are some principles concerning small and large schools that have become accepted as a result of the experience of the states over the years.

1. Maintaining a small school district with only one or two small attendance areas is indefensible in terms of the aims and objectives of present-day education. This does not rule out the obvious fact that some small schools and districts will always be needed in sparsely populated areas of this country.

2. Small school districts and small attendance areas are comparatively inefficient and often represent a waste of tax funds.

3. Small schools suffer from curriculum limitations, even if the wealth of the district makes it financially possible to employ proportionately more and better-trained school staff members.

4. Small schools are often unable to attract the best teachers, regardless of the wealth or the available revenues in those districts.

5. Small schools suffer from lack of special services, such as health, psychological, and counseling programs. No amount of revenue can provide these services if there are not enough pupils to warrant them.

6. Large size of school districts and attendance areas operating with adequate revenue provide the potential for an efficient and effective school system with a high-quality educational product, but it does not and cannot guarantee it.

7. Although the admitted advantages of large school districts over smaller ones are important and can usually be documented, decisions over such matters are nearly always made on the basis of the emotions of the people involved rather than the educational benefits that the pupils will derive.

8. Even though the nation has too many small school districts, it also has some city districts and attendance areas that are too large and unmanageable. The problem of decentralization must be faced in some city districts at the same time that centralization is being emphasized in many other areas.

Although financially the advantages of reorganization of school districts outweigh the disadvantages, there is great resistance from the public when states attempt to impose consolidation on local entities. An example of such resistance occurred in recent years in Illinois when the legislature developed an educational reform package that included an effort to reduce the number of school districts. At the time, Illinois had 1,013 districts, the third highest in the nation (Figure 5.1). The plan was "to eliminate all unit districts with fewer than 1,500 students, all elementary districts with fewer than 1,000 students, all high school districts with fewer than 500 students."[3] Resistance to the proposal immediately arose; small, rural, downstate localities and high-tax enclaves in suburban Chicago were particularly opposed to the prospects of eliminating the small districts. As a result the General Assembly passed a bill that delayed the re-organization plan and "removed the minimum enrollment standards, thereby effectively ending any state pressure for reorganization and consolidation."[4] By 1990–91, the number of districts had been reduced by 57, from 1,013 to 956.

THE ADMINISTRATION OF LOCAL SCHOOL DISTRICTS

Although few people question that the role of local school boards in controlling the operation and financing of schools has changed in the last few years, there is no complete agreement about the causes of this change. As the federal government has extended its financial assistance to schools, its influence over local districts has increased. As the states have increased state monies to school districts and also increased curriculum requirements, certification requirements, levy limitations, and other related requirements, the powers and duties of local school boards have been correspondingly eroded and usurped.

The politics of education has shifted with a rotation about a "state-federal axis rather than a local-state axis." Thus, in the opinion of many, the traditional philosophy and practice of localism has become suspect and is in need of change. In an interview with the authors, Ernest T. Boyer observed, "I think for the first time America is more preoccupied with national results than local school control." Chester Finn, a proponent for less local control, asserts that there already has been a change in practice but theory has yet to be altered. He stated:

> So deeply ingrained in our consciousness is the idea of "local control of education" that few Americans even think about it anymore. Like "separation of church and state," "civilian control of the military," and "equality of opportunity," the phrase rolls off the tongue without even engaging the mind. To suggest that it may be obsolete or harmful is like hinting that Mom's apple pie is laced with arsenic.
>
> The time has come, however, to subject "local control" as we know it to closer scrutiny. It is one of those 19th century school-governance and -finance arrangements that may not serve the country well at the dawn of the next millennium. It is enshrined in neither the Ten Commandments nor the Constitution. It could, therefore, be changed. Indeed, it has already been changing in practice even though we have not yet revamped the theory.[5]

Finn stressed that the governance of schools is antiquated and ought to be abolished. "Boards are not just superfluous, they are also dysfunctional."[6] Taking issue with that point of view, Thomas Shannon, Executive Director of the National School Boards Association, stresses a more traditional concept of local control and expresses the importance of the local board of education:

Local school-board governance consists of several indispensable functions. The board translates federal law and integrates state mandates into local policy action; tests proposed education initiatives against the back drop of community need and sentiment; evaluates on behalf of the entire community the educational program; monitors the work of the superintendent and administrative staff who implement board policy; serves as the final appellate body short of the court system on appeals of citizens and school employees from administrative decisions; cooperatively deals (both as a board and as individual board members) with citizens in school matters in the tradition of responsive, responsible representative governance; and interacts with federal, state, and other local-government entities to ensure that the schools are given the attention they deserve. Each of these functions is so critical that they have given rise to the rubric, "If community school boards didn't exist, we should have to invent them."[7]

Shannon contests that "state legislatures have in fact adopted many oppressive statutes over the years that ruin the type of local school environment needed for innovation. . . . [That] micromanagement by statue hinders local initiative and stifles local imagination by undercutting boards' authority to act as local policy-makers."[8]

Fuhrman and Elmore[9] did extensive research on understanding local control and the degree of change required to conform with new state policies and the capacity to make the required changes. They conclude, among other findings, that "districts often leverage state policies by using local influence networks to reinforce local political agenda and to engage in local policy entrepreneurship. The result is often that the local effects of state policy are greater than those one would predict on the basis of state capacity and that localities often gain influence rather than lose it." Following are other conclusions from the study:

Conventional notions of state and local control in education need to be modified in light of experience and research related to recent state-level reform. The most important modification is to move away from simple zero-sum conceptions of state-local relations, in which each increment of state policy results in an equal and opposite decrease in local control, and toward a conception that allows for the possibility that both state and local control can increase as a result of state policymaking and that recognizes that the exact effect of changes in state policy on state-local relationships is more a function of how states and localities mobilize and use political influence than of state control of local decision.

New conceptions of state-local relations must take account of a range of factors not included in the zero-sum model. Among these factors are the following:

- The volume of state policymaking is not a good indicator of the degree of state control. Rather, the content of state policy, the capacity of states to implement that policy, the degree of variability in local district capacity, and the degree of mobilization of state and local public and professional opinion are key factors in sorting out the relative influence of states and localities.

- Examining the relationship between states and districts is not, by itself, a particularly useful way to characterize state-local relations. Districts are, in fact, multilevel systems, and state influence depends on how state and local priorities are orchestrated around schools and classrooms.[10]

Some of the typical problems faced by local boards of education—including problems related to separation of church and state, providing equal educational opportunities for all students, including minority groups, and control of dissidents and incorrigibles—have been accentuated by a society that is constantly demanding additional services from government. On the other hand, boards of education find themselves subservient to new directives and the new rationale of the state and federal governments that attend the programs to alleviate poverty, extend educational opportunity, and push forward the frontier of knowledge. All these conditions, plus the proposal that seems to be gaining momentum that the states administer the collection and allocation of all funds for education, may seriously curtail the importance of local boards of education and the need for them.

Local Control Not Guaranteed

State responsibility for education is guaranteed by the Tenth Amendment to the United States Constitution and many state constitutions. Local control of schools has long been taken for granted, but there is no guarantee of the extent or the duration of such authority. Since power comes to local districts by delegation from the states, it can be withdrawn at any time at the option of the delegating unit. Consequently, local school districts in each state have always operated at the pleasure of the state's legislature, operating within the limits established by the state constitution. As the states have gradually assumed more and more responsibility for financing education, the role of the local school district in its own governance has decreased commensurately. There is no indication that this trend is about to be reversed.

The great mobility of people has had much to do with the "insolvable" problems of financing education. As the little red schoolhouse has faded out of the picture, the extreme pride of citizens in a particular school has decreased. Average citizens want good schools wherever they go—to a different district or to a different state. The effects of good and of poor education diffuse among the towns and cities of the land. It thus becomes evident that good education is a state responsibility and cannot safely be left to local communities working alone.

Local Fiscal Control

The question of the degree or extent of power local districts should have in the control of their own fiscal operations is controversial and unsettled. If the state provides most of the local school revenue, should it exercise more authority over local school districts than when it provides less? Do the advantages of local districts' control over their own fiscal operations counterbalance the disadvantages? These and other similar questions need to be answered in the states as they continue to increase their proportionate share of public school revenues. Although local districts have traditionally provided more than have the states toward the costs of education, that pattern has changed over the years (Figure 5-2).

Excessive Reliance on Property Taxes

The property tax has not always been local; it has been and still is used by some state governments. It originated during America's colonial period as a selective tax on particular kinds and classes of wealth. For a century or more its base increased until it included both real and personal property. Most of the states have discontinued or minimized the property tax at the state level, in favor of income and sales taxes. But local units of government, including schools, have

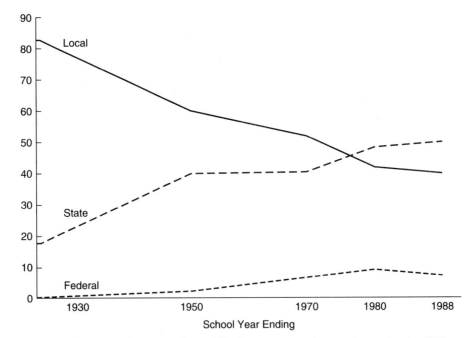

FIGURE 5-2   Sources of revenue for public elementary and secondary schools: 1930 to 1988. (Source: *Digest of Education Statistics 1990*, U.S. Department of Education, National Center for Education Statistics, Office of Educational Research and Improvement (NCES 91-660), February 1991.)

found no adequate substitute for this means of transferring funds from the private to the public sector of the economy.

With all its weaknesses and limitations, the real property tax has been the basic form of taxation for education at the local level of government, and it appears that it will continue to be. Even though taxes on tangible and intangible personal property have been used with varying degrees of success in some states, the real property tax continues to provide most revenues for schools. However, as states have recognized and implemented their financial responsibility for education, the percentage of total school revenue derived from local property taxation has decreased.

A quarter of a century ago, the school districts of this country claimed and received annually about one-third of the local property taxes collected. Even though this tax has been condemned by many tax and educational authorities, and even though the various states have to some degree restricted and denied its unlimited use, school districts now use approximately half of the local property tax revenues collected. They have displaced other units of government—cities and counties—as the principal recipient of such revenues. One of the results of this has been a popular opinion that the property tax is virtually a school tax. Higher property taxes—whatever the purpose or reason for their having been levied—often are considered to be solely attributable to public education.

Local control of education, though strongly embedded in the American mind, has many limiting factors that thwart its purposes and mitigate its effectiveness. Limitations in providing equality of educational opportunity from local tax sources alone are evident in every state. Obtaining adequate local funds for education is complicated by at least two facts. (1) Local revenue is obtained almost completely from taxes on property, which is not a fair measure of the ability of people to pay. (2) Competition for the local tax dollar is becoming increasingly more severe. Most citizens are familiar with the arguments for improvement of local tax administration.

Walker analyzes the use of the property tax in the following:

> Given the history of the local property tax, one might ask: Why keep the tax? The responses are numerous. The tax gets at certain wealth (stock) that the income tax or other taxes on income (flow) do not. Also, the tax is highly visible to local citizens; therefore, local leadership must be more responsive to the body politic. The issue of local autonomy over the schools is inextricably linked to the tax. Moreover, the tax is amenable to small incremental changes in rate. Perhaps most importantly, the tax has been too productive of revenue to be abandoned. It has substantial vertical equity, meaning that it redistributes wealth from the rich to the poor through the schooling process. In addition, the tax tends to increase application of resources to high return human investments, such as education. The list could be extended, but perhaps it is sufficient to state that the prospects for reform of the tax are much greater than the prospects for elimination.[11]

All local institutions and agencies have felt the increasing costs of government. Just as teachers need higher salaries, so do policemen, firemen, and other local government employees. Since local government can seldom go very far afield from a system of local property taxation, competition for these tax dollars has increased and probably will continue to increase. In the light of existing tax conditions, it is understandable that local institutions and agencies, as well as taxpayers, face almost overwhelming financial problems. Thus, complete local responsibility for financing education is unfair and impracticable and makes a mockery of the American dream of equality of educational opportunity for all.

States Limit Local Taxing Authority

The question of whether or not a state may limit the power of voters at the local level to increase their taxes for public education has not yet been definitively answered by the courts. About 70 percent of the states now operate their school finance programs with such a restriction. As a result, poorer districts are severely handicapped if they attempt to provide additional tax revenues with limited tax levies. Of course, wealthy districts can usually provide as good a program as they desire to pay for and still operate within the law. Within recent years, a number of cases contesting state limitations on local tax rates have been before the courts.

At the local level, school district administration of the financial and instructional aspects of the educational program is largely legalistic. Actions of school boards and their employees must be within applicable statutory or other legal authority. Thus, no board of education may act to establish and finance any school program except as constitutional mandate, statute, or court decision provides the specific or implied legal authority. The boards themselves, acting within this framework, may establish their own rules and regulations to govern the schools; these have the force of law.

Inadequate and Unequal Resources

One of the most obvious weaknesses of local control of fiscal operations is that in nearly all states local school districts vary greatly in their access to taxable resources. They must, of course, depend almost completely on property tax revenues for financing education. In poorer districts—those with a low assessed valuation per pupil to be educated—local tax requirements place heavy burdens on some property taxpayers, with the result that citizen pressure to hold down tax rates may result in a level of revenue inadequate for a good school program. Local school systems tend to become conservative and often refuse to inaugurate or operate higher cost programs, regardless of their potential value or the unmet needs of students.

A big problem each state faces in providing equal educational opportunity for all its citizens involves the extreme differences among districts in ability to pay for education, as measured by the assessed valuation of taxable property per student to be educated. One of the strong arguments favoring elimination of many small school districts in most states is that this range of differences in local ability would be sharply reduced by such a process—thereby simplifying the equalization formula to be used. When it is realized that the typical community in the United States derives nearly half of its total school revenue for public education from local sources—particularly the property tax—the significance of wide ranges in local ability to support education becomes evident. The wide disparities that continue to exist in the various states in the amounts of money available for the education of children and youth are a firm reminder of the unfairness of local financing of education with little or no state support. It is true that the extremes in such inequities have been reduced in most of the states, but the problem is still far from being solved. For example, in 1971–72, California's wealthiest district had fifty times as much local wealth per pupil as its poorest. While intolerable, this degree of inequity was an improvement over the 10,000 to 1 ratio that existed in the same state in 1945, or the 129 to 1 ratio that existed in an Iowa county in 1956.

Even more recent reports show that the disparity still exists. In 1991 the Committee for Economic Development noted that, "although poorer districts tax property at a higher rate, the lower tax base usually yields fewer dollars overall and pupil allocations that can be several thousand dollars lower than in wealthier districts. The gap between rich and poor districts is over $2000 per pupil in California, over $6500 in New York, and over $8000 in Ohio."[12] Such imbalances in fiscal ability among the school districts within a state have been the cause of numerous court cases in many states:

> These disparities in local funding are fueling a growing nationwide movement to revamp state education funding mechanisms in order to guarantee more equitable funding of rich and poor school districts. A number of recent state supreme court decisions have declared funding mechanisms used to finance education to be unconstitutional. In the past eighteen months alone, courts have struck down the financing systems of New Jersey, Texas, and Montana. Similar cases are pending in a dozen other states, including Alaska and Connecticut. Some states, such as Kentucky and Oklahoma, in order to avoid having decisions about their financing systems made in the courts, have taken the initiative to redesign their funding systems and make them part of a statewide school-restructuring program. New Jersey recently voted to phase out millions of dollars in state aid now received by the 150 most affluent districts and to increase state support for poor cities and moderate-income suburbs.[13]

The negative effects of inadequate support for schools are most pronounced for families of low income. Affluent families can provide alternatives to a poorly supported school, such as sending their children to more adequately financed public schools, sending them to private schools, employing tutors, or purchasing additional supplies and equipment. No such alternatives are available to low-income families. As pointed out by Benson more than a decade ago:

Lower-income families are trapped in the public education system. Already saddled with heavy tax burdens to support public education, they cannot possibly afford leaving the public sector to find alternatives in private education. To be sure, private education can be an expensive alternative even for wealthier families, but at least it remains an option for them. For poorer families, there is no choice at all. . . . Wealthier families possess the economic and political power to assure them that their desires for educational services will be met. They may form exclusive residential communities providing the kind of public schools they want. They may dominate school boards and, therefore, affect the formulation of educational policy. They can afford private schools that provide the type of special attention they seek for their children.[14]

Local Taxing Power

In the late 1920s the federal government collected approximately one-third of all taxes in the United States. By 1947, it collected three-fourths of the total. The state increased its relative importance as a tax collector by enacting sales and income taxes, and the local unit nearly doubled its property tax revenues. During the same period, state and federal tax revenues nearly tripled. In 1989 property taxes of $117 billion were collected at the local level and $5 billion at the state level. In contrast, $120 billion was collected in sales tax at the state level and $24 billion in sales tax revenue was collected at the local level. Table 5-2 shows the total revenue for elementary and secondary schools from federal, state, and local sources.

TABLE 5-2   Public Elementary and Secondary School Revenue by Source, 1970 to 1980 (in millions of dollars)

Year	Total	Federal	State	Local
1970	38,192	2,767	15,628	19,797
1975	63,047	5,089	27,472	30,486
1980	97,635	9,020	47,929	40,686
1982	113,999	8,419	54,573	51,007
1983	120,778	8,695	57,587	54,496
1984	129,057	8,967	61,657	58,434
1985	140,957	9,524	69,070	62,363
1986	153,696	10,354	75,931	67,411
1987	163,798	10,510	81,650	71,638
1988	174,219	11,190	87,093	75,936
1989	185,122	11,646	93,018	80,458

Source: *Statistical Abstract of the United States, 1990*, U.S. Department of Commerce, Bureau of the Census, January, 1990.

Municipal Overburden

Most of the urban school systems in this country are now facing some degree of financial distress. Their tax bases are either declining or growing too slowly to meet the rapidly increasing costs of education. The financial plight of city school districts is much like that of rural districts historically—unusual conditions that raise the costs of education beyond their ability to pay without additional state revenue. In most areas the rural problem has been "solved" by the use of sparsity factors in state finance formulas, but solutions have not yet been implemented for most urban school systems. Since the unfortunate plight of big-city districts is a relatively new phenomenon, very little has been done to solve the problem.

Municipal overburden results from the fact that public schools and city governments must use the same property tax base to obtain the relatively large revenues required for their operation. The budgets of cities include large sums of noneducational public services such as police and fire protection and health services. The high percent of total city property taxes required to finance these services (as compared to the percent required in small-city and rural areas) limits the property taxing power of city school districts for education.

Most large city school districts must provide education for large groups of high-cost students—minority groups, disadvantaged pupils, and handicapped pupils, many of whose parents migrated there in the hope of finding more satisfactory social and educational programs. The situation became more complicated and the tax burdens more accentuated as affluent inner-city residents moved to the suburbs and were replaced by less affluent citizens who moved there in search of employment. Erosion of the tax base thus accompanied the increase in the need for government services, including education. The high cost of these additional city social and educational services resulted in a higher burden on property taxpayers.

Cities, of course, have made attempts to overcome their problems of overburden. Some have overassessed certain types of property; some have adopted income taxes in order to involve suburban residents in paying part of city government costs; some have appealed to the state and federal governments for financial assistance. A few states have attempted to alleviate this condition by giving big-city school districts additional student weightings or a density factor in their school finance formulas.

Until after World War II, the urban school districts maintained a well-earned position of leadership in education. They had more available resources, expended more money per pupil for education, and generally reacted more favorably to innovation and improvement. But the wheel has turned, and the nation now faces an appalling situation in most of its city schools.

Thus, the financial advantages that most city school districts enjoyed over their rural counterparts no longer exist. The favorable position of city districts that led to the formation of foundation programs to give greater financial strength to small districts has disappeared. This reversal has come as a result of the ever-changing character of cities and their need to provide high-quality education for all their citizens, regardless of race or color or any other contributing factors that might add to the cost of education.

A number of contributing factors relate directly to the overwhelming financial problems now in evidence in urban school districts in all parts of this country.

1. Conditions related to student militancy, student mobility, and integration problems have reversed the traditional trend for candidates for teaching positions to go to the cities, where salaries were more favorable, working conditions were better, and individual initiative could more easily be directed to innovation and experimentation.

2. Problems involving the education of the socially and culturally deprived and the physically and mentally handicapped are accentuated in city districts. Cities must deal with many of these problems, whereas rural school districts, because of lack of numbers, very often minimize them. The inequality thus engendered is accentuated by the great expense of these programs.

3. Increases in city property values have not kept pace with the rapidly accelerating increases in school expenditures. The movement of large numbers of middle- and higher-income people from the core city to the suburbs has curtailed building needs, so property valuations have not risen in cities to the same extent that they have elsewhere.

4. The relative tax-paying potential of city school districts has been reduced by the migration of large numbers of low-income families to the cities. Large demand for compensatory education programs, great need for welfare programs, and the high cost of educating deprived citizens—now in a majority in many of our cities—have combined to downgrade the educational program.

School financing programs have long recognized the fact that small schools are generally more expensive per pupil than larger ones. To compensate for this, school finance formulas have usually included provisions for sparsity factors, which have been accepted as a necessary and fair requirement. Only recently, however, has serious consideration been given to the higher costs of education per pupil in large cities. The density factor in determining costs has not yet been accepted to the same degree as its older counterpart, the sparsity factor. The need for a solution to this financial inconsistency is immediate.

Local Nonproperty Taxes

Accompanying the growing criticism and disillusionment with the property tax has been an increasing attempt by government to provide additional revenue for public schools from local nonproperty taxes. For a number of reasons, this effort has been to a great extent unsuccessful, except in a few large school districts. (1) School districts are not organized to lay and collect taxes; they rely on other units of government for this purpose. (2) Although school districts have fared better than other local institutions in receiving state financial aid in various forms, city and county governments enjoy a much more favorable position in obtaining the receipts from nonproperty taxes such as sales taxes, payroll taxes, and gross receipts taxes. (3) School districts are generally organized in units too small to make certain nonproperty taxes (such as a sales tax) effective; except in large districts, such taxes can be avoided by purchasing goods and services in neighboring communities that do not have such a tax. (4) The net effect of using nonproperty taxes is as disequalizing as the property tax; there is therefore little incentive for extension of such taxes at the local level. (5) The states, having left the property tax almost exclusively to local units of government, are forced to procure their revenues largely from nonproperty tax sources; this, to a great degree, excludes such tax revenue from local school districts.

Some tax and finance authorities have looked with much hope and expectancy at local nonproperty taxes, viewing them as a strong potential supplement to property taxes. Local sales taxes, income or earnings taxes, and others have been used in some communities for school purposes. Unfortunately, the revenues obtained and the inconvenience of collection, plus taxpayer resistance, have made these taxes of doubtful value in many school districts, especially in small cities or communities. Some larger city school districts have, however, used local nonproperty taxes satisfactorily.

Local nonproperty taxes became somewhat popular after World War II, especially in urban centers where the total populations were large enough to make such taxation practicable. Tax authorities who had expected good results from such taxes were disappointed in their applications and their ineffectiveness in smaller districts. Fiscally independent districts have benefited little from such taxes. Some districts, however, have received substantial amounts of money from tax sharing with the state or county in the application of some forms of nonproperty taxation—the sales tax, for example. Up to this time, revenues from nonproperty taxes have been small in comparison with the total costs of education, but the trend may change in the next decade.

States are looking for other sources of revenue. Louisiana, for example, "is the only state in which school districts raise more local revenue from a nonproperty tax alternative than they do from their property taxes. Of the 34 percent provided by local sources in Louisiana, about one-half of these funds was obtained through local taxes on sales."[15]

It appears that local nonproperty taxes will be reserved for the most part as sources of state revenue. At present, nonproperty taxes do not seem to have an encouraging future as a source of local school revenues.

EFFECTS OF LOCAL DISTRICT INADEQUACY

The failure of numerous school districts to maintain full-year school programs in the years of the Depression is a matter of historical fact. One can understand such failures in terms of the impotent economy of that time. On the other hand, it is a source of some embarrassment in this day of unprecedented affluence to note that school districts still face the same problem—some of them without power to resolve it in the midst of the United States' economic prosperity. When some local districts are required to take unneeded "vacations" until local funds can be accumulated in large enough amounts to reopen their doors, and when loyal citizens voluntarily pay their taxes before they are due in order to keep their schools open, it is apparent that local and state partnership plans for financing education in some of the states need to be given greater strength and viability.

ADVANTAGES OF LOCAL CONTROL

The local community and the local school district in the United States are far more influential in their relations to their own educational programs than are their counterparts in other countries. Educational philosophy generally supports the belief that a large degree of local control not only stimulates local interest and support but also more easily permits innovations and improvements. The idea of strong national administrative control of education is repugnant to most of our citizens.

In certain ways the local districts have an advantage over the states and the federal government in obtaining additional funds for education. Those who have observed the long history of federal aid attempts point to the many years of indecision and frustration caused by the bitter debates involving racial discrimination, separation of church and state, political jealousies, and the ever-present fear of federal control. Action at the federal level to shore up the finances of school districts appears to be a practical impossibility. Substantially increased funds at the state level is a reality.

Property taxes for school district revenue, according to the Advisory Committee on Intergovernmental Relations, in September 1991, was 70 percent in the 1950s, 58 percent in the 1970s, and 47 percent in the 1980s. Property taxes remain the mainstay of local own source revenues.[16] Historically, the Committee has pointed out:

> In 1971, property tax revenues were $36.7 billion, or 15 percent of all local, state, and federal taxes. By 1981, property tax revenues were $72.0 billion, or 11.1 percent of all government tax revenues. Between 1971 and 1981, property tax revenues nearly doubled, but state tax revenues and federal tax revenues nearly tripled. Between 1973 and 1978, property taxes increased at an annual rate of 7.8 percent while state sales taxes grew by 12.3 percent, state income taxes rose by 13.3 percent, and federal income taxes increased by 11.9 percent. From 1978 to 1981, property taxes grew by 4.0 percent per year. State sales taxes increased by 9.6 percent, state income taxes increased by 12.0 percent, and federal income taxes rose by 16.4 percent. In 1971, property taxes were approximately 1.98 percent of market value; by 1981, property taxes had decreased by 37 percent to 1.26 percent of property value.[17]

However, according to Augenblick:

> The viability of education finance depends on diverse sources of revenue. Any attempt to eliminate a revenue source (such as the property tax), no matter how well intended, poses a threat to the education system. Rather than doing away with property taxes, policymakers should improve assessment practices, collection systems, and the tax rate setting process. In this way, the equity of a state's school finance system can be balanced against the assurance that adequate revenues will be available to support the education system.[18]

FISCAL INDEPENDENCE OF SCHOOL DISTRICTS

School districts in most States are independent units of government—Maryland, North Carolina, Virginia, and Hawaii represent organizational exceptions. In these states, school systems are dependencies of general governments. In Hawaii, the general government in the State itself; in Maryland, the counties of Baltimore City; in Virginia and North Carolina, county and city governments. In all, about half the states have one or more school systems dependent upon units of general government but these dependent school systems number only 1,608, almost half of which are in the New England States.[19]

The question whether or not the local school board should have autonomy within the law in the use of local tax sources and revenues is relevant in a discussion of local responsibility for education. Many in the fields of economics and political science argue in favor of the fiscally dependent district—a system that places the local district board of education under some degree of jurisdiction by the city or county government. Usually this involves city or county approval of the school district's annual budget. Under this arrangement, city or county officials make final decisions for school budgetary requests, which are based upon deliberations of the board of education without the understanding or active participation of the municipal authorities involved. As a group, educators almost universally favor fiscal independence for school boards.

TRENDS IN LOCAL TAXATION PRACTICES

Many people hope for relief for local property taxpayers, with an increase in the state and federal revenues for education. Current trends are listed next.

1. Property tax administration will be improved; even though taxpayer resistance against such taxes may increase, the property tax will continue to be an important source of funds for operation of public schools. Professionally trained career assessors, more realistic laws concerning property tax administration, the

establishment of larger taxing districts to encourage specialization in tax administration, more adequate and efficient state supervision of the program, and more effective communication between those who administer the tax program and those who pay the taxes—all are reasonable improvements that logically can be expected in the future.

2. Competition among local agencies for the tax dollar will continue to increase; schools will succeed in this arena only if they are able to improve the quality of the educational product that they produce.

3. The urban communities will continue to suffer from revenue shortfall unless given equitable treatment in local, state, and federal allocation of funds.

4. Efforts will be made to make the property tax less regressive and to relieve those who suffer economically from too much emphasis on this kind of taxation. In states that leave the financial responsibility of education almost completely up to the individual local districts, property taxpayers have justifiable cause for complaint.

MEASURES OF LOCAL TAX-PAYING ABILITY

The ability of a local school district to pay the costs of education without state or federal support is a function of two variables: the value of taxable property and the number of pupils to be educated. This is usually expressed as the assessed valuation of taxable property per person in average daily attendance or in average daily membership in school.

For nearly a century, scholars and practitioners of school finance have been studying how to measure the comparative abilities of local units of government to finance education and to provide other services. State equalization programs—particularly those involving power equalization—must use some valid and reliable measure of local fiscal ability if state and federal allocations of funds to local districts are to be justified.

Scholars have conducted extensive research in an attempt to refine the measurement of local fiscal ability. There seems to be little justification for using a theoretically computed index of ability, but there is a strong rationale for using the ability as measured by the tax structure and current system. Little is to be gained in comparing the abilities of school districts in terms of potential taxes and revenue that are not available to those districts. These are measures that may have real value in determining a state's ability to support education, since the state legislative body can make them available by statute, but their value in comparing local districts is limited and questionable.

LOCAL, STATE, AND FEDERAL TAX RESPONSIBILITY

A difficult problem arises in coordinating the taxing system of the three levels of government—federal, state, and local. No one has yet determined the ideal, or even the most practical, combination of taxing powers and authority of these levels of government that will produce maximum social and cultural benefits with maximum taxpayer equity and minimum taxpayer burden and inconvenience. To a very great extent these three units of government operate their tax patterns in isolation from each other. Ideally, their taxing systems should be coordinated. The elements of taxation that are usurped to some degree by any one unit of government would seemingly be sources beyond the powers of the other two units to use. But adequate funds must be provided regardless of source if good education is to be provided for all our citizens.

In most states the local school districts have traditionally had to raise the major part of the tax revenues required to finance their public schools. Reluctantly, the states have assumed important but varying degrees of responsibility for financing education, but the federal government has fluctuated in its participation. For the most part, the latter has remained aloof from the problem. As the states and local districts approach the limits of their taxing power for education, they expect financial assistance from the federal government. The National Education Association has stated: "Public education in the United States is a *joint* enterprise of federal, state, and local government. . . . Federal funds represent a modest supplement directed principally at special populations . . . states and school districts give substance to public education. . . ."[20]

For a long time, the educational establishment has emphasized the potential role of the federal government in collection and distribution of tax revenue to states and local school districts. Federal support for a number of important public functions, such as agriculture, highways, housing, hospitals, and welfare, is taken for granted by the general public. However, the proper role of the federal government in financing education has not yet been determined. Until a significant change occurs in the generally accepted philosophy of financing education, the principle responsibility for that activity will probably continue to rest with the states and their local units.

SUMMARY

Because of the continual increases in funds allocated to public education by most of the states, local control of education is slowly decreasing. This is a source of some concern to many people, who view education as a frontier where people at the local level can exercise some degree of authority in decision making in matters that directly affect them.

Rural areas of the country no longer have the strong influence upon legislation they once enjoyed. On the other hand, urban areas have lost the financial advantage they once had over rural areas. City school districts suffer financially because of higher costs and the need to provide social and welfare services that are minimized in most rural areas.

Although much has been done to decrease the extremely large number of school districts that once existed in the United States, some states still operate far too many small districts. Just as many school districts are too small for efficient operation, many city districts are too large. Most states have been able to provide for the financial needs of small districts, but a satisfactory solution for the municipal overburden of large cities has yet to be found.

The authority and responsibility of local school boards have diminished. Since the prevailing interpretation of the Tenth Amendment to the United States Constitution and the equal protection and education clauses in many state constitutions provide for state responsibility for education, local control is not in any way guaranteed; it may change as the individual states dictate. Historically, there has been a fervor to maintain local control of education, but greater open debate and controversy regarding the effectiveness and usefulness of local boards have emerged in the literature in recent years. Mobility of the population is significant, and people want good schools throughout the nation, but the public may not be willing to pay for them.

The states have always assumed general responsibility for education, but many of them have left the major financial obligation and control with local districts. Only recently has the states' total share of financing education exceeded that of local districts.

The real property tax has been the major source of local funds for education since the early history of the nation. States have recently begun to place limits on such taxes and in a few instances have placed limits on annual expenditure increases for public education.

Local nonproperty taxes are not as effective or productive as they appear to be in theory. Education finance will need to depend on diverse sources of income in the future.

A relatively few school districts are still dependent on some other unit of government for approval of some aspect of their financing. The disadvantages of such a relationship far outweigh the advantages. Dependent school districts are much more likely to become involved in local government politics than are independent districts.

Certain trends are discernible in local taxation practices. Better property tax administration, continued competition for the tax dollar among various agencies and institutions of government, a continuation of the problems created by municipal overburden, more state support for education, and continued resistance to taxes are among the most evident.

ASSIGNMENT PROJECTS

1. Summarize the arguments for and against local control of public education.
2. Reducing the number of school districts in a state will generally reduce the difference in ability to support education between the "wealthiest" district and the "poorest" district in terms of assessed valuation per pupil to be educated. Construct a problem in a mythical state and show that this statement is true.

3. If two school districts appear to have the same number of dollars of taxable property per pupil, but the figure for District A was determined by using the average daily attendance of pupils and that for District B was determined by using the enrollment, which district has the greater ability to support its schools?
4. With the following information, answer questions a, b, and c concerning their relative ability to support education:

District	Students	AV	Percent AV is of SV
A	4,200	$21,210,000	50
B	5,400	28,350	60
C	1,200	4,800	40

    a. Which district has the greatest ability to support education?
    b. Which district has the least ability to support education?
    c. If all three districts were to be assessed at 100 percent of their sale value, which would have the greatest ability to support education?
5. Compare the ability of the following three districts to finance education:

	District A	District B	District C
Assessed valuation	$20,200,000	$30,300,000	$40,400,000
Percent AV is of SV	50	60	40
Students in ADA	1,600	2,200	3,000
Tax levy	16 mills	$1.55/$100	$14/$1,000

    a. Which district can raise the largest amount of money per pupil?
    b. How much?
    c. Considering potential ability (using AV = SV) and using the same tax rates as indicated for each district, which district could raise the greatest amount of money per pupil?
    d. How much?

SELECTED READINGS

Campbell, Roald F., Luvern L. Cunningham, Raphael O. Nystrand, and Michael D. Lisdan. *The Organization and Control of American Schools*, 5th ed. Columbus, Ohio: Merrill, 1985.

Guthrie, James W. *School Finance Policies and Practices, the 1980s: A Decade of Conflict. First Annual Yearbook of the American Education Finance Association*. Cambridge, Mass.: Ballinger, 1980.

Guthrie, James W., Walter I. Garms, and Lawrence C. Pierce. *School Finance and Education Policy: Enhancing Educational Efficiency, Equality, and Choice,* 2nd ed. Englewood Cliffs, N.J.: Prentice Hall, 1988.

Honeyman, D. S., D. C. Thompson, and R. C. Wood. *Financing Rural and Small Schools: Issues of Adequacy and Equity.* Gainesville: University of Florida Press, 1989.

Hooker, Clifford P., and Van D. Mueller. *The Relationship of School District Organization to State Aid Distribution Systems.* Minneapolis, Minn.: Educational Research and Development Council of the Twin Cities Metropolitan Area, 1970.

Verstegan, D. A. *School Finance at a Glance.* Denver, Colo.: Education Commission of the States, 1990.

ENDNOTES

1. *Estimate of School Statistics 1990–91* (Washington, D.C.: National Education Association Data-Search, 1991), p. 5.

2. Lynn Olson, "School Chief Woes Call for a Change of Big-City Boards," *Education Week,* Vol. 10, No. 19, January 30, 1991, p. 16.

3. James Gordon Ward, "Consensus Politics and Local Control: The 1985 Illinois Education Reform Package," *Journal of Education Finance,* Vol. 11, No. 3, Winter 1986, p. 381.

4. Illinois State Board of Education, "The Legislature and the Schools," Vol. 1, No. 34 (March 27, 1986), p. 1, as quoted in Ward, "Consensus Politics and Local Control: The 1985 Illinois Education Reform Package."

5. Chester E. Finn Jr., "Reinventing Local Control," *Education Week,* Volume 10, No. 18, January 23, 1991, p. 40.

6. Ibid.

7. Thomas Shannon, "Local Control and Organizarats," *Education Week,* Vol. 10, No. 21, February 13, 1991.

8. Ibid., p. 32.

9. Susan M. Fuhrman and Richard F. Elmore, "Understanding Local Control," *Educational Evaluation and Policy Analysis,* Spring 1990, p. 94.

10. Ibid., pp. 93–94.

11. Billy D. Walker, "The Local Property Tax for Public Schools: Some Historical Perspec-

tives," *Journal of Education Finance,* Vol. 9, No. 3, Winter 1984, p. 288.

12. *The Unfinished Agenda: A New Vision for Child Development and Education* (New York: Committee for Economic Development, 1991), p. 61.

13. Ibid.

14. Charles S. Benson et al., *Planning for Educational Reform* (New York: Dodd, Mead, 1974), p. 96.

15. David S. Honeyman, "An Examination of Fiscal Neutrality in Louisiana: Using Alternative Measures of School District Wealth," *Educational Considerations,* Vol. 17, No. 2, Spring 1990, p. 33.

16. *Fiscal Trends* (Washington, D.C.: Advisory Committee on Intergovernmental Relations, September 5, 1991), p. 3.

17. *Significant Features of Fiscal Federalism in 1981–82* (Washington, D.C.: Advisory Committee on Intergovernmental Relations, April 1983).

18. John Augenblick, "The Importance of Property Taxes to the Future of School Finance," *Journal of Education Finance,* Vol. 9, No. 3, Winter 1984, p. 393.

19. *State Aid to Local Government* (Washington, D.C.: Advisory Commission on Intergovernmental Relations, April 1969), p. 34.

20. *Estimate of School Statistics 1990–91,* p. 3.

Chapter 6

Education:
A State Function

State policy makers continually face the dilemma of achieving excellence in public education . . . Given the financial resources and political constraints that many states face, this achievement is perhaps improbable within the near future. Additionally, there is no compelling evidence to suggest that either the potential constraints or limited financial resources will change over the next several generations. —R. CRAIG WOOD, DAVID S. HONEYMAN, 1990

Education appears to have been considered important in colonial times largely because of its presumed preventive effect in fortifying people to resist evil. Important as that purpose may have been, the rationale for the establishment and operation of schools has changed considerably since that era.

Establishing and operating a system of public schools has been recognized as a function of government rather than of private enterprise since the settlement of the first Europeans in what is now the United States. Early colonists recognized the importance of education in building and maintaining a democratic government and properly developing individuals and organizations to serve it. The general tone toward schools and education was succinctly expressed in the statement the Continental Congress included in the Northwest Ordinance of 1787: "Schools and the means of education shall forever be encouraged." The spirit of that declaration continues to be a part of the national ideal.

The present relation of government to education has evolved over two centuries. For the most part, the practical "partnership" of federal, state, and local levels of government has worked well, at least until recent years. Each state has been responsible for its own system of education, with power to delegate whatever degree of control it chose to local districts of the kind and number it desired. As a result, there have been fifty versions of that relation in as many states. The federal government over the years has held an advisory position, with very little real authority over education.

Changes and innovations are an integral part of the continuing development of our educational system. The need for improvement of education is becoming more observable year after year. But how shall the course of the three-level governmental relation to education be determined? Is the stage being set for more state and less local responsibility for financing education? Have the traditional arguments favoring local control become obsolete? Should the federal government be a full-fledged partner in the business of public education? Such questions demand serious consideration as the nation moves to meet the imposing challenges which face it in the years ahead.

EARLY DEVELOPMENT OF STATE RESPONSIBILITY

The word *education* is conspicuous by its absence in the United States Constitution. The writers of that document avoided any specific designation of responsibility for the pattern that formal education should take in this country. The reasons for such an important omission are presumed to have been as follows. (1) Certain other needs of the newly formed states were more urgent at that time. (2) Many of the leaders of government presumed that a controversy over educational responsibility might lead to an impasse, or at least add greatly to the already overwhelming problems about which there was great dissension. (3) The original thirteen colonies had already established their own patterns of school organization and had recognized and accepted their individual obligations for education, at least to some degree, by previous action and legislation during the colonial period.

The Constitution should be interpreted and evaluated in terms of the unique conditions under which it was adopted rather than in terms of its presumed deficiencies or its areas of emphasis. The United States of America was born as a legal entity after a period of stress that resulted in the American Revolution. The colonies won that bitter conflict after almost superhuman effort and sacrifice on the part of many, but not all, of their citizens. The founding fathers, recognizing their break with the philosophy of government of that day, were vitally concerned with how to establish perpetuity of government. They felt a need to avoid endowing the federal government with powers that might at some time overbalance the powers of the state governments. This they hoped to achieve by delegating certain powers to the federal government while strengthening the structure and framework of the individual states. Such an arrangement appears to have been necessary to assure formal adoption of the Constitution by the thirteen individualistically oriented and mutually suspicious colonies that would form the foundation of the new country.

It should not be assumed that early Americans were indifferent to education or had little interest in it. The establishment of Harvard in 1636, the Laws of 1642 and 1647, and the Ordinances of 1785 and 1787 (passed by the Continental Congress under the Articles of Confederation, which makes federal aid to education predate the Constitution) are examples of their actions to provide for some important aspects of an educational program. Education had been at low ebb during the Revolution. It was provided mostly by private schools, with only local community support and with little or no cooperation among schools. The real battle for free public schools under colonial or state supervision had not yet begun.

Undoubtedly, the framers of the Constitution believed that the governmental framework they were creating implied provision for education. James Madison proposed the establishment of a university; Thomas Jefferson advocated appropriations of public lands for education; George Washington pressed hard for a national university. With such support for specific aspects of education by these and other leaders of that time, few historians believe that education was not considered by the founding fathers.

In the minds of many interpreters of the Constitution, Article I, Section 8 gives Congress the authority to provide educational support. "The Congress shall have power to lay and collect taxes . . . to pay the debts and provide for the common defense and general welfare of the United States. . . ." Education is part of the general welfare of the nation.

Some of the deficiencies of the Constitution were evident as soon as it was adopted. It was apparent immediately that it did not protect individual rights to the extent expected or desired. Consequently, the first ten amendments were adopted in 1791 as the Bill of Rights. These, especially the Tenth Amendment, form much of the legal basis for our present system of education. The Tenth Amendment provides that "the powers not delegated to the United States by the Constitution, nor prohibited by it to the States, are reserved to the States respectively, or to the people." Thus, education has been and continues to be primarily a function of state government. This responsibility is further documented by state constitutional provisions acknowledging and accepting this power, plus numerous court decisions supporting it.

State Interpretation of Educational Responsibility

The fifty states have not all accepted the challenge and obligation to sponsor education with the same degree of enthusiasm. Some have created large numbers of local districts and left most of the problems of education in the hands of local boards of education. Some have exerted very little administrative control or leadership over local units; others have developed an almost complete state school system. Although some of the states have accepted a large degree of financial responsibility for education, a few have almost completely ignored the problem at the state level.

The state school systems developed from local units. State responsibility for education was accepted in theory, but little leadership at this level was in evidence until the early nineteenth century, when a few educational leaders, particularly Horace Mann and Henry Barnard, began their historic efforts to develop a state foundation for education.

Development of Decentralized Educational System

Education historians have noted that local units of diverse sizes and philosophy dominated the United States scene:

It was not unnatural, during the days of the frontier, that education, though plainly enough a legal function of the state, should have been carried on with a very large measure of local operational discretion. The frontiersman disliked governmental restraint and found it especially odious when it touched a matter so personal and domestic as the rearing of his children. So long as these frontiersmen sent their children to school and did not press for financial assistance the most exacting state government was willing to let them alone.[1]

Thus, the story of the development of the fifty state school systems is one of diversity, struggle, and dedication to the idea of a decentralized system of education, without a national system, a minister of education, or any national control. Thurston and Roe, in 1957, described the situation well:

In tracing these developmental influences one is struck by the awareness that events and situations surely and inevitably seemed to be drawing this new country toward state-established universal free public education as the only logical solution which would correlate with a system of government based on the freedom and dignity of man. The struggle within the colonial government over the perplexing problem of localism and state rights versus national power shaped eventually our curious trilogy of educational control and cast the mold of our legal structure of education. The solution today seems natural—with the state maintaining legal supremacy and acting as the fulcrum to provide proper balance for the local community on the one side, where schools can be kept close to the people, and the national government on the other, where the general welfare of the nation can be safeguarded.[2]

The actions of many state legislatures in recent years reflect a more serious attitude toward state school finance problems and their solutions.

The typical citizen tends to think of the state school systems as having existed as they now are from the beginning of the nation, but our patterns of education, including our financial formulas and schemes, are the products of more than two centuries of development under a grassroots process of building—a process that was often erratic. However, appreciation for these systems, with all their limitations, comes quickly to the conscientious student of educational history. Those who understand the contributions of such men as Washington, Jefferson, Franklin, Paine, Barnard, and Mann must share some degree of pride in our systems of education, which have made such rich contributions to this country.

Thus it seems that the omission of specific educational provisions from the Constitution has proved to have been wisdom on the part of those who were responsible for the "oversight." Sound philosophy espousing decentralization, a willingness to involve people at the local and state levels, and national patience have proved to be better developers of our state school systems than anything that could possibly have been planned by the foresight of earnest educational and governmental leaders two centuries ago. From this process there emerged the best organizational pattern of education the world has yet produced.

DEVELOPMENT OF SCHOOL FINANCE POLICIES

The history of financing public school education in the United States is an interesting one. Actually, it is fifty separate stories of controversy, fumbling, false starts, long periods of inaction, and application of various forms of informal local and state action. In the early part of the nation's history, most of the costs of school operation were defrayed with nonmonetary services, provided by school patrons to the school itself or to the teacher. Fuel, custodial services, board and room for the teacher, and similar services were provided in lieu of salaries, insurance, and fringe benefits.

As the schools grew in size and complexity, so did the methods of financing them. These finance systems, and even the processes used to develop them, represent diversity and lack of standardization in the fullest meaning of those terms. Too often, the states profited little by the experiences of other states. Much too often, the states seem to have regarded variety as virtue and following the leader as vice. The lessons learned in one state seldom reduced the learning period required by taxpayers and professional leaders in another.

Land Grants and Other Nontax Funds

It is difficult to determine the exact beginning of state support for public education. Paul Mort reported that by 1890 the existing states provided about $34 million—almost 24 percent of that year's total school revenue. Since some of that state revenue was obtained from land given to the states by the federal government in the famous Northwest Ordinance of 1787, Mort included federal funds in the category of state funds.

Although the Tenth Amendment to the Constitution states that all powers not delegated to the United States are reserved to the states respectively, or to the people, that statement was not immediately recognized as a mandate to the states to provide financial support for education. State support of education developed slowly even though some educational finance theorists contend that the Tenth Amendment is tantamount to positive law. When the twentieth century began, only 17.2 percent of public school district revenues came from state sources.

The states generally provided means of legalizing local school taxes in their early statehood years, but equalization and sound theories and practices of state-local partnership in financing education were developments of the twentieth century for the most part.

In the early history of the colonies, land grants for the establishment and support of schools were common, especially in Massachusetts. As an example, from the early pioneer work in the field of land grants by Massachusetts was to emerge the state of Maine. Other more or less popular sources of the limited funds used to establish and maintain schools in the colonies included gifts, rate bills, and lotteries. Before taxation became the accepted method of financing schools, most of the known ways of collecting money were used in one or more of the thirteen colonies to obtain school funds. The early settlers brought with them the traditions of their European homelands, which had little relation to practical methods of financing decentralized schools as they began to emerge in the United States. Thus, there followed a long period of conflict over how to solve this important problem.

In the early United States, with its seemingly unlimited expanses of land and other valuable resources, it was natural that the granting of lands should become a significant reality in financing education. This policy reached a climax with the Northwest Ordinance of 1787, which was enacted by the Continental Congress primarily to stimulate migration to the West and secondarily to foster education. This law provided for the survey of the western lands and the reservation of Section 16 of every township for education, stating its purpose in the now famous statement, "Religion, morality, and knowledge being necessary to good government and the happiness of mankind, schools, and the means of education shall be forever encouraged."

The land grants of 1787 became effective with the admission of Ohio to the Union in 1802. When California became a state in 1850, the grant included two sections per township. Arizona, New Mexico, and Utah received four sections per township on becoming states in the latter part of the nineteenth and early part of the twentieth centuries.

The effect of the land grants on education was monumental. However, the lands were mismanaged in some of the states; the funds obtained from the rent or sale of the land were sometimes squandered. As a consequence of such mismanagement and inefficiency in many of the states, the potentially large revenues from this source were never fully realized. The same carelessness that characterized the use of natural resources in much of the western migration seemed to pervade the operation of the school land program.

The land-grant states relied to a great extent on the land grants to supply school funds until the end of the nineteenth century. The size of the grant was great, even in terms of the enormous expanses of unsettled territory of that day. Twelve states received the sixteenth section per township; fourteen states received sections 16 and 36; and three states received sections 2, 16, 32, and 36 per township. Kentucky, Maine, Texas, Vermont, West Virginia, Oklahoma (which when settled was Indian land), and the thirteen original states received no federal lands.

Since the original grant of land, the federal government has granted additional lands to some of the states, including salt lands, swamp lands, and internal improvement lands. Altogether, the land grants have been estimated to be more than 154 million acres, which is a land mass greater than Illinois, Indiana, and Ohio combined, and a value of billions of dollars—not including statehood grants to Alaska and Hawaii. In spite of the inefficient management of some of these lands, the funds derived therefrom provided many of the states with the means required to establish and operate schools while their state and local tax structures were being developed. They antedated state property taxes and thus became the revenue source for state improvement programs in extending the quantity and improving the quality of school services during the early development of state school systems, especially in the midwestern and western states.

Early Taxation Patterns

The taxation patterns for education in the newly formed United States were largely permissive, creating a situation that generally favored the city school districts, which were progressive, and penalized the rural areas of the country, which were more tax-resistant. The taxing policies of the several states emerged gradually from the patterns that had been used in the New England States. By 1890, all the states then in the Union had tax-supported public educational systems. About one-fourth of them provided more than half of their public school costs from state funds, and only eleven states provided less than 15 percent of their public school costs. The states not only felt certain responsibilities to help build sound educational programs but were also concerned with the settlement of the West. Hence, the first quarter of the nineteenth century saw the real beginning of a taxing pattern for the support of public education. By then most of the nontax sources—gifts, lotteries, bequests, and rate bills—were beginning to vanish from the scene. Their complete abandonment took several decades, and a few of these practices are still evident today.

THE DEVELOPMENTAL STAGES OF SCHOOL FINANCE THEORY

The development of public school finance theory and practice can be divided into five stages or periods. Admittedly, the periods overlap, and no specific dates divide them. Although theories have developed logically, their acceptance and use by the states have often been sporadic or almost nonexistent. Examples may be found of states that even now are in each one of the five stages of development. Of course, the size of a state, its educational finance needs and traditions, and its educational leadership may have equipped it for easier and freer transition and movement, compared with other states, into a modern and realistic stage of school finance theory and practice. Although a few states have continually pushed forward the frontier of educational finance theory, some are still trying to operate twentieth-century school programs with nineteenth-century financing practices.

The five stages of development of state-local relations (disregarding the federal level for the moment) are (1) the period of local district financial responsibility, with little or no assistance from the state; (2) the period of emerging state responsibility, with the use of flat grants, subventions, and other nonequalizing state allocations to local districts; (3) the emergence of the Strayer-Haig concept of a foundation program; (4) the period of refinement of the foundation program concept; and (5) the presently emerging period of "power" or "open-end" (shared costs) equalization practices and emphasis on high-quality education.

Period One: Emphasis on Local Responsibility

Since schools were first established in the United States on a local basis, it was natural for school finance to be a local community or church problem. The original colonies used rate bills or tuition charges, a procedure that they brought from their European homelands, but some of the New England towns began very early in their history to use property taxes to help finance education. Massachusetts and Connecticut were the leaders in this field, and each used this practice to some extent during the latter half of the seventeenth century. Tax support was used to a limited extent in the original southern states and in some Middle Atlantic States for the support of pauper schools.

The permissive property tax laws that existed when the colonies became states gradually became mandatory toward the end of the eighteenth century and the early part of the nineteenth. As the westward movement of settlers accelerated and the number of local school districts began to multiply, the popularity and acceptability of the local property tax as the mainstay of the school financing program increased. By 1890, with the closing of the frontier, all of the states were using property taxes, supplemented in many instances with revenue from the land grants and from other sources.

Even though most of the states were supporting local tax effort in school districts with the allocation of some state funds as early as 1890, some of them have continued to ignore this important financial responsibility even up to the 1965–66 school year, when ten of the fifty states provided less than one-fourth of the total revenue required for operating their public schools, and four of them provided even less than 15 percent.

The gross weaknesses and limitations of financing education at the local level are all too evident. Extremely wide differences in local tax-paying ability to meet the costs of education in hundreds of school districts (in a few instances more than a thousand) in a state make a mockery of the theory of equality of educational opportunity for all school pupils, unless the state does something to help financially weak districts. Since each district is almost completely on its own as far as finances are concerned, the place of each pupil's residence becomes the all-important determinant of the quantity and quality of education available. Local initiative and local ability, important as they are in our philosophy of decentralization in education, should never be allowed to become the determinants of the caliber of education that the citizens in any community receive.

The weakness of complete local financing of education becomes more evident as the property tax becomes less and less based on the ability-to-pay principle of taxation. It is evident that the greater the number of school districts in a state, the greater the likelihood of wide disparities in wealth, so states with hundreds of school districts can least afford to confine themselves to this obsolete approach to the school finance problem.

In the early twentieth century, as rural communities and neighborhoods grew into larger ones, without accompanying expansion of taxable wealth, the need for state support of education became more evident. States were slow to move in this direction, however, until the Depression of the 1930s showed the hopelessness of financing education by complete reliance on local property taxes.

Some forms of state support had existed for some time before the Depression. The early work of Cubberley in 1905 was the beginning of an era of study and experimentation in devising state plans that might assure equality of educational opportunity for all and at the same time improve school programs and equalize the tax burden.

Period Two: Early Grants and Allocations

About the turn of the century public schools in most population centers acquired their present structure—12 grades and a nine-month school term— and came to represent a greater cost to local taxpayers. As States legislated local programs of this scope, the issue of inequality in local wealth surfaced. Rural communities in particular found it increasingly difficult to impose tax rates stiff enough to meet the State mandated programs. Cities with their concentration of valuable properties could and did provide high level educational programs with moderate tax effort.[3]

From the very beginning of public financing of schools, a few states recognized and implemented their responsibilities in the matter. A number of reasons may be given for this early development. (1) The extreme inequalities that local property taxation generated among local school districts were soon obvious. (2) The funds that the sale and rental of the public lands provided were intended to find their way into the treasuries of local districts where control of education existed. (3) Many leaders in the educational movement recognized that the responsibility for education that the Tenth Amendment thrust on the states encompassed financial responsibility as much as any other kind.

In the early part of the twentieth century, Ellwood P. Cubberley was the pioneer and foremost figure in the serious consideration of state apportionments of funds to local school districts. Some of the principal tenets of his philosophy of school finance are expressed in the following:

Theoretically all the children of the state are equally important and are entitled to have the same advantages; practically this can never be quite true. The duty of the state is to secure for all as high a minimum of good instruction as is possible, but not to reduce all to this minimum; to equalize the advantages to all as nearly as can be done with the resources at hand; to place premium on those local efforts which will enable communities to rise above the legal minimum as far as possible; and to encourage communities to extend their educational energies to new and desirable undertakings.[4]

Cubberley's study of state allocations of funds to local districts, including flat grants, percentage grants, and others, showed that such allocations did not reduce inequalities and may even under certain circumstances have increased them. He saw little evidence that state fund allocations had reduced the wide range in the quality of education produced in school districts or the great disparity in ability to finance their programs. He made the first scientific study of the problem.

Cubberley was dedicated to the principle of equality of educational opportunity for all. Most of his ideas of how to provide such equality were far ahead of the practices of his time, even though most of them have been revised and improved in recent years. Noteworthy among the ideas and principles that Cubberley espoused were:

1. The belief that education was indeed a financial responsibility of the states, which they could not and should not ignore.

2. The firm conviction that state financial support was in addition to local effort, not intended as justifiable tax relief to local districts.

3. The awareness that existing methods of allocating state monies not only did not equalize the financial ability among local districts but may actually have increased financial inequalities among districts.

4. The need to increase the number of educational programs offered in the schools with attendant increases in state money for those districts with such extensions. This was his widely known version of reward for effort.

5. The wisdom of using aggregate days attendance over census, enrollment, average daily attendance, or any other measure used in determining the amount of state funds to local districts. This would encourage the extension of the school year and would penalize those districts that shortened the total length of their school year.

6. Distribution of some part of the state funds on the basis of the number of teachers employed in a district. He felt that this provision would aid the rural districts, which usually had a low pupil-teacher ratio.

Most of the Cubberley-inspired theories of school finance have become discredited and outmoded. It is easy to show that he was right in condemning flat grants, percentage grants, and subventions as nonequalizing. It is likewise easy, however, to show that his reward-for-effort principle was also nonequalizing. The wealthy districts already were employing more teachers, conducting more and better school programs, and holding more days of school per year than the poorer ones were. Thus, his reward for effort was applicable in the wealthier districts and much less applicable in the less wealthy ones.

Some of the states still use a few of the features of Cubberley's finance proposals. Fortunately, some of these practices are in combination with other, more equalizing methods of allocating state funds. Although some nonequalizing grants may have justification in school finance formulas, they are not justified if used alone. They represent progress beyond local effort alone, but they are glaring examples of some of the inconsistencies so readily discernible in the Cubberley concept.

It must be emphasized that there are some potential dangers involved in allocating state funds to local districts, regardless of how this is accomplished. Two principal risks are (1) the state could increase its control over local districts as it increases its financial support and (2) state monies may be used to replace rather than supplement local monies for education.

The first of these two considerations requires little discussion, for the state already exercises plenary power over its school districts. The degree of state authority and power over education is entirely a legislative matter that the will of each successive session of each state's legislative assembly controls and regulates. The extent of such control need not be in direct relation to the fiscal policies of the state as far as education is concerned, and it has not been so.

The purpose of state financial support of education is not to replace or reduce local effort unless that effort has been considered unduly burdensome to local taxpayers. Its purpose has been to supplement local tax revenues in order to provide an acceptable school program. The obvious answer to this problem is to require minimum school district levies before state funds are forthcoming.

Period Three: Emergence of the Foundation Program Concept

Modern school finance theory had its origin in the monumental work of George D. Strayer and Robert M. Haig. The real theory of equalization with its foundation program concept began with the findings of the Educational Finance Inquiry Commission of the schools of New York in 1923. The equalization of educational opportunity through the inception of a foundation or of a minimum program came as a direct result of the Strayer-Haig intensive studies of school finance programs built around the Cubberley philosophy and practiced in several states in the United States, particularly New York.

The Strayer-Haig studies discovered that in the school finance program of the state of New York, built as it was primarily around the distribution of state funds on a "per teacher quota basis," favored "the very rich and the very poor localities at the expense of those which are moderately well off." From this and other discoveries of deficiencies in the state finance plans of that era, Strayer and Haig advocated their *foundation*, or minimum program, concept. Their plan centered on several fundamental factors or standards:

1. A foundation program should be devised around the rich district idea—each local district would levy the amount of local tax that was required in the richest district of the state to provide a foundation, or minimum, program. The rich district would receive no state funds; the other districts would receive state funds necessary to provide the foundation program.

2. All foundation programs should guarantee equality of educational opportunity up to a specified point, but all local districts should have the discretionary right to go beyond that point and provide a better program through tax-levy increases.

3. The program should be organized and administered to encourage local initiative and efficiency.

4. The features of the program should be defined in the law and should be objective and apply to all school districts of the state.

5. Foundation programs should be constructed, after thorough study and careful planning, around the needs and resources of each individual state.

6. The cost of the foundation program should include a major part of the total cost of public education in that state.

7. The program should be organized so that no district receives additional funds because it is underassessed for property taxation purposes at the local level; uniform property assessment is essential in all foundation programs.

8. The plan should encourage the reorganization of school districts into a reasonable number and the consolidation of attendance areas wherever practicable, but provision must be made to avoid penalizing necessary small schools.

9. The foundation program should be a minimum and not a maximum program; local initiative and increased expenditures above the foundation program must be practicable in all the districts of a state.

The Strayer-Haig concept of equalization is summarized in the following brief statement:

> The Strayer-Haig approach became the model for numerous State adaptations. Compromises with the strict application of the equalization objective were made in most States to accommodate: (a) the long-standing tradition of flat grants; (b) the reluctance of State officials to increase State taxes to fully finance an equalization plan; and (c) the desire of some localities to finance truly superior public schools. In most States the foundation plan ended up providing the poorest district with a basic educational program at a level well below that which many school districts willingly supported. Wealthy districts were left ample local tax leeway to exceed the minimum foundation plan level without unduly straining local resources. Retention of flat grants as part of most State school financing plans left the wealthiest communities free to forge ahead.[5]

Period Four: Refinement of the Foundation Program Concept

The foundation program concept opened the gates for widespread experimentation and refinement of this method of approaching equal educational opportunity. In New York State, Paul Mort, working with Strayer and Haig, developed a program providing a degree of equalization plus the use of flat grants. The question of whether or not to take "surplus" monies from wealthy districts to help the states obtain equalization revenue was often debated and "settled" in various states. The question of the reasonableness of continuing the Cubberley concept of payment for effort was likewise debated by the individuals and commissions that were facing the problem of improving state finance programs. Wide differences in interpretation of the foundation program concept were developed and experimented with during this period.

Some important changes have followed experimentation with the Strayer-Haig concept of equalization in the last half-century:

1. There began an early movement away from the levy of a statewide property tax, the proceeds of which were to be distributed to schools on a school population or average daily attendance basis.

2. Fiscal independence of school districts was attained in most sections of the country.

3. The change from state property taxation to local property taxation brought intricate problems of obtaining fair and equitable property assessments.

4. The Depression years saw the establishment of laws in most states limiting the taxing power of school districts. (The restrictions have been eased to some extent since the end of World War II.)

5. Beginning efforts have been made in the use of local nonproperty taxes. These, however, have been insignificant except in a few large local districts.

6. The Cubberley emphasis on improvements and reward for effort with state funds was undercut by the Mort emphasis on equalization.

Mort found that this concept of equalization was incompatible with Cubberley's emphasis on reward for effort:

> The conclusion follows that these two purposes (equalization and reward for effort) that have controlled attempts to build state aid systems since the work of Cubberley two decades ago are found to be incompatible. We are, therefore, faced with the necessity of choosing one or the other. It is a choice between meeting the demands of a principle that cannot be met without state aid—the equalization of educational opportunity—and the use of one of many methods for meeting another principle.[6]

The Advisory Commission on Intergovernmental Relations noted some of the ways in which the Mort program improved on the Strayer-Haig theories:

> Perfecting amendments to the basic Strayer-Haig equalization thesis were developed as States enacted their foundation plans. For example, Paul Mort and other practitioners showed that educational costs differ for elementary and secondary pupils and that the unit of need in the foundation plan should be appropriately weighted to reflect these differences. . . .

The physically and mentally handicapped children became the subject of special solicitude.[7]

Modern school finance theories were spawned and developed by a relatively few well-known leaders in the field, such as Cubberley, Strayer, and Mort. Their contributions are known to all who read the literature of school finance. But historians generally seem to have forgotten or minimized the importance of others' contributions to the field. This apparent oversight may have been due to the unpopularity or lack of acceptance of their ideas at the time of their introduction.

Two school finance pioneers of the early part of this century whose contributions to the field were important but who have not always occupied their rightful positions in school finance history were Henry C. Morrison and Harlan Updegraff. Their theories, while not particularly popular in their own time, are relevant in today's finance reform movement with its emphasis on increased state support for education and district power equalization.

Henry C. Morrison emphasized that the methods of financing education in the early 1900s were unsatisfactory. Local school districts, by their organizational structure, were perpetuating unequal educational opportunities for the school children of each state. The allotment of state funds or grants to districts for special purposes was not bringing the kind or amount of equalization its advocates expected. Morrison favored a new and different approach to the problem. He theorized that if the state were one large district, it could not only equalize the tax burden but could also distribute the funds derived without complicated formulas such as were being used. Some of his main ideas—use of the income tax, full state funding, and considering the state as one large district—are much more acceptable today than they were in Morrison's own time. For example, several states now use the income tax to relieve the unfair and regressive property tax from some of its traditional burdens, and Hawaii has become a one-district state under many of the conditions Morrison advocated.

The unpopularity of Morrison's view resulted from his lack of support of a philosophy of local control of education and his willingness to replace "popular" property taxes with "unpopular" income taxes. Changes in two conditions have brought a degree of popularity to Morrison's ideas: (1) local control has lost some of its traditional glamor; and (2) the property tax—even though still necessary at the local level—has sunk to the bottom of desirability as a major source of school revenue.

Harlan Updegraff in 1922 developed a formula that would combine equalization and reward for effort without the objectionable features of the Cubberley plan. This was simply allowing the state to provide funds for program improvement (as well as for equalization), with each local district free to determine what the improvement program should be. (Updegraff's work in New York preceded the work of Strayer-Haig, but his contribution to the philosophy of school finance is more related to this period than to that of Cubberley.)

As indicated elsewhere in this text, the states have moved somewhat blindly from one form of state and local financing of education to another. The foundation program was accepted as the best method of leveling the inequalities that seemed to persist among the districts within every state. But even the foundation program has not proved to be a panacea. The high costs of compensatory education, the financial problems that result from municipal overburden, the unfairness among districts that varying policies and degrees of property underassessment create, and the inability of poor districts to go very much beyond the minimum program are evidence of the need for improving the minimum, or foundation, program concept in its current form.

Period Five: Emerging Power Equalization

The foundation program concept was an improvement over the older methods of distributing state funds to local school districts. In spite of that, however, school districts of differing financial capacities continue to have unequal abilities to exceed the foundation program. Thus, in the less wealthy districts the foundation program has been not only a "minimum" but also a near "maximum" program, for tax levies above the foundation, or base, without state help remit such small amounts of revenue that they discourage local effort to exceed the base program.

The predominant theme in school finance practice for the first half of this century was "equalization of educational opportunity." The wealth of the state was to be taxed to educate all the children of the state regardless of where they lived or the tax-paying ability of their parents or their school district. Various devices and formulas have been tried and notable improvements made. Equalization meant that the state and local districts were exercising a degree of partnership in establishing and paying for a basic program of education for every school-age child in the state.

In the midpart of this century, Paul Mort and others advocated a new concept of equalization—a "new look" in incentive financing. Their proposal guarantees a foundation program at state and local expense for all districts and also encourages local initiative for a better educational program by continuing to maintain a high degree of state-local partnership for whatever level above the foundation program the local district cares to go. Wisconsin used a variation of this concept between 1949 and 1969. Rhode Island, Alaska, New York, Maryland, and a few other states initiated similar plans in the 1970s and 1980s.

This open-end (shared cost or power) equalization plan for state and local financing of education is not really a new idea; in the early 1920s, Updegraff proposed such a plan, but it was too far ahead of the financial practices of the time. Its increasing favor and limited adoption have resulted from wider acceptance of state financial responsibility for education. It tends to be more acceptable in states that supply a high percentage of the total public education at state expense. In those states that exert only a minimum effort to finance education, the plan is ahead of their financial philosophy and therefore acceptance has been slow.

In its simplest terms, the open-end, or shared-cost, equalization plan proposes that a foundation program be established, with determination of the percentage of this program to be paid by each individual district and by the state. This percentage of state funds would be high for poor districts and low for wealthier ones. Once that determination has been made for each district, the same partnership ratio would be maintained to pay the total cost of the school program in each district. Each local board of education would still determine the levy to be made, thus preserving local control of education. There would be many variations and applications of this basic principle, but the fundamental premise of the program remains the same: state partnership throughout the complete finance program and thus a guarantee of a sound educational program for every district within the borders of every state.

Running through the educational finance philosophy of the last half-century, but almost submerged and forgotten until recently, is this far-reaching policy, first enunciated by Harlan Updegraff, of an equalized matching formula that would combine equalization and reward for effort. In contrast to Cubberley, Updegraff would have the state help to provide the finances for improved programs but leave the expenditure decisions to the local school boards. Under the guidance and initiative of Paul Mort, this principle has been activated in a few of the states, but its use is not yet widespread.

DISTRICT POWER EQUALIZATION

In the development of school finance theory, various terms have been used to describe what has become known as district power equalization. Equalized percentage matching and open-end equalization are being used in this text synonymously with district power equalization in referring to this form of reward for effort incentive for school districts. Perhaps the term *power* is more appropriate than any of the others, because the principle literally provides a poor school district with the power to obtain as much revenue per student as more wealthy districts making the same local tax effort.

Burke summarizes the philosophy concerning extension and improvement of the foundation program concept in the following:

> Some new possibilities have been seen by some in the reward-for-effort theory as first developed by Harlan Updegraff in 1919 and as applied in Wisconsin in 1949 and Rhode Island since 1960, and as proposed in a number of other states such as New York. Under these plans, a given unit of tax effort in a locality with low fiscal ability is made to produce the same number of dollars of revenue per pupil as would result from the same effort in a district with average or above-average fiscal capacity. Thus, the level of the state-

supported equalization program rises with local tax effort in the ready and willing local units and with the success of the state and/or local leadership in overcoming nonfiscal limitations in others.[8]

Some states require state equalization at the same rate for the entire educational program as is determined in the foundation program. The local district determines the limits of the local effort, and the state maintains financial responsibility for the entire program. This open-end equalization program is often referred to as equalized percentage matching (EPM). It is sometimes viewed as a means of opening a state's financial coffers to every local district. It is extremely effective in obliterating financial advantages for one district over another in providing for high-quality education rather than simply a minimum or foundation program.

Table 6-1 is a simplified example of how a district power equalization program might work. In this example, four mythical districts of widely varying assessments of property per pupil to be educated are compared in the calculation of a foundation program with an expenditure of $1,600 per weighted-pupil unit (WPU) and a required local levy of 20 mills. The local and state revenues are then determined, and the ratio of local revenue to state revenue is calculated for each district. In District A (the wealthiest one) the local revenue is one and two-thirds times as great as the state revenue; in District D (the poorest one) the required state revenue is fifteen times as high as the local amount.

If the Strayer-Haig concept of equalization were to be followed, each district would then be on its own to go above the foundation program. Herein lies an obvious weakness, for District A is able to raise $50/WPU for each mill of tax, whereas District D would raise only $5/WPU. In a power equalization program, the state is required to continue its degree of partnership for the full program. Thus, if a $2,000/WPU expenditure is considered an arbitrarily established optimum, the state would contribute $750/WPU to District A (assuming a 25-mill levy

TABLE 6-1   An Example of District Power Equalization

District	Assessed value/ student	Tax levy	Guaranteed amount/WPU	Local revenue	State revenue	Local-state ratio
A	$50,000	0.020	$1,600	$1,000	$ 600	5:3
B	40,000	.020	1,600	800	800	1:1
C	10,000	.020	1,600	200	1,400	1:7
D	5,000	.020	1,600	100	1,500	1:15
					Foundation program	
A	$50,000	0.025	$2,000	$1,250	$ 750	5:3
B	40,000	.025	2,000	1,000	1,000	1:1
C	10,000	.025	2,000	250	1,750	1:7
D	5,000	.025	2,000	125	1,875	1:15
					Optimum program	

as in the table) and $1,875/WPU to District D. By this process, financially weak districts are able to offer as good a program as wealthier ones.

At first glance it may seem that this creates a standard program for every district within a state. Such is not the case, however, for each local district would have the right and the responsibility to determine what the local tax rate would be over and above the mandated foundation program levy. In this way local control is assured and state partnership responsibility mandated.

The EPM concept was given strong support by the decisions in court cases of the 1970s, beginning with *Serrano v. Priest* (1971).[9] It lost support, however, with the Supreme Court's reversal of *San Antonio Independent School District* v. *Rodriguez* (1973)[10] when the principle of equalized percentage matching was not required in Texas and, by inference, in other states, depending on state constitutions. The majority opinion of the court stated that education was not a federal constitutional right; the responsibility for education should be left to lawmakers at the state level, through the democratic processes that elect them. However, the ruling does not disallow the equalized percentage matching concept. It is still valid, even if not required. Justice Powell, in speaking for the court, called upon the states to develop a concept such as EPM when he stated that the Court did not place a judicial imprimatur on the status quo and that the need for tax reform was evident.

The movement has received renewed impetus in the 1990s through litigation in several states, once again in Texas (*Edgewood Independent School District* v. *Kirby*),[11] and in Kentucky (*Rose v. Council for Better Education*).[12] Connelly notes the need for an efficient, adequate and equitable financing of education based on those decisions:

> [T]he *Rose* and *Edgewood* decisions may be critical to the design and implementation of efficient, equitable, and adequate state financing schemes in many states. Certainly both cases have called attention to the affirmative duty imposed on state legislatures to provide an efficient system of public free schools where states have chosen to make education a fundamental right. This calls for adequacy of funding and uniformity in the delivery of educational opportunities to children from rich and poor districts alike. A child should not fall victim to his place of residence.[13]

Equalized percentage matching may be a solution.

Opponents of the EPM principle of power equalization fear that it will deplete already overburdened state treasuries. This reasoning remains the chief deterrent to adoption of this principle in state school financing, but studies and experience point up the obvious merits of the EPM approach. Local control of the educational program rests with each individual school board, but the state cannot escape its proportionate financial responsibility. Districts are encouraged to make adequate tax effort, for if they spend less they lose more. Complete equalization is achieved in spending as well as in tax effort. Since there is no ceiling in tax effort, the inequalities encountered between wealthy and poor districts, which are so obvious in a typical foundation program are lessened or disappear. The only restriction to an adequately financed program thus becomes the willingness or unwillingness of the people at the local level to tax themselves within reasonable tax limits. With the state matching the local district on a predetermined basis in terms of local ability, the previously unrealistic tax requirements for a high-quality education program in a poor district are reduced greatly or even eliminated.

It would be difficult to conceive of many valid arguments against the shared-cost philosophy. The principal deterrents to early acceptance of some form of this simple financial plan are apathy, traditional acceptance of archaic plans of school finance, lack of state leadership in the much needed improvement of property tax administration (especially in assessment practices), too many kinds and numbers of school districts with differences in taxing and spending powers, and widespread realization that such a program may liberalize the financing program in a great many of the school districts in this country. However, a significant step forward is long overdue in most states, and progress appears to be imminent.

THE VARYING STATE ROLE

Cubberley's emphasis on incentive grants for special purposes, with less stress on equalization, was a reasonably satisfactory approach to state school finance policy during the early part of this century. The states were using state property taxes to obtain revenue to be distributed to local school districts. Cubberley advocated state incentive grants to promote specific improvements, with less emphasis on equalization needs.

During the 1920s, the states generally gave up their state property taxes and placed almost complete responsibility on the local districts and the counties for administering the property tax. Equalization became a necessity to get state funds for financially weak school districts. Strayer, Haig, Mort, and their colleagues began to emphasize the foundation program and to minimize incentive grants.

During this period of change, the states found it imperative to modify somewhat their finance laws and practices to help solve the problems created by leaving all property tax responsibility with the local districts. Some of the main problems were (1) the need to provide the best possible equalization program to make equal educational opportunity available to all—even in the financially weak school districts created by this change in taxing procedure; (2) the need to provide fiscal independence for all school districts, in an effort to give school boards budgetary power and authority commensurate with their educational responsibility; (3) the need to provide assistance to local districts in their administration of the local property tax, in which they sought equality in assessing practices, efficiency in tax collection procedures, and other improvements; (4) the need to expand the tax base and provide some property tax relief by using nonproperty taxes where practicable; and (5) the need to give local districts greater autonomy in administering the property tax by reducing or eliminating state-imposed restrictions on levies—a carryover from the Depression years.

Much progress has been made in solving these problems, but the finance laws and the state-local partnership are far less acceptable than they might be. Sound financial theories are far ahead of the practices of most states, including those that have been leaders in experimenting with new programs. Present conditions—such as inadequate local revenues and municipal overburden—in many beleaguered school districts dictate the need for increasing and improving the role of the state in financing education. The state must increase its partnership responsibility, preferably by continuing its support through the full educational program in every district on an equalization basis. Although many people think of this as a new and radical idea, the experience of the last fifty years validates it as a sound approach to the perennial financial problems facing the public schools of this country.

Describing the complex school finance systems of the states is an exhaustive process. There are as many finance programs as there are states. However, some commonality exists in a type of basic or foundation program, a relationship between state and local contributions and a design for categorical programs. Changes occur frequently as legislatures meet and courts influence interpretations of various state constitutions. Following are brief descriptions of five state finance programs that will give the reader a sense of the diversity in plans.

California

The California school finance law has been greatly influenced by the *Serrano* v. *Priest* case (1971) which was finally "declared closed in the spring of 1989."[14] Funds for school districts are based on average daily attendance (ADA) of students and feature designated revenue limits, categorical aid, lotteries, and "extras which depend on local circumstances."[15] There is a minimum funding level guarantee for all children attending school in the state. The California constitution mandates that schools are free, and students must attend from age six to eighteen or until they receive a diploma or equivalent. Over 60 percent of public education is supported by state revenues, mostly generated from sales and income taxes. Twenty percent comes from local property tax, 3.5 percent from lotteries, 7.5 percent from federal sources, and some funds come from miscellaneous local sources such as food sales, money for debt repayment, and interest. The state guarantees support that is the "*greater* of the previous year's amount per student adjusted for inflation and growth *or* the percent of the states General Fund allocated to education in 1986–87."[16] There are voted leeway and bond election options.

Sixty percent of the total school money in California is for general purposes and forty percent is for categorical aid. Each district has a revenue limit per student. ADA multiplied by the district's revenue per ADA equals its total revenue limit. In 1991, of the 1,012 districts, 44 received their revenue limit entirely from property taxes. These 44 districts can retain all their property tax revenue even if it exceeds their limit; thus recapture is not used. They also receive the "per-pupil basic aid" from the state. Categorical aid (the one-fourth) includes special education, preschool child care, desegregation, teacher's retirement, transportation, vocational education, adult education, nutrition, driver training, drug prevention, migrant, compensatory, gifted and talented, instructional materials, mentoring, reading, school improvements, and year-round incentives.[17]

Utah

The Constitution of the State of Utah indicates that "the legislature shall provide for the establishment and maintenance of a uniform system of public schools, which shall be open to all children of the State, and free from sectarian control."[18] In order to accomplish that mandate, the state operates a school finance foundation program which guarantees a certain basic level of expenditure for each student, with a minimum uniform local property tax rate that each district must levy. The minimum local property tax levy in fiscal 1993 was 21.375 mills which is converted to a rate with 1 mill equal to .0002 percent in the school finance formula. The state-guaranteed amount for fiscal 1993 was $1490.00 per weighted-pupil unit. Average daily membership (ADM) is used in the calculations. Pupils are weighted to reflect the costs associated with providing special services and used to allocate state aid under the foundation program. Therefore, the students in ADM including weighting factors multiplied by the state-guaranteed amount per WPU minus what the local property tax levy yields equals the amount of state aid each district will receive for the basic program. The educational responsibility of each student becomes a function of the total taxable wealth of the state and is not limited to the taxing ability of each local school district.

In 1992–93 three of the state's forty districts met the guarantee from the .02124 mills because local property assessed value was high in relation to the number of students to be educated. Utah recaptures funds from those three districts to help support the uniform school fund.

State aid is provided by income tax, which by constitutional fiat, is totally earmarked to the Uniform School Fund for the "schools established by the legislature."[19] Other sources of funds come from school land income, corporation franchise tax, mineral production and other minor sources. Additional support must be transferred from the general fund in which the state sales tax is the largest revenue source for the state.

Over 60 percent of the money spent for education in the state is for the regular school foundation program. Categorical programs use the remainder for social security and retirement payments for educators; special purpose programs such as productivity studies, transportation, insurance, career ladders, year-round schools, outcome-based education, technology, regional service centers, and small schools; handicapped programs; youth in custody; vocational and technical education; adult and driver education.

Iowa

The 1989 Iowa legislature enacted a new school finance law that sunsets July 1, 2001. The new law provides for a student-driven formula. Students are counted on the third Friday of September. Weighting factors (WPU) are used. The enrollment of one year is used in the subsequent year. For example, the student count on the third Friday of September 1993 will be used to determine the 1994–95 budget. If significant enrollment shifts occur, the state can adjust the budget to meet exigencies.

The 1992–93 state cost per pupil was $3,336.00. Supplementary weightings for special education, pupil sharing, teacher sharing, whole grade sharing, shared administration, advanced algebra and above, chemistry, advanced chemistry, physics, advanced physics, and second year and above foreign language are used. Local districts must levy a uniform tax of $5.40 per $1,000 assessed valuation. The state provides the difference between 83 percent of the state cost per pupil and what the uniform levy generates. These state funds come from state income of sales tax.[20] The local district is required to levy an additional property tax to make up any remaining funds that are necessary to meet the approved budget.

Categorical aid is available for transportation assistance; removal, management, or abatement of environmental hazards; dropout prevention; gifted and talented program; programs for non-English speakers; at-risk students; early childhood education; educational excellence; and instructional support. Enrichment levies can be utilized for instructional support, physical plant and equipment, adult service, and management.

Connecticut

The state goal for Connecticut is to provide excellence and equity in public school programs. [21] The State Board of Education, under Section 10-4 of the Connecticut General Statutes, is charged with:

> "general supervision and control of the educational interests of the state, which interests shall include preschool, elementary and secondary education, special education, vocational education and adult education; shall provide leadership and otherwise promote the improvement of education in the state. . . ." This charge includes implementing the Connecticut General Statutes and federal legislation relating to education. The State Board of Education has direct responsibility for the Department of Education, the Regional Vocational-Technical Schools, and the state's vocational rehabilitation services. [22]

This proviso of funding education is met through a cost-sharing method. In fiscal 1992, the state provided 40.3 percent of public education funding; the local share was 55.5 percent. The trend in the previous five years was for more state funding, going from 31 percent to its current level and the local funding dropped from 60 percent to its current level.

Equalization is a goal for Connecticut in its Education Cost Sharing Program, which is designed to provide funds for education to equalize programs and reduce disparities in per-pupil expenditures. Tax rates are targeted for equalization as well. Funds are to be distributed in accordance with an equalizing formula establishing a minimum spending level in each town.

Categorical support is used for health services, school buildings, service centers, interdistrict programs, teacher standards, professional development and training for teachers, adult education, compensatory education, bilingual education, drug education, summer school, and early childhood programs.

Louisiana

The salient feature of the Louisiana public education finance system is the Minimum Foundation Program (MFP). Its goal is to ensure a basic minimum education program for all its public elementary and secondary schools. The cost of the basic MFP in Louisiana is based on two major components: (1) the regular education program and (2) the special education program. The costs of these two programs are summed to obtain the total MFP cost for each school district. The amount of local funds generated from a state-mandated uniform levy of 5.5 mills is subtracted from the cost of each district's total MFP. The difference between the total MFP cost and the local funds represents the state's obligation, referred to as "the necessary funds to equalize" in each district. The MFP formula does not include measures for local fiscal capacity or consider local tax effort. The formula provides statewide minimum salaries for allotted school positions and incorporates state aid to school districts for programs such as a sabbatical leave provision with pay for teachers, a minimum salary schedule for school bus drivers, and a retirement plan for school lunch employees.

In Louisiana the respective contributions made by all three governmental levels in the support of education remains relatively stable. The state provided approximately 53 to 55 percent of the total revenue for the public schools throughout the 1980s, whereas local governments generated 34 to 37 percent of the funds, and the federal government contributed 10 to 12 percent. The average expenditure per pupil in average daily attendance was $3,500. The state's share of revenues for its public schools during the 1980s was derived primarily from taxes on mineral resources. By the late 1980s, however, retail sales taxes surpassed severance taxes as the primary source of state tax revenue.

School districts in Louisiana have considerable leeway to raise local revenues to supplement the state's contribution. The flexibility afforded school districts in raising local revenues from the property tax and the sales tax serves to increase interdistrict differences in local revenues. As in most states, there is considerable variation among school districts in Louisiana in fiscal capacity or "ability" to finance schools. [23]

TABLE 6-2 Percent of State Budgets Spent on Education; Expenditure per Pupil by State

	State	% of budget	Expenditure per pupil
1	Utah	42.7	2,733
2	Indiana	42.1	4,126[a]
3	Arkansas	42.0	3,272
4	North Carolina	41.9	4,386
5	Vermont	41.5	5,418[a]
6	South Carolina	40.8	3,731
7	Iowa	40.4	4,590
8	Texas	40.0	4,056
9	Wisconsin	39.5	5,703
10	Nebraska	39.0	3,874[a]
11	Missouri	38.8	4,226
12	Kansas	38.6	4,706
13	Alabama	38.5	3,314
14	Virginia	38.5	5,000
15	Montana	38.2	4,147
16	West Virginia	38.2	4,146
17	Michigan	38.1	5,073
18	North Dakota	38.0	3,581[a]
19	Oregon	38.0	5,085
20	Washington	38.0	4,638
21	Arizona	37.8	3,853
22	Oklahoma	37.7	3,484
23	Mississippi	37.5	3,151
24	Wyoming	37.3	5,281
25	Delaware	37.0	5,848
26	Colorado	36.9	4,580[a]
27	Idaho	36.8	3,037[a]
28	New Mexico	36.8	4,180
29	New Hampshire	36.5	5,149
30	Ohio	36.4	4,394
31	Pennsylvania	35.9	5,670
32	South Dakota	35.4	3,312
33	Kentucky	35.4	3,824
34	Georgia	35.1	4,456[a]
35	Maine	35.1	5,577
36	Illinois	33.9	4,853
37	Maryland	33.8	5,887
38	Minnesota	33.8	5,114
39	Tennessee	33.1	3,503
40	New Jersey	32.8	8,439
41	Rhode Island	32.2	6,523[a]
42	Florida	31.7	5,051
43	California	31.1	4,598
44	Connecticut	31.1	7,934
45	Louisiana	30.4	3,457[a]
46	Nevada	29.6	4,387[a]
47	New York	28.9	8,094
48	Massachusetts	28.1	6,170
49	Hawaii	27.1	4,504
50	Alaska	22.8	7,252[a]
51	District of Columbia	16.9	7,407

Source: Percent of state budgets—*Digest of Education Statistics, 1990,* U.S. Department of Education; Estimated expenditures per pupil—*Rankings of the States, 1990,* National Education Association, Research Division.
[a]Data estimated by NEA.

The budgets of the various states are influenced greatly by the number of students to be educated and the revenue available. Figures in Table 6-2 show the relationship between the percent of the state budget spent on education and the amount of revenue generated on a per pupil basis. The percent of the state budgets spent on education varies from 42.7 percent in Utah to 22.8 percent in Alaska. The expenditures per pupil range from $2,733 in Utah to $8,439 in New Jersey.

The slow development of state support for education has not necessarily been a result of continuous lack of interest on the part of the people involved. Much of the indecision has come from a lack of knowledge of the solution of school finance problems. Passage of time has increased the acuteness and difficulty of these problems, but it has also provided some answers. The principles and the theories to mold a justifiable state-local relationship in financing education have been developed and proven; they should now be utilized.

PURPOSES OF STATE FINANCIAL SUPPORT

While people in general favor additional state financial support for education, few would like to see greater state control with attendant elimination of local responsibility in the matter. What then are the main purposes of state support? Several have been emphasized and have had their advocates; few are controversial. The following are some of the most important of these:

1. Providing state support to promote local school improvements was championed by Cubberley. It is particularly important to have state support for local educational programs that are too expensive for the weaker school districts to finance.

2. State funds are needed to equalize educational opportunity for all children of the state. Strayer, Haig, and Mort stressed the need for state-supported foundation programs for this purpose.

3. State support is required to provide incentives for greater local tax effort. Mort's work in Rhode Island and New York, conceived around the Updegraff equalized matching formula concept that combined equalization and reward for effort, illustrates the practical result of this form of state financial support.

4. State support broadens the tax base of school support. To the local property tax revenues, the state adds funds that have been collected from many kinds of nonproperty taxes. Thus, the burden to property taxpayers for educational services is made lighter, and more elements of the private sector are involved in financing education.

FEDERAL FUNDS AND STATE SUPPORT OF EDUCATION

It is generally agreed that state funds should not be used to reduce local tax effort, except in instances of obvious overburden. Likewise, federal funds should not be used to replace state funds for education. The costs and the administrative responsibility for education should rest as near as possible to the people receiving educational services. State support is provided when reasonable local taxes produce inadequate revenue, and federal support is defensible only when local and state revenues resulting from reasonable effort are insufficient for an excellent school program throughout the state. Also, if a specific national need is determined, then a national program should be funded to solve that need, such as the G.I. Bill after World War II and the National Defense Education Act after the launching of Sputnik.

Most states, especially those that have provided only small general-purpose grants to local districts and those that provided only a small percentage of education costs from state sources, ignored PL 874 (federal aid for federally impacted areas) in determining fund allocations to public schools. That is as it should be, for federal funds should not decrease state funds. However, some other states—particularly those that have provided a high percentage of the total amounts that their local districts used—have reduced their allocations of state monies to those local districts receiving PL 874 funds. Various processes have been used to make such an adjustment, but it has usually been by some percentage of the amount of federal funds that local districts received under this program. This was a source of great controversy until the federal government made it illegal for a state to receive credit for federal funds under this program by any reduction in the amount of state funds to be allocated to any district. The concept holds true with present federal aid regulations which require that funds must "supplement" not "supplant" local or state funding.

STATE ABILITY TO SUPPORT EDUCATION

Measurement of a state's ability to support education is difficult. Local districts must confine their main tax effort to the property tax, but the states have no such limitations. Sales taxes, income taxes, and many others are available for state use, thereby complicating the problem of measuring and comparing total tax effort and ability.

The ability of the states to support education varies greatly, regardless of the criteria or devices used in its measurement. Here again, as with measurement of local ability, the question arises as to whether tax-paying ability should be measured in terms of potential revenues from all sources, many of which are not legally authorized, or in terms of the tax system that is authorized and operable. Does a state have the ability to produce any given amount of school revenue from a state sales tax if such a tax is not being used? Another unanswered question is related to the relative economic effects of varying forms and kinds of taxation. For example, what property tax rate is equivalent to a 6 percent sales and use tax?

Some old ways of measuring state taxing ability have outworn their usefulness. An example is the use of per capita wealth as measured by the assessed or the real value of taxable property within the state. The deemphasis or complete elimination of the state property tax and the introduction of sales and state income taxes have resulted in the demise of this method of comparing the abilities of states to finance education.

The most common method now used to compare the financial ability of states to support education seems to require the inclusion of income. The close relationship between some state income tax systems and the federal income tax program makes determination of total income relatively easy. Relating the total personal income to the total population does not consider the disparity among the states in the ratio of school-age children to total population. Using the average daily membership or average daily attendance of pupils in public schools does not consider the wide variation among the states in the numbers of pupils attending private or parochial schools. Some authorities in the field support the seemingly justifiable method of using total personal income minus total federal income taxes paid by the people of a state divided by the total number of children of school age as the best method of measuring state ability to pay for education. Still others advocate complex combinations of data and mathematical formulas, which are difficult to determine but which, once obtained, lend some validity to such methods of comparing the ability of states to finance education.

Since the ability of the fifty states to support education naturally varies, and since each spends a different amount per child being educated, it follows that their taxing efforts also vary. Those less wealthy states whose citizens choose to have good educational programs must necessarily make a greater effort than their more fortunate counterparts in more wealthy states. *Effort* is an elusive term, requiring complicated means of measurement. The important point is that real differences continue to exist among the states in their ability to finance education.

SUMMARY

Early settlers apparently recognized the importance of education to the future of the United States, but they left the various states with the responsibility for its implementation and development. Education was not referred to specifically in the United States Constitution; interpretation of the Tenth Amendment delegated that responsibility to the individual states. Each state in the Union has interpreted its responsibility differently. Hence, there is no single public school system, but rather fifty distinct systems.

The states have developed their school finance systems largely by trial and error, with considerable difficulty and sacrifice. Public schools were originally financed largely by land grants, fees, tuition charges, and other nontax funds; as schools became more numerous, property taxes were introduced as a source of local revenue.

The Northwest Ordinance of 1787 and later land grants did much to help the states develop public education. At first, local districts financed education with little or no state assistance, and there were vast differences in district ability to provide quality education programs. By the early part of the twentieth century the states were making grants to local districts, for the most part based on the philosophy of Ellwood Cubberley. A quarter of a century later the equalization principles of George D. Strayer and Robert M. Haig were being applied to school finance systems. Paul Mort and others did much to improve the equalization concept during the middle years of the century. Currently, stress is placed on district power equalization, greater state funding, and educational reform.

There is great variety among the states in the methods used to allocate funds to local disticts. Describing the finance system of the 50 states is complex. Some commonalities include a basic or foundation program, a relationship between state and local contributions, and utilization of the categorical funding method. The trend is toward greater state responsibility for financing public education in all states, resulting in greater state control and an erosion of the power and authority of local school boards.

ASSIGNMENT PROJECTS

1. Trace the development of the school finance program in your state through the various stages, as outlined in the text. Indicate areas or aspects of the program that may still be in some of the earlier stages, such as state grants per pupil or other nonequalizing grants.
2. Develop your own classification or history of school finance. Indicate what you consider to be the most desirable school finance system that could be established.
3. Develop arguments for and against full state funding of education.
4. Propose a program of district power equalization that you think would be desirable for your state.
5. Relate state financing of education with state control. Is it possible to have local control of education with complete state financing? Justify your answer.

SELECTED READINGS

Cohn, Elchanan. *The Economics of Education.* rev. ed. Cambridge, Mass.: Ballinger, 1979.

Fuhrman, Susan, and Alan Rosenthal, eds. *Shaping Education Policy in the States.* Washington, D.C.: Institute for Educational Leadership, 1981.

Grubb, W. Norton, and Stephan Michelson. *States and Schools.* Lexington, Mass.: Lexington Books (D. C. Heath), 1974.

Guthrie, James W., Walter I. Garms, and Lawrence C. Pierce. *School Finance and Education Policy: Enhancing Educational Efficiency, Equality, and Choice.* 2nd ed. Englewood Cliffs, N. J.: Prentice Hall, 1988.

Honeyman, D. S., D. C. Thompson, and R. C. Wood. *Financing Rural and Small Schools: Issues of Adequacy and Equity.* Gainesville: University of Florida Press, 1989.

Johns, Roe L., Edgar L. Morphet, and Kern Alexander. *Economics and Financing of Education.* 4th ed. Englewood Cliffs, N.J.: Prentice Hall, 1983.

Jordan, K. Forbis, and Nelda H. Cambron-McCabe. *Perspectives in State School Support Programs. Second Annual Yearbook of the American Education Finance Association.* Cambridge, Mass.: Ballinger, 1981.

McDonnell, Lorraine, and Milbrey Wallin McLaughlin. *Education Policy and the Role of the States.* Santa Monica, Calif.: Rand Corp., 1981.

Mort, Paul R. *State Support for Public Education.* Washington, D.C.: American Council on Education, 1933.

Odden, Allan, and L. Dean Webb. *School Finance and School Improvement Linkages for the 1980s. Fourth Annual Yearbook of the American Education Finance Association.* Cambridge, Mass.: Ballinger, 1983.

ENDNOTES

1. Lee M. Thurston and William H. Roe, *State School Administration* (New York: Harper & Row, 1957), pp. 137–38.

2. Ibid., p. 11.

3. *State Aid to Local Government* (Washington, D.C.: Advisory Commission on Intergovernmental Relations, April 1969), p. 40.

4. Ellwood P. Cubberley, *School Funds and Their Apportionment* (New York: Teachers College, Columbia University, 1906), p. 17.

5. *State Aid to Local Government,* p. 40.

6. Paul R. Mort, as quoted by Erick L. Lindman in *Long-Range Planning in School Finance* (Washington, D.C.: National Education Association Committee on Educational Finance, 1963), pp. 38-39.

7. *State Aid to Local Government,* p. 40.

8. Arvid J. Burke, "Financing of Elementary and Secondary Schools," in Warren E. Gauerke and Jack A. Childress, eds., *Theory and Practice of School Finance* (Chicago: Rand McNally, 1967), p. 127.

9. *Serrano v. Priest,* 96 Cal. Rptr. 601, 487 P.2d 1241 (Calif. 1971).

10. *San Antonio Independent School District* v. *Rodriguez,* 411 U.S. 1, 93 S. Ct. 1278 (1973), rehearing denied.

11. *Edgewood Independent School District* v. *Kirby,* 777 S.W. 2d 391 (Texas 1989).

12. *Rose* v. *Council for Better Education,* 790 S.W. 2d 186 (Ky. 1989).

13. Mary Jane Connelly, "Recent Developments in School Finance Litigation: The Kentucky and Texas Cases," *Educational Considerations,* Vol. 17, No. 2, Spring 1990, p. 25.

14. *California K-12 School Finance System,* *EdSource,* (Menlo Park, Calif.: California Department of Education; Fiscal Policy Planning and Analysis Division, 1991), p. 6.

15. Ibid., p. 7.

16. Ibid., p. 3 (emphasis added).

17. Ibid., pp. 1–8.

18. Article X, Section I, Utah Constitution.

19. Ibid.

20. Summary of Iowa's New School Finance Law (Chapter 257), p. 5.

21. Budget Brief 1991–1992, Connecticut State Board of Education, p. 1.

22. Ibid.

23. Terry G. Geske and Barbara La Cont, "An Examination of Fiscal Neutrality in Louisiana Using Alternative Measures of School District Wealth," *Educational Considerations,* Vol. 17, No. 2, Spring 1990, pp. 31–37.

Chapter 7

Federal Interest in Education

A clear federal commitment to meeting the special educational needs of America's children is encouraging as we confront the tasks facing our education system in the final decade of the 20th century.
—MARY JEAN LE TENDRE, 1991

The history of education during the twentieth century was one of almost continuous controversy over the question of the federal government's role in financing education. Certainly, there have been few domestic political issues that have generated more discussion and more indecisive debates about who should pay the costs of education than this one. In spite of federal legislation such as the National Education Defense Act of 1958, the Elementary and Secondary Education Act of 1965, and the Education Consolidation and Improvement Act of 1981, the question of the rightful place of the federal government in education still has racial, religious, and political overtones. The issue continues to divide citizens on emotional and philosophical grounds. Unfortunately, as the twenty-first century approaches, the determination of ideal federal-state-local relations in financing education has not yet been made.

HISTORICAL ROLE OF THE FEDERAL GOVERNMENT

Historically, the federal role in education has been minor; its function was to conduct research, disseminate information, and provide advisory assistance to the other two levels of government—to exercise interest in education without direct responsibility or control. At various times, however, the federal government has provided some financial support for education, usually eschewing extensive federal controls in the process. In its forays into providing financial assistance, the government has appeared to sense that inadequate or poor education is a result of inadequate financing. For the most part, it has attempted to

191

assist low-ability states more than higher-ability states, leaving decision making and administrative controls with the individual states.

The legal relation of the federal government to education is largely indirect. Federal courts rule on alleged violations of constitutional rights by the states and their local school districts. However, the impact of such federal court decisions upon education, even though indirect, has been of great consequence and will continue to be so. The nationwide effect of the Supreme Court's desegregation ruling in *Brown* v. *Board of Education* (1954),[1] as well as the impact of Title IX of the Education Amendments of 1972 (sex discrimination), Section 504 of the Rehabilitation Act of 1973 (discrimination against the handicapped), and court cases at various levels are excellent examples of how indirect controls may strongly influence schools and their organizational and administrative operations.

Constitutional Role

The Constitution of the United States provides indirectly for the federal government to exercise a minor role in the three-way partnership of government responsibility for education. The Tenth Amendment has been interpreted as legal sanction for state responsibility for this important service of government. The framers of the Constitution viewed with fear the possibility of a nationally controlled school system. Their distrust of a strong central power was a break from the philosophy of government in the European countries. They feared concentration of power, whether it was political or religious. The colonists' main purpose in coming to America—political and religious freedom—seemed to be antithetical to strong centralization of power in a national unit of government.

Very early in the nation's history, the federal government began a policy of deference to the states in matters of education. Even before the Constitution was ratified, the government in power passed the Northwest Ordinance, which provided for land grants to new states to foster education. These grants provided some incentive for the settlement of western lands and was the first act of federal aid to education. As the colonies became states and relinquished their land claims, the newly formed federal government began to establish a policy for their disposition as gifts to the newly formed states to finance state-sponsored public education systems.

A Sound Partnership

Even the severe critics of education in the United States recognize that the state-local-federal partnership in education worked well for over a century. State constitutions and court decisions at all levels recognized and supported this relation. The public schools, recognized as one of the truly great contributions of this country to the world, were developed under the aegis of this partnership system. Their vitality and accomplishments attest to the validity of this relation.

Thus, for most of the duration of the republic, the constitutionally authorized advisory role of the federal government was accepted and followed, with only minor exceptions. The grass-roots level of school control that has been so vigorously defended seemed to be working well. The United States became a leader in many areas of science and culture; the schools played an important part in that achievement. Even the perennial problem of financing education was solved in most areas of the country with little or no involvement of the federal government.

To be sure, the federal government vacillated in its role. Periodic—even spasmodic—innovations and policy changes came and went without panic on the part of those who were dedicated to preventing change in the federal role. To a great degree, the occasional venture of the federal government into educational matters represented the philosophies of those in positions of power in the federal hierarchy rather than real changes in the educational philosophy of society in general.

In recent years, the generally accepted roles of the three levels of government in sponsoring and financing education have been in a state of flux. In particular, the role of the federal government has become more enigmatic; its relation to state and local government has been in an unprecedented state of confusion and controversy. To a great extent, the increasing role of specific national interests and of the federal government has come as a result of the accelerating disability of the other two levels to fulfill their traditional responsibilities in the educational structure.

Historically, the states and their local school districts have faced almost complete financial responsibility for education. Recently the problem has become too great for their inadequate taxing machinery. At the same time, the federal government has developed a powerful and responsive taxing system, although it has had only advisory obligation to the broad field of public education.

FEDERAL INVOLVEMENT—A FLUCTUATING ROLE

The role of the federal government in education during the twentieth century can best be described as fluid. When the United States entered World War I, the national government became actively involved in vocational education. It was determined to be necessary to meet the challenges of the war effort. The 1920s was a decade of minor involvement, except for efforts in Indian education for federally operated schools.

While the nation was in the depths of a depression in the 1930s, federal interest was accelerated to meet the demands facing an impoverished nation. During this period legislation established the Federal Surplus Commodities Corporation to distribute surplus food for student lunches. The National Youth Administration and the Civilian Conservation Corps were established to provide work and training for youth. The Public Works Administration made grants available and extended loans for school construction.

During World War II, the country was focused on funding the war effort, leaving few resources for educational programs. However, in 1943 the Vocational Rehabilitation Act was passed and in 1944 the G.I. Bill was passed for veterans to receive vocational and educational opportunities.

After the war there were efforts in Congress and with the president to provide general aid. Many proposals surfaced, but broad federal support could not be engendered. Issues such as no federal funds to segregated school and school districts, church-state ramifications and fear of federal control thwarted many funding efforts.

This changed with the launching of Sputnik by the Russians in 1957. There was great interest at the federal level to rally support for education. The National Defense Education Act (NDEA) was passed, which provided revenue for math, science, foreign language, media, and counseling services. A decade later, in 1965, the Elementary and Secondary Education Act (ESEA) was passed with the primary tenet (Title I) being to provide federal support for districts and schools in low-income areas, including pass-through provisions to private schools.

In 1972 and 1978 amendments that slightly modified the 1965 Act were passed, adding some programs and increasing allocations for education. Federal support shifted when Congress passed the Education Consolidation and Improvement Act (ECIA), which took effect in July 1982. The new program included a change from Title I to Chapter I, eliminated many categorical programs and replaced them with block grants to states. Under the legislation 20 percent of the allotment could remain at the state level and 80 percent would flow through to the local districts.

In 1980, recognition was given to education at the federal level with the establishment of the Department of Education. Two years later, the cabinet position was in jeopardy as a new administration proposed that it be disbanded. Many attribute the survival of the Department to the "A Nation at Risk" report developed under then Secretary of Education, Terrel H. Bell.

The renewed interest in education had its effect. Reports by members of the committee that wrote "A Nation at Risk" were given at eleven sites throughout the United States; it was made clear that most of the proposed reforms could be accomplished without additional funds. No such funds were promised by the federal government; it was stressed that the responsibility for reform rested with the states and local entities.

In 1988 the Hawkins-Stafford School Improvement Amendments were passed. These amendments are really a synthesis of federal interest in education, for they repeal and change numerous laws and programs. The Education Consolidation and Improvement Act was repealed. Chapter I (formerly Title I of the Elementary and Secondary Act of 1965), Chapter II, magnet school programs, science and math teacher training, foreign language programs, and impact aid were all substantially amended. The Amendments created a program for gifted and talented students, a high school basic skills program, a dropout prevention program, a program to educate disadvantaged preschoolers and their illiterate parents together, a program for effective schools, a fund for innovative programs, and another fund for teachers to solve education problems. All of these elements for simplicity's sake are called the Hawkins-Stafford Amendments. Le Tendre states:

> These amendments represent a major step at the federal level to bring the benefits of the education reform movement of the 1980s to our nation's disadvantaged students.[2]

DECREASE IN FEDERAL EXPENDITURES

A look at recent federal budgets indicates that, although the dollar amounts remain constant, the percentage of the federal budget allocated to education, employment, and training decreased.

In 1985 Congress passed the Gramm-Rudman-Hollings Balanced Budget and Emergency Deficit Control Act (Gramm-Rudman Act), aimed at balancing the federal budget. The debt in 1980 was less than a trillion dollars, and when the decade ended, it was in excess of three trillion—a three-fold increase. The largest expenditures were to manage the debt, direct payment to individuals (primarily social security benefits), and defense. Many individuals and groups who believed the Gramm-Rudman Act unconstitutional challenged the act in court in 1986. The Supreme Court ruled one section of the law unconstitutional but upheld the rest of the act. The unconstitutional section provided for the comptroller general to decide on budget cuts if the president and Congress were unable to agree on the cuts. The Court ruled that the comptroller general's involvement would infringe on the constitutional power of the executive branch, violating the principle of separation of powers. The Court said:

> Since the powers conferred upon the Comptroller General as part of the automatic-reduction process are executive powers, which cannot be constitutionally exercised by an officer removable by Congress, those powers cannot be exercised and therefore the automatic deficit reduction process cannot be implemented.[3]

The Court did not strike down the statute itself, nor the mandated deficit targets. Members from the administration and the Congress stated that even though that one provision was struck down, the law will still be enforced, and the president and Congress will work to make the law effective by making the cuts.[4]

During the 1980s, funding for the Department of Education declined as a percent of the total budget, from 2.5 percent to an estimated 1.8 percent. The proportion of the education department's outlays for human resource programs fell from nearly 5 percent of the total outlays to an estimated 3.9 percent. The federal share of total expenditures for elementary and secondary education programs also declined over the last eight years, from 8.7 percent to 6.2 percent.[5]

One can only conclude that the decade was a time of relentless "chipping away" of federal aid to education.[6] No one can predict what the federal role will become in the 1990s and the twenty-first century, but everyone knows that a new pattern will develop—not systematically, perhaps, but inevitably.

LIMITED FEDERAL AID: A REALITY

The first federal aid for education, the Northwest Ordinances, are older than the United States Constitution, and various forms of categorical aid have appeared at an accelerating pace since World War II. As conscientiously as one may search for valid opposing arguments, or as boldly as one may decry federal involvement in educational matters, the die is cast. No longer is the debate whether or not the federal government can be involved as a partner in funding education. The questions are: (1) what percentage of the total education budget should the federal government assume? (2) Should the process of funding be through block grants, categorical aid, or general aid?

Some of the most vociferous critics of federal programs permit their children to participate in school lunch programs, attend agricultural colleges, pursue vocational education, and participate in many other federally subsidized programs. The most radical critic of federal assistance to education can find little to condemn in the tremendously important land grants or in the G.I. Bill, which provided federal funds for the education of war veterans. Both of these programs were significant federal contributions to education. On the other hand, the most ardent advocate of federal aid can point to some programs that seem to have gone beyond generally acceptable limits in federal usurpation of control or domination of responsibility for education.

Various classifications have been used to differentiate the many programs of federal aid, depending on their purpose or their supporting rationale. Reference is often made to such common and understandable divisions of assistance as *general-purpose, categorical, block grants,* and *emergency aid* for certain groups of citizens for whom the government assumes responsibility.

The American Association of School Administrators described the following five kinds of federal aid: (1) aid to promote the cause of education; (2) aid to broaden the scope of education; (3) aid to educate individuals for whom the federal government accepts responsibility; (4) aid to improve the quality of education; and (5) aid to compensate for deficiencies in the school tax base. Some federal assistance serves more than one of these purposes, however, and is therefore not accurately categorized in any one classification.

Still another way of classifying federal aid may involve only three subdivisions: (1) federal aid to states to help promote and finance already established educational programs; (2) federal aid provided by the operation of federal programs that supplement state-established educational offerings; and (3) federal aid made available to nonpublic schools.

FEDERAL FISCAL ADVANTAGES AND DISADVANTAGES

The federal government's role in financing public education may be characterized as having begun as advisory and supplementary. The contribution of the federal government to the present state of development of public schools has been important, in spite of the disadvantages that this unit of government encounters as a partner in the system of education. It is the unit in the hierarchy of governance that is at the greatest distance from the ongoing process of education. By constitutional design, the federal government was to have only limited interest in educational matters. Education is the only function of the local school district and is an important function of state government, but it is only one of many important responsibilities at the national level. The federal government has a myriad of problems and programs that of necessity often upstage the federal interest in education—especially in periods of crisis or national emergency.

Superior Taxing System

The federal government has certain advantages that the other units of the partnership lack and that tend to give high moral, if not legal, responsibility to assist in the operation of this important and expensive service of government. Chief among these is its unchallenged position as the greatest tax collector. Using the highly graduated income tax, it has become a tax-collecting agency without peer in efficiency and effectiveness.

The federal government uses the graduated income tax as its predominant source of revenue. Total income, with proper deductions for dependents and other tax exclusions, provides a good comparison of the ability of people to pay their obligations to government. The income tax represents a positive segment of a sometimes maligned tax system. It produces large amounts of revenue at a relatively low collection rate. It is collected for the most part by withholding taxes and is therefore a "convenient" tax to pay. It is paid by a high percentage of citizens, although it is too easy to evade, under certain conditions. Features of the tax can be regulated in such a way as to alter the economic pattern of the country. With all its limitations and unfairness in the treatment of some individuals or companies, the income tax remains the backbone of this country's tax structure. Inherent inequities in its application are its greatest deficiency; its power to produce large amounts of revenue while using the ability principle of taxation is its greatest virtue.

Neutral Position

The federal government enjoys a position of neutrality as far as providing educational advantages is concerned, for all the people are citizens of a nation, not just citizens of local communities and states. The national interest requires some means of ensuring universal equality of educational opportunity that is not confined to rich districts, states, or any other level of structure. Potentially, federal tax money can be used in any state for education or in any school district, for every citizen can be viewed at the national level as being as important as every other one. It is much more difficult for state officials in a wealthy state to practice such a philosophy when considering the pupils in another less fortunate state.

DISTRIBUTING FEDERAL FUNDS

Although the need to provide federal programs and monies for education in the states has been established, there has been no definitive decision concerning the method or process of distribution. The method that is considered to be the most acceptable (general aid) has not yet been authorized by congressional action. Nor has Congress seen fit to distribute federal funds to the states on an equalization basis.

Federal Equalization

The battle has been won for equalization of state funds to local districts, but no such arrangement has been authorized for distribution of federal monies to the states. Certainly the arguments for equalization are as valid when applied to the allocation of federal funds as when applied to distribution of state funds. State boundaries, like school district boundaries, should not relegate some pupils to poor education while elevating others to superior education. Place of birth should not arbitrarily determine the kind and amount of education a student should receive, for the principle of equality of educational opportunity applies to all citizens.

That federal financial assistance should be distributed to the states on an equalization basis is supported by the following arguments:

1. The states have wide differences in their ability to pay for education, regardless of the devices or methods used to measure such comparative figures. This has a great deal to do with the wide range of annual expenditures per pupil, although other factors are involved. Some of the less wealthy states cannot finance an optimum or even an average educational program without excessive taxation, whereas others can do so with minimum tax effort.

2. Modern education does not confine its social or economic benefits to the area covered by the school district, the state, or even the nation. Conversely, the bad effects of poor education follow the recipients wherever they go. The problems created by inadequate education in a poor state accompany the school dropout or the graduate who moves to a more affluent area in search of job opportunities. Thus, it is to the advantage and interest of even the wealthy states that every state provide a good education for all its citizens. The best known method of assuring a sound educational program in every state is providing an equalized finance base.

3. A strong and viable educational program in every state strengthens the nation as a whole—its defenses, its economic productivity, and its support for the basic principles of democracy. Democratic or representative government can function successfully only with enlightened citizens in a society devoid of caste or class structure. Educational opportunity tends to erase or mitigate social class distinction.

The method for distributing federal funds has its critics who may have an influence in the 1990s. The formula for allocating funds has been based on the states' per-pupil expenditures. The rationale is that those states that spend more per pupil should be rewarded for making a greater effort. Opponents contend that such a policy is inequitable, as many states are shown to be making a greater effort when the per capita income within the state is considered in the formula. Senate Bill 755, 102nd Congress (1991), notes that when a calculation is made of the correlation between the average per-pupil expenditure and per capita income, these two factors are closely related; that is, states with relatively high (or low) personal income per capita also have relatively high (or low) average per-pupil expenditure.

In practice, a state's average per-pupil expenditure can be influenced by many factors, such as personal income, school age population, transportation, utility costs, number of private school students, and number of students with special needs. To allocate federal funds based merely on the states' per-pupil expenditures raises an equity question in the minds of some educators.

Categorical versus General Federal Aid

Three types of federal aid to education can be described as follows:

1. Categorical aid. Under this approach, Congress designates the exact purposes for which federal funds shall be used.

2. Block grants. The term has sometimes been used as if it were synonymous with general aid, but this is not the way the block grant concept has come to be understood among most people in education. Educators see block grants as related to the categorical approach, but involving broader categories and greater discretion within these categories.

3. General aid. In its pure form this type of aid involves only a general expression of purpose or priority by the federal government, such as improving education at the elementary and secondary levels. It also implies far less accountability, reporting, and evaluation.

Many educators have accepted block grants and categorical aid programs of the federal government even though they believe that general aid is more desirable but impossible to obtain under present conditions. Various practical realities foredoom any federal aid programs that have been or might be introduced by Congress:

1. The forms of federal aid that purport to provide universal equal opportunity would require differential amounts of money per pupil among the various states, according to some measure of need. Members of Congress from wealthy states, whose election to office is determined periodically by their respective voting constituencies, can hardly be expected to vote for larger allocations to needier states than to their own—unless they see education as a national as well as a state responsibility.

2. Since the federal government, through decisions of the Supreme Court, has ordered the end of segregation in this country, members of Congress are constrained to vote against general federal aid, without controls, until integration has been implemented and the "separate but equal" philosophy of an earlier era has suffered complete demise.

3. There is at present no nationwide agreement concerning use or nonuse of federal monies for nonpublic schools. A few states legally provide state funds for nonpublic school purposes, which may be vetoed by court decisions; others reject the idea. It will be difficult if not impossible to get congressional approval of general federal aid until such monies are used in every state with the same interpretation of church-state relations in financing education.

4. The fear of federal control of education pervades the thinking of the average citizen when he or she considers extension of federal support to the states. Thus, if additional federal activities are inaugurated, the degree of control must be set at a point where state or local responsibility for education is not in serious jeopardy.

It would seem that the odds against obtaining general federal aid in any substantial amount are high at the moment. Perhaps it is more meaningful to consider the practical pros and cons of the categorical aid programs that have inundated the state and local districts.

The chief arguments raised against categorical aid are the following: (1) It tends to give the federal government too much power and control in determining where the money is to be spent. (2) It often results in imbalances in the curricula and programs that the schools sponsor. There is hope in the belief that just as the states began their appropriations to local districts in categorical grants and later moved to more general aid, so may the federal government move toward more generalized aid programs in the future.

Future general federal aid programs, to be effective, must embody certain characteristics. (1) They must not be used to allow state and local support monies to be decreased. The main responsibility for financing education must remain at those levels; federal assistance must assume an "icing on the cake" function.

(2) Funds should be based on the principle of equalization, but each state should expect to receive some funds, depending on its comparative wealth and need. (3) Funds should be provided for some specific programs that are in the national interest but that may be neglected because of their high costs, inconvenience, or emergency nature—education of the disadvantaged, the handicapped, the exceptional, and similar groups.

The traditional solution to overcoming the inflexibility of categorical programs is the block grant. Though funds still flow to the states on a formula basis, much broader discretion is permitted in the allocation of the funds at the state and local levels. States are given much more administrative responsibility in monitoring, and local education agencies still have the flexibility to choose from a variety of programs.

FEDERAL-STATE-LOCAL FINANCE SHARING

To what degree should each level of government participate in financing public education? The answer to that very reasonable question has never been made with any consensus. What proportion of local-state-federal sharing should be accepted as standard? Are there criteria that can be applied to determine a more realistic and valid basis on which to base each level's partnership responsibility? As the costs of education increase and states and local districts become increasingly less able to finance education, how shall the role of the federal government be determined? The questions in this regard are easy to formulate and numerous; the answers are evasive. The problem remains.

Governmental Responsibilities Change

From the beginning of this nation, education has been part of state government. It has been a direct responsibility of the states, but the onus for financing education has chiefly been on the local school districts. Certain operational realities make it likely, however, that there will be significant changes in this condition in the immediate future.

Ironically, Americans continue to trumpet the merits of local, decentralized control of the educational system at the same time that local inadequacies have brought the state and its centralization tendencies into more responsible action in financing education, in certifying teachers, and in standardizing curricula. Changing demands of society for more governmental services, including education, put additional pressures upon government for more controls, more definitive guidelines, and stricter regulations, with commensurate loss of local power.

The shifting of responsibilities of the three levels of government for educational needs and services is not a new phenomenon. For example, financing education, once a local function only, is now largely a local-state partnership responsibility; promotion of pupils at certain grade levels was once virtually a state-controlled operation, but now it is completely within the jurisdiction of the local district. As functional responsibilities shift, changes come also in the degree of centralization emphasis. Just as any increase in state financial support for education may represent some degree of encroachment upon local control, so additional federal support increases the possibility of centralization of power and lessening of state and local autonomy in operating public schools.

State and federal regulations and power over public school operation have increased slowly but surely in the last two decades. As districts reach out to become recipients of state and federal revenues, which are more equitably imposed and more economically collected than those at the local level, they must weigh the advantages received against the possible losses of power.

Partnership Proposals Vary

No compelling method exists for determining the proportion of public school costs to be paid by each level of government. Those opposed to federal aid would divide the responsibility between the local units and the state. The strong supporters of the status quo would leave the proportions at somewhere near the present percentages. There are a comparative few who would continue to maintain the unrealistic position that the finances should be provided almost completely at the local level to assure local control of education. A number of citizens are advocating complete state support of education in order to simplify and improve equalization. Some support has been engendered for still another relationship among the members of the partnership in education: equal percentage participation by each—a one-third partnership at each level of funding.

There are some strong arguments in favor of much greater participation by the federal government in financing education. Chief among these is that most state and local units do not seem to possess the financial muscle necessary to do the job as it should be done. In confronting such a problem, school administrators look longingly at the possibility of securing greatly expanded federal financial support.

FEDERAL AID IN LIEU OF TAXES

Federal aid to education does not represent a purely altruistic position by an affluent "uncle" to some financially inept relatives (state and local school districts). Rather, some federal programs have been organized and implemented because of the financial obligations that the federal government has to the states. A prime example is the obligation the federal government has to make payments in lieu of the taxes that would ordinarily be paid on the tremendous amount of land that it owns, particularly in the western states. About one-third of the land area of the country is owned by the federal government; this removes it from the reach of state, county, or school district property taxes (Figure 7-1).

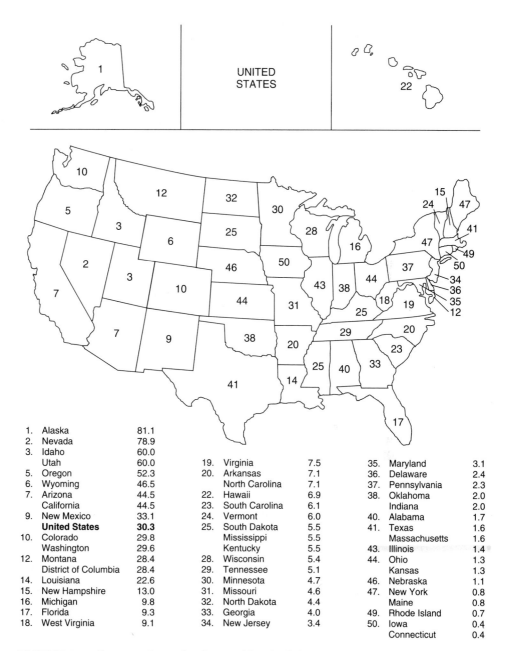

UNITED
STATES

1.	Alaska	81.1						
2.	Nevada	78.9						
3.	Idaho	60.0						
	Utah	60.0	19.	Virginia	7.5	35.	Maryland	3.1
5.	Oregon	52.3	20.	Arkansas	7.1	36.	Delaware	2.4
6.	Wyoming	46.5		North Carolina	7.1	37.	Pennsylvania	2.3
7.	Arizona	44.5	22.	Hawaii	6.9	38.	Oklahoma	2.0
	California	44.5	23.	South Carolina	6.1		Indiana	2.0
9.	New Mexico	33.1	24.	Vermont	6.0	40.	Alabama	1.7
	United States	**30.3**	25.	South Dakota	5.5	41.	Texas	1.6
10.	Colorado	29.8		Mississippi	5.5		Massachusetts	1.6
	Washington	29.6		Kentucky	5.5	43.	Illinois	1.4
12.	Montana	28.4	28.	Wisconsin	5.4	44.	Ohio	1.3
	District of Columbia	28.4	29.	Tennessee	5.1		Kansas	1.3
14.	Louisiana	22.6	30.	Minnesota	4.7	46.	Nebraska	1.1
15.	New Hampshire	13.0	31.	Missouri	4.6	47.	New York	0.8
16.	Michigan	9.8	32.	North Dakota	4.4		Maine	0.8
17.	Florida	9.3	33.	Georgia	4.0	49.	Rhode Island	0.7
18.	West Virginia	9.1	34.	New Jersey	3.4	50.	Iowa	0.4
							Connecticut	0.4

FIGURE 7-1   Percent of state land owned by the federal government, fiscal year 1989. (Source: *Public Land Statistics 1989*, U.S. Department of Education.)

INCREASED GOVERNMENTAL SERVICES

It is impossible to understand the point of view that favors extended federal financial support for education unless one understands the change in philosophy about government services that has pervaded the country in the last several decades. The "hands off" and "government do as little as possible" view of the earlier years of the nation's existence is no longer acceptable, desirable, or practicable. Traditionally the federal role was accepted as one of maintaining law and order, providing for some degree of protection to individuals and their property, and in general maintaining a laissez-faire policy toward most other problems. Such a role was justifiable and worked for the maximum development of individual initiative and growth. Economists and political scientists supported this policy, and it served the country well for a long period of its early history.

The "let alone" policy of government is no longer justifiable. The increasing complexity of social institutions, the economic order, and the political structure has resulted in increased services of government. The dangers of unlimited extension of such services are great, however. Thus, determining the services that should be provided by each level of government and those that should be left to the individual is now of paramount importance. The assumption here is that each unit of government is responsible for providing those services that will result in maximum benefits to the greatest possible number of citizens.

EDUCATIONAL LEADERSHIP NEEDED

It seems likely that the present ferment in education, related to the controversial role of the federal government, will disappear when a proper mixture of educational leadership at all levels is achieved. At the moment, no one is prepared to prescribe the ingredients necessary for maximum results from our tremendous monetary investment at all levels of government. In the past, American ingenuity has been noteworthy for its ability to solve the problems of society when they have arisen. Solving current problems involving the increased participation of the federal government in education should be no exception to this tradition. In the meantime, if the interests of boys and girls are to be considered in their proper perspective, the massive difficulties now before the nation should not be allowed to curtail or thwart the purposes of the federal commitment or to reduce its thrust. The problems of education, and the national, state, and local interest in solving them, have never been greater. The programs now in operation, as well as future ones, will have important consequences for education for many years to come. No state or local school district should fail to take advantage of the programs that are available. This will require leadership, imagination, and dedication from people at all levels of operation if maximum individual and social benefits are to be obtained.

IMPACT OF FEDERAL AID TO EDUCATION

It is difficult to assess objectively the impact that federal aid has had on education in the United States. Berke and Kirst, in their study of the financial factors that affect public education and their analysis of the impact of federal school aid in California, Massachusetts, Michigan, New York, and Texas, came to some generalizations concerning this that are worth considering:

1. In the most urbanized areas there was a unique crisis in educational finance caused by a general deterioration in their fiscal situation combined with higher demands and costs—for education and for other public services—than existed in neighboring communities.

2. Central cities received more federal education aid than their suburbs, but the amounts were too small to compensate for the suburban advantage in local wealth and state aid.

3. There were significant differences in the patterns of individual programs.

4. If fiscal capacity to support education is seen only in terms of property value per pupil, there is little compensating effect through federal aid.

5. If one takes the proportion of poor and minority pupils in a district as one proxy for educational need . . . federal aid tends to be significantly related to educational need.

6. Over the four-year period of their study, amounts of federal aid reported by individual school districts varied erratically because of the bizarre timing of federal fund appropriation and administration.

7. The failure to concentrate funds on the students most in need of compensatory education has frequently resulted in a superficial veneer of fragmented programs and new equipment, rather than in an integrated, high impact intervention to achieve major educational change.

8. Although federal aid is intended to provide strategically useful funds for educational purposes not otherwise receiving adequate support, the amounts of aid are simply too small in view of the problems that confront education.[7]

THE FUTURE OF FEDERAL AID-TO-EDUCATION PROGRAMS

Concerning the future of federal assistance to education, the following facts now seem to be apparent:

1. The widespread and complex involvement of the federal government in helping to finance public education programs is likely to fluctuate little in the near future. There is some evidence that the specific programs to be sponsored or financed may change considerably as they are influenced by changing philosophies and changing leaders in the three branches of the federal government.

2. Federal, state, and local experience in working with current and future programs will help immeasurably in solving some of the fermenting problems that are now big hurdles in establishing an appropriate federal-state-local partnership in public education.

3. If order is to be established in the administration of federal programs, it will be necessary to center primary responsibility in fewer educational agencies at the national level. The United States Department of Education is the logical agency to administer most, if not all, of the federal programs directly related to education.

4. Additional federal financial programs need not—indeed, should not—greatly increase the degree of control over education at the national level. However, there is a need to give national purpose to education. The confining boundaries between school districts, counties, and states that were of such consequence half a century ago are now imaginary and meaningless. Funds for education, regardless of their source, should be directed toward achieving national as well as state and local community goals of education.

5. Although categorical aid and block grants contribute greatly to the educational program, the goals of education demand that some form of general aid should be recognized as desirable. This should be initiated at the earliest possible time to help dissolve the barriers preventing equal educational opportunity for every citizen, regardless of color, race, creed, or place of residence.

The opinions of people concerning the role of the federal government have changed greatly in recent years. Some federal responsibility for education was once defended largely by a "liberal" segment of the social milieu. While still somewhat controversial, some federal involvement is now supported by a majority of citizens regardless of political party affiliation, race, religion, or any other designation. As the programs and official responsibilities of the public schools increase, greater participation and support are required at each of the three levels of government. As the costs of high-quality education continue their spiral upward, it is inconceivable that the solutions to the increasing problems of education should rest on only one or two of the parties concerned—the states and the local school districts. For the system to work as intended, each partner must assume some share of the additional responsibility for the educational programs that citizens will continue to demand in the years ahead.

Over the century, many federal funding elements have endured, and are likely to continue in the future, primarily in the areas of Indian education, vocational education, compensatory education, education for the handicapped, land grants, school foods, federal payments in lieu of taxes, and support through loans and grants to students in postsecondary and higher education institutions.

THE DEPARTMENT OF EDUCATION

For 113 years the federal government's main thrust in the performance of its educational function came through the operations of the United States Office of Education. The agency was founded in 1867 and called the Department of Education, although not represented in the cabinet. The newly designated agency had three major functions: (1) to collect such statistics and facts as would show the condition and progress of education in several states and territories; (2) to diffuse such information respecting the organization and management of schools and school systems, and methods of teaching, as would aid the people in the establishment and maintenance of efficient school systems; and, (3) otherwise promote the cause of education throughout the country. The first Department of Education was quickly downgraded to the status of a department within the Bureau of Interior and remained there for 72 years, functioning as a small record-keeping office and collecting information on the modest federal education efforts.

Proposals for a separate department surfaced periodically but were given little support. In 1939 the Office of Education was transferred to the Federal Security Agency, which became the Department of Health, Education and Welfare (HEW) in 1953.

With the tremendous expansion of federal education programs in the period after World War II, arguments for a separate department grew more compelling. During the 1960s, several studies of government organization recommended establishment of a separate department, as well as further reorganization that would bring all education programs under the administration of a single department.

In 1972 Congress established an Education Division, headed by an Assistant Secretary of Education within the Department of Health, Education and Welfare. Despite this reorganization, administration of federal education programs continued to be confusing and sometimes contradictory. In 1978, administration of the hundreds of education programs was spread over more than 40 different agencies. In September 1979, Congress approved the creation of the Department of Education, with cabinet-level status. The legislation established a Department of Education, headed by a secretary to be appointed by the president and approved by the Senate. It formed within the department six offices: elementary and secondary education; postsecondary education; vocational and adult education; special education and rehabilitation services; education research and improvement; and civil rights. Also established was an office of education for overseas dependents and an office of bilingual education and minority languages.

The legislation emphasized that the primary responsibility for education was reserved to the state and local school systems and specifically prohibited the department from increasing federal control over education or from exercising any control over the curriculum, administration, personnel, library resources, textbooks, or other instructional materials of any school, except to the extent authorized by law.

In an executive order issued May 2, 1980, President Jimmy Carter stated the new department's purposes in the following:

> Now, to meet the needs of generations to come, we have established a Department of Education to express our national commitment to education, to promote equal educational opportunity, to assist local authorities in their efforts to improve our schools, and to administer federal education programs more efficiently.
>
> I call upon all parents and students, all teachers and administrators, all lawmakers and public officials—I call upon all my fellow citizens to celebrate this day. As a people, let us dedicate ourselves anew to building an educational system which will cherish young people, instill self-discipline and prepare students for tomorrow's world; which will encourage scientific curiosity and foster artistic creativity; which will support research, reward good teaching and honor high intellectual achievement.
>
> Only by making this commitment can we pass on a tradition of educational excellence and equal opportunity to Americans of the twenty-first century and give them the tools they will need to shape their own interpretations of the American dream and make their own contributions to life, liberty and the pursuit of happiness.[8]

The election of Ronald Reagan in November 1980 brought new challenges to the year-old Department of Education. Terrel H. Bell was appointed Secretary of Education, with the mandate to abolish the department "as quickly as possible." The demise of the Department of Education was thwarted through the impact "A Nation at Risk" had on the country. The focus was turned toward the need to make improvements in education.

In 1991, President George Bush appointed Lamar Alexander, former Governor of Tennessee, as the fifth Secretary of Education. One of his challenges was to expedite a greater business-education relationship with the establishment of the New American Schools Development Corporation. To emphasize the partnership "the president sought a high profile deputy secretary of education . . . David T. Kearns, the chairman of Xerox Corporation."[9] While many educators embraced the business sector joining the fight for better schools, many voiced concerns that the alliance may be short-lived.[10] Without greater financial support from federal sources, states as well as businesses may become disenchanted with the concept.

One of the major challenges of the department as it makes grants and disburses funds to states and school districts throughout the nation is that of establishing a proper balance in the federal government's "partnership" relationship with state and local educational systems to bring educational excellence to all the nation's schools.

SUMMARY

The role of the federal government in education has long been a controversial one that has had racial, religious, and political overtones. Historically, federal involvement with the public schools has been minor. The framers of the Constitution seemed to have feared the establishment of a nationally controlled school system. In effect, the adoption of the Tenth Amendment in 1791 relegated the federal government to an advisory role as far as education is concerned. Throughout the history of the United States, the comparative roles of the three levels of government have been in a state of change.

Federal education activities began in 1785 with the land grants that were given for the purpose of establishing schools. Later, the Morrill Acts provided land for the establishment of land-grant colleges. These were followed by supplemental acts and by various vocational education grants. School lunch, relief and emergency programs, war on poverty, and payments in lieu of taxes have all been a part of the federal involvement in financing education. Federal emphasis has been given to programs designed to help eliminate racial and sex discrimination, stress cultural awareness, and provide funds for specialized categorical programs.

The federal government has certain advantages over state and local levels of government in financing education. Chief among these is the ability to collect taxes in an efficient and inexpensive manner. One of its major concerns is how to determine the best method for distributing funds equitably. It has been politically impossible for Congress to agree on distributing funds to the states and school districts on an equalization basis. Consequently, federal funds are usually categorical in nature, with the result that the states and local school districts lose some of their control of the curricula.

There is still wide disagreement among the people of the nation as to the degree to which the federal government should participate in financing public education. However, the "let alone" policy of past years is no longer justifiable. A proper mixture of leadership at all levels of government is needed if public education is to continue to improve and to provide the kind and amount of instruction that is so necessary for the youth of the nation. It is hoped that the Department of Education will help to determine the proper role for the federal government in financing education as the nation moves into the twenty-first century.

ASSIGNMENT PROJECTS

1. Trace the development of the Department of Education from its beginning to its present position. List the advantages and disadvantages of having a department of education at the national level.

2. Determine which of the long list of federal acts for financing education that have been in operation through the years have been generally accepted with little controversy and which have engendered great controversy.

3. Distinguish between general federal aid and categorical federal aid in terms of their advantages and disadvantages, their value to the states and to school districts, and the problem of getting each type enacted by Congress.

4. Determine the extremes among the several states in terms of the percentages of total school district revenue obtained from federal funds. Defend or criticize these differences.

5. Trace the development of land grants by the federal government and indicate the disposition of these lands in your state.

6. Select a categorical grant of the federal government and trace how it is allocated to the states, to school districts, and to various schools. Determine what controls the government has put on how the funds are spent, how the funds are administered, and how expenditures are reported to the federal agency.

7. Trace the rationale behind the proposal for 1/3-1/3-1/3 funding for education. Where are the funds to come from on each level? Who is to determine how the funds are spent? Who will benefit from this funding pattern?

SELECTED READINGS

The Fiscal Year 1987 Budget, Summary and Background Information. Washington, D.C.: Department of Education, 1986.

Grant, W. Vance, and Thomas D. Synder. *Digest of Education Statistics 1985–86.* Washington, D.C.: U.S. Government Printing Office, 1986.

Guthrie, James W., Walter I. Garms, and Lawrence C. Pierce. *School Finance and Education Policy: Enhancing Educational Efficiency, Equality, and Choice.* 2nd ed. Englewood Cliffs, N.J.: Prentice Hall, 1988.

Honeyman, D. S., D. C. Thompson, and R. C. Wood. *Financing Rural and Small Schools: Issues of Adequacy and Equity.* Gainesville: University of Florida Press, 1989.

Plisko, Valena White, and Joyce D. Stern. *The Condition of Education.* 1985 ed. Washington, D.C.: National Center for Education Statistics, 1985.

Schools, People, and Money. Washington, D.C.: President's Commission on School Finance, U.S. Government Printing Office, 1972.

Stump, Mary M., ed. *1985 Guide to Federal Funding for Education.* Arlington, Va.: Education Funding Research Council, 1985.

Thomas, Norman C. *Education in National Politics.* New York: David McKay, 1975.

Timpane, Michael, ed. *Federal Interest in Financing Schooling.* Cambridge, Mass.: Ballinger, 1978.

Verstegan, D. A. *School Finance at a Glance.* Denver, Colo.: Education Commission of the States, 1990.

Webb, L. D., Martha M. McCarthy, and Stephen B. Thomas. *Financing Elementary and Secondary Education.* Columbus, Ohio: Merrill, 1988.

ENDNOTES

1. *Brown* v. *Board of Education* (I), 347 U.S. 483, 74 S. Ct. 686 (1954).

2. Mary Jean Le Tendre, "Improving Chapter I Programs: We Can Do Better," *Phi Delta Kappan,* Vol. 72, No. 8, April 1991, p. 578.

3. *Bowshar* v. *Synar,* 106 S. Ct. 3181 (1986)

4. "Handing Congress a Hot Potato: The Supreme Court Nullifies a Key Budget Balancing Provision," *Time,* July 21, 1986, p. 24

5. Deborah A. Verstegen and David L. Clark, "The Diminution in Federal Expenditures for Education during the Reagan Administration," *Phi Delta Kappan,* October 1988, pp. 134–38.

6. Ibid., p. 135.

7. Joel S. Berke and Michael W. Kirst, *Federal Aid to Education: Who Benefits? Who Governs?* (Lexington, Mass.: Lexington Books (D.C. Heath), 1972), pp. 2–4.

8. Jimmy Carter, as quoted in *Education Times* (Washington, D.C.: George Washington University, May 12, 1980), p. 1.

9. Jonathan Weisman, "Educators Watch with a Wary Eye as Business Gains Policy Muscle," *Education Week,* July 31, 1991, p. 25.

10. Ibid.

Chapter 8

The Influence and Climate of the Courts

With the recent, sweeping state supreme court decisions overturning school finance structures in Kentucky, New Jersey, and Texas, and active or planned cases in nearly half of the states, education finance litigation and school finance reform have rebounded to high places on state education policy agendas. —ALLAN ODDEN AND LORI KIM, 1991

Over the years, major changes and improvements have usually been difficult to effect in state school finance programs. Legislative action is almost always necessary, and this process normally involves disturbance of the state's taxing and funding systems. Changes almost always require additional funds, and this arouses taxpayer criticism and resistance. As a consequence, public schools are often in some form of financial crisis. In such emergencies the machinery for school financing is patched up, and little effort is directed toward major revamping or replacement of obsolete finance programs. Thus, many states have been financing late twentieth-century schools with early twentieth-century finance patterns.

Nowhere in the broad spectrum of activities in education is there a better example of recent reversal of attitude toward change than in public school finance. Although periods of crisis do not always appear to lend themselves to the difficult process of changing and innovating, evidence concerning what is now being done in school financial theory and practice contradicts such a view. For several years the public has been aware of an impending crisis in the financing of public education in the United States. Taxpayer revolts against increased bond or even current expenditure levies, early closing of schools because of depleted budgets, severe reductions of school services, and similar happenings have become commonplace. Inadequate revenues have been distributed inequitably, and the burden of providing such funds has been shared with little regard to fairness for individual taxpayers. While these and many other financial problems plagued the schools, little constructive action was taken until the pressure of the courts made it imperative.

COURTS OFTEN GENERATE CHANGE

One has only to read the history of American education to be reminded of the many times the courts have altered its course. The *Kalamazoo* case of 1874[1] established a legal system of taxation for funding secondary education; the *Brown* case of 1954[2] pushed aside the indefensible doctrine of "separate but equal" facilities and opportunities for minorities; the "one man-one vote" decision of 1962[3] changed the organization of state legislative bodies and ultimately obliterated the requirement that voters must pay property taxes in order to vote in certain school elections. In 1971 the *Serrano* decision of the California Supreme Court[4] put legal pressure on the state legislature to revise the state finance formula to effect greater equity and equality for the students in all school districts within the state. The Supreme Court in *Rodriguez*[5] upheld the Texas school financing system in 1973, stating that education is not a fundamental interest under the federal constitution. Since then a plethora of cases in state courts have altered (or sustained) school finance systems.

COURT DECISION GUIDELINES

Generally, the courts tend to reflect the values and attitudes of a majority of the people toward the issues and questions on which they are ruling. Numerous recent court decisions illustrate the changing attitude of the general public toward some of the legal principles involved in financing education. This changing of attitude can be illustrated by the controversy over Supreme Court nominees. When the president nominates someone to the Court, often the nominee's political—not judicial—philosophy becomes the target of the inquiry. Certain general guidelines have emerged from the numerous state and federal court decisions about financing education. Some of the most important of these are the following:

   1. The courts are generally inclined to construe statutes concerning taxation strictly. They usually favor the taxpayer over the school district. A Florida court, for example, pointed out that "in deciding questions relating to procedure employed by a governmental taxing agency one must bear in mind at the outset that laws providing for taxation must be construed most strongly against the government and liberally in favor of the taxpayer."[6]
   2. School finance funds, including tax monies, are state funds, not local ones. Local school districts are agencies of the state and are in reality acting for the state. The courts are therefore inclined to require the same care and efficiency in the administration of school funds that is required for other state agencies and institutions.

3. The courts have held consistently to the opinion that school taxes need not be imposed so that a direct relation exists between the benefits individual taxpayers receive and the amount of taxes they pay. In the words of one court, "The benefits are intangible and incapable of pecuniary ascertainment, but it is constitutionally sufficient if the taxes are uniform and are for public purposes in which the whole city has an interest."[7]

4. The legislature of each state has complete power to control public school funds and to determine how the public schools shall be financed, subject only to the restrictions imposed by the constitution of the state involved. Consequently, the legislature has wide discretion in determining how school funds shall be apportioned, so long as the basis for such apportionment is just and not arbitrary.

POWER OF THE COURTS

Most citizens are aware of the fact that education is a state function in which some responsibility is delegated to the local school unit. They know, too, that each state's legislative body exercises plenary power over its own educational system. However, they sometimes disregard or underemphasize the subtle but strong power the judicial system has over educational matters. As a consequence, the average person is often startled when a major court decision shows the effect a higher federal or state court brings to bear on the educational systems of the states.

Until the early 1970s most higher courts refused to interfere or to rule in certain types of school finance cases, with the rationale that the methods used to collect and distribute funds to local school districts were a legislative, not a judicial problem. For example, in *Sawyer* v. *Gilmore* (1912)[8] the Supreme Court of Maine said, "The method of distribution of the proceeds of such a tax rests in the wise discretion and sound judgment of the Legislature. If this discretion is unwisely exercised, the remedy is with the people and not with the court."

No one seriously question the philosophy of the *Sawyer* court—least of all the courts that have ruled on similar disputes. Courts have not rewritten state school finance laws to meet the conditions they may have ruled against, although some have threatened to do so. The function of the courts to interpret laws and constitutions does not go that far. They have, however, sometimes given states a reasonable time in which to make the court-required changes through the normal channel of legislative action.

EQUAL PROTECTION AND THE COURTS BEFORE 1971

Perhaps the most publicized court case before 1971 that involved the provision of unequal revenues per pupil in different school districts in the same state was

McInnis v. *Shapiro* in Illinois in 1969.[9] The complaint was that there was inequality in the provision of funds in various school districts in the state. The complaint was dismissed by a three-judge court even though it recognized the wide range of expenditures among Illinois school districts. The court ruled that the Illinois plan for financing public education reflected a rational policy that was consistent with the mandate of the Illinois Constitution. It stated that the unequal expenditures per pupil did not amount to an invidious discrimination and that the laws that permit such unequal expenditures were neither arbitrary nor unreasonable. It further ruled that equal educational opportunity was not a constitutional requisite and that the court could not decide the issue.

The plaintiffs appealed the case (now *McInnis* v. *Ogilvie*) to the United States Supreme Court. The Court, without hearing the case, affirmed the decision of the lower court. The trial court had emphasized judicial lack of power or authority to change state school finance programs when it said, "The courts have neither the knowledge, nor the means, nor the power to tailor the public moneys to fit the varying needs of these students throughout the state. We can only see to it that the outlays on one group are not invidiously greater or less than that of another. . . ."

In the *McInnis* case, educational advocates of equal protection had projected their thinking to include all children eligible for such by constitutional guarantee under the Fourteenth Amendment. Hence, educators were disappointed at the failure of the Court to take positive action to alleviate the disparities in the case.

DEVELOPMENT OF EQUAL PROTECTION THEORY

While the courts were refusing to take positive positions concerning the equal protection questions being raised regarding inequitable state school finance systems, certain school finance scholars and researchers were engaged in developing a rationale and defense against such inequities in nearly all of the states. Arthur E. Wise, John E. Coons, William Clune, and Stephen Sugarman were some of the leaders who argued that the quality of education within a state should not be a function of wealth, race, or geography. Wise, in recommending that school resources be distributed equitably according to the degree of social or economic disadvantage borne by school students, suggested three forms of school finance revision: (1) state collection and distribution of all school revenues to local school districts; (2) equalization of the tax bases of local school districts by redrawing district lines; and (3) manipulation of equalization formulas. Coons, Clune, and Sugarman emphasized the "power equalization" theory that was first enunciated by Harlan Updegraff over half a century ago: equal tax effort should generate equal resources in all school districts. The positive effect of their scholarly work, along with that of many other school finance authorities with similar concerns, was soon to be evident in *Serrano* v. *Priest* in 1971 and similar decisions that followed quickly in other states.

SERRANO v. *PRIEST* (1971)

A landmark decision that reversed the general view of state school financing formulas occurred on August 30, 1971, when the California Supreme Court ruled that John Serrano's complaint against the state's public school financial pattern was justifiable and that the pattern must be revised to make it constitutional.[10] At the time the *Serrano* suit was brought to court, educational expenditures per person in California ranged from $274 in one district to $1,710 in another, a ratio of 1 to 6.2. In the same year, two districts in the same county (Beverly Hills and Baldwin Park) expended $1,223 and $577 per pupil, respectively. This inequity was due to the difference in the assessed valuation of property per pupil to be educated ($50,885 in Beverly Hills and $3,706 in Baldwin Park—a ratio of nearly 14 to 1). The taxpayers in Baldwin Park paid a school tax of 54.8 mills ($5.48 per $100 of assessed valuation) while those in Beverly Hills paid school taxes of only 23.8 mills ($2.38 per $100 of assessed valuation). Thus, a tax effort in the poorer district twice as high as that in the wealthier one resulted in school expenditures of only 47 percent of that in the wealthier district.

The disparities in school funds available per pupil that led to the *Serrano* lawsuit could have been found in nearly all of the fifty states. It should be noted that the differences in ability to pay for education in Beverly Hills and Baldwin Park were not exceedingly great when compared with the extremes in the entire state or with those that could have been found in other states. Had the case been concerned with the extremes then existing in all of California, they would have been about 50 to 1, about 14 to 1 in New York, and 6 to 1 in Utah. Thus, the issue in *Serrano* was concerned with differences in ability to pay—not necessarily in the size of those differences.

In *Serrano*, the California court considered questions related to the comparative wealth of districts, the classification of education as a *fundamental interest*, and whether or not the financing system was necessary to the attainment of any compelling state interest. In a 6 to 1 opinion, the court declared the state's public school financing system to be unconstitutional. It declared that dependence on local property taxes was the "root of the constitutional defect." It noted what school finance analysts have long known: under such a system, with heavy reliance on property taxation, school districts with a low value of taxable property per child cannot levy taxes at high enough rates to compete with more affluent districts; in many instances they cannot even provide funds for a minimum program of education.

The following statement summarizes the rationale of the court in the *Serrano* v. *Priest* decision:

> The California public school financing system, as presented to us by the plaintiff's complaint supplemented by matters judicially noticed, since it deals intimately with education, obviously touches upon a fundamental interest. For the reasons we have explained in detail, this system conditions

the full entitlement to such interest on wealth, classifies its recipients on the basis of their collective affluence and makes the quality of a child's education depend upon the resources of his school district and ultimately upon the pocketbook of his parents. We find that such a financing system as presently constituted is not necessary to the attainment of any compelling state interest. Since it does not withstand the requisite "strict scrutiny," it denies to the plaintiffs and others similarly situated the equal protection of the laws. . . . If the allegations of the complaint are sustained, the financial system must fall and the statutes comprising it must be found unconstitutional.[11]

The trial court held that the California system of financing public education violated the equal protection provisions of the *California* constitution and the Fourteenth Amendment to the U.S. Constitution because a disparity of tax money to support education existed among the districts of the state. According to the court, it made no difference that the existing system might provide an adequate education for all the children of the state. The disparity in the amount of money available for the education of children among the districts was constitutionally significant because it permitted some school districts to offer a higher quality of education than others. This differential treatment of children was in the area of the fundamental interest of education and was not justified by any compelling reason. Therefore, the court reasoned, the disparity must be corrected within a reasonable period of time. It ordered the state to provide a better equalization program by August 1980.

The trial court asserted that providing a school finance law was a responsibility of the California legislature, but it took the liberty of suggesting four possible plans to meet the requirements of equal protection:

1. Full state funding with statewide imposition and control of real property taxes.

2. Reorganization of the 1,067 then existing school districts into about 500 districts, with boundary realignments to equalize assessed valuations of real property among all school districts.

3. Retention of the school district boundaries but removal of commercial and industrial property from local taxation for school purposes.

4. School district power equalizing is based on the concept that school districts could choose to spend at different levels; but for each level of expenditure chosen, the tax effort would be the same for each school choosing such level, whether it be a high-wealth or a low-wealth school district.

Demurring in 1971, the California Supreme Court looked past all previous contrary decisions of other courts. Previous rulings in such states as Michigan, Virginia, Texas, and Illinois had implied that the equal protection clause of the Fourteenth Amendment did not apply to school financing patterns. Thus, *Serrano* became a landmark case—the first major decision by a higher court ruling against a state's school finance program on the basis of violation of equal protection for all the school pupils of a state.

CONSEQUENCES OF *SERRANO*

The following statements are representative of the reactions of school finance scholars and writers to the *Serrano* decision:

> Despite the fact that the school-finance systems of every state but Hawaii were subjected to fundamental challenge, the decision was widely hailed on all sides. The press, legislative groups, educators at all levels in the administrative hierarchy, and taxpayer organizations were all enthused. Liberal civil rights adherents rejoiced at the apparent triumph of egalitarianism and conservative property owners rejoiced at the apparently impending demise of the local property tax. . . . [12]

Wickert, writing in 1985, stated: "A new era was introduced with California's *Serrano* v. *Priest* court decision, which required school funding to be determined on some basis other than district property wealth."[13] However, many members of the educational community viewed the *Serrano* decision with a degree of skepticism. They feared that rather than being a great promise for the future in the field of educational finance, it might bring a leveling of the growth curve of revenues provided for education. A period of retrenchment was anticipated for taxpayers, who were beginning to rebel against the local property tax. Educators, along with numerous lay citizens, were quite concerned with the spiraling costs of educational programs and services that the public continued to demand in spite of their cost.

The *Serrano* decision was followed with some inaccurate statements and faulty interpretations concerning what the California Supreme Court had actually said in condemning the finance law in that state. The following statement clarifies some of the misunderstandings that developed:

> Since the *Serrano* decision is a major factor in setting the criteria for education finance reform, it is important to be clear about what the court did and did not say. The court did not say that equal dollars had to be expended per child. It did not explicitly rule out plans providing more funds to higher cost pupils—such as disadvantaged, vocation, gifted, or handicapped students—as long as the distribution of these funds is not related to district wealth. Finally, the court did not exclude the property tax as a basis of education finance, but rather said that the level of educational expenditures could not be a function of district wealth. Thus a statewide property tax with redistribution of the revenues raised on the basis of any of a number of criteria, except district wealth, may be permissible.[14]

The immediate consequences of the *Serrano* decision were overwhelming in matters of school finance. Within five months after the announcement, three other state courts had made similar rulings. States that formerly seemed to be satisfied with maintaining their traditional financing programs began to study and restyle them with a zeal well beyond any previously demonstrated. Most of them encouraged, or even demanded, formal studies to modernize their school financing formulas. Such prompt state action was considered necessary in the face of an apparent legal threat of nationwide school tax and funding reform. The traditional local property tax, which had formed the chief framework for financing education in some states, appeared to be doomed. Although the *Serrano* decision did not condemn property taxes per se, it did condemn the unfairness that resulted from their use in California. State officials faced with apprehension the prospect of providing equitable school finance formulas if local property taxes were reduced or eliminated. They viewed with alarm the possibility of *Serrano*-type litigation in their states. Consequently, research studies were organized to correct formula inequities before court action was initiated.

Van Dusartz v. *Hatfield* (Minnesota, 1971)

In October 1971, only six weeks after *Serrano*, Minnesota became the second state to have its system of financing education declared unconstitutional.[15] A federal district court judge accepted the California arguments and findings as being equally applicable in Minnesota. According to him, "the level of spending for a child's education may not be a function of wealth other than the wealth of the state as a whole." The court recognized that pupils in publicly financed schools have a right under the equal protection guarantee of the Fourteenth Amendment to have money spent on them "unaffected by variations in the taxable wealth of their school districts or their parents." The court said:

> This is not the simple instance in which a poor man is injured by his lack of funds. Here the poverty is that of a governmental unit that the State itself has defined and commissioned. The heaviest burdens of this system surely fall defacto upon those poor families residing in poor districts who cannot escape to private schools, but this effect only magnifies the odiousness of the explicit discrimination by the law itself against all children living in relatively poor districts.

Robinson v. *Cahill* (New Jersey, 1972)

On January 19, 1972, the New Jersey Superior Court of Hudson County ruled that the state's educational financing system created inequities that violated the state constitution's educational provisions and also the equal protection clause of the Fourteenth Amendment.[16] The court said that pupils living in districts with low assessments of property per child were being discriminated against and that such a system likewise discriminated against taxpayers, who shoulder unequal burdens in providing funds for education. It also declared that it was not suggesting "that the same amount of money must be spent on each pupil in the state. The differing needs of pupils would suggest to the contrary."

The New Jersey Supreme Court, by unanimous vote, declared the state's system of financing public education to be unconstitutional, saying that it failed to fulfill an 1875 mandate in the state constitution concerning equal educational opportunity. The court did not declare the state's local property tax to be unconstitutional, but it did rule that any system that continued to rely primarily on local property taxes for financing public schools would be so declared.

The court gave the state legislature until January 1975 to approve a new program for public school financing with less dependency on local property taxes, or face further court action. The directive to the state involved the establishment of a finance program for a "thorough and efficient" public school system. It further stated that if the legislature failed to guarantee all pupils equal tax support, it would issue an order for that purpose—a strong threat of court enactment of taxing legislation. Since the case was tried in state courts and the rulings were based on compliance with the state constitution, the case was never heard by the U.S. Supreme Court, despite numerous attempts to appeal it.

That the New Jersey Court recognized its responsibility to be that of judging the constitutionality of the law and that of the legislature to enact the law is shown in the following statement of that court:

> We do not go further for several reasons. We continue to be hesitant in our intrusion into the legislative process, forced only so far as demonstrably required to meet the constitutional exigency. As well, it would be premature and inappropriate for the court at the present posture of this complex matter to undertake, a priori, a comprehensive blueprint for "thorough and efficient" education, and seek to impose it upon the other Branches of government. Courts customarily forbear the specification of legislative detail, as distinguished from the obligation to judge the constitutionality thereof, until after promulgation by the appropriate authority. . . .

Spano v. *Board of Education* (New York, 1972)

Of the numerous court cases decided since *Serrano* concerning the financing programs of the various states as they relate to the equal protection clause, the first to decide against the charges of the plaintiffs, came in New York.[17] Andrew Spano and other residents and property holders in Lakeland Central School District No.1 sued the board of education and various state officials because of the alleged unfairness of New York's legislative and constitutional provisions for levying and distributing school tax funds. Although the charges were much the same as in *Serrano*, the court based its decision on two previous cases (*McInnis* v. *Ogilvie*, Illinois, 1969; and *Burruss* v. *Wilkerson*, Virginia, 1969).[18] While acknowledging that there may be inadequacies and unfairness in state school financing systems, the New York Supreme Court indicated that in its view changes to correct such inequities should be the duty of the legislature rather than the court. It further stated that the "one scholar–one dollar" version of the "one man–one vote" mandate would have to be the prerogative of the Supreme Court.

SAN ANTONIO INDEPENDENT SCHOOL DISTRICT v. RODRIGUEZ (1973)

In 1970, three urban school districts in Texas brought suit against the Texas board of education and the state commissioner of education to determine whether or not the Texas system of allocating state funds for education was unfair. This case was based on the charge that underassessment in many rural school districts of taxable property resulted in their obtaining disproportionate amounts of state funds.[19] In late 1971, a federal court ruled that the Texas financing system violated both the federal and the Texas constitutions. The court went a step beyond the California and Minnesota decisions by giving Texas two years to reorganize its school financing system. The court threatened that if the legislature should fail to act, the court "will take such further steps as may be necessary to implement both the purpose and spirit of this order."

The *Rodriguez* case was accepted for review by the United States Supreme Court and became the first and only equal protection case concerning school finance to be considered by the high court to date. The facts of the case were as follows:

1. The financing of elementary and secondary schools in Texas came from state and local funding.

2. Almost half of the revenues came from the state's Minimum Foundation Program, which was designed to provide a minimum educational offering in every school in the state.

3. To provide for this program, the school districts as a single unit provided 20 percent of the funding.

4. Each district contributed its share as determined by a formula designed to reflect its relative tax-paying ability. These funds were raised by property taxes.

5. All districts raised additional monies to support schools.

Rodriguez held that the revenue source varied with the value of taxable property in the districts, thus causing great disparities in per-pupil spending among districts. The lower courts concluded that the Texas system of public school finance violated the equal protection clause of the Fourteenth Amendment, finding that wealth is a "suspect" classification and that education is a "fundamental" interest. On March 21, 1973, the U.S. Supreme Court, by a vote of 5 to 4, reversed the lower court decision, which also nullified the *Van Dusartz*[20] decision in Minnesota and negated all related pending federal court actions. In general, the Court ruled that reforms with respect to state taxation and education are matters reserved for the legislative processes of the various states. Education is not a constitutional federal interest, and the Texas school finance system did not discriminate against any class of persons considered suspect, because it dealt with property-poor school districts, not individuals. As stated by Leland Melvin:

The court rejected the suspect classification based on the fiscal neutrality standard. The court held that the defendants failed to show that any class of citizens had been denied an education—they only showed that some districts received a lower quality education than others. The court also held that education was not among the rights protected by the U.S. Constitution. Determining that neither a suspect classification or fundamental interest existed, the court applied the rational relationship test to the issue and held the Texas school finance system to be constitutional.[21]

Since *Rodriguez* was heard in federal court and the decision related to the equal protection clause of the Fourteenth Amendment to the United States Constitution, it did not directly affect actions of a similar nature in state courts, such as *Serrano* and *Robinson*. Melvin continued:

The U.S. Supreme Court decision in *Rodriguez* effectively removed school finance reform litigation from the federal courts. Further court action was forced to rely on violation of state constitutional provisions if any relief was to be afforded. Ten years have passed since the U.S. Supreme Court handed down its decision in *Rodriguez* and the state courts have been very active.[22]

That the Court did not support or agree with the disparities in per-pupil expenditures so evident in the *Rodriguez* case is indicated in the following statement by Justice Powell:

We hardly need add that this Court's action today is not to be viewed as placing its judicial imprimatur on the status quo. The need is apparent for reform in tax systems which may have relied too long and too heavily on the local property tax. And certainly innovative new thinking as to public education, its methods and its funding is necessary to assure both a higher level of quality and greater uniformity of opportunity. These matters merit the continued attention of the scholars who already have contributed much by their challenges. But the ultimate solutions must come from the lawmakers and from the democratic pressures of those who elect them.

Therefore, the Court found current methods of financing education chaotic and unfair, but it could not say "that such disparities are the product of a system that is so irrational as to be invidiously discriminatory." On the other hand, Justice Thurgood Marshall, in his dissenting opinion, charged that the Court's decision "is a retreat from our historic commitment to equality of educational opportunity."

This action of the Supreme Court in effect supported property taxation as a source of local school financing, but it did not stop the momentum generated in several states for school finance reform. State courts were faced with interpreting their constitutions in light of the *Serrano* philosophy and the *Rodriguez* decision.

STATE COURT CASES

Since *Rodriguez* was tried in federal courts, and because the United States Supreme Court stated that education is not a federal constitutional right, the ruling moved similar cases away from the federal court system to state courts. This shifting was made possible in part by the U.S. Supreme Court's decisions that state constitutional law can be separated from federal interpretation. In *Oregon* v. *Hass*,[23] the Court stated that a "State is free *as a matter of its own law* to impose greater restrictions . . . than those this Court holds to be necessary. . . ."

In fact, the Supreme Court refused to hear cases from Wyoming, Ohio, and California (*Serrano* II),[24] verifying that school finance is a state matter. Melvin stated:

> The Supreme Court of the United States has spoken and it is clear that the problem of reform must be handled by the states. The decision in *Rodriguez* pointed out that the high court considered the matter one for states to solve. This posture has been strengthened by the fact that the high court has refused to review decisions of state supreme courts in this area since *Rodriguez*.[25]

In their interpretations of state constitutions and school finance statutes, state courts have ruled in opposing ways, some in favor of the *Serrano* doctrine, some in favor of the *Rodriguez* philosophy. Those that have used the *Serrano* decision as precedent have ruled on the basis that school finance formulas violated the equal protection or equal educational opportunity clauses of their state constitutions or that education is a fundamental interest protected by the state constitution.[26] Those state courts that have followed the *Rodriguez* philosophy have been unable to find a rationale in state constitutions for equalizing per-pupil expenditures.[27] The Michigan and New York high courts originally overturned their school finance systems based on the *Serrano* decision, but these courts later reversed those rulings, citing *Rodriguez*.[28]

Thompson v. *Engelking* (Idaho, 1975)

In May 1975, the Idaho Supreme Court in its decision in *Thompson* v. *Engelking* ruled that the Idaho school finance law did not violate the state constitutional requirement of a uniform system of public schools and that it did not deny equal protection of the law.[29] The suit (similar to the *Serrano* case) argued that the law prevented the maintenance of a general, uniform, and thorough system of public, free, common schools for all children. The court decided that education was not a fundamental right, citing *Rodriguez*, and that children need not have equal facilities and receive equal services. It further declared that unequal amounts of money may be spent per pupil and that the amount may be dependent in part on the tax base of the district in which the pupil resides.

Serrano v. *Priest* (II) (California, 1977)

The question of the constitutionality of California's school financing formula was raised a second time, in light of the *Rodriguez* decision in the Supreme Court, in *Serrano* II.[30] The state supreme court again ruled for equality of per-pupil expenditures, citing the equal protection clause of the state constitution. The quality of education in California could not be dependent upon the wealth of parents or the residence of students.

Under *Serrano* II, the trial court retained jurisdiction over related school finance questions. In 1986 a suit was filed alleging that unacceptable disparities in money expended per pupil existed among school districts. In this compliance hearing, the court ruled that categorical aid for special needs programs could not be included when determining wealth-related disparities. The $100 range specified in *Serrano* II as the acceptable wealth-related disparity may not have to be rigidly observed.

Seattle School District No. 1 of King County v. *State of Washington* (Washington, 1978)

A school finance program in the state of Washington reached the courts in the late 1970s when the Seattle school district could not provide adequate funding because the voters in the district repeatedly failed to approve necessary tax levies. In *Seattle School District No. 1 of King County* v. *State of Washington*,[31] the state supreme court ruled in favor of the plaintiffs and gave the legislature until July 1, 1981, to enact a school finance program in compliance with the mandate of the court.

In the view of the court, excess levies were permissible in Washington and were required so as to permit school districts to provide a basic education for resident children. Hence, the state must provide a means of implementing its public education mandate. The court found that the Washington state constitution placed a duty on the state to make *ample* provision for the education of school children.

Levittown v. *Nyquist* (New York, 1978, 1982)

On June 23, 1978, the New York State Court of Appeals, the state's highest court, declared the state's school finance system unconstitutional.[32] Although the decision was reversed in 1982, it is significant because it was the first school finance case where the problem of municipal overburden was an important factor.

The court found that the New York system of financing education failed in its obligation to give "all the state's schoolchildren the opportunity to acquire at least those basic skills necessary to function in a democratic society." The original charge by twenty-seven low-wealth districts held that the law discriminated against students in poor districts and failed to provide a "free system of common schools wherein all children may be educated," as provided for in the constitution of the state. When the four large metropolitan districts joined the suit as intervenors, the charge was brought that the state finance system discriminated against them by not taking into account their special needs and higher costs—municipal overburden. In addition, they claimed that they were penalized as a result of the law's providing state monies on the basis of student attendance rather than enrollment.

In the 1982 reversal of this decision, the court of appeals ruled that the state school financing system did not violate the equal protection clauses because the state allowed for a minimum foundation program from state funds augmented by local monies.

Board of Education of the City School District of Cincinnati v. Walter (Ohio, 1979)

On June 14, 1979, the Ohio Supreme Court held that Ohio's school finance system was constitutional,[33] citing *Rodriguez*. The court held that there was no evidence indicating that the state had not provided a thorough and efficient educational program for the children of the state. It ruled that funding was adequate, that it provided a minimum standard program, and that there was a rational basis for the inequities that may have existed. The court said that "thorough and efficient education" does not have to be "more than simply adequate or minimal," as was maintained in *Robinson* v. *Cahill*[34] in New Jersey in 1973. "The fact that a better financing system could be devised which would be more efficient or more thorough is not material," said the court. The U.S. Supreme Court declined without explanation to review the case.

Lujan v. Colorado State Board of Education (Colorado, 1982)

The Colorado Supreme Court upheld the state school financing system, even though it admitted that disparities due to differences in district wealth existed.[35] There is no discrimination, invidious or otherwise, in a school finance system that applies a uniform subsidy formula on a statewide basis while promoting community control by means of local taxation. The state school financing system did not violate the state constitutional mandate for provision of "thorough and uniform" educational opportunities. Local control is the objective of the school finance system, and the court upheld this view even though local property taxes resulted in disparities in per-pupil expenditures.

Hornbeck v. Somerset County Board of Education (Maryland, 1983)

The state high court in Maryland ruled that the state's system of financing public schools did not violate state or federal equal protection clauses because education was not a fundamental right in Maryland.[36] That educational resources in poorer school districts are inferior to those in rich school districts does not mean that there is insufficient funding provided by the state's financing system for all students to obtain an adequate education. Maryland's education system did not have to be "equal" in the sense of mathematical uniformity, as long as efforts were made to minimize the impact of undeniable and inevitable demographic and environmental disadvantages on any given child.

Dupree v. *Alma School District No. 30* (Arkansas, 1983)

This case struck down the Arkansas system for financing public schools because equal protection was denied to school districts (and their students) that were "property poor."[37] The court ruled that inequalities are inherent in a financing system based on widely varying local tax bases; the system actually widens the gap between the property-poor and property-wealthy districts in providing educational opportunities.

East Jackson Public Schools v. *State* (Michigan, 1984)

This suit challenged Michigan's school financing system because it produced unequal per student funding between districts.[38] The court of appeals held that education is not a fundamental right under the state constitution; the state's obligation to provide free public education was not synonymous with an obligation to provide equal per-student funding between districts. The state had a minimum foundation program, whereby poor districts received state aid to raise their per-pupil expenditures to a minimum level.

Horton v. *Meskill* (Connecticut, 1977, 1985)

In 1977 the Connecticut Supreme Court declared that the right to education is so basic and fundamental in that state that infringement must be strictly scrutinized.[39] Therefore, the court declared unconstitutional the state school financing system, which depended primarily on a local property tax base without regard to the disparity in the financial ability of the towns to finance an educational program, with no significant equalizing state support.

In 1985 the court again was asked to rule on Connecticut's system of financing schools. At that time, it upheld new legislation (enacted in 1979 after *Horton* I) because it did equalize expenditures per pupil. This court defined the process for scrutinizing the state's finance formula in light of education being a fundamental right:

1. Plaintiffs must show that disparities in educational expenditures are not de minimis and do jeopardize fundamental rights to education.
2. The burden shifts to the state to justify disparities as advancing a legitimate state policy.
3. If the justification is acceptable, the state must show that disparities are not so great as to be unconstitutional.

Papasan v. *Allain* (Mississippi, 1986)

This Mississippi case relates to school land grants. The northern twenty-three counties in the state were held by the Chickasaw Indian Nation at the time the state was granted the sixteenth section of land for the support of schools. The Chickasaw land was later ceded to the United States through a treaty, but no sections were designated for education. Congress provided lands to the state in lieu of section 16. Under state statutes the sixteenth sections and lieu lands were to be held in a trust for the benefit of schools, with all revenue derived from the land allocated directly to the township in which they were located. The state legislature sold the lieu lands and invested the proceeds in loans to railroads, which were later destroyed during the Civil War and never rebuilt. Though the lieu lands were not replaced, the state continued to award minimal interest payments to the twenty-three counties.

The case arose in 1984 when local school officials on behalf of the school children from the Chickasaw Cession area filed suit in federal district court against state officials, challenging the disparity in the level of school funds—only $0.63 per pupil in the Chickasaw Cession counties, as compared to a state average of $75.34 per pupil in the other counties. The district court dismissed the complaint, holding that the claims were barred by the Eleventh Amendment to the United States Constitution, and the court of appeal affirmed the decision. However, the United States Supreme Court ruled that the Eleventh Amendment did not bar a claim that unequal distribution of school land funds violated equal protection.[40] The case was remanded to the trial court to determine whether a legitimate state interest existed for the disparity in distribution of benefits from public school lands.

Helena Elementary School District v. *State* (Montana, 1989)

This case centered around the educational clause in the Montana state constitution which stated:

> It is the *goal* of the people to establish a system of education which will develop the full educational potential of each person. *Equality of educational opportunity* is guaranteed to each person of the state.[41]

The state's position was that the clause was an aspirational *goal*. The plaintiffs' position was that *equal educational opportunity* was guaranteed by the clause. Experts and educational officials testified that (1) substantial disparities existed in the quality of education among the districts, (2) wealth in the districts was disparate with the spending per pupil in similar districts to be as much as 8 to 1, (3) comparable tax rates in different districts still allowed richer districts to raise twice as much as poorer districts and spend twice as much, (4) higher spending provided better educational opportunities. The court agreed with the plaintiffs, experts, and educators and declared that the "total educational spending per district must be essentially equal since the guarantee of *equality of educational opportunity* applies to every person in the state of Montana."

Rose v. *Council for Better Education* (Kentucky, 1989)

The constitution of Kentucky states that the General Assembly shall, by appropriate legislation, provide for an efficient system of common schools throughout the state. The Supreme Court of Kentucky examined what was meant by an *efficient* system by looking at indications of educational achievement. The court determined that the poorer districts were in worse condition than the richer districts. They probed deeper, noting that 35% of Kentucky's adult population were not high school graduates, that Kentucky ranked nationally in the lower 20 to 25 percentile in virtually every educational category dealing with achievement, and that inadequate performance was a reality in almost all districts. The court determined that Kentucky's funding system was underfunded and inadequate, as well as unequal and inequitable, and that educational funding must be increased and become equitable.[42] The court declared the funding system to be unconstitutional, based on the educational clause, and ordered the legislature to revise the state funding system to comply with the mandated efficient system of common schools.

Edgewood Independent School District v. *Kirby* (Texas, 1989)

The Texas Supreme Court held that the state's educational finance system was unconstitutional, violating the *efficiency clause* of the state constitution, which mandates that the state provide an "efficient system of public schools."[43] The facts in the case were not disputed: There was a 700 to 1 ratio between the value of taxable property in wealthiest and poorest districts, and district spending per student varied from $2,112 to $19,333. The state (Kirby) argued that the word *efficient*, as used by the 1875 Texas Constitutional Convention, meant a simple and inexpensive system. In contrast, the plaintiffs (Edgewood Independent School District) contended that *efficient* did not mean simple and inexpensive but *effective* and *productive*. The court agreed with the plaintiffs and stated that "in mandating 'efficiency,' the constitutional framers and ratifiers did not intend a system with such vast [financial] disparities as now exist."

The court maintained that resultant inequities from such financial disparity were "directly contrary to the constitutional vision of efficiency." The court determined that equality was the norm, not a minimum foundation program espoused by *Rodriguez*, and directed the state legislature to provide a system that repaired the constitutional defects. The Texas legislature passed Senate Bill 1, which the Governor signed into law June 7, 1990. The plaintiffs returned to court, arguing that the legislature had not met its constitutional obligation as Senate Bill 1 did not change the school finance system enough to bring about equity. The court agreed with the plaintiffs, calling the system a "Band-Aid," and directed the legislature to change the system and make it efficient. To be efficient, the court said, the financing system must "draw revenue from all property at a substantially similar rate." Further, a justice in a concurring statement reaffirmed the doctrine of allowing the legislature to develop the system and that" [we] should not speculate or interfere with the ongoing legislature debate as to how to meet the mandates of *Edgewood*. . . ."

Abbott v. *Burke, Abbott II* (New Jersey, 1990).

The first time this case was before the New Jersey Supreme Court (*Abbott I*), the court directed that the educational funding system in New Jersey should be contested before an administrative agency. The second time this case appeared before the court, the funding issue was specifically addressed.

The *Abbott* cases were a continuation of a series of *Robinson* v. *Cahill* cases brought before the courts in New Jersey. In *Robinson I* the court found the funding system in New Jersey to be in violation of the state education clause in their state constitution. The *Robinson* series of cases continued to *Robinson V*, in which the court declared that a 1975 New Jersey Public School Education Act was facially constitutional even though the possibility existed that some districts might not provide the required *thorough and efficient* education.

The plaintiffs in the *Abbott II* case contended that the Public School Education Act was not only unconstitutional as applied to certain districts, but that such financial disparities existed and the Act was unconstitutional in its entirety.[44] The court began its review by examining the meaning of *thorough and efficient* and concluded that this phrase relates to a climate of change, and that *thorough and efficient* is consistent with "continually changing environment." The court painstakingly examined a number of social ills such as crime, drug abuse, unwanted pregnancy, and child abuse and linked the lack of education to a rise in crime. Finally, the court ruled that the legislature had to bring forth a system to ensure that children in property-poor districts receive an education substantially equal to that of children in the property-rich districts.

Coalition for Equitable School Funding v. *State of Oregon* (Oregon, 1991)

In 1991, Oregon's school funding system was upheld as constitutional even though the method resulted in disparities between state standards and the amount of state funding, as well as disparities among school districts in financial benefits or tax burdens.[45]

The Coalition, composed of school districts, taxpayers, parents, and students, challenged the state's system as violating three provisions of the state constitution: (1) an article establishing a uniform and general system of common schools; (2) an article requiring that taxes be uniform on the same class of subjects within the territorial limits of the authority levying the tax; and (3) an article prohibiting denial of equal privileges for immunities.

The court held that the state's financing method was valid under a subsequently enacted "Safety Net" constitutional provision governing school districts' levying of property taxes for operating purposes. The court interpreted the Safety Net to contemplate the kind of disparities of which the plaintiffs complained. The provision expressly recognized the permissibility of relying on local property taxes to fund public schools.

The court explained that "when a party argues that a *general constitutional provision* forbids the state from doing something, that argument may be answered by a *later-adopted constitutional provision* that allows the state to do that very thing." Because of the Safety Net provision, Oregon's system of funding public education was upheld.

The denouement of the aforementioned court cases has been perplexing. Seventeen states testing their school finance formula in light of the state constitution have followed the *Rodriguez* doctrine and have had their systems upheld. Ten state supreme courts have declared that their systems of educational finance violate their state constitutions. States upholding their systems are Arizona, Colorado, Georgia, Idaho, Illinois, Maryland, Michigan, Minnesota, New York, North Carolina, Ohio, Oklahoma, Oregon, Pennsylvania, South Carolina, Virginia, and Wisconsin. Those that have held their system unconstitutional are Arkansas, California, Connecticut, Kentucky, Montana, New Jersey, Texas, Washington, West Virginia, and Wyoming.[46] The influence of the courts is great; but the climate is changeable: historically, geographically, and ideologically.

PRINCIPLES ESTABLISHED BY RECENT COURT DECISIONS

The court decisions of *Serrano*, *Rodriguez*, and other related state cases have seemed to agree, with only minor exceptions, with the following general principles or conclusions:

1. Education is considered to be an important interest of the state.

2. Since educational needs vary from district to district, the state does not have to require all of its school districts to spend the same amount of money per pupil or offer identical educational programs.

3. Although local property taxes discriminate against the poor, state legislatures are not required to eliminate them in favor of taxes on other sources of revenue.

4. Schools may make additional expenditures for programs for exceptional children, compensatory programs for culturally disadvantaged children, and programs for other educational needs that are significant and worthy of special treatment.

5. No specific plan or plans have been mandated to achieve equitability in school finance formulas.

PRESSURE FOR REFORM

After the *Rodriguez* decision, many feared that the school finance reform process would be slowed if the court actions alone were used. Therefore, the school finance court decisions resulted in general pressure on most state legislative bodies to bring reform to school finance systems. Kirp wrote:

> The Supreme Court's decision in *Rodriguez* demolished the hope that the courts would lead a school finance revolution of national scope. Although suits premised on equal protection and specific educational provisions in state constitutions have subsequently been filed, the judicial response has been at best mixed. But even as the courts' involvement in this issue has diminished, legislatures in eighteen states, most of them states where no authoritative judicial decision was rendered, have revised their financing systems to reduce the impact of disparities in local wealth. . . . [47]

Legislative bodies, whether or not they are faced with mandates from the courts, have had much activity in developing legislation dealing with the equity issue. Following Justice Powell's admonition in *Rodriguez* that these matters merit the continued attention of scholars, lawmakers and the people, some different prerogatives were used. They included full state funding with elimination or reduction of local tax levies; use of a statewide property tax; increase in state income taxes, sales taxes, or both; assumption by the state of all capital-outlay costs; increases in school expenditures in poor districts, with or without a decrease in expenditures in more affluent ones; provisions for additional local revenue to supplement a state-funded school program; and advocacy of greater federal participation in financing education.

In the past, problems in school finance practices have generated efforts for improvements. For example, excessive taxpayer burdens in some districts and the lack of adequate revenue to support desirable educational programs in some poor districts led to flat and percentage grants in the early 1900s. The second quarter of the century saw the establishment and implementation of crude foundation programs. The 1950s and 1960s fostered improved state equalization formulas. During that period the federal government sponsored categorical aid programs to help the country rebound from the shock of Sputnik. Since 1954, as a result of the *Brown* desegregation decision by the Supreme Court, the emphasis has been on providing equal rights for minority groups.

Thus, striving for school finance improvements is a never-ending struggle. Only occasionally, however, does the effort become so concerted and visible as to be classified as a "reform" movement. Such a reform effort began in the early 1970s as a result of the court decisions that ruled some state school finance laws unconstitutional. Nearly all states began a strong post-*Serrano* effort to provide greater equality in the allocation of their education resources.

FINANCE STUDIES AND REFORM EFFORTS

During the 1960s, 1970s, and 1980s, several studies had an impact on state school finance programs. They included a 1968 report from the National Education Finance Project which stated that there was a growing awareness of the importance of providing an adequate education for all citizens, and an increasing recognition of the need for differential educational programs for individuals and groups having special learning needs. In addition, there needed to be a developing understanding of the importance of human capital to the well-being of the "brain intensive" economic system. Therefore, state financial systems needed to be improved to make them more equitable. Most states needed to adopt equalization programs that considered the ability of local districts to pay as well as variations in unit costs and pupil costs. The report noted that the cost differentials for various classes of pupils fluctuated. Finally, the report stated that federal aid to education should be general rather than categorical.

A 1972 report from the President's Commission on School Finance stated the following: Each state should assume responsibility for raising and allocating the funds required for education but leave control of education at the local level; state allocation should include differentials based on educational need such as for education of handicapped and disadvantaged students; states should reorganize their school districts to provide more equal tax bases; and consideration should be given to financial assistance to nonpublic schools.

The Advisory Commission on Intergovernmental Relations proposed a model in 1973 that would require states to assume substantially all elementary and secondary education costs. Its proposal for equality would cross state lines, but if such a plan could not be effected, it recommended equalization across metropolitan areas. The financing method would use the power equalization principle, a uniform property tax, and "recapturing" of excess funds in wealthy districts by the state. Its alternate to this plan would be full state funding.

Perhaps the most controversial and influential report was "A Nation at Risk: The Imperative for Educational Reform." The report maintained that a major cause of the once unchallenged preeminence of education in the United States affecting commerce, industry, technology, and innovation was mediocrity in America's public schools.

Verifying public sentiment, the report from the National Commission on Excellence in Education to President Ronald Reagan in 1983 indicated that the American schools inadequately met the challenges of global competition. The commission, appointed by Secretary of Education, Terrel H. Bell, consisted of 18 members under the chairmanship of David P. Gardner. The now famous document frankly stated:

> Our nation is at risk. Our once unchallenged preeminence in commerce, industry, science, and technological innovation is being overtaken by competitors throughout the world. This report is concerned with only one of

the many causes and dimensions of the problem, but it is the one that under-girds American prosperity, security, and civility. We report to the American people that while we can take justifiable pride in what our schools and colleges have historically accomplished and contributed to the United States and the well-being of its people, the educational foundations of our society are presently being eroded by a rising tide of mediocrity that threatens our very future as a nation and a people. What was unimaginable a generation ago has begun to occur—others are matching and surpassing our educational attainments.

If an unfriendly foreign power had attempted to impose on America the mediocre educational performance that exists today, we might well have viewed it as an act of war.[48]

The Commission viewed the decline in standardized test scores, illiteracy rates, and poor achievement in mathematics and science as a disaster. They called for increased high school graduation requirements in English, mathematics, science, social studies, and computer science. More time for education by extending the school day or the school year was recommended. Teachers were to work longer, have career ladder opportunities, and act as mentors, if experienced, or be mentored if novices.

There have been many state school finance and reform studies. In *The Unfinished Agenda: A New Vision for Child Development and Education,* the Committee for Economic Development notes that nearly every state is at some stage of seriously addressing its educational problems. For example:

- Nearly every state now has some form of statewide student accountability testing. Some states, such as Georgia and Florida, expanded existing programs; and others, such as Pennsylvania and Ohio, mandated statewide student testing for the first time.
- Forty-three states have increased or specified for the first time their high school graduation requirements.
- Thirty-three states have some alternative route to teacher certification that allows qualified individuals to bypass traditional state-certified teacher-training programs. As recently as 1983, only eighteen states provided such alternative routes.
- More than twenty states have passed or are considering legislation to expand public school choice.
- About twenty states are in the process of redesigning their school-funding systems in order to distribute funds more equitably to less wealthy districts.
- Nine states (New Jersey, Ohio, Arkansas, Georgia, Kentucky, New Mexico, South Carolina, Texas, and West Virginia) have enacted provisions for intervening in academically bankrupt districts.
- More than two-thirds of the states have taken steps to reduce the incidence and costs of teen pregnancy, and nineteen states have expanded Medicare coverage to include pregnant women and young children in families with incomes up to 133 percent of the federal poverty level.[49]

FACTORS LIMITING SCHOOL FINANCE REFORM

For the most part, education studies during the 1980s have centered on reform. Though not specifically related to the study of school finance formulas, these reform reports on local districts and state funding patterns have had great impact. After "A Nation at Risk," governors from many states assumed leadership for education, pressuring state departments of education and legislative bodies to mandate reform measures. The school reform movement saw the development of two distinct groups of citizens seeking reform, with divergent backgrounds and approaches to the problems they were trying to solve. In the first group were those with professional experience in education, many of whom had vested interests and some degree of expertise and practical understanding of the problems to be solved. These were school finance professors, public school administrators, and specialists in state departments of education—the "friends" of public education. These were the "authorities" in the field, working for improvement of their profession.

The second group of reformers included those who saw the problem from a different perspective—lawyers, economists, political scientists, representatives of the disadvantaged, members of state legislatures, representatives and members of minority groups, and others with only secondary interest in education per se. This group usually worked with community and state political leaders to bring about reform sufficient to avoid *Serrano*-type court decisions or to revise or defeat proposed laws that would repudiate their state school finance systems.

Unfortunately for the schools, these two groups did not always agree about goals or methods. Communication and collaboration were often neglected or minimized, and consequently the results were not always satisfactory.

Other problems plagued the advocates of school finance reform. The differences that have always existed among urban, suburban, and rural districts were not decreased in the struggle to improve the financing of education. For example, there was seldom any solution to the question of providing additional funds for city districts to compensate for municipal overburden. The problem of getting laws enacted to satisfy the rulings of courts was always difficult when such proposals were thrown into the political arena. Many legislative bodies found it politically impossible to enact legislation that would meet the "requirements" established by courts in the same state—largely due to the fact that any school finance program would inevitably favor one kind of school district over another.

CALIFORNIA'S PROPOSITION 13

Students of physics frequently cite the law, "Action equals reaction." They observe the swing of the pendulum that moves an apparently equal distance in two opposite directions. Applying such observations to the real world outside the laboratory, one can observe this physical law operating with more dramatic and perhaps more consequential results in the realm of the social sciences. Everywhere are examples of the inevitability of movement to the liberal side bringing reverse action to the conservative, and vice versa. The progress of a society and its institutions in the direction of their ultimate goals is too often marked by a few steps one way, followed immediately by almost equivalent steps in the other direction.

This phenomenon has been observed many times in the field of public school finance. California's Proposition 13, said by its ardent sponsors to be a panacea for a tax-paying society, came more quickly and with more force and national influence than was generally anticipated. In one massive effort, the voters of California, by almost a 2 to 1 margin, voted to restrict property taxes to 1 percent of the 1976 assessed market value of such property, thus reducing property tax revenues by about 57 percent. The act also provided that a two-thirds favorable vote of the legislature would be necessary to increase future annual tax assessments to a maximum of 2 percent.

Although the quick and convincing passage of Proposition 13 caught many people by surprise, some voter reaction to inflationary costs of education and increasing taxes had long been anticipated by knowledgeable people in the field of school finance. Persistent resistance to taxes could be seen on every hand— defeated bond and school budget elections, increases in the number and size of circuit-breaker and other tax relief measures, and increases in high-cost services to elderly and handicapped persons were strong and persuasive indicators of difficulties to come in providing adequate funds for public education and other government services.

California was an extremely fertile ground for tax retrenchment. In addition to high property values due to extreme inflation, it had a highly progressive income tax, a high sales tax, and a record of high and steadily increasing property taxes. Its system of keeping assessments in line with the inflationary market value of property, although philosophically desirable, also worked to the benefit of the instigators of Proposition 13. Increases in market values were quickly transformed into higher personal taxes on real property, while in many other states increased assessments tended to lag far behind market value increases. Then, too, it appeared to be "popular" practice in California to keep the tax structure producing revenues greater than expenditures, with a consequent buildup of reserves that could be used in emergencies. Present, too, was the political notion that a surplus of state government revenues represented high efficiency in state administration rather than simply excessive taxation. The California legislature seemed to be reluctant to enact a satisfactory tax relief measure in spite of numerous attempts to do so.

The passage of Proposition 13 instantaneously affected other states. A survey of all 50 states conducted one year later revealed the following: Twenty-two states reduced property taxes; eighteen states reduced income taxes; fifteen states curtailed in some fashion the collection of sales taxes; eight states voted spending limits; and a dozen states have repealed or reduced various other taxes.[50]

Proposition 13 was not immune from judicial review. Over time Proposition 13 resulted in dramatic disparities in the taxes paid by persons owning similar pieces of property. Long-term owners paid lower taxes, while newer owners paid higher taxes. One such new owner, Stephanie Nordlinger, claimed the "scheme violated the Equal Protection Clause of the Fourteenth Amendment" and brought suit in Nordlinger v. Hahn.[51] The County Superior Court dismissed the complaint and the state Court of Appeal affirmed. Nordlinger appealed to the U.S. Supreme Court and on June 18, 1992 the case was decided with the Court ruling (8-1) that Proposition 13 and its attendant tax disparity did *not* violate the Equal Protection Clause.

Speaking for the Court Justice Blackman stated:

> The Equal Protection Clause of the Fourteenth Amendment commands that no state shall "deny to any person within its jurisdiction the equal protection of the laws." The Equal Protection Clause does not forbid classifications . . . and as a general rule "legislatures are presumed to have acted within their constitutional power despite the fact that, in practice, their laws result in some inequality . . . and judicial intervention is generally unwarranted" . . . and we must decline petitioner's request to upset the will of the people of California. The judgement of the Court of Appeal is affirmed.[52]

FINANCE REFORM OR TAX REDUCTION

Various measures limiting taxation powers were enacted between 1976 and 1984. New Jersey, Texas, Colorado, Michigan, Tennessee, Arizona, and Hawaii were among the first states to pass such legislation; California gained the greatest attention by passing Proposition 13 in 1978, and Proposition 2$\frac{1}{2}$ in Massachusetts followed in 1980.

There was a brief relaxing of spending limitations as the reform movement gained momentum. However, a lagging economy, cutbacks in federal aid, and the realization that reform was expensive spurred new interest in curtailing expenditures for public services.

In each case where limits have been imposed, the state faces the paradox of substantially reducing property taxes while preserving school programs. To the degree that tax reductions are made and/or school services reduced, it appears that the friends of education have failed to make a legitimate case for the high costs of school services. That there is conflict between the forces favoring school finance reform and those favoring tax reduction is shown in the following statement:

> There is an impending clash between two major public finance movements. One is stimulating large increases in state/local public spending while the other is galvanizing a trend toward lower expenditures. The first is known

as the "school finance reform movement." Its supporters have been working since the turn of the century but have developed a new focus on equity in recent years. The second movement is led by a strong network of state policy makers who are pushing for tax or spending limitations. They have succeeded already in pushing the center of state politics to the right. . . . [53]

Thus, the "battle" between those who view education as an investment in human capital and those who feel that tax reduction is a panacea for societal ailments was reopened. It was apparent that taxpayers were demanding some relief from the heavy burden of high taxes. Gradual decreases rather than abrupt and destructive decreases in taxes, placing reasonable limits on the expenditures of government, the establishment of tax levy limits, the liberalization of circuit-breaker laws for the tax relief of the poor and the handicapped, and greater centralization and consolidation of schools in many areas of the country are better methods of obtaining taxpayer justice than indiscriminate cuts that slowly destroy social institutions.

SUMMARY

For the first time in the history of education in the United States, the courts exert considerable pressure on the states to improve their school finance systems. Out of their decisions there emerged certain guidelines, which emphasized equity and equal protection in school finance formulas.

Serrano v. *Priest* (1971) in California was one of the most influential court cases involving school finance to be decided during the decade. As a result of *Serrano*, almost every state made efforts to improve its method of financing education. Although *San Antonio Independent School District* v. *Rodriguez* (1973) ended appeals in the federal courts, the school finance issue continued in state courts. States that followed the *Serrano* philosophy found education to be a fundamental right for the students of that state, according to the state constitution, or found school financing patterns to be in violation of state education clauses. States that followed the *Rodriguez* philosophy found no justification for equal per-pupil expenditures in their state constitutions.

Twenty-seven states have had their school finance scheme challenged in the courts. Seventeen of them have ruled in the *Rodriguez* doctrine, ten in the *Serrano*. As the 1980s ended and the 1990s began, cases in four states seemed to indicate a trend toward the *Serrano* philosophy, but in 1991 Oregon's supreme court ruled that their state's finance formula was constitutional.

School finance reform was evident in nearly all of the states at some time during the decades of the 1970s and 1980s. Unfortunately, the groups working for reform did not always cooperate in proposing changes in school finance laws. Several national and individual state studies influenced state finance reform.

The impact of the courts is altered by a tax reduction movement heightened by the passage of Proposition 13 in California, which provided for a radical reduction in local property taxes and weakened local control and financing of public education in that state. Several states followed California's lead in reducing taxes. The long-term effect of finance reform and tax reduction in the states is not yet known.

ASSIGNMENT PROJECTS

1. Review some of the important court cases not included in the text that have stimulated or retarded school finance reform in recent years.
2. Trace the history of tax-restrictive legislation in one particular state. Indicate the major forces favoring such tax restrictions as well as those opposing it.
3. Produce the evidence to show that tax-restrictive legislation penalizes schools more than any other function of state and local government.
4. In class, organize into groups and debate the consequences of Proposition 13.
5. Interview a school finance professor, a public school administrator, and a school finance specialist in a state department of education about financing of education in the next ten years. Then interview a state legislator, a tax lawyer, an economist, a political scientist, a spokesperson for the disadvantaged, and a spokesperson for a minority group about the same subject. Compare and contrast their opinions and viewpoints.
6. Write a position paper on the role of parent-teacher organizations in the school finance reform movement. Why have they not been more involved? Should they be? If so, how can they become more involved?

SELECTED READINGS

Data Research, Inc. *Deskbook Encyclopedia of American School Law.* Rosemont, Minn: Data Research, Inc., 1989.

Doyle, Denis P., and Terry W. Hartle. *Excellence in Education: The States Take Charge.* Washington, D.C.: American Enterprise Institute for Public Policy Research, 1986.

Gee, E. Gordon, and David J. Sperry. *Education Law and the Public Schools: A Compendium.* Newton, Mass.: Allyn and Bacon, 1978.

Guthrie, James W., Walter I. Garms, and Lawrence C. Pierce. *School Finance and Education Policy: Enhancing Educational Efficiency, Equality, and Choice.* 2nd ed. Englewood Cliffs, N.J.: Prentice Hall, 1988.

Honeyman, D. S., D. C. Thompson, and R. C. Wood. *Financing Rural and Small Schools: Issues of Adequacy and Equity.* Gainesville: University of Florida Press, 1989.

McCarthy, Martha M. *A Delicate Balance: Church, State, and the Schools.* Bloomington, Ind.: Phi Delta Kappan Educational Foundation, 1983.

Odden, Allan R., and Lawrence O. Picus. *School Finance: A Policy Perspective.* New York: McGraw-Hill, 1992

Strahan, Richard D., and L. Charles Turner. *The Courts and the Schools.* New York: Longman, 1987.

Thomas, Gloria Jean, David J. Sperry, and F. Del Wasden. *The Law and Teacher Employment.* New York: West Publishing Company, 1991.

Underwood, Julie K., and Deborah A. Verstegen, eds. *The Impact of Litigation and Legislation on Public School Finance: Adequacy, Equity and Excellence.* New York: Harper & Row, 1990.

Valente, William D. *Law in the Schools.* Columbus, Ohio: Merrill, 1987.

Verstegan, D. A. *School Finance at a Glance.* Denver, Colo: Education Commission of the States, 1990.

Webb, L. D., M. M. McCarthy, and S. B. Thomas. *Financing Elementary and Secondary Education.* Columbus, Ohio: Merrill, 1988.

ENDNOTES

1. *Stuart* v. *School District No. 1 of the Village of Kalamazoo,* 30 Mich. 69 (1874).

2. *Brown* v. *Board of Education* (I), 347 U.S. 483, 74 S. Ct. 686 (1954).

3. *Baker* v. *Carr,* 369 U.S. 186, 82 S. Ct. 691 (1962).

4. *Serrano* v. *Priest* (I), 96 Cal. Rptr. 601, 487 P.2nd 1241 (Calif. 1971).

5. *San Antonio Independent School District* v. *Rodriguez,* 411 U.S. 1, 93 S. Ct. 1278 (1973).

6. *Lewis* v. *Mosley,* 204 So.2d 197 (Fla. 1967).

7. *Morton Salt Co.* v. *City of South Hutchinson,* 177 F.2d 889 (10th Cir. 1949).

8. *Sawyer* v. *Gilmore,* 109 Me. 169, 83 A. 673 (Me. 1912).

9. *McInnis* v. *Ogilvie* (*Shapiro*), 394 U.S. 322, 89 S. Ct. 1197 (1969).

10. *Serrano* v. *Priest* (1) 5 Cal. 3d 584, 96 Cal. Rptr. 601, 487 P.2d 1241 (Calif. 1971).

11. Ibid.

12. Paul D. Carrington, "Equal Justice Under Law and School Finance," in *School Finance in Transition* (Gainesville, Fla.: National Conference on School Finance, 1973), p. 162.

13. Donald Wickert, "Some School Finance Issues Related to the Implementation of Serrano and Proposition 13," *Journal of Educational Finance,* Spring 1985, p. 535.

14. Betsy Levin et al., *Paying for Public Schools* (Washington, D.C.: Urban Institute, 1972), p. 8.

15. *Van Dusartz* v. *Hatfield,* 334 F. Supp. 870 (D.C. Minn. 1971).

16. *Robinson* v. *Cahill,* 289 A.2d 569 (N.J. Super. 1972).

17. *Spano* v. *Board of Education,* 328 N.Y.S.2d 229 (N.Y. 1972).

18. *Burruss* v. *Wilkerson,* 310 F. Supp. 572 (W.D. Va. 1969), *cert. denied,* 90 S. Ct. 812 (1969).

19. *San Antonio Independent School District* v. *Rodriguez,* 411 U.S. 1, 93 S. Ct. 1278 (1973).

20. *Van Dusartz* v. *Hatfield,* 334 F. Supp. 870 (D.C. Minn. 1971).

21. Leland D. Melvin, "The Law of Public School Finance," *Contemporary Education,* Spring 1984, p. 149.

22. Ibid.

23. *Oregon* v. *Hass,* 420 U.S. 714, 719 (1975).

24. *Washakie County School District No. 1* v. *Herschler,* 606 P.2d 310 (Wyo. 1980), *cert. denied,* 101 S. Ct. 86, 449 U.S. 824 (1980); *Board of Education of the City School District of Cincinnati* v. *Walter,* 390 N.E.2d 813 (Ohio, 1979); *Serrano* v. *Priest* (II), 557 P.2d 929 (Calif. 1977), *cert. denied,* 432 U.S. 907 (1977).

25. Melvin, "The Law of Public School Finance," p. 153.

26. *Horton* v. *Meskill*, 376 A.2d 359 (Conn. 1977); *Horton* v. *Meskill*, 486 A.2d 1099 (Conn. 1985); *Seattle School District No. 1 of King County* v. *State of Washington*, 585 P.2d 71 (Wash. 1978); *Washakie County School District No. 1* v. *Herschler*, 606 P.2d 310 (Wyo. 1980), *cert. denied*, 101 S. Ct. 86, 449 U.S. 824 (1980).

27. *Shofstall* v. *Hollins*, 515 P.2d 590 (Ariz. 1973); *Thompson* v. *Engelking*, 537 P.2d 635 (Idaho 1975); *Olsen* v. *State of Oregon*, 554 P.2d 139 (Ore. 1976); *State ex rel. Woodahl* v. *Straub*, 520 P.2d 776 (Mont. 1974); *Knowles* v. *State Board of Education*, 547 P.2d 699 (Kans. 1976); *Blase* v. *State of Illinois*, 302 N.E.2d 46 (Ill. 1973); *People of Illinois ex rel. Jones* v. *Adams*, 350 N.E.2d 767 (Ill. 1976); *Lujan* v. *Colorado State Board of Education*, 649 P.2d 1005 (Colo. 1982); *McDaniel* v. *Thomas*, 285 S.E.2d 156 (Ga. 1981); *Board of Education of the City School District of Cincinnati* v. *Walter*, 390 N.E.2d 813 (Ohio 1979).

28. *Milliken* v. *Green*, 203 N.W.2d 457 (Mich. 1972); *Milliken* v. *Green*, 212 N.W.2d 711 (Mich. 1973); *Board of Education of Levittown Union Free School District* v. *Nyquist*, 408 N.Y.S.2d 606 (Nassau Co. Supreme Court 1978), *aff'd*, 443 N.Y.S.2d 843 (1982), *rev'd*, 453 N.Y.S.2d 643, 439 N.E.2d 359 (N.Y. 1982).

29. *Thompson* v. *Engelking*, 537 P.2d 635 (Idaho 1975).

30. *Serrano* v. *Priest* (II), 557 P.2d 929 (Cal. 1977), *cert. denied*, 432 U.S. 907 (1977).

31. *Seattle School District No. 1 of King County* v. *State of Washington*, 585 P.2d 71 (Wash. 1978).

32. *Board of Education of Levittown* v. *Nyquist*, 408 N.Y.S.2d 606 (Nassau Co. Supreme Court 1978), *aff'd*, 443 N.Y.S.2d 843 (1982), *rev'd* 453 N.Y.S.2d 643, 439 N.E.2d 359 (N.Y. 1982).

33. *Board of Education of the City School District of Cincinnati* v. *Walter*, 390 N.E.2d 813 (Ohio 1979).

34. *Robinson* v. *Cahill*, 289 A.2d 569 (N.J. Super. 1972).

35. *Lujan* v. *Colorado State Board of Education*, 649 P.2d 1005 (Colo. 1982).

36. *Hornbeck* v. *Somerset County Board of Education*, 458 A.2d 758 (Md. 1983).

37. *Dupree* v. *Alma School District No. 30*, 651 S.W.2d 90 (Ark. 1983).

38. *East Jackson Public Schools* v. *State*, 348 N.W.2d 303 (Mich. App. 1984).

39. *Horton* v. *Meskill*, 376 A.2d 359 (Conn. 1977), *aff'd*, 486 A.2d 1099 (Conn. 1985).

40. *Papasan* v. *Allain*, 106 S. Ct. 2932 (1986).

41. *Helena Elementary School District* v. *State*, 769 P.2d 684 (Mont. 1989).

42. *Rose* v. *Council for Better Education*, 790 S.W.2d 186 (Ky. 1989).

43. *Edgewood Independent School District* v. *Kirby*, 777 S.W.2d 391 (Texas 1989).

44. *Abbott* v. *Burke* (*Abbott II*), 575 A.2d 359 (N.J. 1990).

45. *Coalition for Equitable School Funding* v. *State of Oregon*, 811 P.2d 116 (1991).

46. The 27 states that have examined their educational funding systems are: Arizona (*Shofstall*, 515 P.2d 590); Arkansas (*DuPree*, 651 S.W.2d 90); California (*Serrano II*, 557 P.2d 929); Colorado (*Lujan*, 649 P.2d 1005); Connecticut (*Horton*, 376 A.2d 359); Georgia (*McDaniel*, 285 S.E.2d 156); Idaho (*Thompson*, 537 P.2d 635); Illinois (*Blase*, 302 N.E.2d 46); Kentucky (*Rose*, 790 S.W.2d 186); Maryland (*Hornbeck*, 458 A.2d 758); Michigan (*Milliken*, 203 N.W.2d 457); Minnesota (*Van Dusartz*, 334 F. Supp. 870); Montana (*Helena*, 769 P.2d 684); New Jersey (*Abbott II*, 575 A.2d 359); New York (*Levittown*, 439 N.E.2d 359); North Carolina (*Britt*, 357 S.E.2d 432); Ohio (*Walter*, 390 N.E.2d 813); Oklahoma (*Fair School Fin. Council*, 746 P.2d 1135); Oregon (*Coalition for Equitable School Funding* v. *State*, 811 P.2d 11.(1991); Pennsylvania (*Danson*, 399 A.2d 360); South Carolina (*Richland County*, 364 S.E.2d 470); Texas (*Kirby*, 777 S.W.2d 391); Virginia (*Burruss*, 310 F. Supp. 572); Washington (*Seattle School Dist.*, 585 P.2d 71); West Virginia (*Pauley*, 255 S.E.2d 859); Wisconsin (*Kukor*, 436 N.W.2d 568); and Wyoming (*Washakie County School Dist.*, 606 P.2d 310).

The 10 states that have declared their funding systems unconstitutional are: Arkansas (*Du Pree*, 651 S.W.2d 90); California (*Serrano II*, 557 P.2d 929); Connecticut (*Horton*, 376 A.2d 359); Montana (*Helena*, 769 P.2d 684); Kentucky (*Rose*, 790 S.W.2d 186); New Jersey (*Abbott II*, 575 A.2d 359); Texas (*Kirby*, 777 S.W.2d 391); Washington (*Seattle School Dist.*, 585 P.2d 71); Wyoming (*Washakie County School Dist.*, 606 P.2d 310).

47. David L. Kirp, "Law, Politics, and Equal Educational Opportunity: The Limits of Judicial Involvement," *Harvard Educational Review,* Vol. 47, No. 2 (May 1988), pp. 122-23.

48. The National Commission on Excellence in Education, "A Nation at Risk: The Imperative for Educational Reform," Washington, D.C.: April 1983, p. 5.

49. *The Unfinished Agenda: A New Vision for Child Development and Education* (New York: Research and Policy Committee, Committee for Economic Development, 1991), pp. 66-67.

50. *Phi Delta Kappan* (October 1979), p. 84.

51. *Nordlinger* v. *Hahn,* 1992 WL 132447 (U.S. 1992)

52. Ibid.

53. Michael W. Kirst, "The New Politics of State Education Finance," *Phi Delta Kappan* (February 1979), p. 427.

Chapter 9

Patterns for Developing School Finance Systems

America has a long tradition of state and local control of schools. The U.S. Constitution says nothing about education, and what does not belong to the Federal government becomes the province of each of the states. In education the state is the ultimate responsible agency. —ELLIOT W. EISNER, 1991

Court cases continue to send the strong message to states that reform is necessary in school finance systems. Strong signals were heard even prior to the landmark *Serrano* v. *Priest* [1] case in 1971. Several years earlier, taxpayer resistance to the continually increasing costs of education had been slowly building. Wide disparities in tax levies and school revenues had been changing school finance problems from local-state to state-national concerns. Ravitch viewed it this way: "The new politics of education rotated about a state-federal axis rather than a local-state axis which bypassed educational authorities by working directly with sympathetic congressional committees and by gaining judicial supervision."[2]

At the same time, school finance scholars were presenting evidence that the state school finance programs in existence did not provide the equal educational opportunity they were devised to provide. The foundation program concept had fallen short of the objectives its proponents had set for it. Equalization programs with local options that provided little or no state support eroded the effect of the foundation program concept as a guarantor of equal protection of school students in different districts. As implemented, it left the wealthy districts with more total funds per student than poor ones, with consequent disparities in curricular offerings as well as in tax burdens.

CONCERN FOR EQUAL RIGHTS

Since the founding of the United States, factors have worked to extend and protect the rights of citizens. With the ratification of the U.S. Constitution, the

Bill of Rights was adopted to provide greater and more specific protection of individuals. Since that time, society itself has been making slow but consistent progress in improving and equalizing the rights of individual citizens in numerous ways. As early as 1874, in the *Kalamazoo* case,[3] high school students were assured of an education on the same taxing basis as elementary students. In the *Brown* case of 1954,[4] black citizens were guaranteed equal educational opportunities with whites. By the mid-1960s the courts had eliminated or reduced geographic discrimination in legislative bodies by deciding that "the value of one's vote could not be diluted or debased when compared with the votes of others in the same circumstances," and had determined that lack of financial ability could not be used to deny criminals equal protection of the law.

Some important historical events in the United States increased the need for, and helped accelerate implementation of, plans for greater equality of educational opportunity and equal protection for school-age citizens. Industrialization increased the discrepancies in the financial ability of school districts and states to finance education. The Depression brought defaults in the payment of property taxes, greatly reduced incomes, and other economic distresses, which emphasized the need for increased state support of floundering school systems. World Wars I and II brought attention to the extremes in unequal education that were being provided in various sections and school districts throughout the country, because of the extremely unequal rates of rejection of potential military servicemen due to education deficiencies. Sputnik, in 1957, pointed up the need to improve public school educational programs if the United States intended to remain competitive in exploring outer space. The "A Nation at Risk" report in 1983 warned that American preeminence in commerce, industry, science, and technological innovation was being challenged worldwide and knowledge, learning, information, and skilled intelligence were the new raw materials of international commerce with the United States falling behind other nations. In 1991, *AMERICA 2000* called for a more stringent curriculum, including the United States dominance in the world in math and science by the year 2000. These are only a few indicators of the need to equalize and improve educational opportunities for school-age youth.

Although the *Serrano* case appeared to be an abrupt reversal of popular public and court opinion, it was in reality an extension of the trend toward greater protection of the rights of citizens in many aspects of the constitutional guarantee of equal protection for all citizens. Equalization was not, as some have thought, a completely novel idea, without precedent. As far back as 1905 Cubberley stated: "All the children of the state are equally important and are entitled to the same advantage."[5] In 1983 Berne and Stiefel concluded, "from 1940 to 1970 only the decade of the 1960s failed to show improvement in horizontal equity in an overwhelming number of states. This is a noteworthy result in the light of the school finance reforms that were concentrated in the next decade of the 1970s."[6]

The early 1970s saw great activity in the courts, in school board meetings, and in legislative halls. One of the most noticeable results was a reemphasis on certain tenets of school finance philosophy and theory that had been sponsored by such theorists as Updegraff and Morrison. Some of their ideas of how to provide equality of educational opportunity—which had not been popular when introduced, nor given an opportunity for practical development—began to be recognized as potentially valuable. Morrison's ideas concerning greater state control and virtual elimination of local districts now seemed logical to many who favored full state funding of public education. Updegraff's concept of reward for effort now reappeared under the name *power* (or open-end) *equalization*. Rather suddenly, these half-century-old ideas, hidden away in textbooks, seemed to offer the best solution to the problems in school finance.

There appear to be only two plans of state school finance that would meet the conditions now being implied by the courts. These are (1) full state funding and (2) district power equalization. These two plans are not equally acceptable to all states or to all people. The long and cherished tradition of local control of education seems to be threatened by such radical departures from past practices, especially by the almost revolutionary concept of full state funding. Certainly, few states could function as one district, as Hawaii does. Yet it was known that flat grants, percentage grants, foundation programs with or without local options, or any combination of these methods did not achieve equal protection.

FULL STATE FUNDING

The idea of full state funding of education certainly could not be considered radical or unacceptable to the people in those states that were providing more than half of their public school revenues from state sources. Earmarked state property taxes, sales taxes, income taxes, and others were common and could be expanded if full state funding were to be adopted. However, the difficulty of accepting the idea of full state funding in those states that provide much less than half the public school revenues presents a much greater problem. Many voters and decision makers look askance at increased state support, because of the possibility of increased state control over local schools.

At various times in United States history, exponents of complete state financing of education have put forth such proposals, with little popular support. They point out that more than half a century of state effort to equalize educational opportunity and school tax burdens by state-local partnership finance formulas has not achieved this goal. They reason that all states could attain this objective if they collected and controlled the disposition of all school funds.

Three different degrees of state participation are possible for financing and operating public schools.

1. State operation of public schools, with substantial reductions in the administrative and operational responsibilities of local school boards.

2. Complete state support, with elimination of locally raised funds but with state basic programs increased to adequate levels.

3. The foundation program approach, with state funds added to local tax funds to produce a state-guaranteed level of school support.

Graham noted the need for more complete state support:

We have witnessed an astonishing transformation in the role of the states in shaping the future of our nation. We—the states—now have more freedom to do what we know we must do. As a result of this increased flexibility, the states are free to become innovators instead of caretakers. But along with that new-found freedom comes added responsibility.

State leaders have a responsibility to the citizens to lead the states and nation into the 21st century. And, to do that we must lead by example: by doing, by taking risks, by providing the impetus for change ourselves.[7]

Models 9-1 and 9-1a are illustrations of two plans for full state funding of education, with minor adjustments that could be used. Model 9-1 illustrates full state funding without allowance for local options. All districts would receive the same number of dollars per weighted-pupil unit. Its disadvantage is that the state legislature would determine by itself the maximum number of dollars per pupil to be provided. Local needs, local desires, and local initiative would be ignored under this type of financing. Model 9-1a provides almost full state funding, with limited local options to go beyond the state-sponsored program. Although this plan purports to provide for local preferences, it is nonequalizing and favors wealthier districts, as do all finance plans where local effort is not state supported.

The plan shown as 9-1 provides exactly the same amount of revenue per weighted-pupil unit in each district. This has some serious limitations:

1. It makes the state-determined program a minimum as well as a maximum program.

2. It provides no way for a school district to enrich its program beyond that which the state mandates.

3. It removes fiscal responsibility from the control of local school boards.

4. It may tend to jeopardize local school programs when the state's revenue will not seem to support full state funding at a desirable level.

When this model is used, the result is nonequalization among districts of varying taxable wealth per weighted pupil. Thus, when all three districts use the maximum 10-mill levy, the net effect is that District L has available only $180 per mill per weighted-pupil unit while District H has $240 per mill per weighted-pupil unit. By the use of nonsupported local optional levies, the equalization accomplished with full state funding has been neutralized to some degree. Of course, if the state provides funds for nearly all the cost of school district programs, with only minimal local optional levies, the latter may not seriously upset the overall equalization that the program produces.

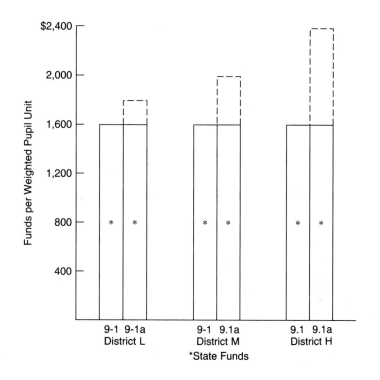

Full state funding			
Districts	Assessed valuation	State funds per WPU	Required local levy
L	$20,000,000	$1,600	Nil
M	40,000,000	1,600	Nil
H	80,000,000	1,600	Nil

Almost full state funding with minimum local options			
Additional local levy	Local funds per WPU	Total funds per WPU	Total funds per M per WPU
District L—10 M	$200	$1,800	$180
District M—10 M	400	2,000	200
District H—10 M	800	2,400	240

MODEL 9-1   Full state funding; 9-1a Almost full state funding with local levy option (10 M).

Ramifications

Full state funding under any plan raises some questions about an attendant increase in state control of local schools and a corresponding decrease in the power and authority of local school boards. Some feel that recent increases in state support of local school revenues have already reduced the role of local school boards in administering schools to an undesirable and irreversible point. Others suggest that the high degree of local control of half a century ago may not be possible or desirable in today's world.

As the name implies, full state funding places the burden for providing a good public school program completely upon the state itself. There is little promise that the typical legislature, in the face of extreme pressure for state funds from all state institutions, would year after year provide the money necessary for the high-level educational program desired by the citizens of its various school districts. Determining the amount of money necessary for education could very well become an "average practice" minimum program, completely lacking in local incentives.

Full state funding is an acceptable plan for districts that would be "leveled up" to expenditure levels or standards above their previous position. But "leveling down" or forcing some districts to remain at their current expenditure level could result. It is doubtful that leveling down or maintaining the status quo could be operable in any state. Hence, the state itself would be forced to find a system or rationale for providing funds above the established amount for expensive or high-expenditure school districts.

Probably the most negative aspects of full state funding are the following. (1) The state would exercise the power to determine the amount of revenue in every district with little regard for the educational needs or desires of the local citizenry. (2) There is no way to determine, on a rational and objective basis, which districts should be given the funds necessary to explore innovative practices or encouraged to become exemplary. Since local districts would make no tax effort on their own to finance education, the state would lack a legal framework or device with which to determine which schools or in what amount state funds should be allocated to "deserving" districts.

It is likely that full state funding would lead to the extended use of sales and income taxes, with less emphasis upon the property tax. There is much to be said in favor of this change, but the plan tends to discourage, if not obliterate, local initiative and special tax effort to provide better schools than those legislated by the state. Thus far, the states have found no satisfactory substitute for the incentive grants that have been used to provide better programs than are financed in districts where there is no expressed desire to extend local district effort to obtain such excellence.

Advantages and Disadvantages

Full state funding has some advantages and disadvantages. Its advocates claim that full state funding would:

1. Meet the requirement of the court decisions that the education of a student should be dependent only upon the wealth of the state, not upon the wealth of the parents or the school district.

2. Equalize the revenue among school districts and at the same time provide greater equity among the taxpayers of the state.

3. Reduce interdistrict competition for state funds, which can lead to the possible elimination of small and inefficient school districts.

4. Relieve local districts of the problem of obtaining funds, so that more local effort could be devoted to the improvement of the curriculum.

Those who point to the disadvantages of full state funding say that it would:

1. Result in a loss or reduction in the amount of local control of the educational program.

2. Result in loss of revenue in many districts now making additional tax effort to support better school programs, thus resulting in a leveling-down process.

3. Curtail innovative and high-cost programs, regardless of their need or worth.

4. Put public schools in more direct competition with other state agencies, such as higher education institutions, for state revenues.

5. Make a minimum program the maximum program by not providing a way for any district to go beyond the state-mandated and state-supported program.

6. Penalize districts with comparatively high salaries and operational costs.

Although current systems of financing education generally result in local competition for financial resources, full state funding would seem likely to result in having professional organizations of teachers negotiating at the state level as the major thrust for greater expenditure of funds for education. Local needs, local desires, and local problems of a unique nature would probably become subordinate to the collective bargaining process, with the end result that it would create centralized school operations, in contrast to the decentralized pattern now in existence in all states except Hawaii.

Full State Funding Not Defined Accurately

Part of the problem in considering the philosophy of full state funding lies in its definition. If taken literally, *full* state funding has some distinct limitations in its application to several districts within a state (as pointed out in this chapter). However, if the term *almost full* state funding is used, there could be options available to local districts that could mitigate or eliminate most of the disadvantages of this system of financing education. The latter definition is the one most commonly used, even though it is incongruent with the term itself.

DISTRICT POWER EQUALIZATION

An alternative to the full state funding model that would meet the requirements of recent court decisions is *district power equalization* (DPE). By definition, DPE means that each local district mill levy should produce the same number of dollars of total school revenue per mill per weighted student in every district, and the last mill to be levied should produce the same total funds as the first one. It was advocated in 1922 by Updegraff but found little support until the early 1970s. Its later popularity came largely as a result of the lack of support for full state funding as a means of providing equal protection as mandated by court decisions and recommended by several school finance studies.

Power equalization is sometimes viewed by its critics as a process of depleting a state's financial resources. Thus far, there is little evidence to support this view. Its value lies in the fact that it is extremely effective in obliterating the financial advantages of one district over another in providing the funds required to produce a quality education program rather than simply providing a minimum or foundation program.

Model 9-2 illustrates district power equalization with full state support for each mill of tax levy. Model 9-2a shows the same principle, but with all levies above those of the foundation program supported by the state at a fractional part of the original amount. This, of course, flattens the graph line (see model), thereby decreasing the state percentage and increasing the local percentage of revenue produced. The program remains equitable, however, so long as the level is kept above the amount the wealthiest district could produce locally or if all surpluses were recaptured by the state.

It should be noted that the steeper the line in a DPE formula graph, the greater the so-called raid on the state treasury and the less the effort required at the local level. Increased costs by this process would probably cause a state to flatten the DPE line and thereby increase the local district's share of the cost of the educational program. By this process the state should be able to control the degree of depletion of its treasury this program would bring.

The following is a simplified example of how an equalized percentage or power equalization program might function.

In the above example, four mythical districts of widely varying assessments of taxable property per weighted-pupil unit (WPU) are compared in the calculation of a foundation program with an equalization program of $1,000 per weighted-pupil unit with a required local levy of 10 mills. District A has its local revenue matched by the state on a 1:1 basis, District B on a 2:3 basis, District C on a 1:9 basis, and District D on a 1:19 basis. This, of course, is a simple foundation program. If each district goes 2 mills above the foundation program on a DPE basis, District A gets a $1,200 per WPU program, with $600 local and $600 state revenue; District B has the same program, with $480 local and $720 state revenue; District C has $120 local and $1,080 state revenue; and District D has $60

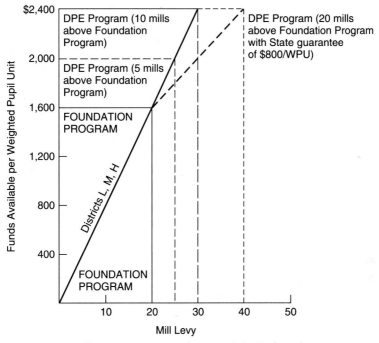

MODEL 9-2 District power equilization; 9.2a Reduced percentage power equalization.

			Foundation program			
				Revenue/WPU		Local-state ratio
District	Assessed value/WPU	Mill levy	Guaranteed amount/WPU	Local	State	
A	$50,000	10	$1,000	$500	$500	1:1
B	40,000	10	1,000	400	600	2:3
C	10,000	10	1,000	100	900	1:9
D	5,000	10	1,000	50	950	1:19
			Program above the foundation			
A	$50,000	2	200	100	100	1:1
B	40,000	2	200	80	120	2:3
C	10,000	2	200	20	180	1:9
D	5,000	2	200	10	190	1:19

local and $1,140 state money. Thus, a power equalization program requires the state to continue its degree of partnership with each district for the full program. By this process, financially weak districts (such as District D in the above example) are able to offer as good a program (in terms of cost) as wealthier ones. This is the essence of the philosophy of equality of educational opportunity.

At first glance it may seem that this creates a standard program for every district within a state. Such is not the case, however, for each local district would have the right and the responsibility to determine what the local tax rate would be over and above the mandated foundation program levy. In this way local control is assured and state partnership responsibility is mandated. To illustrate this, suppose that District A elected to levy 1 mill above the mandated foundation program, District B decided on a 2-mill increase, District C a 4-mill program, and District D a 5-mill increase. The result of this would be as follows:

		Optional program above foundation program				
District	Increased tax levy	Guaranteed amount per WPU	Local revenue	State revenue	L-S ratio	Total per/WPU
A	1 M	$100	$50	$ 50	1:1	$1,100
B	2 M	200	80	120	2:3	1,200
C	4 M	400	40	360	1:9	1,400
D	5 M	500	25	475	1:19	1,500

It can be seen that equal levies bring equal dollars in all districts, but each district is free to choose the level at which its program will be supported. This preserves the element of local control in decision making, but at the same time it requires the state to support the entire program to whatever level the law permits local districts to operate.

As previously indicated, fear that local determination of mill levy increases under this program will be so high as to deplete state treasuries is the greatest deterrent to adoption of this form of district power equalization. However, studies conducted in some states that have used the concept to a limited extent do not seem to justify such apprehension.

The merits of district power equalization are readily discernible. Local control of the extent to which the educational program goes above the state minimum rests with each individual school board, but the state cannot escape its proportionate financial responsibility. Districts are motivated to make adequate tax effort, for if they spend less they lose more. Complete equalization is possible in spending as well as in tax effort. If there is a high enough ceiling on local tax options, the inequalities encountered between wealthy and poor districts, which are obvious in a typical foundation program with unsupported local options, disappear. The only restriction to an adequately financed program thus becomes the willingness or unwillingness of the people at the local level to tax themselves within reasonable limits. With the state matching the local district on a predetermined basis in terms of local ability, the previously unrealistic tax requirements for a quality education program in a poor district are reduced greatly or even eliminated.

The Utah legislature enacted a limited power equalization program that has changed little since 1973. All school districts are required to assess the same tax levy, and each receives the same number of dollars per weighted-pupil unit. The local voted leeway option is available up to 10 mills above the basic program, with the power equalization principle essentially applied on the first 2 mills. Eighteen of the forty districts in Utah use some part of this leeway, and only one uses it to the legal maximum. State support of the leeway program has an unequal effect only on school districts with a level above 2 mills. Figure 9-1 is an example of the limited power equalization concept. Of the forty districts shown, four provide 100 percent of the basic program. Note that only 32 percent (the state average) of the total maintenance and operation basic program is provided from local property tax when all districts assess a required 22 mills. The 68 percent state guarantee of $2000 per weighted-pupil unit comes from state resources. The limits are controlled by the $2000 guarantee.

In Figure 9-1, District 17 is used to further clarify the concept. There are 14,500 students in average daily membership with various weighting factors that provide the district with 18,000 WPUs. The state guarantees $2000 per WPU or $36 million for the basic program. The district is required to assess 22 mills (.022) against property with an assessed value of $409,090,909, which raises $9 million locally or 25 percent of the needed revenue. The state provides the other 75 percent or $27 million to guarantee an equalized dollar figure for the district. The inequities of a nonstate-supported voted leeway are discussed in Chapter 3 (see Table 3-1).

PROPERTY REASSESSMENT AND LOCAL DISTRICT REVENUES

Many of the states have found it difficult to raise their finance programs beyond the state equalization requirement. It is often difficult to get the voting public to approve leeway or override levies in the face of already high property taxes. This is particularly difficult at times when property assessments have just been increased, a practice that is mandatory at stated intervals in several states. Those who do not understand the equalization principle often have the idea that property assessment increases automatically bring local property tax revenue increases. They thereby assume that local leeway increases are unnecessary under those conditions and vote against them.

Using District 17 in Figure 9-1 in a further example; if after a reappraisal of property the assessed valued increased by 10 percent (or to approximately $450 million), 22 mills would raise $9.9 million, which provides a "windfall" of

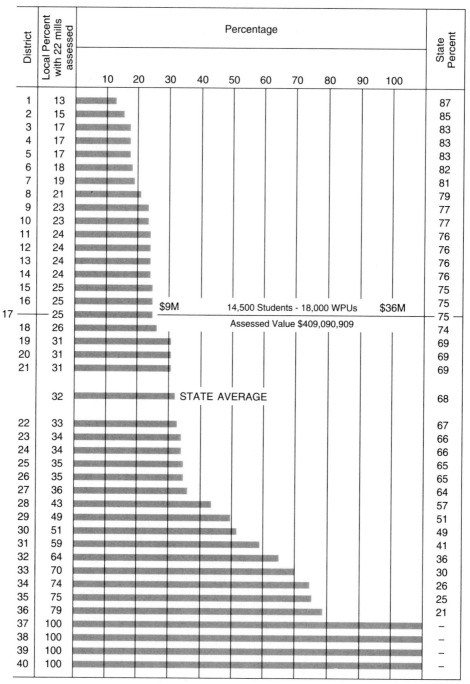

District	Local Percent with 22 mills assessed	Percentage	State Percent
1	13		87
2	15		85
3	17		83
4	17		83
5	17		83
6	18		82
7	19		81
8	21		79
9	23		77
10	23		77
11	24		76
12	24		76
13	24		76
14	24		76
15	25		75
16	25		75
17	25	$9M 14,500 Students - 18,000 WPUs $36M Assessed Value $409,090,909	75
18	26		74
19	31		69
20	31		69
21	31		69
	32	STATE AVERAGE	68
22	33		67
23	34		66
24	34		66
25	35		65
26	35		65
27	36		64
28	43		57
29	49		51
30	51		49
31	59		41
32	64		36
33	70		30
34	74		26
35	75		25
36	79		21
37	100		–
38	100		–
39	100		–
40	100		–

FIGURE 9-1 Limited power equalization—percent of local revenue raised toward the basic maintenance and operation state guaranteed program of $2000 per WPU when a minimum of 22 local mills is required.

$900,000 to the state rather than to the local district. Of course, if the program is not state supported, increases in assessment bring commensurate increases in local revenue.

The state would participate in a leeway to the same degree as in the basic equalization program, if it was involved in a power equalization program. The amount of total funds available to the district would be the same—regardless of the extent of property assessment increase. The voted leeway program would then be as follows:

Voted leeway program with power equalization

Before reappraisal	After reappraisal
1. Total local funds raised from a 2-mill property tax $80,000 (40,000,000) (.002)	1. Total local funds raised from a 2-mill property tax $160,000 (80,000,000) (.002)
2. State funds $720,000 (Using the state-local ratio of basic program) 9:1	2. State funds $640,000 (Using the state-local ratio of basic program) 4:1
3. Total leeway program $800,000	3. Total leeway program $800,000

On the other hand, if the override or leeway portion is not state supported, increased assessments do bring additional local tax revenues, as shown in the following example. Here a 2-mill override produces twice as much local revenue when the assessment is doubled.

Voted leeway program

Assume that the district (by a favorable vote of the people) decides to levy an additional 2 mills *above* the foundation program. (This voted leeway is *not* state supported.)

1. Total local funds raised $80,000 (40,000,000) (.002)	1. Total local funds raised $160,000 (80,000,000) (.002)
2. State funds nil	2. State funds nil

When the state-supported foundation program and a nonsupported leeway program are considered together, the percent of total budget increase in a "poor" district is considerably less than in a "rich" district, as shown in the following illustration. These are small percentage increases in spite of doubling the assessment of the property, because the additional leeway is only a small part of the total program.

Total foundation and leeway programs		Total foundation and leeway programs	
Foundation program	$10,000,000	Foundation program	$10,000,000
2-mill voted leeway	80,000	2-mill voted leeway	160,000
Total	$10,080,000	Total	$10,160,000
		Percent increase to total district funds due to reappraisal	.8%

	Property reapplraisal in two districts			
	Before	After	Before	After
Assessed valuation	$20,000,000[a]	$40,000,000	$120,000,000[b]	$240,000,000
Foundation program Local funds (25 M)	$ 500,000	$ 1,000,000	$ 3,000,000	$ 6,000,000
State funds	$ 4,500,000	$ 4,000,000	$ 2,000,000	$ (1,000,000)[c]
Total foundation program	$ 5,000,000	$ 5,000,000	$ 5,000,000	$ 5,000,000
Voted leeway program Local funds (2 mills)	$ 40,000	$ 80,000	$ 240,000	$ 480,000
Total of both programs	$ 5,040,000	$ 5,080,000	$ 5,240,000	$ 5,480,000
Percent of total budget increase as a result of property reappraisal		.8%		4.6%

[a]Poor district.
[b]Rich district.
[c]Local funds placed in the State Uniform School Fund.

Computerization has made it possible for counties and states to reevaluate property on a yearly basis. For many years, the reassessment was a continual job, and some properties may have gone for years without updated values. Extremes were very noticeable when properties, in some cases, were not reassessed for over 20 years. To control local districts from gaining a "windfall," legislators often reduce the required mill levy in a power equalization program and limit increases in voted leeway and capital outlay budgets. In some cases it might be a percentage cap in relation to the previous year's revenue or require a "truth in taxation" hearing to provide the public the opportunity to express concerns over tax increases brought about by increased property values.

DETERMINING THE BEST FINANCE PLAN

There are many plans available to states for the allocation of funds to local districts. Various combinations of equalizing grants, adaptations of the foundation program principle, and varying degrees of power equalization may be used to utilize the advantages and eliminate the disadvantages of each. The state may use categorical or special-purpose funding to encourage the introduction or stimulation of innovative programs. It may use instructional programs or units as the basis for determining the size of state allocations to local districts, or it may set up state standards or guidelines and use state committees to negotiate with local districts for budget plans that meet the unique needs of districts. Thus, the number of potential state financing patterns is almost unlimited.

The choice of financing programs is great, but at this point in school finance reform there are no perfect systems for distributing state funds to local school districts. Each plan has limitations and falls short of equalizing financial resources to the complete satisfaction of all the people concerned. Some systems are better than others, and some states make greater efforts to improve than others. Given the inequities that exist in almost every state plan, there is no room for complacency in viewing school finance reform in any state. Certainly, there is little justification for maintaining or preserving traditional methods until a panacean formula is discovered.

It has been estimated that the various states use nearly 400 kinds of state aid to local districts, including the minimum program, transportation, salary-schedule allowances, and shared state taxes. No one way is generally accepted as the best, in terms of its popularity over all other plans, for organizing the state-local partnership for financing education. Programs now in existence vary from Hawaii's one-district system, where the district covers the state and is the sole taxing and financing unit for the operation of all its public schools, to programs in which state-level allocations to local districts involve only a relatively small part of the total funds available to local districts. All other states come somewhere in between these two extremes.

It is safe to assume that school financing plans of the future will emphasize greater state involvement and proportionately less local responsibility. Since the property tax is the realistic source of local revenue and since its utilization has reached most extreme proportions, it is evident that state tax sources will have to be increased to meet the surging costs of education. Of the big revenue producers, the sales tax and income tax are used mostly by state government. These taxes are probably destined to bear the brunt of the tax increases that appear to be necessary now and in the future to finance the high-quality education programs that nearly all our citizens demand.

EQUALIZATION OF SERVICES

One idea on future state financing of education, whether through complete state financing or some degree of state-local partnership, involves state equalization of services rather than of dollars. One of the chief problems in state allocation of funds revolves around the incontrovertible fact that equal dollars provided to unlike districts result in unequal units of service. Similar amounts of money never result in equal purchases of instructional services, since some districts must pay much higher salaries than others. The costs of school buses, of gasoline, or of any other required services or supplies vary considerably in all the districts of all the states. The fairest measure of equalization, then, would be the program that equalizes the required school services in all school districts. Such a principle needs no justification, but much more research and experience will be required before it replaces present-day equalization of dollars among the school districts of any state.

EMPHASIS ON WEIGHTING FACTORS

Determining the funds necessary to operate a school program, regardless of the process or formula used, is a function of the "need" of the school district. Need is related first of all to the number of pupils to be educated. There are many other determinants of need, but the number of pupils in average daily attendance (ADA) or the number of students in average daily membership (ADM) forms the basic unit of measurement. Although schools have used, and continue to use, the idea of providing equal dollars for all children in the state as the measure of equality of educational opportunity, such a concept is really not valid. Equal dollars per student do not produce equal products or equal results. As Kirst said:

> Although the scope of school finance research has grown with the growth of the public sector, research has stopped at the schoolhouse door. Researchers in economics, political science, administration, and applied finance have for the most part looked at large-scale problems of equity by comparing policies and funding formulas among schools, among districts, or among states. Only rarely have they looked at the smaller scale problems of equity posed by the distribution of resources within schools. . . . They have ignored the cost implications of curriculum tracking, watered-down textbooks, and how teachers spend their time. . . . One reason most researchers have not investigated equity or efficiency inside schools is that their training provides neither the theory nor the tools they need for the investigation.[8]

Further, unequal educational opportunities are certain to result when funding does not consider such common variables as racial origin, physical and mental handicaps, socioeconomic backgrounds, language deficiencies, and many other diverse characteristics of students.

In addition to differing student characteristics, the cost of an educational program is related to such existing variables as the size of the school district and the size of the school attendance area, for the cost of educating 25,000 pupils is not necessarily exactly 100 times that of educating 250 pupils. Similarly, the cost of operating a high school of 500 pupils may not be the same as that of financing 500 elementary pupils. Schools with a high percentage of disadvantaged pupils cost more than those with a lower percentage. Sparsity factors make the cost of education in small rural communities higher than in average-sized towns. On the other hand, the unique problems of large cities and metropolitan areas make the cost of education proportionately higher, even though some might expect economies of scale to apply.

Weighting factors are perhaps the best measures of the amount of additional resources and services needed to provide all students, regardless of their personal or environmental handicaps, with reasonably equal educational programs. Fortunately, there are relatively few citizens who continue to challenge the humanistic view that children who have physical or mental handicaps, or who attend school in exceedingly small or extremely large and disadvantaged schools, should benefit from educational programs that are more costly than "normal" ones.

Although some have thought that the weighted-pupil concept was a direct discovery of the *Serrano* era of school finance reform, only its degree of acceptance in recent school finance programs is new. Mort and Reusser pointed out the long tradition of this fundamental principle more than forty years ago:

> The weighted-pupil unit (or its mathematical equivalent—the weighted-classroom unit) is the most systematically refined of all measures of educational need and has been in practical use for a quarter of a century in state-aid laws, in expenditure comparisons of various types of districts, and in comparisons of ability to support schools.[9]

The many inequalities that exist force states to recognize that the number of pupils by itself does not indicate the operational need of school districts. Disparity in fiscal needs arises from the composition of the pupil populations. That being true, it becomes necessary for weighting to be made if fairness and equality of educational opportunity are to be achieved.

Weightings would lose their importance and become superfluous if the schools to be served had the same proportions of variables that appear to require weightings. If 40 percent of the pupils in every school district are secondary school pupils, there would be little need for weighting this factor. If every district had 10 percent of its pupils in small or isolated school attendance areas, there would be little need for weightings here. However, these factors are never constant from district to district. Weighting tends to put the extra costs incurred in providing maximum quality education for pupils with special or more than average problems where they belong—on the state. Many of these discriminating problems, if left to local districts, are minimized or ignored.

PRINCIPAL TYPES OF WEIGHTINGS

In any consideration of the number of pupils as a determinant of the money needs of a district, several important weightings must be considered: (1) the sparsity or isolation of pupils in rural areas; (2) the density of pupils in heavily populated metropolitan areas; (3) the grade levels of pupils; and (4) the degree of disadvantage certain classes of pupils may suffer, such as the handicapped or those who require special education services. Consideration should also be given to the training and experience of the professional staff members of each district. To consider all pupils to be of equal worth or cost is no more erroneous than to consider all teachers to be of equal worth or cost to a school system.

Sparsity Factors

The need to provide additional funds to help finance the small schools that operate in nearly every state has long been recognized and accepted. Bass notes:

> Small rural school districts face a wide variety of problems, from difficulty in hiring and retraining quality teachers to the inability to field competitive athletic teams because of the limited number of students. But by far the most critical and pervasive problems deal with costs and revenues. Small schools, if they are to provide educational programs similar in breadth and quality to those of larger schools, will inevitably incur higher per-pupil costs due to limited enrollment, small pupil-teacher ratios, higher utility and other operational costs per pupil, and other factors that limit economies of scale.[10]

State legislatures, mostly rurally dominated until recently, have usually made provisions for the protection of small and expensive schools and districts. The methods used may vary from state to state, but the end results are much the same. Typically, the process used involves weighting such pupils in the finance formula so as to require the state to pay its proportionate share of the higher cost involved in the education of pupils in small groups. At the same time, some states give the state board of education the responsibility of determining when such privilege may be rescinded or withdrawn, as when some small schools might reasonably be expected to be consolidated or reorganized into larger and more efficient units.

Sparsity weighting factors are difficult to construct without inequalities. For example, the following formula, developed by the National Educational Finance Project,[11] leaves some discrepancies in the funds that would be provided for certain sizes of schools.

Elementary school size	Weighting factor
Fewer than 100	1.30
100–149	1.20
150–200	1.10

Under this formula, a school with 99 students would get a total weighting of 128.7, but a school with 100 students would get a weighting of only 120. All schools with enrollments of 94 to 99 would receive more funds than the school with 100 students. At the high expenditure levels of schools today, this becomes too great a difference for schools of this size to ignore.

In an attempt to eliminate such inequalities, Utah uses a somewhat complicated formula in which every additional student enrolled in small, isolated schools generates additional dollars of revenue. A sample from the present formula for small, isolated schools (to compare with the National Education Finance Project formula) follows:

	Necessarily existent small schools formula table			
Students (#)	6-Yr High WPU/ADM	4-Yr High WPU/ADM	Jr./Mid. WPU/ADM	Elem. WPU/ADM
10	3.00000	3.00000	3.00000	3.00000
20	2.42886	2.41096	2.38567	2.15297
30	2.09810	2.06967	2.02997	1.67384
40	1.86546	1.82927	1.77992	1.34406
50	1.68658	1.64415	1.58776	1.09611
60	1.54171	1.49399	1.43221	.89993
70	1.42030	1.36796	1.30194	.73947
80	1.31607	1.25959	1.19016	.60515
90	1.22496	1.16471	1.09251	.49080
100	1.14419	1.08047	1.00600	.39220
110	1.07180	1.00484	.92851	.30635
120	1.00632	.93631	.85846	.23102
130	.94664	.87376	.79466	.16453
140	.89191	.81628	.73619	.10556
150	.84144	.76319	.68230	.05307
160	.79468	.71391	.63241	.00624

Source: *Utah Public School Finance System*, Utah State Office of Education, 1990.

By the use of this formula, a school with 165 students would be given credit for 165.5 WPUs. This is smaller than the 166 that would be given to a school with one more student in a school with no weighting for sparsity. This may appear to be unnecessary manipulation in order to obtain equality, but in a state with many small schools it is an important factor in maintaining harmony and goodwill among school boards and administrators who know the size and funding of their neighboring schools.

Density Factors

The sparsity factor has long been accepted and applied in finance parlance and in practice, but allocation of additional funds per pupil to large city school districts is relatively new and has had only limited application. Municipal overburden, large numbers of disadvantaged and exceptional children, the practical problems and additional costs needed to implement racial integration, and the higher salaries and operational costs resulting from strong union organizations are all a part of the finance problem of large urban areas. The best answer to this complex problem appears to be weighting of pupils. This would guarantee that the state would share in paying for these additional expenses, which are largely beyond the control of the districts involved.

There is an understandable reluctance on the part of people, even many of those who are knowledgeable in school finance matters, to recognize and solve this problem. For many years, the city school districts enjoyed financial and cultural advantages over their rural counterparts. Less reluctance to exploit the property tax, better-prepared teachers and administrators, more cultural opportunities to abet the school program, and less citizen resistance to accept change and innovation all added their part to the natural advantage that city schools enjoyed over rural schools. Hence, the city schools provided much of the leadership for improving the curriculum and increasing the monies available for education.

The problem today is not the same and neither is its solution. The cities have been losing many upper- and middle-class citizens to suburbia, at the same time as less affluent and less well-educated citizens move to the cities to obtain employment. The tax base has thus been weakened while the problems of city school systems are increasing. The problems attending migration of people to and from the core of large cities, such as lower tax-paying ability, increased competition for the tax dollar to provide better police protection, greater social problems in the ghettos, and additional services required of government have placed the cities at a financial disadvantage for the first time in the nation's history. Burke summarized the problem of using density factors in school finance formulas:

> What we have in big cities is a complex set of conditions making it difficult to muster sufficient support for public education at a time when the educational needs of these cities are more critical than ever before. It was not poverty alone but outdated school district structure, public values, and many other factors which resulted in the deplorable educational conditions found in the rural areas of the state during the first three decades of this century before the state equalization program brought some relief. To the extent that the density correction brings relief it can be defended. Many other aspects of state equalization programs have had no better justification than that.[12]

Grade Level Weighting

Traditionally, weightings for secondary pupils as compared with elementary pupils were widely accepted and implemented. The pupil-teacher ratio was lower, the average salary of teachers was higher, the cost of instructional materials and equipment was higher, and the student activities and out-of-school programs were more extensive and expensive for the secondary level. The validity of the assumption that secondary school pupils should have a weighting when compared with elementary pupils is more seriously questioned now than ever before. The chief argument favoring the weighting is that pupil-teacher ratios are lower in secondary schools, thereby increasing the cost per pupil. There are, however, a number of arguments that build a strong rationale against such weighting. (1) There is little difference in salaries between the two levels in most states, since single-salary schedules make no differentiation. (2) With the emphasis on the use of computer laboratories, instructional media, and improved libraries for elementary schools, the differences in costs have largely disappeared. (3) Activity and field-trip programs are no longer restricted or limited to secondary schools.

Special Education Weightings

Some aspects of the school's program will be more expensive than others: vocational education, compensatory education, and education for physically or mentally handicapped pupils, for example. If one accepts the thesis that public education of the kind and extent that will allow all students to develop to their maximum potential should be provided, one must accept the corollary that these pupils or their programs must receive a weighting in the school finance plan. Programs in these areas were stalemated or nonexistent until states and school districts gave them weighting commensurate with their needs. Here again, the weightings may take many forms, such as special appropriations or grants and weightings of the individual students in such programs.

Following is a weighting approach that might be utilized to develop a finance structure for special education students:

Communicative disorder	1.1
Visually impaired	1.6
Other health impaired	1.8
Intellectually handicapped	2.4
Learning disabled	2.4
Severely intellectually handicapped	2.6
Hearing impaired—hard of hearing	2.7
Hearing impaired—deaf	2.9
Behavior disordered	2.9
Orthopedically disabled	2.9
Multihandicapped	3.4

Students of school finance need to be aware of difficulties in defining special education categories and the significant task legislators have in financing programs adequately. As a safeguard to state treasuries, *prevalence* limits may need to be applied, capping totals that would be available for each category. For example, in the area of learning disabled noted previously, a percentage of the total of student population could be applied at both the state and local district level. In such a formula if a percentage of .03 were established in a district of 10,000 students, each state through the legislature would provide funding for up to 300 students who are learning disabled. Although the financing structure is dependent on some type of special education identification, any form of labeling of students is unfortunate. Such designations should be handled with caution.

Teacher Qualification Considerations

Universal high-quality education is being stressed everywhere; it seems to be one of the absorbing concerns of the professional educator at the moment. The prevalence of single-salary schedules throughout the country strongly implies that increased academic preparation and increased experience in the field improve the teacher and thereby improve the quality of instruction.

The finance problem enunciated by this dilemma can be seen very easily. The foundation program provides money for teachers and other operational costs in terms of the number of weighted pupils to be educated and also for other specialized employees or services. But the teacher requirement places the school district in a precarious position. If in the employment of professional personnel the superintendent strives to improve the quality of instruction, he or she will usually recommend hiring the teachers with the most training and experience—with attendant higher salaries. This leaves little or no state-equalized foundation program funds for operational costs. These would then have to be paid with local funds. If, however, a less qualified teacher is employed, funds from the foundation program can be used for other expenses, but this does little to improve the quality of the instructional program. The net result is that the wealthy districts employ the personnel they think will do most to improve the quality of instruction, but the poorer districts are forced to employ those with least demands on the salary schedule, regardless of other factors.

State foundation programs should include weightings that consider the qualifications of the professional employees, so that the state will pay its proportionate share of the cost of employing a better-qualified staff. Otherwise, the onus for improving instruction by employing better-trained and more experienced teachers rests strictly on the local district. If it is to the advantage of the local school district to employ personnel with more training and experience, it is also to the advantage of the state to help see that this is possible financially.

To picture the simplest possible use of the teacher-training and experience allowance in the foundation program, assume that Districts A, B, and C in the following illustration have equal amounts for all pertinent factors except the training and experience of their teachers.

District	Assessed value	Class-room units	State-guaranteed amt/CRU[a]	Required levy	Number of teachers	Average teacher index
A	$40,000,000	100	$15,000	15 mills	80	1.20
B	40,000,000	100	15,000	15 mills	80	1.35
C	40,000,000	100	15,000	15 mills	80	1.55

[a]CRU means classroom unit.

The average teacher index is calculated by placing each teacher's name in the proper training and experience slot on an index salary schedule, adding the index figures for all teachers, and dividing that total by the number of teachers. In the example below, District A (which obviously has a predominantly young and not-too-well-trained staff), with an average index of 1.20, is entitled to an additional 20 percent of its total of 80 teacher-earned classroom units. District B would receive 35 percent of 80 as additional units; and District C would receive 55 percent. The calculations for the foundation program would then be as follows:

New foundation program

District A
1. Minimum program need—(100 + 16)(15,0000)   = $1,740,000
2. Local tax effort—(40,000,000)(0.015)   =   600,000
3. State allocation—(step 1 minus step 2)   =   1,140,000

District B
1. Minimum program need—(100 + 28)(15,000)   = $1,920,000
2. Local tax effort—(40,000,000)(0.015)   =   600,000
3. State allocation—(step 1 minus step 2)   =   1,320,000

District C
1. Minimum program need—(100 + 44)(15,000)   = $2,160,000
2. Local tax effort—(40,000,000)(0.015)   =   600,000
3. State allocation—(step 1 minus step 2)   =   1,560,000

District C, with its better-trained, more experienced, and therefore more expensive staff of teachers, would receive considerably more state money than District A or District B. The state thereby shares the additional costs of better-qualified teachers. Under such an arrangement, no district would be forced to employ inexperienced and poorly trained teachers simply because they cost less. Teachers with greater experience and more extensive training would then be able to compete for positions with current-year college graduates and others with limited experience and training.

The arguments favoring weighting teacher qualifications in the foundation program do not go uncontested. It has been pointed out that rural districts and less wealthy districts usually employ less well-qualified personnel than other districts do. To the extent that this is true, such allowances for training and experience may reduce instead of induce equalization. But even this argument falls flat when it is realized that without such allowances the only means the poor districts have of competing with wealthier ones in hiring the best-qualified teachers would necessarily come through greater local tax effort. With teacher-qualification weighting, however, the possibility of poor districts increasing the qualifications of their teachers becomes a reality. Concern over what the wealthy districts can do in this matter should be of little consequence, for most of the costs of such improvement in the more or less impoverished districts would come from all the taxpayers of the state rather than only from those who live in the school district.

Miscellaneous Weighting Factors

Many other weighting factors can reasonably be expected in state foundation programs. Notable examples include provision of funds for transportation, administrative and other professional nonteaching personnel, and capital outlay or debt service. Unfortunately, the incidence of such factors is low, and there is too little state acceptance of these in foundation programs. Many of these, however, are covered by special grants or appropriations of a nonequalizing nature. Certainly, greater interest and more state support need to be developed in these areas, especially in providing stronger and more equalized state support for capital outlay and debt service expenditures.

SUMMARY

Two plans of financing education appear to meet the criteria the courts have mandated: full state funding and district power equalization. Full state funding of public education has been advocated by some writers for several years. Such a plan raises some important questions about increased state control and the problem of financing districts that desire to maintain special higher-cost programs.

District power equalization involves the principle of state-local partnership, where each local district mill levy would produce the same number of dollars of revenue per mill per weighted student (state and local) in every district. Its main disadvantage is the fear that such a principle might open the doors of the state treasury.

Property reassessment upward does not necessarily increase the total revenues made available to school districts. Typically, it increases the local district's share and decreases the state's share of funds—provided the program includes some form of equalization.

The use of weightings is increasing in school finance formulas. Also, the use of weighted pupils is gradually replacing the use of the actual number of pupils in determining the financial needs of a school district. Sparsity and density factors are also being used more extensively in determining the budgetary needs of local education agencies. During the 1990s, states will continue to refine and expand weighting factors in school finance programs.

ASSIGNMENT PROJECTS

1. Using the following information about two school districts, solve the indicated problems.

District	Assessed valuation	Weighted pupil units
A	$40,000,000	2,000
B	15,000,000	900

	Foundation program	Board leeway	Voted leeway
State guarantee	$900/WPU	$500/WPU	$200/WPU
Required levy	20 mills	$1.40/$100 AV	$10/$1,000 AV

			District A		District B	
Foundation	1. Need (in $)	$	____	(1)	$	____(13)
program	2. Local effort		____	(2)		____(14)
	3. State allocation		____	(3)		____(15)
Board leeway	1. Need (in $)		____	(4)		____(16)
	2. Local effort		____	(5)		____(17)
	3. State allocation		____	(6)		____(18)
Voted leeway	1. Need (in $)		____	(7)		____(19)
	2. Local effort		____	(8)		____(20)
	3. State allocation		____	(9)		____(21)
All three	Total local funds		____	(10)		____(22)
programs	Total state funds		____	(11)		____(23)
	Total funds		____	(12)		____(24)

2. **Power Equalization**
   From the previous problem, calculate the following:

	District A	District B
Ratio of state revenue to local revenue (Foundation program)	(25)____:____	(26)____:____

   Under the power equalization principle, how much money would the state provide for each of these districts using all three programs?

District A—$ _____ state money (27)
District B—$ _____ state money (28)

Total amount of
money/WPU   District A—$ _____ (29)
                   District B—$ _____ (30)

Comparing the old program with power equalization, compare the total amounts of money available per WPU for each of the two districts if A levied a total of 36 mills and B a total of 38 mills.

	Old program		Power equalization program	
District A	(31) $_____	/WPU	(33) $_____	/WPU
District B	(32) $_____	/WPU	(34) $_____	/WPU

Repeat the problem, with A levying 38 mills and B levying 36 mills.

	Old program		Power equalization program	
District A	(35) $_____	/WPU	(37) $_____	/WPU
District B	(36) $_____	/WPU	(38) $_____	/WPU

SELECTED READINGS

Alexander, Kern, and K. Forbis Jordan, eds. *Constitutional Reform of School Finance.* Lexington, Mass.: Lexington Books (D.C. Heath), 1973.

Benson, Charles S., Paul M. Goldfinger, E. Gareth Hoachlander, and Jessica S. Pers. *Planning for Educational Reform: Financial and Social Alternatives.* New York: Dodd, Mead, 1974.

Carnegie Forum on Education and the Economy. *A Nation Preparing Teachers for the 21st Century.* Washington, D.C.: 1990.

Chubb, J. E., and T. M. Moe. *Politics, Markets, and America's Schools.* . Washington, D.C.: Brookings Institution, 1990.

Dreeben, Robert, and J. Alan Thomas, eds. *The Analysis of Educational Productivity, Volume 1, Issues in Microanalysis.* Cambridge, Mass.: Ballinger, 1980.

Elmore, R. F., and associates. *Restructuring Schools: The Generation of Educational Reform.* San Francisco: Jossey-Bass, 1990.

Guthrie, James W., Walter I. Garms, and Lawrence C. Pierce. *School Finance and Education Policy: Enhancing Educational Efficiency, Equality, and Choice.* 2nd ed. Englewood Cliffs, N.J.: Prentice Hall, 1988.

Honeyman, D. S., D. C. Thompson, and R. C. Wood. *Financing Rural and Small Schools: Issues of Adequacy and Equity.* Gainesville: University of Florida Press, 1989.

Mueller, Van D., and Mary P. McKeown. *The Fiscal, Legal and Political Aspects of Elementary and Secondary Education. Sixth Annual Yearbook of the American Education Finance Association.* Cambridge, Mass.: Ballinger, 1986.

Odden, Allan R., and Lawrence O. Picus. *School Finance: A Policy Perspective.* New York: McGraw-Hill, 1992.

Thomas, Gloria Jean, David J. Sperry, and F. Del Wasden. *The Law and Teacher Employment.* New York: West Publishing Company, 1991.

Webb, L. D., Martha M. McCarthy, and Stephen B. Thomas. *Financing Elementary and Secondary Education.* Columbus, Ohio: Merrill, 1988.

ENDNOTES

1. *Serrano* v. *Priest* (I), 96 Cal. Rptr. 601, 487 P.2d 1241 (Calif. 1971).

2. Diane Ravitch, *The Troubled Crusade* (New York: Basic Books, 1983); reviewed by Deborah A. Verstegen,"Book Reviews," *Journal of Educational Finance,* Winter 1986, p. 388.

3. *Stuart* v. *School District No. 1 of Village of Kalamazoo,* 30 Mich. 69 (1874).

4. *Brown* v. *Board of Education* (I), 347 U.S. 483, 74 S. Ct. 686 (1954).

5. Elwood P. Cubberley, *School Funds and Their Apportionment* (New York: Teachers College, Columbia University, 1905), p. 17.

6. Robert Berne and Leanna Stiefel, "Changes in School Finance Equity: A National Perspective," *Journal of Educational Finance,* Spring 1983, p. 420.

7. Robert Graham, "Education and Economic Growth: The State Role," *Journal of Educational Finance,* (Fall 1982), p. 135.

8. Michael W. Kirst, "A New School Finance for a New Era of Fiscal Constraint," in *School Finance and School Improvement Linkages for the 1980s, Fourth Annual Yearbook of the American Education Finance Association,* Allen Odden and L. Dean Webb, eds. (Cambridge, Mass.: Ballinger, 1983), pp. 1, 3.

9. Paul R. Mort and Walter C. Reusser, *Public School Finance,* 2nd ed. (New York: McGraw-Hill, 1951), p. 491.

10. Gerald R. Bass, "Isolation/Sparsity," *Journal of Education Finance,* Fall 1990, p. 180.

11. *Alternative Programs for Financing Education* (Gainesville, Fla.: National Education Finance Project, 1971), p. 272.

12. Arvid J. Burke, "The Density Correction in the New York State School Aid Formula," in *Long-Range Planning in School Finance* (Washington, D.C.: National Education Association Committee on Educational Finance, 1963), pp. 136-37.

Chapter *10*

Public Funds and Nonpublic Schools

Providing for the education of schoolchildren is surely a praiseworthy purpose. . . . [E]ven a praiseworthy, secular purpose cannot validate government aid to parochial schools when the aid has the effect of promoting a single religion or religion generally or when the aid unduly entangles the government in matters religious. —AGUILAR V. FELTON (1985)

Since the early separation of church and state functions, the predominant philosophy of government has been that some services can be supplied better by the public sector. Education is a notable example. Relatively few people would favor removing the responsibility of government for this important public service. At the same time, however, privately sponsored schools have been encouraged for those groups and individuals who are willing to support them financially in addition to participating in financing the public school system.

A CONTROVERSIAL ISSUE

The illegality of direct government support for private and parochial schools is well established in the codes of the states and at the federal level. However, some state governments are enacting legislation that provides some state-collected tax funds for use by nonpublic schools. The courts, particularly the U.S. Supreme Court, have consistently disallowed direct state financial support to private and parochial schools. However, they have allowed Congress and state legislatures to provide support that promotes a secular principle, does not foster government entanglement, and does not advance or inhibit religion.

Those who favor direct public aid to nonpublic schools base their arguments on the following points:

1. Parents should have freedom of choice in the education of their children. Proponents cite the case of *Pierce* v. *Society of Sisters* (1925) as a guarantee of such choice. Said the court, "The fundamental theory of liberty under which all governments in this union repose excludes any general power of the State to standardize its children by forcing them to accept instruction from public teachers only."[1]

2. There is no evidence to support the fear that divisiveness in education will be caused by the existence and operation of nonpublic schools.

3. The failure of nonpublic schools would create a tremendous impact on the financing of public education. From the economic point of view it would be better to finance nonpublic schools to the extent necessary to keep them solvent.

Opponents of direct aid to nonpublic schools argue that:

1. Parochial aid represents a backward step, since this country once maintained such a system of education but has since altered the concept.

2. Private schools tend to discriminate against students in terms of race and religious background.

3. Such a practice violates the First Amendment.

4. Solution of the problem should be based on principle, not on economic considerations.

One of the basic principles of American education that has received general acceptance through the years is that public funds cannot legally be used for sectarian or other nonpublic schools. However well the principle has been accepted in theory, the issue is still debated, as indicated in the following opinion expressed by Justice Brennan in *Aguilar* v. *Felton* (1985):

> We have often grappled with the problem of state aid to non-public, religious schools. In all of these cases, our goal has been to give meaning to the sparse language and broad purposes of the cause while not unduly infringing on the ability of the states to provide for the welfare of their people in accordance with their own particular circumstances. . . . We have noted that the three-part test first articulated in *Lemon* v. *Kurtzman* guides the general nature of inquiry in this area (*Mueller* v. *Allen*, 1983). . . . First the statute must have a secular legislative purpose; second, its principal or primary effect must be one that neither advances nor inhibits religion; finally, the statute must not foster an excessive government entanglement with religion.[2]

The courts have relied on the so-called *Lemon* test since 1971 in all cases involving the sensitive relationship between government and religion in the education of children.[3] Although not directed to the finance issue, the *Lee* v. *Weisman* case, which was decided in 1992, was a catalyst in reaffirming the three-pronged *Lemon* test. The case involved the constitutionality of ceremonial prayer at public school events such as graduation. The Justice Department, in their friend-of-the-court brief had urged the Supreme Court to scrap the so-called *Lemon* test and allow "... for greater 'civic acknowledgements of religion in public life.'"[4]

NONPUBLIC SCHOOL ENROLLMENTS

About 11 percent of the students in the United States in grades kindergarten through twelve are in nonpublic schools.[5] The problem of church-state relations in financing education of nonpublic schools is not merely a question of the number of students or the number of schools involved; there is also the question of where those schools and students are located. Nonpublic schools and students are concentrated in certain states, and particularly in large cities. Failures of nonpublic schools in such states as Oklahoma and Utah (where only 1.5 percent of school children attend nonpublic schools) or North Carolina (where approximately 5 percent attend nonpublic schools) would not cause a significant financial adjustment. On the other hand, major closing of nonpublic schools in Rhode Island (with an enrollment of 22 percent of the students in nonpublic schools), New York (21 percent), or Pennsylvania (16 percent) would cause a tremendous financial burden on the public schools.[6]

It would seem that the states with the highest percentage of students attending nonpublic schools would be the biggest losers if public monies were diverted to such schools. However, in one of those states (New York), the Fleischmann Commission, in its post-*Serrano* report, estimated that it would be $415 million cheaper for the state to pay additional school costs for students in nonpublic schools than to assimilate them into public schools. The commission was opposed to providing public funds to nonpublic schools.

THE LAW AND CHURCH-STATE RELATIONS

Determining an acceptable relation of church and state has been a concern in this country since its founding. The early New England colonies, except for Rhode Island, made the Congregational Church their official church, whereas the colonies south of Maryland were Anglican. New York had a "multiple establishment" pattern of church-state relationship. Only Rhode Island, Pennsylvania, and Delaware had no officially established church. Vestiges of church-state relations have continued to exist in one form or another.

Legal Provisions for Separation

Article VI, Section 3 of the U.S. Constitution, especially the First Amendment that was included in 1791 in the Bill of Rights (ten amendments that delineated the rights of individuals), placed in American law the principles of freedom of religion and separation of church and state. Article VI provided that "no religious test should ever be required as a qualification to any office or public trust under the United States." The First Amendment, in establishing church-state separation, states: "Congress shall make no law respecting an establishment of religion, or prohibiting the free exercise thereof." The intended meaning is clear enough, but how to provide the proper and complete application of the principle is highly controversial. The Fourteenth Amendment, often referred to as the "due process" amendment, was established in 1868. In the years since that time, it has been interpreted by the courts as applying the First Amendment and other federal guarantees to the states. It provides that "no state shall make or enforce any law which shall abridge the privileges or immunities of citizens of the United States; nor shall any State deprive any person of life, liberty, or property without due process of law, nor deny any person within its jurisdiction the equal protection of the laws."

The Courts and the Child-Benefit Theory

The Supreme Court of the United States has ruled a number of times on the legal relation of church and state as intended by the amendments to the Constitution. For the various state legislative bodies and for the people generally, the Court's decisions have had varying degrees of palatability. The lack of complete support by the states for the federal position is partially vindicated by the general lack of unanimity among the Court members themselves in many of these decisions, some of which were made by the narrowest possible vote of the Court.

In *Cochran* v. *Louisiana State Board of Education* (1930),[7] the United States Supreme Court upheld the practice of Louisiana in providing free textbooks, paid for by tax funds, for pupils attending nonpublic schools. In the view of the Court, this was not a violation of the First or Fourteenth Amendments and was therefore legal. The basis for this reasoning was the "child-benefit" theory, according to which the children, not the churches they represented, were the beneficiaries of the funds expended. This view of the problem has never been supported by more than a few of the states.

In the verdict in *Everson* v. *Board of Education* (1947),[8] the U.S. Supreme Court, by the closest possible margin (5 to 4), held that using New Jersey tax funds allocated to school districts to reimburse parents for the cost of bus fares to attend nonpublic schools was legal and did not violate the First or Fourteenth Amendments. Seeking the protective cloak of the child-benefit theory, the Court regarded the action as safe, legal, and expeditious public welfare legislation.

A few of the states have reacted in support of the *Cochran* decision; about half of them have accepted the essence of the *Everson* verdict. State courts in Alaska (1961), Wisconsin (1962), Oklahoma (1963), and Delaware (1966) "have struck down enactments authorizing free busing of children attending denomination schools."[9] Pennsylvania (1967) and Connecticut (1960) upheld some variations of the *Everson* decision.

In 1975, the U.S. Supreme Court (*Meek* v. *Pittenger,* 421 U.S. 349, 95 S. Ct. 1753 (1975)) allowed textbooks to be loaned to nonpublic school students but disallowed the use of public funds for services, equipment, and instructional materials. In 1977 the Court (*Wolman* v. *Walter,* 433 U.S. 229, 97 S. Ct. 2593 (1977)) ruled that the provision of books, testing and scoring, and diagnostic and therapeutic services was constitutional, based on the child-benefit theory. State support of field trips, instructional materials, and equipment was ruled unconstitutional, as they aided schools rather than children per se. In 1986, in *Witters* v. *Washington Department of Services for the Blind* (106 S. Ct. 748 (1986)), the Court ruled that a blind student who was studying at a Christian College to become a minister, and who had been denied vocational assistance, could receive it. The basis of the decision was that aid for the *student* was acceptable.

Nearly all of the fifty state constitutions contain provisions that prohibit spending public funds for sectarian purposes. With rare exceptions these provisions have been followed, and the defense against using state funds for operating nonpublic schools has been relatively airtight until recent years.

FEDERAL AID AND NONPUBLIC SCHOOLS

Many proposals of members of Congress for federal support to public education have stirred controversy. Despite pressures to provide funds to "save the parochial schools from financial disaster," the line has generally been held. However, each skirmish on the issue has found the defense lines weakened and more vulnerable to future conflicts.

One of the first setbacks for opponents of using state funds for parochial schools came in Pennsylvania. In 1968, that state passed an act authorizing the state superintendent of public instruction to contract for the purchase of secular education services for students from nonpublic schools located in the Commonwealth of Pennsylvania. It provided that certain revenues from state harness racing should go into a nonpublic elementary and secondary education fund for the financing for all of these expenditures. No public school funds were involved.

Because the Pennsylvania legislation was controversial and might potentially influence other states, litigation was expected. It soon materialized; suit was brought in June 1969 against the state superintendent of public instruction and the state auditor general. The plaintiffs, including many professional and religious groups, charged that the legislation violated the First and Fourteenth Amendments to the U.S. Constitution. Late in 1969, a federal court ruled on the case, and *Education U.S.A.* reported:

> Catholic educators are hailing a federal court decision in Pennsylvania as a legal breakthrough supporting state aid to nonpublic schools. The ruling upheld the nation's first state aid law for nonpublic schools by dismissing a

suit challenging the constitutionality of the 1968 Pennsylvania statute. The 2 to 1 majority decision approved the state statute which provides for $21 million this year and $41 million next year in state aid to nonpublic schools. The court said the law neither creates nor supports the establishment of religion.[10]

SUPREME COURT RULINGS

Acclaim for the decision in Pennsylvania was short-lived. In June 1971, the U.S. Supreme Court overruled the district court decision and declared the Pennsylvania law to be in violation of the principle of separation of church and state. The decision was accompanied, however, by a contrary one regarding public support of nonpublic colleges and universities in Connecticut.

In these rulings, the Supreme Court acted simultaneously on three appeals of cases concerned with the use of public funds for nonpublic schools. These cases included *Tilton* v. *Richardson* (public funds for higher education in Connecticut), *Lemon* v. *Kurtzman* (public funds for providing educational services in nonpublic elementary and secondary schools in Pennsylvania), and *DiCenso* v. *Robinson* (public funds to provide supplements to the salaries of teachers in certain nonpublic elementary schools in Rhode Island).[11]

In considering the three cases, the Court looked at a number of issues. (1) Is aid to church-related colleges and universities constitutionally different from similar aid to church-related elementary and secondary schools? (2) May the state or the federal government or both provide direct aid to nonpublic schools, or must they confine themselves to indirect assistance like that already approved in the *Everson* and *Cochran* cases? (3) To what extent do these cases support or violate the establishment clause, which requires avoidance of excessive government involvement or entanglement with religion?[12]

In *Tilton* the Court sustained the Connecticut law for public aid to colleges and universities. In *Lemon* it rejected the Pennsylvania law to aid nonpublic elementary and secondary schools, and it also rejected the Rhode Island plan for supplementing teacher salaries in nonpublic schools. These cases determined that there is less likelihood of state involvement or entanglement in the affairs of a church-related college than in a church-related elementary or secondary school.

Evidence of the controversial nature of many other state and federal plans for using or not using public funds for nonpublic schools is shown by the following representative examples of many laws and court rulings:

- The U.S. Supreme Court ruled against tax benefits for any private segregated school set up in Mississippi to avoid integration.
- The Maine Supreme Court ruled against church-state-related legislation. The court pointed out that financial conditions created by closing parochial schools were not the issue—the Constitution, not economics, was at stake.

- In 1969, the California legislature made profit-making enterprises not connected to their tax-exempt purpose (religion) subject to the state's 7 percent tax on net income.
- The West Virginia Supreme Court ruled in 1970 that county school systems must furnish bus transportation to parochial school students.
- A New York law that would have provided $33 million a year to church-related schools for teacher salaries, instructional materials, and other costs of instruction was declared unconstitutional by a three-judge federal panel in 1971.
- Ohio's law permitting aid to nonpublic schools was upheld by the Ohio Supreme Court in November 1971, but in October 1972 the U.S. Supreme Court affirmed the decision of a federal district court that had ruled against the state's making direct grants to parents of children attending nonpublic schools.
- The National Defense Education Act, the Elementary and Secondary Education Act, and the Education and Consolidation and Improvement Act of 1981 have all provided federal funds to public school districts that aid students in nonpublic schools through the "pass-through" provision.
- In June 1983 the Supreme Court handed down its opinion in *Mueller* v. *Allen*. [13] By a 5 to 4 vote, it approved a Minnesota law that permits taxpayers to deduct from their state income tax expenses for tuition, textbooks, and transportation. The deduction is neutrally available to every family with children of school age but is especially beneficial for parents who send their children to private schools.
- In *Aguilar* v. *Felton* (1985), [14] the Supreme Court held that the practice of nonpublic schools being used part-time as public schools and receiving state aid was unconstitutional, because nonpublic schools in that situation are "pervasively sectarian."
- In May 1991, the U.S. Eighth Circuit Court of Appeals unanimously overturned a lower court decision in a Missouri case (*Pulido* v. *Cavazo*) which held that the U.S. Department of Education allocation of Chapter I funds that provided "off the top" money to provide leased mobile vans or portable classrooms for pupils in religious schools was unconstitutional. In a split vote, the panel also overturned the lower court's ruling that such vans and portable units could not be placed on the property of a church-affiliated school. The circuit court said that the units would be viewed as "religiously neutral" under proper circumstances. [15]

The proponents of plans to allocate state monies to nonpublic schools, especially in New York and Pennsylvania, have made numerous attempts to enact laws in harmony with the types of such aid the Supreme Court had agreed upon in previous years. At the same time, they have endeavored, with little success, to answer the Court's objections in previous cases. For example, after the *Lemon* v. *Kurtzman* decision in 1971, the advocates of aid to parochial schools tried to enact legislation that met three criteria established by that court for determining whether or not a law meets the establishment clause requirements: (1) the statute must have a secular legislative purpose; (2) its principal or primary effect must be one that neither advances nor inhibits religion, and (3) the statute must not foster excessive government entanglement with religion. These are the three prongs of the *Lemon* test.[16]

In June 1973, in *Sloan* v. *Lemon*,[17] the U.S. Supreme Court held that Pennsylvania's Parent Reimbursement Act for Nonpublic Education was unconstitutional. The act provided funds to reimburse parents for some of the tuition expenses they paid to send their children to nonpublic schools. On the same day, the Court held unconstitutional a New York statute that provided funds for nonpublic schools serving low-income families. The funds were to be spent for the maintenance and repair of buildings, for tuition grants, and for certain tax benefits for low-income parents of students attending nonpublic schools.

The major arguments presented against the Pennsylvania and New York laws were:

1. Providing state funds for nonpublic schools violates the First Amendment to the Constitution.

2. Such allocation of funds could have a serious effect on the capability of the public schools to discharge their responsibility.

3. Such funding would divert money from public education to private education.

4. This funding would tend to renew the conflict over church-state relations.

5. Such funding would increase the number of students in nonpublic schools and change the mix of students in public schools.

In reviewing *Sloan* v. *Lemon* (Pennsylvania) and *Committee for Public Education and Religious Liberty* v. *Nyquist* (New York),[18] the Supreme Court, by margins of 8 to 1 and 6 to 3, respectively, rejected both statutes. It held that the "maintenance and repair provisions violate the Establishment Clause because their effect, inevitably, is to subsidize and advance the religious mission of sectarian schools." It held that the tuition reimbursement parts of both statutes fail the "effect" test for the same reason as those governing the maintenance and repair grants. It ruled that the tax benefit to parents of nonpublic school children did not fit the pattern of property tax exemptions sustained in *Walz* v. *Tax Commission* (1970).[19] (In the view of the Court, tax exemptions for property used solely for religious purposes tended to reinforce the separation of church and state and to avoid excessive government entanglement with religion.) The controlling factor, in the view of the Court, was that although both statutes would aid all nonpublic schools, 90 percent of the students affected were attending schools controlled by religious organizations. Thus, the statutes had the practical effect of advancing religion.

In *Aguilar* v. *Felton* (1985) the point at issue was that nonpublic schools were being used (and reimbursed by the state) as "part-time public schools." These religious schools identified themselves as public during the time they were teaching secular subjects. The Supreme Court held that the procedure was unconstitutional, stating:

Schools in this case are thus "pervasively sectarian," [and] the challenged public school programs operating in the religious schools may impermissibly advance religion in three different ways. First, the teachers participating in the programs may unintentionally or inadvertently inculcate particular religious tenets or beliefs into the curriculum. Second, the programs may provide a crucial symbolic link between government and the school indicating a support of the religious denomination operating the school. Third, the programs may have the effect of directly promoting religion by impermissibly providing a subsidy to the primary religious mission of the institutions affected.[20]

EDUCATIONAL CHOICE

The topic in education receiving the greatest exposure in the literature during the past decade is *choice,* and many list it as "the hottest education issue of the 1990s." The subject is greatly debated because of the national attention it has garnered from high political offices. President George Bush emphasized that it is a necessary step in redefining education, calling it a "national imperative." A special choice outreach office with the Department of Education was established late in 1989,[21] and governors throughout the country endorsed the concept as a way to restructure education.

On June 25, 1992, Secretary of Education Lamar Alexander proposed a federal "choice" program called the "GI Bill for Children." The recommendation would provide $1,000 scholarships to students from low or middle-income families who could spend the money at public, private or parochial schools. It was presented as a pilot program costing $500 million. Education officials generally reacted with disdain.

Choice is not a new issue. Since the founding of the United States, it has often been discussed whether the public or the private sector should be charged with the major responsibility of providing education. The negative claims against the public schools have included their alleged discrimination against the gifted and the handicapped, their presumed failure to teach students the fundamental skills, and their reputation for fostering inequality among the races and between the sexes. These and numerous other charges have resulted in various proposals for radical changes in the organization and administration of schools. Some of these proposals purport to be panaceas; others are proposed as partial solutions to the many problems that education critics claim are not solvable under the present public school systems of the fifty states.

Education Vouchers

A frequently proposed solution to the choice issue is that of providing a voucher to be spent at the school selected by the parents and student. Numerous versions of this approach have been suggested since this idea was originally espoused by

Milton Friedman in his 1962 *Capitalism and Freedom*. Reduced to its simplest form, his plan recommended: (1) determination of a minimum level of education by each state, (2) the issuance to parents of vouchers that could be used in approved schools to purchase the education obtainable in that school, and (3) the payment by parents of the additional amount of money required by a particular school over and above the amount of the voucher.

It is claimed that such an arrangement would allow parents a choice among the educational programs available to their children by paying the amount required above the cost allowed by the voucher. The schools could be of any type—private, parochial, or public—provided they met the established state standards.

Advantages and Disadvantages

It is relatively easy to see limitations and possible defects in this organizational system. It seems apparent that the affluent would be able to purchase education at the more expensive and prestigious schools, whereas the less affluent would be forced to purchase education for their children at less expensive institutions. Undoubtedly, this would accentuate undesirable economic segregation and social class distinction. Although such a program might offer a choice of schools and curricula for students in central cities or in other areas of dense population, the idea of competitive schools in rural areas is not feasible from the point of view of basic economics, considering the limited number of students available. In places where parochial schools predominated, such a system would likely foster the promulgation of church dogma and values.

Some of the advocates of a voucher system argue that it would result in greater decentralization of schools. This, they say, is highly desirable, since it would bring the schools closer to the people whose children attend them. However, chaos could potentially develop if each school were allowed to set its own standards of values, to determine the subjects to be taught, and to establish its own costs of attendance.

Advocates say that such a plan would give parents a wider choice of education for their children, and that the schools would be better as a result of the natural competition that would arise. They point to the fact that the public schools now maintain a natural monopoly and are very slow to react to public pressure and criticism, but that private schools that are dependent upon favorable public opinion react quickly to the desires and needs of their students.

One of the premises of the voucher theory is that such a competitive system would increase the efficiency of school operation, just as competition does in other fields of activity, but certain limiting factors tend to discredit such an assumption. For example, the ability of parents or students to select schools of higher quality than others (assuming that the system is large enough to provide schools of varying quality) is open to question, and it raises concerns described by Wise and Hammond:

In the worst case scenario, unregulated vouchers could result in at least certain classes of parents not being able to secure the quality of education they want for their children. This would be true under the various definitions of quality if the entire voucher system were to be underfunded by the state, if parents did not have adequate information to make sound decisions about school options, if the marketplace did not produce desired educational options in all neighborhoods, or if the educational resources, processes, or philosophies selected by parents were not to result in the learning outcomes they desire. Furthermore, if tuition and admissions policies are unregulated, low-income parents and those parents of children with whatever the excluded characteristics might be from schools practicing selective admissions (ability, gender, ethnicity, language dominance, etc.) would have fewer opportunities to choose the quality of education they want for their children. To avoid any one of these potentially undesirable consequences, the state would have to become involved in policies about the state financing and private supplementation of vouchers, the extent and accuracy of the information system for parents, the location of educational alternatives of various types, the technology of education, and/or the admissions policies of schools.[22]

The fragmentation of large schools into numerous small ones (as some of the proponents of voucher schools advocate) would certainly increase unit costs and introduce many other negative characteristics of small schools—limited curricula, high per-pupil administrative costs, and provincialism to name only a few. There is little evidence available to indicate that small schools would be extremely competitive in terms of students, faculty, or courses of study. The history of public education in this country has been one of combining small schools to provide more opportunities for specialization and to eliminate the innate inefficiency, and other deficiencies of small units. This was emphasized by Roe L. Johns and others in the following:

> [T]he creation of a large number of competing schools could lead to substantial diseconomies of scale. This would be especially true in the case of secondary schools where the thrust for many years has been to eliminate small, inefficient high schools. The diseconomies of scale which would arise with many small private and public schools in competition for students could easily reduce their output per dollar expended for education rather than producing the greater efficiency in the use of the resources allocated to education.[23]

A coalition of education associations condemned the use of vouchers, stating, "often veiled as choice, [vouchers] are examples of unwise public policy because they undermine our nation's system of public schools." The forum argues that:

- Voucher advocates often have an ulterior motive—shifting public education funding to private schools—when they propose choice.
- Voucher proposals do little for long-term education reform by deflecting
  attention away from other potential reforms.
- Choice programs that include private schools have the potential to cir-
  cumvent provisions for educational quality control and public accountability; safeguards against racial and social class isolation; restrictions on
  the use of funding for religious purposes; and rules forbidding racial,
  ethnic, "and other invidious" discrimination.[24]

Until recently the voucher system has gotten little exposure, and there has
been limited actual experience with it. One of the few experiments of note was by
the Alum Rock Union School District in California, on a pilot basis from 1972 to
1975. Friedman and Friedman (1980) declared it to be a success, but they agreed
that it was hardly a proper test, as it was limited to only a few public schools.
Doyle described the project as so radical that Alum Rock was the only district in
the nation that was willing to accept federal funds to serve as a demonstration site.
The limited scope of the project made it difficult to assess vouchers, especially
because of the intense anxiety and extensive publicity surrounding it.[25]

A plan that would provide more data in testing the voucher system has been
made possible by the Wisconsin legislature that passed a bill allowing 1,000
public school students the option of attending nonsectarian private schools at
state expense. The measure is specifically aimed at low-income students currently enrolled or who have dropped out of school. John Coons praised the
legislation: "People who have been pretty much entombed in segregated public
schools will have a chance to get their civil rights vindicated in the private
sector."[26] Under the program, which will last five years, students will be able to
enroll in nonsectarian schools that agree to accept the approximately $2,500
provided as full reimbursement for tuition costs. By September 1990, a total of
635 students had applied to participate in the program.[27] Some feel the few
numbers for the program for the first year were because of bad publicity and the
fact that the voucher program was being challenged in the Wisconsin courts.
"Although the Milwaukee program was struck down by the state court on a
technicality, there is support at the state level for reimplementing and expanding
the program."[28]

Like many other innovative ideas, vouchers have become more complex in
theory after years of discussion and consideration. Several variations on the plan
are now found in the literature. One of the principle adaptations is the "family
power equalizing" plan developed by John Coons and Stephen Sugarman of the
University of California at Berkeley Law School. Champions of the choice movement for over a quarter of a century, they have attempted to unsuccessfully get
the issue on California's election ballot on several occasions. With the success in
other states and the national thrust, proponents in California are encouraged,
and at this writing a new initiative had been formally filed with prospects of
attaining the required valid signatures to include the measure on a ballot. Following are the basic principles of choice described by Coons and Sugarman:

1. Any system of choice must aim to reduce the class and racial segregation characteristic of the present order.

2. In order to assure equality of access to all participating public and private schools, choice must tilt toward the poor.

3. School systems must guarantee transportation for reasonable distances to those who cannot afford to pay for it themselves.

4. The choice system must make special efforts to direct information to families unaccustomed to choosing schools for their children.

5. Government-operated schools must be able, if they wish, to free themselves from regulations not imposed on private schools.

6. The plan should not encumber private schools with new regulations governing hiring, curriculum, or choice of facilities.

7. The value of the scholarships should suffice to stimulate new providers.[29]

Tuition Tax Credit

An option open to proponents of aid to nonpublic schools is the tuition tax credit plan. Such an arrangement would indirectly divert some public funds to the support of nonpublic schools. A proposed Tuition Tax Credit Act in 1977 (the Packwood-Moynihan bill) was an example of a federal device to get public funds to nonpublic schools. It proposed that parents who paid tuition for children in nonpublic schools should be given a tax credit. Its sponsors argued that the public had a responsibility to support the bill, as it would assist public schools financially by keeping children in nonpublic schools where enrollments were decreasing. Those opposed to the measure felt that it violated the First Amendment, benefited the rich and middle classes, and was only slightly less objectionable than the controversial voucher system. The proposed act was defeated in 1978.

Another attempt to promote tuition tax credits came directly from the president's office in April 1982. The press release from the White House followed most of the same reasoning used by others who have promoted the concept. It noted the following:

- All parents have a fundamental right and responsibility to direct the education of their children in a way that best serves their individual needs and aspirations. Private schools provide an essential means for many in fulfilling their aspirations.
- The President's draft tuition tax credit proposal provides tax relief to the working families of nonpublic school students, and expands the ability of American parents to exercise educational freedom of choice.
- Educational opportunity and choice in a pluralistic society require a diverse range of schools—public and private.
- This choice raises issues of tax equity for those who carry the double burden of supporting both private and public school costs.

- A tuition tax credit would assist these working families in meeting the increasing costs of nonpublic education. While still paying local taxes to support public schools, these families would be able to recover up to half the cost of each child's tuition.[30]

The president's program allowed for nonrefundable credits, phased in over a three-year period—from $100 the first year to a maximum of $500. There was little support for the measure, and Congress took no action.

The issue of tuition tax credits remained popular with the Republican Party. It was included as part of the 1988 political platform. However, by April 1989, President George Bush stated that he did not favor tuition tax credits, noting that "we can't afford to do that. . . . So I think that everybody should support the public school system." Although the President's remarks appeared to indicate a clear departure from the previous administration, the turn of events was not entirely surprising to those associated with private education.[31] One proponent noted, "It's an idea whose time has come and passed, or not come at all."[32]

Supporters of tax credits were encouraged in late 1990 when a bold move by a town in New Hampshire authorized a tax abatement for property owners who sponsored high school students attending private school—either secular or religious. Under the plan, property owners could receive property tax relief of as much as $1,000. An interesting sidelight to the abatement is that the property owner may sponsor any student whether a relative or not. It is anticipated that several court cases will challenge the law, but the selectmen of the town of Epsom are relying on the 1983 U.S. Supreme Court decision, *Mueller* v. *Allen*, to pass constitutional muster.[33]

APPROACHES TO CHOICE

States and local districts that have ventured into choice provide students with options in the following categories: open enrollment, magnet schools, postsecondary concurrent programs, schools within a school, alternative schools in and out of the district, high school graduation incentives, and area learning centers. Part of the choice controversy is that the term has not been clearly defined. Supporters claim to favor choice, "but when it comes to the specifics of actual choice plans, their superficial consensus breaks down. To the extent the movement for choice can be called a movement at all, it is an extremely fragmented and conceptually shallow one. It lacks mission."[34]

Enthusiasts for educational choice have been motivated by the work of social scientists John Chubb and Terry Moe. Their scholarly work, *Politics, Markets, and American Schools*, outlines elements that they recommend for developing an educational choice program. "The guiding principle is that public authority must be put to use in creating a system that is almost entirely beyond the reach of public authority." The authors present formidable criteria in the areas of

"The Supply of Public Schools," "The Funding of Public Education," "Choice Among Schools," "Governance and Organization of the Public Schools," and "Overview: Choice as a Public System."[35] "At least twenty states and a significant number of municipalities have made choice a key strategy for educational improvement, and many more are considering it."[36]

THE CONTROVERSY NOT SOLVED

The relation of church and state and now the broader issue of choice have serious implications for school finance, some of which become more apparent each year. For example, the constantly increasing costs of education for nonpublic schools have caused the sponsoring agencies to take a serious look at the operation of such institutions. There is some merit to their argument that some governmental financial assistance may be required to keep their operation solvent so that they can continue to supplement and abet the educational programs of the public schools. Their contention is that nonpublic school bankruptcy would bring hundreds of thousands of abandoned students back into the public education system, at a very high cost.

Despite the obvious fact that nonpublic school failures will result in higher costs of public education, most citizens prefer to view the church-state issue on the basis of principle rather than economics. Either approach to the problem has its limitations, its defenders, and its critics. Consequently, litigation in this area of financing education is becoming more common and controversial than ever before in history.

The state legislature in Minnesota introduced a bill that allows parochial schools to receive public funds for education. Adopted in May 1991, the legislation provides for certain students between the ages of 12 and 21 to enroll in nonprofit private schools. Students who are at least 16 years old and qualify for the program may enroll in church-sponsored schools. The sectarian schools must not exclude students based on religious beliefs and must provide "nonsectarian education services." The local school district is the contracting agent and provides 88 percent of the basic state funding to the participating nonpublic school.

A similar measure allows high school juniors and seniors to attend college, including religious institutions, at district expense. The program was deemed constitutional by a federal district judge, indicating that it did not violate the establishment clause.[37]

Unfortunately, even though many courts have ruled on the problem, there is no clearly determined answer to whether or not statutes adopted in some of the states are contraventions of the First or Fourteenth Amendments. The controversy over the church-state conflict and the implications of sharing public revenue with private schools pose many questions for both private and public school administrators. The future is difficult to predict, but one thing is certain: the courts and legislators will be challenged with this issue again and again.

SUMMARY

The principle of separation of church and state is lauded in this country, but it has caused a dilemma of some importance in the field of education. Direct government financial support for private and parochial schools has continually been repudiated by the courts. Proponents of financial aid to nonpublic schools argue that parents should have a choice in the type of school their children attend, that nonpublic schools cannot function properly without financial support, and that the elimination of such schools would cause economic stress on public schools.

Opponents argue that parochial aid represents a big step backwards in educational philosophy, that the practice would violate the First Amendment to the U.S. Constitution, and that the problem should be solved on the basis of principle rather than its economic effect. The principle of separation has generally been observed, but interpretation of it has sometimes changed. The courts have sometimes supported a child-benefit theory and some forms of tax credit payments for elementary and secondary school students, if such action passed the *Lemon* test.

The topic of *choice* is receiving much exposure in the literature, noted by some to be "the hottest education issue of the 1990s." A frequently proposed solution to the choice issue is that of providing a voucher to parents to be spent at the school they wish their child to attend. Tuition tax credits is another option that expands the possibilities for choice and at the same time proposes a way to divert federal and state public funds to nonpublic schools.

The church-state controversy has had and will continue to have an important effect on state school finance systems. Nonpublic schools, like public schools, are being adversely affected by continually rising costs, which sometimes force nonpublic schools to discontinue their services. This, of course, places a greater financial burden on the public schools.

The issue of financial support to nonpublic schools remains unresolved. The debate over its merits and drawbacks goes on unabated, with no satisfactory solution yet in evidence.

ASSIGNMENT PROJECTS

1. Trace the history of the church-state controversy in education in your own state since the adoption of the U.S. Constitution.
2. Review three important court decisions that have had an effect on public financing of church schools.
3. Summarize the arguments in favor and those opposed to the granting of public funds for the support of nonpublic schools.

4. Some states have made greater efforts than others to provide public funds for nonpublic schools. Trace the history of a particular state in its efforts to come to a satisfactory solution to this problem.

5. The "choice" issue has implications for diverting public funds to nonpublic schools. Prepare a paper presenting the pros and cons of this point of view.

6. Prepare a paper indicating your position on the question of using public funds to help support nonpublic schools.

7. Defend Supreme Court decisions on church-state issues in financing education against critics who claim that such decisions are actually anti-religion.

SELECTED READINGS

Abramowitz, Susan, and Ann Stackhouse. *The Private High School Today*. Washington, D.C.: National Institute of Education, 1982.

Berne, Robert, and Leanna Stiefel. *The Measurement of Equity in School Finance*. Baltimore, MD.: Johns Hopkins University Press, 1984.

Chubb, J. E. and T. M. Moe. *Politics, Markets, and America's Schools*. Washington, D.C.: Brookings Institution, 1990.

Coleman, James, Thomas Hoffer, and Sally Kilgore. *Public and Private Schools*. Washington, D.C.: National Center for Educational Statistics, 1981.

Coons, John E., and Stephen D. Sugarman. *Education by Choice: The Case for Family Control*. Berkeley: University of California Press, 1978.

Everhart, Robert. *The Public School Monopoly: A Critical Analysis of Education and the State in American Society*. Cambridge, Mass.: Ballinger, 1982.

Kirkpatrick, David W. *Choice in Schooling: A Case for Tuition Vouchers*. Chicago: Loyola University Press, 1990.

McCarthy, Martha M. *A Delicate Balance: Church, State and the Schools*. Bloomington, Ind.: Phi Delta Kappan Educational Foundation, 1983.

Nathan, Joe, ed. *Public Schools by Choice: Expanding Opportunities for Parents, Students, and Teachers*. St. Paul, Minn.: Institute for Learning and Teaching, 1989.

Odden, Allan R., and Lawrence O. Picus. *School Finance: A Policy Perspective*. New York: McGraw-Hill, 1992.

Williams, Mary Frase, Kimberly Small Hancher, and Amy Hunter. *Parents and School Choice: A Household Survey: School Finance Project*. Washington, D.C.: U.S. Department of Education, 1983.

ENDNOTES

1. *Pierce* v. *Society of Sisters*, 268 U.S. 510, 45 S. Ct. 571 (1925).

2. *Aguilar* v. *Felton*, 105 S. Ct. 3232 (1985).

3. *Lemon* v. *Kurtzman*, 403 U.S. 602, 91 S. Ct. 2105 (1971), *rehearing denied*.

4. Mark Walsh, "Court Opens Term with Several Major School Cases on Docket," *Education Week*, October 2, 1991, p. 25.

5. *Educational Governance in the States* (Washington, D.C.: U.S. Department of Education, 1983), pp. 86–87.

6. Ibid.

7. *Cochran* v. *Louisiana State Board of Education*, 281 U.S. 370, 50 S. Ct. 335 (1930).

8. *Everson* v. *Board of Education*, 330 U.S. 1, 67 S. Ct. 504 (1947), *rehearing denied.*

9. National Education Association, *Research Bulletin 45*, No. 2 (May 1967), p. 44.

10. *Education U.S.A.* (Washington, D.C.: National School Public Relations Association, Dec. 8, 1969), p. 86.

11. *Tilton* v. *Richardson*, 403 U.S. 672, 91 S. Ct. 2091 (1971); *Lemon* v. *Kurtzman*, and *DiCenso* v. *Robinson*, 403 U.S. 602, 91 S. Ct. 2105 (1971), *rehearing denied.*

12. The Supreme Court previously addressed this question in *Walz* v. *Tax Commission* (397 U.S. 664, 90 S. Ct. 1409) and upheld by an 8 to 1 vote a constitutional and statutory provision in New York exempting church property from taxation.

13. *Mueller* v. *Allen*, 463 U.S. 388, 103 S. Ct. 3062 (1983).

14. *Aguilar* v. *Felton*, 105 S. Ct. 3232 (1985).

15. Mark Walsh, "Court Backs Rule on Chapter 1 in Religious Schools," *Education Week*, May 29, 1991, pp. 1, 23.

16. *Lemon* v. *Kurtzman*, 403 U.S. 602, 91 S. Ct. 2105 (1971), *rehearing denied.*

17. *Sloan* v. *Lemon*, 413 U.S. 825, 93 S. Ct. 2982 (1973).

18. *Committee for Public Education* v. *Nyquist*, 413 U.S. 756, 93 S. Ct. 2955 (1973).

19. *Walz* v. *Tax Commission*, 397 U.S. 664, 90 S. Ct. 1409 (1970).

20. *Aguilar* v. *Felton*, 105 S. Ct. 3232 (1985).

21. Mark Pitsch, "Cavazo Creates Outreach Office to Promote Choice," *Education Week*, December 12, 1990, p. 30.

22. Arthur E. Wise and Linda Darling Hammond, "Educational Vouchers Regulating Their Efficiency and Effectiveness," *Educational Researcher*, Vol. 12, No. 9 (November 1983), p. 11.

23. Roe L. Johns et al., *Financing Education: Fiscal and Legal Alternatives* (Columbus, Ohio: Merrill, 1972), p. 79.

24. Mark Pitsch, "Coalition Assails Private School Vouchers as Unwise Public Policy," *Educa-tion Week*, December 12, 1990, p. 30. Ten of the eleven-member consortium signed a statement of support. They are: the American Association of Colleges for Teacher Education, the American Association of School Administrators, the American Federation of Teachers, the Council of Chief State School Officers, the National Association of Elementary School Principals, the National Association of Secondary School Principals, the National Association of State Boards of Education, the National PTA, the National Education Association, and the National School Boards Association.

25. Denis P. Doyle, "Private Interests and the Public Good," *College Board Review*, No. 130 (Winter 1983–84), p. 9.

26. Quoted by William Snider, "Voucher System for 1,000 Pupils Adopted in Wisconsin," *Education Week*, March 18, 1990, pp. 1, 14.

27. Lynn Olson, "Milwaukee Choice Program Enlists 391 Volunteers," *Education Week*, September 12, 1990, p. 14.

28. *The Unfinished Agenda: A New Vision for Child Development and Education.* (New York: Committee for Economic Development, 1991), p. 48.

29. John E. Coons and Stephen D. Sugarman, "The Private School Option in Systems of Educational Choice," *Educational Leadership*, December 1990/January 1991, Vol. 48, No. 4, p. 55.

30. The White House Office of the Press Secretary, for release at 10:30 A.M. CST, Thursday, April 15, 1982. Tuition Tax Credit Fact Sheet.

31. Ann Bradley, "Tax Credits Are Too Expensive, Bush Asserts," *Education Week*, April 5, 1989, pp. 1, 17.

32. Ibid., quoting Denis Doyle.

33. Karen Diegmueller, "Town in N.H. Grants Property-tax Break as Choice Incentive," *Education Week*, January 9, 1991, pp. 1, 17.

34. John E. Chubb and Terry E. Moe. *Politics, Markets, and American Schools* (Washington, D.C.: The Brookings Institute, 1990), p. 207.

35. Ibid., pp. 218–25.

36. *The Unfinished Agenda*, p. 47.

37. Mark Walsh, "Minnesota Law Allows Church Schools to Get Public Funds," *Education Week*, October 9, 1991, p. 24.

Chapter 11

Financing School Facilities

Public schools across the U.S. are deteriorating faster than they can be repaired or replaced. One problem is that construction hasn't kept up with needs; another is short shrift for maintenance. —ALLAN C. ORNSTEIN, 1990

The uncomplicated and formerly satisfactory nineteenth-century system of financing public school capital outlays with funds raised almost solely by local property taxes is obsolete and impractical for present-day use. Before the 1900s there was little need for extensive state participation in this important aspect of financing education. Most school districts had been able to finance their own capital-outlay expenditures without assistance. Their school building problems had not yet reached the magnitude they have attained in recent years. There were many reasons for this:

1. A smaller percentage of the school-age population attended school.
2. Building costs were much lower for a number of reasons: buildings were much less pretentious, labor costs were much lower, and fewer special areas and less expensive equipment were required.
3. There was no accumulation of need for buildings, as there has been during much of this century.
4. Since extensive changes and innovations were minimal, relatively few facilities or buildings were discarded because of obsolescence.
5. The assessed value of taxable property per child to be educated was much more favorable, in terms of the taxes to be raised, than it is now.

As the need for state involvement increased in the early years of this century, a few states made feeble gestures toward helping finance school district capital outlays. About half a dozen southern states provided emergency funds to the hardship districts least capable of providing school buildings with local tax funds alone.

Since the problems of financing public school facilities are much the same as those of financing current expenditures, it would seem that reforms and improvements in one would bring similar improvements in the other. Such had not been the case, however, as the movement toward equalizing capital outlay has been slow. Walter G. Hack noted the similarities and differences in these two related problems of financing education in the post-*Serrano* reform period:

> Both types (financing current expenditures and financing facilities) have apparently felt the effects of the economic slowdown, double-digit inflation, and the wrath of the taxpayers' revenge. There is one major difference, however, significantly more recent attention has been given to problems related to financing the current expense programs. This attention is certainly legitimate and logical, given the proportion of school dollars expended between the two programs. It appears now, however, that attention could and should be at least shared with needs to finance capital outlay expenditures.
>
> Thus far in the decade, the *Serrano* and *Rodriguez* cases have occupied center stage in the educational finance theater. As a consequence of, and sequel to, the original cases, many states have mounted studies and enacted legislation to provide more equity in educational programs and financing. In much of the reform legislation which has been enacted, little or no modification has been made in the system to finance capital outlay. . . . [1]

COMPLETE LOCAL SUPPORT

One of the strong traditions that began to develop early in school finance history was that capital-outlay costs were of local concern only, in spite of strong and almost universal acceptance of state responsibility for education. The soundness of such a position is open to serious debate, but the general acceptance of this local responsibility, and the almost complete indifference on the part of state governments, is a matter of open record. In spite of recommendations for state participation in capital outlays by such finance planners as Updegraff and Mort, the main concern of most authorities in the Strayer-Haig era of influence was with state support of current operational costs only. This may have been because current expenditures included about 85 percent of the total school budget, with only 15 percent being spent for capital outlay.

Complete local support for financing capital outlays was an appropriate and practical method of collecting the money to build and equip new school buildings for many years. The rationale for such a method of collecting capital outlay and debt service funds has virtually disappeared in the face of newer and certainly fairer methods of financing education. Some of the changes in school finance philosophy include the following:

1. Since responsibility for education is legally a state function, responsibility for its financing rests firmly upon each state.

2. There is no justification for financing capital outlays on a different basis from current expenditures. If state financing of current operations is fair, so is state financing of capital outlays.

3. There is no defense for the traditional method of financing school facilities by relying completely on a regressive and unfair local property tax when more equitable tax sources are available at the state level.

4. It is false economy to indebt school districts for long periods of time, with excessive interest costs.

5. It is paradoxical to provide adequate funds for current expenditures for all districts and then deny some of them good educational programs because low assessed valuations and state-imposed limitations on debt service maximums limit their fiscal ability to provide satisfactory facilities.

6. Just as no district, regardless of its wealth, should enjoy pecuniary advantages over another in obtaining current operation funds, neither should any district enjoy resource advantages over another in providing school facilities.

Complete local responsibility for financing the current expenditures of school districts was eliminated in most states in the early part of this century, with the advent of state grants of various kinds to local districts. But financing the construction of school buildings has not yet made such progress; such financing is still almost completely a local responsibility in most of the states. In terms of the Coons, Clune, and Sugarman version of fiscal neutrality, the kind, number, and even the quality of school buildings and facilities available to most school children is still a function of the wealth of their parents, neighbors, and the school district in which they live. Financing school facilities is more than half a century behind our practices in financing current expenditures, and the gap is widening rather than decreasing.

The school finance court decisions in the early 1970s were concerned largely with inequities and inequalities in financing current expenditures. Only by implication can it be said that they were requiring the same improvements in financing capital expenditures. The problems in improving the latter are tremendously greater than they are in improving state finance programs for current expenditures. The problem of overcoming tradition and then directing attention and action toward equalization in financing capital outlays will require much time, effort, and money.

FACTORS RESTRICTING LOCAL RESPONSIBILITY

A big factor working against local responsibility for building school facilities, especially before the recent reorganization trend, was the low assessed valuations in thousands of small school districts. Regardless of the statutes and the willingness of people to tax themselves, bonding small districts to build school buildings was often mathematically impossible. In some school districts, for example, the cost of a new building might well exceed the assessed valuation of the entire district, whereas in other districts in the same state a small tax levy would be adequate to build needed buildings on a pay-as-you-go basis. Such inequity undermines the concept of providing equality of educational opportunity for all children within a state.

Another argument against complete local responsibility for construction of school buildings is that such costs would then be paid almost entirely by payers of property tax. Some people would then escape paying their share of these capital-outlay costs. The property tax may once have been a reasonably fair measure of tax-paying ability, but it is not so today. Using property tax payments exclusively for capital outlays repudiates our long-held belief in taxing people in terms of their ability to pay for education. Only state participation in such costs can provide parity for this inequity. Such relief should be provided on an equalization basis. This would bring some relief to payers of property taxes and would broaden the tax base to include revenues from many different kinds of taxes, an absolute necessity in any tax system.

LOCAL CAPITAL OUTLAY FINANCE PLANS

During the many years of almost exclusive local support for financing capital outlays, several different plans and procedures have evolved in the states. Chief among these have been pay-as-you-go, use of tax reserve funds, and bonding.

Pay-as-You-Go Financing

Pay-as-you-go financing, which has been feasible in some large and relatively wealthy school districts, is an ideal way to finance capital outlays. It is the quickest and perhaps the easiest way of getting the necessary resources from the private sector to the public sector of the economy. It eliminates the expenditure of large sums of money for interest, the costs of bond attorney fees, and election costs. It is convenient and tends to reduce the time required to obtain school facilities. This is particularly important in periods of high interest rates and inflation. As the costs of education have risen year after year, fewer districts have been able to take advantage of this method without creating a hardship for some payers of property tax.

Pay-as-you-go plans usually do not produce adequate revenue to finance school plant construction because of two factors: (1) relatively low assessed valuations in small and average-sized districts compared with the high cost of building; and (2) low tax levies due to restrictive legal limitations and high tax rates on property for obtaining the revenue for current expenditures. Many school districts that used this plan successfully in the years of relatively low-cost construction have found it impractical in recent years.

Building Reserve Plan

The accumulation of tax funds to be held in reserve for future building needs has been practiced in a few states; in some others it is illegal. This plan provides for spreading construction costs over a period of time *before* the buildings are erected—as contrasted with bonding, which spreads the cost over time *after* the schools are constructed. At first consideration, this reserve plan would appear to be a good method of solving this financial problem. However, there are a number of legitimate (and also some controversial) objections to this process:

1. The accumulated funds paid by taxpayers before the money was needed will have cost them the use of such funds with interest that might have been earned, and in many instances they may be funds that were borrowed by taxpayers at rates considerably higher than those available to the school district if these accumulated funds had been invested until they were needed.

2. Changes in the membership of the board of education, changes in the apparent needs of the school district, or both may sometimes result in diversion of these reserve funds to purpose other than those for which they were collected.

3. Some taxpayers who pay into the reserve fund may never receive the attendant benefits because they move from the school district.

4. Inflation tends to erode the value of the reserve and reduce its purchasing power, rather than increase it as a result of interest accumulation.

5. Some argue, rather feebly, that all those who use the buildings should pay their fair share of the cost of such facilities. This is possible only when the costs are paid over a long period of time—not feasible when pay-as-you-go or pay-in-advance procedures are used.

The validity of this "intergeneration equity" philosophy is open to question. If one espouses the point of view that each generation should pay for the benefits it receives from use of school facilities, one is rejecting the ability-to-pay principle of financing education and reverting to the benefit principle, an untenable position that has long since been rejected in school finance theory. At this point, too, it seems reasonable to assume that each generation will be called upon to make sizable payments for school facilities without concern for which generation is getting more or less than its share of benefits.

Although it is usually illegal to combine funds from the current-expenditure budget and the capital-outlay budget, except under certain legally established conditions, the effect of high tax rates in one area is that taxpayer resistance often forces lower tax rates in the other. Thus, the high rates necessary for pay-as-you-go or pay-in-advance payments for capital outlay may force lower rates for current expenditures, resulting in district curtailment of educational programs and services or other presumed economies such as reduced salary increases or increased pupil-teacher ratios.

Some districts that use the building reserve plan make a practice of earmarking certain voted revenues that are accumulated in a sinking fund to finance capital outlays. In practice, the plan is much like the pay-as-you-go process.

Under certain conditions, surpluses may be transferred from current expenditures at the end of a fiscal period to building reserve funds. The use of building reserves is usually subject to prior approval by the eligible voters of a district. In some states its potential utilization is limited to new construction; in others it may be used for any construction, including renovation and remodeling.

Bonding

The most common of all local programs for financing capital-outlay and debt-service expenditures is bonding. The process involves obtaining taxpayer favor for the district to issue long-term bonds to obtain funds to construct buildings and provide other facilities. Bond retirement involves levying property taxes to obtain funds to repay the principal and accrued interest. Bonding practices are required in districts with low assessed valuations of property, where tax revenues are not large enough to finance building costs on a current basis, and where the accumulation of reserve funds is either impracticable or illegal.

The principal advantages of the bonding system of raising school construction monies are the following:

1. Relative stability may be maintained in the tax levies necessary for construction. The tax burden is usually small enough each year so that it does not disturb the taxing plan for current-expenditure revenue.

2. Most districts can bond for large enough amounts to meet their building needs, whereas pay-as-you-go financing does not usually provide this opportunity.

3. School buildings and facilities necessary to operate a new program can be obtained when they are needed. Waiting for new construction until the required funds are in the school treasury would result in the denial of many educational benefits to the unfortunate students who were going through the school program when the facilities were needed but not provided.

4. The generations of people who get the greatest use of the facilities would be the ones to pay for them.

5. In an inflationary period, building costs may exceed interest costs.

There are also some disadvantages to the use of a bonding process for school building construction. These drawbacks include:

1. Total cost of the facilities is greater due to the necessity of paying large amounts of interest. However, the position of most school finance authorities is that the interest cost is small when compared with the benefits obtained by the almost immediate procurement of school facilities when they are needed.

2. Deferred payments often result in the construction of larger and more elaborate facilities than are needed; cash payments tend to reduce the desires of those who supply the funds at the time of purchase.

3. Bonding puts the entire cost of school construction on payers of property tax.

Bonding Authorities

The tightening of budgets and tax-limiting legislation has made it necessary for states and local districts to seek creative ways to finance new facilities and to make better utilization of existing buildings. Some states are broadening the concept of bonding authorities and bond banks to provide some flexible alternatives in solving capital-outlay problems. Camp and Salmon describe the concept in this way:

> The bonding authority concept, first developed at the turn of the century to circumvent constitutional debt limitations, and the bond bank concept, introduced in the early 1960s to consolidate the issues of subordinate political entities under the auspices of a state corporation issue, have evolved in many cases as effective and efficient methods of assisting local education agencies in financing school facility construction and other capital improvement programs. A series of these public corporations has developed in varying forms in over one-third of the states by entering into lease-purchase agreements with or purchasing bonds of local education agencies, thus supplying badly needed funds for the construction and improvement of local school buildings.[2]

The authors list the following as characteristics of a public bonding corporation:

1. It acts as an alternative financing vehicle which provides credit assistance to local governments, and acts as an intermediary between the investment market and the local government. It is an autonomous governmental corporation that issues its own bonds for the purpose of constructing public elementary and secondary school buildings. It does not enter into the assessment of need or initial evaluations surrounding the determination of physical characteristics of the buildings, and it does not participate in the actual operation of the facilities following construction. It acts primarily in a financing capacity.

2. It operates as a "quasi-business" organization with strong exclusion-principal and/or private-good characteristics. In general, it operates without yearly state appropriations even though it can use certain state accounts as a reserve to secure better bond ratings. In addition to its other services as a financial intermediary, it is empowered to accept certain state grants, helping to defer a portion of the costs to local districts.

3. It has the power to incur debt and issue bonds which are not considered a debt of the state, but it cannot tax except in special emergency conditions. The proceeds of the issue are used to purchase bonds and other evidences of indebtedness, including leases for the purpose of school construction. Receipts from rents, fees, or bonds are used to secure and service bonded indebtedness.

4. It purchases revenue or general obligation bonds from or enters into leases with the local school governing units, and issues revenue bonds and/or general or moral obligation bonds.

5. It assists local units with marketing debt issues and often creates a market of size for the debt of small local education agencies.[3]

Refunding Bonds

Lower interest rates and the need for additional capital outlays have motivated some districts to refund outstanding bonds. The concept is similar to an individual borrowing money to consolidate debts, paying off existing obligations, extending the months (or years) of payments, and making only one payment to a single lending source. The advantages of refunding or refinancing are: (1) interest rates are generally lower; (2) obligations are consolidated, and there is only one expiration date; and (3) a lower payment frees capital for other needed projects. Disadvantages include: (1) the public does not have the opportunity to vote on the measure, except in board meeting hearings; (2) the obligation is spread over a longer period of time; and (3) total interest throughout the full transaction may be greater.

Table 11-1 shows a cash flow analysis for a school district after refunding bonds of $4,705,000. The goal was to lower debt-service payments and collect revenue toward future capital costs. Outlined in the table are the principal and interest due yearly, a comparison with the prior issues, and the savings accrued from refinancing over the eight-year period. Needless to say, when school administrators and boards of education refund bonds, much analysis of the fiscal position of the district is needed.

Salmon and Wilkerson emphasize another caution dealing with refunding:

> Advance refunding of municipal bonds by school districts is legally permissible in many states and would be a desirable policy option for all states. The Internal Revenue Service (IRS) has promulgated a series of regulations that provide the framework for such refunding (Code of Federal Regulations). The primary intent of the IRS regulations is to deny unreasonable profits to the underwriters and to prohibit issuance of tax-exempt securities by governmental units that invest the proceeds in materially higher yield, taxable securities. However, if the IRS regulations are not followed properly, such municipal bonds might be classified as "arbitrage bonds" and the school district could lose its tax-exempt status (United States Code Service 1983).[4]

TABLE 11-1 Refunding $4,705,000 Bond Issue—Cash Flow Analysis and Savings Report

Date	Principal	Coupon	Interest	Total	Prior D/S	Savings	Cumulative Savings
			Proposed debt service				
11/1/91			71,918.13				
5/1/92	130,000.00	4.900000	143,836.25	345,754.38	380,340.00	34,585.63	34,585.63
11/1/92			140,651.25				
5/1/93	65,000.00	5.300000	140,651.25	346,302.50	380,340.00	34,037.50	68,623.13
11/1/93			138,928.75				
5/1/94	70,000.00	5.600000	138,928.75	347,857.50	380,340.00	32,482.50	101,105.63
11/1/94			136,968.75				
5/1/95	690,000.00	5.900000	136,968.75	963,937.50	995,340.00	31,402.50	132,508.13
11/1/95			116,613.75				
5/1/96	830,000.00	6.100000	116,613.75	1,063,227.50	1,094,990.00	31,762.50	164,270.63
11/1/96			91,298.75				
5/1/97	870,000.00	6.200000	91,298.75	1,052,597.50	1,087,090.00	34,492.50	198,763.13
11/1/97			64,328.75				
5/1/98	985,000.00	6.250000	64,328.75	1,113,657.50	1,147,960.00	34,302.50	233,065.63
11/1/98			33,547.50				
5/1/99	1,065,000.00	6.300000	33,547.50	1,132,095.00	1,166,475.00	34,380.00	267,445.63
	4,705,000.00		1,660,429.38	6,365,429.38	6,632,875.00		267,445.63
Accrued							
	4,705,000.00		1,660,429.38	6,365,429.38	6,632,875.00		267,445.63

Dated 8/1/91 with delivery of 8/1/91
Average coupon (interest):   6.186687
Average life: 5.704304
Net present value savings at: 6.5933% equals 215,939.75 or 4.5896% of par of the current issue
                                                     or 5.0809% of par of the prior issue

Smith Capital Markets, Salt Lake City, Utah.

Other Alternatives

An option some districts are using and many states are encouraging is the fuller utilization of buildings through the adoption of a year-round schedule. Students attend the prescribed number of days of school, but they are spread throughout the year in various combinations (e.g., 45 days in school, 15 days out). Theoretically, on a four-track system, one-fourth more students can attend the school, saving the costs of a new building for every four schools on the plan. Proponents of the year-round schedule point out that other savings accrue in the maintenance and operation area.

Earthman discusses options for meeting facility needs and freeing capital outlays. He suggests: (1) selling or exchanging existing school facilities or property, (2) entering into lease agreements, (3) leasing air rights over a school site, and (4) cooperating with other agencies in sharing facilities. He summarizes:

> None of these alternatives are complete solutions to the crunch that school systems feel for housing students and none of the alternatives are even new ideas to most educational administrators, but the identified alternatives might be means that can be used in combination to help meet a need. Because of unstable demographic conditions and subsequent change in program demand, the schools may need to more fully explore the use of these alternatives than previously. The phenomena of an increase in student population in the future, plus the rapid growth of selected programs in the schools, and the great need to keep facilities in better repair is beginning to have a profound impact upon the ability of the national school system to respond to capital needs. This, coupled with the prospect that capital funding of local projects may be shifting to the state capital will mean the local school administrator will be even more hard pressed than ever before to obtain capital funds to meet local facility needs. The movement of the veto power for capital funds from the local electorate to the state bureaucracy may well change the manner in which local school administrators obtain capital funds.[5]

CAPITAL OUTLAY FINANCING SINCE WORLD WAR II

Actions at the federal level of government brought the seriousness of the nation's school building problem into focus shortly after the close of World War II. The National School Facilities Survey of school building needs in the early 1950s brought attention to the dimensions of the problem. The passage of Public Law 815 in 1950, which provided federal capital-outlay funds for school districts in areas affected by federal installations and defense projects, was substantial evidence of federal recognition. The study showed that a number of events and conditions made necessary a reconsideration of the roles of the state and local school districts in financing capital outlays. In the first place, the building needs of school districts had increased for a number of reasons, including the following:

1. The backlog of needed school buildings had been increasing and had reached a phenomenal high by the end of the war. The economic effects of World War I, the Depression of the 1930s, and World War II had taken their toll in unbuilt school buildings. From 1914 until 1945 there had been few years when current building needs had been met.

2. A sharp upturn in birthrates during and immediately after World War II necessitated sharp increases in the number of school buildings to be built.

3. During the long periods of inactivity in the construction of school plants, particularly during and after World War II, changes in educational objectives and instructional procedures rendered many school buildings obsolete, in urgent need of replacement.

4. School reorganization programs, particularly from the late 1940s through the 1950s, had done much to create school building needs. Larger plants were needed to accommodate larger groups of pupils, at the same time that the small buildings in sparsely populated areas were no longer located where they were needed.

5. The greater mobility of people saw a large group moving toward the suburbs, with low potential for building the facilities required, and the migration of minority groups, particularly from the South to urban centers in the North. These were primary factors in creating imbalances of facilities.

A second important condition that helped force changes in school construction responsibilities was that as the districts faced increasing pressure to build new schools, many intervening factors reduced their ability to do so without additional state or federal financial assistance:

1. Increased costs of education, including construction costs, made the financing of capital outlays with accumulated reserves or on a pay-as-you-go basis less feasible than ever before. Many districts that had used one or both of these methods in earlier years now found them totally impossible to implement.

2. The indebtedness limitations that most states had placed on local capital outlay levies had become unrealistically low in many instances. These tax levy ceilings had been placed on local districts to protect property owners from excessive taxation when they were suffering from the financial difficulties accompanying the Depression of the 1930s. The result of these limitations was that in many districts where the people were willing to incur indebtedness for adequate capital outlays, state restrictions made such solutions impossible.

The pros and cons concerning state restrictions upon bonding power tend to counterbalance each other. According to Knezevich and Fowlkes:

Although legal restrictions on incurring indebtedness are onerous, they are not necessarily bad in themselves. Those that promote better management, such as the requirement that only serial bonds can be issued, are commendable. Statutory or constitutional requirements which promote the careful regulation of the school's debt can make bonds easier to market and command a more favorable rate of interest. Legal restrictions, such as holding the debt limitation of schools to an unrealistically low percent of the assessed valuation of property, can result in the impairment of the fundamental purposes of the school district.[6]

3. State requirements for voter approval for districts to incur long-term indebtedness made such approval difficult or impossible to obtain. Requirements such as that a two-thirds favorable vote be required for approval, or that a real property tax payment be made by all eligible voters, made it particularly difficult to vote bonds for the large sums necessary to finance capital outlays solely by local property taxation.

LOCAL SCHOOL BONDING PRACTICES

Local school districts that are in need of large capital-outlay funds find it necessary, like individuals, to borrow money from some source, to be repaid with interest over a relatively long period of time. Typically, the individual borrowing money signs a short-term note and receives the amount of the loan in cash or credit, to be repaid at an agreed-upon rate of interest over a predetermined period. The process is much the same for a school board needing capital-outlay funds. The board, after receiving formal approval from the school patrons (required in nearly all states), issues and sells bonds to one or more competing companies on the basis of the lowest bid for interest rates. Usually the principal and interest on these bonds are to be paid according to an agreed-upon plan, usually over a 10-, 20-, or 30-year period.

Types of Bonds

Registered bonds, as the name implies, require that all payments be made solely to the registered owners on record with the school district that issued them. Historically districts have used bearer or coupon bonds rather than registered bonds because of the lack of need to keep meticulous records, negotiability, and easy transferability of ownership. That option no longer exists.

Since 1983, bonds sold by school districts must be registered, a result of the Tax Equity and Fiscal Responsibilities Act (TEFRA). The purpose of the law is to increase revenues for the federal government. Sponsors of the law believed that owners of bearer bonds were not paying their fair share of taxes. With bearer bonds no list of owners is kept. Interest is paid to the owner by taking the bond coupon from a booklet and presenting it for payment. To transfer ownership, a person merely gives the bond to another. Because no one can positively identify the bearer, one could avoid paying taxes. A person could use bearer bonds as gifts and not have to report the transfer. The IRS believed that in excess of 100 million dollars of unreported income was the result. The act has not gone unnoticed in the courts. South Carolina filed suit, and the National Governor's Association joined, but the Supreme Court upheld TEFRA.

Now school districts must issue bonds in registered form and keep records of the owners' names, addresses, and social security numbers. Interest paid and ownership transfers must be recorded. School districts are to comply with TEFRA, which means increased costs for maintaining records.

Bond Attorney

The increasing complexity of state requirements for bonding and the increasing legal and financial problems facing the school administrator make it almost mandatory for school districts to employ a bond attorney when a bond issue is contemplated. The attorney's experience and training provide the school board and superintendent with advice and legal information necessary to complete this important aspect of financing the construction of school facilities. Services include securing legally accepted affirmation of bonding by the voters and arranging proper and advantageous sale of bonds to the best interest of the school district.

Bonding Power

Bonding is not an implied power that school districts may use at their discretion and convenience; it must be expressed in the body of state law. The legislature has full power to determine the conditions required for bonding and the limits of bond issues available to each district. Likewise, it has plenary power to determine the qualifications of voters, how the bonds are to be sold, and any other pertinent conditions surrounding the transaction. However, the statutory conditions concerning bonding are often directory rather than mandatory, and courts usually support bond business where substantial compliance with the law has existed. Strict compliance is expected, but the intent of the statutes is to determine the will of the voters. Consequently, the legality of bond elections and sales is usually determined by whether or not the procedures have determined what the people actually wanted.

Bonds Are Debentures

School district bonds are debentures acknowledging a debt that the school district owes to the bondholder; they do not have collateral backing or ordinary mortgage rights, however. They are not mortgages in the typical sense of the word, for they do not permit bondholders to foreclose and take over the physical

assets of a district in the event of default in payment. The various lawmaking
bodies and the courts, while recognizing that taking possession of school property by an unpaid bondholder would be against the interest of the people in
general, protect the bondholders by requiring that certain tax funds be earmarked and set aside in special funds or accounts for bond redemption.

BOND TYPES

There are several ways to classify bonds: according to the agency (municipality
or state) issuing them, the degree of security protecting bondholders, or the
procedure to be used in paying them. The most common way of classifying them
is by the method used to pay or retire the bond principal. Under this classification, there are two main types: serial bonds and straight-term bonds.

Serial Bonds

The advantages offered by the serial type of bonding are such that its use is
required in most of the states. This kind of bond provides for payment of accrued
interest each year and also for retirement of part of the principal each year on an
amortized basis. This reduces the total interest cost, since interest is charged only
on the unpaid balance of the principal. It also affords an extension of further
bonding capacity as the amounts on the principal are paid. It is not necessary
under this type of bonding to amass large surpluses or sums of money in a
sinking fund in anticipation of bond maturity at a later date. Taxes can be held to
the total amount required to pay the predetermined costs of debt retirement each
year. Such a plan is inflexible and may cause problems in periods of unantici-
pated decline or reduction in yearly tax receipts for such purposes.

Straight-Term Bonds

Straight-term bonds that mature at the end of the bonding period have very little
real value to a school district. Although they are said to have been important and
useful in financing capital outlays in years past, their history has been one of
mismanagement and poor planning. Hence, they are not used extensively today.
There is little to be gained by a district's delaying retirement of a debt until the
end of the bonding period. The arguments were forcefully stated by *The Bond
Buyer* in the following:

> The debt retirement plan should provide for: (1) the retirement of principal at
> least as rapidly as the capital assets acquired while the proceeds depreciate;
> (2) declining debt service on existing debt, otherwise the almost inevitable
> sale of emergency or unanticipated issues will result in debt service having a
> decidedly upward bias; (3) a maturity schedule that does not add undue
> rigidity to the budget.[7]

A variation of the straight-term bond saw the development of legal requirements for establishing and maintaining "sinking funds" for the payment of bonded indebtedness. These requirements called for the proceeds of debt retirement tax levies to be placed in a specific fund for payment of the bond principal at maturity. The usually anticipated problems of administering reserve funds—proper and safe investment, protection against mismanagement, and avoidance of making loans or transfers to other accounts—have continued in the administration of this kind of bond.

Callable Bonds

Bond amortization plans are usually rigid and prevent adjustment over the period of their retirement. Bonds that are sold during a period of high interest rates may thereby become a heavy burden if interest rates drop appreciably during the life of the bond issue. For that reason, "callable," or "refundable," options are available to the school district at the time of the original issue of the bonds. These provide for premature payment of the debt, with reissue of the bonds at a more favorable rate of interest. Since this feature protects only the school district from falling interest rates (with no protection to the bonding company for increasing rates), the cost of such an option makes callable bonds a little more expensive than ordinary serial or straight-term bonds.

Bond Sales

Bonds are most often issued in $1,000 or $5,000 amounts. They are sold through competitive bidding. Interest rates are determined by the economic conditions at the time they are sold, the extent and degree of competition in the market, the bond rating, and the length of the term for which they are issued. Bonds are attractive investments because of their exemption from federal and state income taxes.

AMORTIZATION SCHEDULES

The selection of the best schedule for a district to retire a bond issue depends on whether or not additional bonds will be involved before the issue in question is repaid. It requires no particular skill to amortize one issue over a period of years, keeping total interest and principal payments (and consequently tax levies) at a nearly constant figure. The problem is rather complicated, however, in districts that require frequent bond issues of varying amounts and with varying interest rates.

Long-range planning in school districts involves anticipation of school construction and bonding for several years ahead. Although there is no mathematical or exact rule for amortizing bond issues, a few practical guidelines may help the school administrator plan when frequent issues are expected:

1. The bond principal should be retired in an orderly fashion as soon as possible, in order to reduce bond interest cost and to increase future debt capacity.

2. Bond levies should ordinarily be kept somewhat constant, with the highest levy being set at the time of voter approval and with legal reserves being kept reasonably high. (Taxpayers often resent frequent increases in tax rates, particularly when they come as a result of poor planning or lack of foresight by the school board.)

3. Promises made by school personnel concerning bond-redemption tax levies should be made only on the basis of careful long-range planning. Such promises should be kept.

4. Surplus sums of money held in anticipation of bond payments should be invested within the restrictions of state law.

5. Bonds should be refunded whenever it is to the financial interest of the district to do so.

6. School boards should utilize consultant help from finance authorities in planning long-range bonding programs.

7. Bond and debt service levies should not be so high that taxpayer resistance forces a reduction of the levy for current expenditures.

8. The people should be kept informed concerning the long-range construction and bonding plans of the school district.

9. Indices of amortization can often be used to advantage in preparing complex amortization schedules.

10. So far as possible, bond payment schedules should anticipate future school facts and figures that affect fiscal matters. Changes in projected school population, expected fluctuations in property assessment values, economic trends, and changes foreseen in the policies of the community and state toward indebtedness and future educational needs are a few of the most important matters to consider.

STATE CAPITAL-OUTLAY FINANCING

States did little to help in financing local public school capital outlays until the second quarter of this century, as Thompson pointed out:

> State involvement in assisting local communities with facilities funding provides a checkered history. At various times the effort has been enthusiastic, but at other times denial of responsibility has been evident. In general, there has been less than enthusiastic support among the states for the concept of state participation in school building costs.[8]

Early State Capital-Outlay Programs

Since an initial action of Delaware in 1927 that provided for significant state support for local district debt-service costs in the foundation program, most of the fifty states have made some progress in this aspect of school finance. By 1965, about 80 percent of the states had used some method of assisting local districts in financing capital outlays and debt service. Legislative grants and appropriations, including, for example, a part of the foundation program, state loans, state guarantees of local indebtedness, and state purchases of local district bonds, are the most important devices used by the states to help local districts finance capital outlays. An indication of the extremes among the states in financing such expenditures can be seen from the following:

> State participation in financing local facilities ranges from Delaware's major support to California's billion dollar loan plan, from the Pennsylvania State School Building Authority to Indiana's and Kentucky's "do it yourself" holding companies—originated in the 1920's—from Florida's, Washington's, and New York's scientifically conceived state grant programs to South Dakota's purchase of local bonds and Oregon's support of construction of junior colleges only. In 1965, state school officers in only 10 states responded, "We have done nothing in the way of state support or loans for local school construction in postwar years."[9]

Current Programs

During its existence, the United States Office of Education did much to stimulate the states to provide plans for helping local districts to finance capital outlays. In 1951, it proposed that each state should include capital-outlay financing in its foundation program for current and long-range building programs. State departments of education were to establish specific programs and help administer them. Current funds were to be used and reserves were to be established when practicable.

A few states have adopted a policy of making loans to districts for capital-outlay purposes. The conditions of repayment usually include a standard effort for each district. The districts unable to repay the loans with a preestablished degree of tax effort receive the unpaid part of the loan as a state grant. The plan works well but sometimes results in overburdening certain districts with tax effort in order to meet stated requirements for eligibility to use such loans. Such handling of loan grants provides a degree of equalization, for the more wealthy districts would have no chance to default in repaying their loans, but poorer districts would often find it impossible to do otherwise.

The current situation on state financing of local district capital outlays is characterized by the following points:

1. Emergency state grants often precede regular appropriations or provision for capital-outlay funds in a state's foundation program. Relatively few districts share in the use of such emergency funds. The success of these plans is largely a function of the objectivity of the guidelines and standards required for participation. Over time, these emergency programs very often develop into more or less permanent patterns for such diversion of funds for school construction.

2. Only a few states include capital outlays as a part of the foundation program. Flat grants, incentive funds (such as matching funds or reorganization grants), emergency grants-in-aid, special grants to financially feeble districts, repayable loans, building authorities, and equalized foundation grants are the main ways used to allocate state funds to local districts for financing capital outlays.

3. There is little similarity among the methods used by the states for providing capital outlays and debt-service funds to school districts; state appropriations and state loans are probably the two most used methods. While flat grants and incentive grants help all districts, they are not equalized and therefore tend to be limited in scope and in their effect on solving the capital-outlay problem. Some of these grants have been utilized to encourage school district reorganization and attendance area consolidation. Matching grants used by some states have given greater aid to wealthy than to poor districts; on that basis they are not satisfactory.

4. Many states use more than one main program or device in getting state school money converted into local buildings; some allow local districts to accumulate funds for future building needs.

5. The state usually supervises rather carefully the expenditure of state monies for local school building construction, as it does with other state funds. The state often provides such supervision even when no state funds are directly involved in local school construction. This often involves required state approval of plans for new construction, observance of state-established building standards, and the services of state school-building consultants in the planning of local schools.

6. Building authority plans offer a temporary solution to the problem of obtaining adequate buildings in some school districts. However, many of the financially weaker districts are hard pressed to provide funds for the high cost of such building authority rentals. There seems to be no more reason for the state to subsidize weak district rental costs than to subsidize and liberalize the construction practices involved in building their own buildings in the first place. As pointed out by Johns and Morphet, "The question might well be raised as to whether the state is gaining anything from a long-range point of view by establishing indirect procedures for doing something that could be done even better by setting about to solve the problem directly."[10]

The use of school building authorities is an oblique attack on the problem of providing adequate school buildings. Under this plan, the building company constructs a building and rents it to the school district. The chief virtue of the plan is that it provides facilities for use by financially weak districts that could not bond to build their own because of low assessed valuations and unduly restrictive debt limitations.

School building authorities, provided for in some of the states, have not proved desirable for all school building purposes. Adequate planning, construction of school plants with modern educational specifications, and the difficulties involved in fitting changing programs to inflexible facilities are some of the problems that this kind of program generates.

7. Some degree of increased control and supervision of local districts seems to accompany the provision of state funds to help pay local school building costs. Local school boards and citizens sometimes interpret the provisions some states attach as guidelines and standards for school construction as usurpation of some of the authority commonly vested in the local school board.

STATE SUPPORT: A TREND

Most states were grossly unprepared to offer solutions to postwar school building needs. Some of them sought solutions by making grants from accumulated surpluses; others provided equalized matching plans; and still others experimented with including capital-outlay monies as a fundamental part of their foundation programs. Variety in the solutions to the problem and inadequacy of funds were the chief ingredients of such state-local partnership plans. In recent years, it has become evident that changes will have to be made in the method of financing capital outlays. Many financially weak districts have been unable to meet their own building needs. There now must be an increased demand that states come to the rescue of local districts with plans to provide substantial amounts of capital-outlay money, with little if any increase in state control.

Naturally, the sum in question is not meager. In an extensive study of school facilities, Ornstein and Cienkus estimate repair bills to be about \$48.2 billion or about 4.4 percent of the 1991 school revenues.[11] The Results in Education 1989, published by the National Governor's Association reports that maintenance costs for local schools have increased by 64 percent in a six-year period and existing plans to renovate and build schools is expected to cost \$84 billion. Individual states are feeling the pressure. Evidence provided in Texas indicates that a total of \$5.4 billion would be needed to fund facility projects by 1996.[12] The New Jersey State Supreme Court calculated that capital spending would be \$3 billion as they studied the *Abbott* v. *Burke* issue.[13] The administrative law judge noted:

> It is quite obvious on this record that facilities present a statewide problem. Besides the differences in the quality of school facilities between poor urban districts and wealthy districts, our school facilities generally need modernization. . . . Similarly, I do not believe that widely differing physical plants can be justified on an equal protection basis. . . . I FIND [judge's emphasis] that a more systematic way of dealing with replacing and renovating outmoded physical plants should be incorporated into the financing system.

The trend toward greater participation for financing facilities at the state level was heightened by the outcome of *Pauley* v. *Bailey* (1984)[14] in West Virginia, which established that adequate facilities are a necessary part of a thorough and efficient education system. West Virginia legislators and education leaders were given the challenge of developing a system of equitable financing for the schools, including capital outlays. Since facilities ranged from deplorable to exemplary and there was a wide variation of resources among the counties, the state needed to assume a greater role in funding school facilities. The estimate for bringing buildings up to a basic standard was over $800 million. The state proposed a bond election in 1986 for $200 million for building needs, in an attempt to meet the requirements of the court order. However, the voters of West Virginia rejected the bond issue on three occasions. Still determined to meet the court order, lawmakers created the independent School Building Authority. A total of $800 million is expected to be expended for school construction through 2001.[15]

Thirty-one states have provisions for capital-outlay assistance for school construction ranging from full state funding in Hawaii, Maryland, and Maine to a loan fund program in two states. Nineteen states have no provisions for capital-outlay support for local school districts.[16] Utah provides local qualifying districts with "critical building aid." An attempt was made to equalize capital outlay in the 1991 legislature. The measure did not pass. One wealthy district losing school population indicated that if the legislation was enacted they would file a lawsuit, while a financially poor district with increasing enrollment indicated that if it did not pass, a *Serrano*-type case would be filed.

Honeyman stresses the need for both local and state agencies to be involved in solving the capital outlay problem:

> Deferred maintenance and school construction needs are a serious concern throughout the United States. The problems associated with financing of facilities by school districts place many school districts in potential distress. The problem is crucial to the long-term success of many rural and poor school districts that lack an adequate tax base to support the levels of debt needed to resolve the problem. Regardless of the mechanisms that can be used to resolve deferred maintenance and facility needs, local districts and state education agencies must plan to address this growing problem.[17]

DEBT LIMITATIONS LIBERALIZED

> In addition to the many direct methods that the states used to facilitate construction of needed school buildings—grants, loans, creation of building authorities, inclusion of such costs in foundation programs, and others—there were indirect provisions that allowed some local districts to solve their own problems. One of the most important of these indirect provisions was the liberalization of school district debt and tax-levy limitations. Debt limitations, usually expressed as some percentage of the assessed value of taxable property, were changed in one or more of several possible ways. Some states changed the total debt limitation of a school district from a percentage of assessed value to a similar percentage of true value. Others increased the limit by a stated dollar amount; still others provided for additional tax-rate levies.

The matter of relating a school district's debt limits to a specified percentage of the assessed valuation is open to serious question, as Barr and Garvue have indicated:

> Debt limits should not be related to the amount of local assessed evaluation. A more appropriate overall limit for financing capital outlays would be a limit of 25 percent of school revenue allocated to reserve funds, debt service, lease rental, and current construction. Experience has shown that this, or even higher allocation of public school revenues for school building purposes is feasible [and] prudent, and does not adversely affect bond ratings.[18]

THE FEDERAL GOVERNMENT AND CAPITAL OUTLAYS

Participation of the federal government in programs to aid school districts with their capital-outlay expenditures is of relatively recent origin. The prevailing opinion that school plant construction was exclusively a local problem was not challenged by federal relief until the emergency programs of the Depression years were undertaken.

Federal aid to education is often opposed because of fear of federal control, among other reasons. If it is assumed or admitted that federal control follows federal funds for local district current expenditures, no such acknowledgment is made when the funds are used for the construction of school facilities. For example, the Public Works Administration and the Works Progress Administration constructed many school buildings in the 1930s and then released them to local school boards with no federal control over their use.

General federal aid has often been characterized as a strongly political issue, with racial and religious overtones. But federal aid for the construction of local school buildings was advocated in political campaigns more than a quarter of a century ago by both dominant political parties. Both candidates for the presidency spoke in favor of such aid as the beginning point and least controversial aspect of federal aid. In spite of that, no significant bill for federal aid for school construction has yet been enacted.

EQUITY IN FINANCING EDUCATIONAL FACILITIES

The persistent efforts of many states to provide equity of educational opportunity following *Serrano* and the other major school finance court decisions of the 1970s have not been paralleled in the matter of financing capital-outlay expenditures. As a result, most of the inequities that have plagued this area of public school finance in the past still exist. Unfortunately, reform has been virtually off-limits to this branch of school finance. However, the courts are showing a much greater interest regarding school districts having the ability to provide adequate facilities. Examples from "Tennessee (*Small Schools*, 1988), New Jersey (*Abbott*, 1988), Texas (*Edgewood*, 1986), Missouri (*Jenkins*, 1986), Alaska (*Kenai*, 1987) and West Virginia (*Pauley*, 1979, 1982) address facility issues in these states."[19]

Some of the discrepancies and imbalances that continue to exist between financing school programs and financing the physical facilities that house such programs are subtle and are therefore given slight attention by most casual observers of the education scene. The most significant of these include:

1. It is unfair, discriminatory, and certainly unjustified for the state to provide equalization funds for ongoing school programs and at the same time do virtually nothing to provide proper facilities in which to house those programs. Such oversight or calculated neglect may at best require less wealthy districts to burden their citizens with additional high tax obligations over long periods of time; at worst, these districts may find it impossible to provide minimum or standard facilities, even with maximum local property tax effort.

2. The long-term bonding debts incurred by taxpayers in less wealthy districts are often considerably higher than in wealthier districts because of the more favorable interest rates obtainable on bond issues in the latter.

3. There is a high degree of unfairness to those districts that are required to build and equip several buildings each year, as compared to those that do not face such requirements. Increases in district school population caused by the mobility of people are a problem of the state, not simply of the districts affected by increases in student enrollment.

4. Districts with higher-than-average or typical percentages of students requiring high-cost facilities are penalized under the existing system because they are required to provide the needed buildings and other facilities at local expense. Such programs for vocational education, education of the handicapped, and education of minority and compensatory students are often found in property-poor school districts, where their financing is difficult and certainly inequitable in comparison with that of the typical district.

5. Financing of school facilities usually requires voter approval, which is often extremely difficult to obtain in less wealthy districts because of already heavy property tax burdens. Wealthy districts usually have less difficulty with this problem.

6. Bonded debt revenue from property tax levies increases criticism and the inequity of the property tax within a given district. All the unfairness, regressivity, and the actual shifting of the tax payment to others for whom the tax was not intended are increased in districts that not only have to finance the local district's share of an equalization program by property taxation, but also have to repeat the process in order to obtain funds to defray capital-outlay expenditures.

EQUALIZATION OF SCHOOL BUILDING COSTS

The point has already been made that equalization in the financing of local district capital outlays is just as important, justifiable, and necessary as equalization in financing current expenditures. It is equally true that there is no fairness in financing capital outlays exclusively from property tax revenues. Most of the states now provide some state financial assistance, but the time has arrived for states to allocate such funds on the same basis as they provide for current expenditures.

Numerous proposals have been made for revamping the antiquated system of building school buildings with local property tax revenues only. States have frequently come to the rescue of poorer districts, some of which lack the property valuation required to finance buildings even on a long-term bonding basis, given the large expenditures for interest.

In reality, school buildings belong to the state, rather than to the community in which they are located. That being true, the state is obligated to assume major responsibility for their construction. There is no point in state equalization of current expenditure funds if some local districts cannot provide the funds to build adequate facilities for school programs. There is not complete equity in financing education if a wealthy school district can provide luxurious buildings and facilities with very little tax effort at the same time that property-poor districts cannot provide minimum or acceptable facilities even with tremendous effort.

One proposal to solve the problem of providing school facilities through equal effort in poor districts as in rich ones, while relieving property taxpayers of some of the burden of that responsibility, is reviewed here. In its very simplest terms, it provides that the state would:

1. Levy a small statewide property tax to be collected by the state for school building purposes.

2. Match the amount received (in some multiple or ratio as determined by state law) from that tax with revenue from other sources—income taxes, sales taxes, or others utilized in that particular state.

3. Combine the two amounts into a state school building fund to be used for that purpose only.

4. Determine the need for and priority of school buildings to be built for a fixed period of time. (This, of course, may be changed as conditions and the needs of school districts change.)

5. Finance the buildings approved on a pay-as-you-go basis, thereby eliminating the high interest costs now being paid by most local districts that are required to borrow money over a long period of time.

Those who favor local financing of school construction—usually people in property-rich districts—point to one possible weakness of such a plan: Not all districts would be able to get their needed buildings each year because of the extremely high cost. They also say that the political influence of larger districts would give them higher priority and that state control would be complete—an undesirable result. However, they overlook the fact that large sums of money are wasted each year by districts that are not properly equipped to carry on the studies and provide the services needed to build functional and economical school buildings. It is difficult to deny the assertion that state control of school buildings is fairer and much more desirable than state control of the financing and administration of the school program; once the buildings are built, the state cannot control their use and certainly has no reason to.

SUMMARY

Providing funds for school construction is as much a state responsibility as providing operating funds. However, most states have required local districts to use property taxes for capital-outlay expenditures. The financing of local school district facilities at the state level has been a low-priority item, and few states have yet developed an equalization formula for this purpose. Court cases in Tennessee, New Jersey, Texas, Missouri, Alaska, and West Virginia are providing impetus for greater state involvement. The costs are not meager, with estimates for repair bills alone reaching nearly $50 billion. Tax limitation laws and court cases such as *Pauley* v. *Bailey* (1984) may provide impetus for greater state involvement in the near future.

One of the major factors that has restrained many districts from needed construction has been the low assessment value of their taxable property. Largely because of such low assessment values, most school construction has been financed by some form of bonding. Pay-as-you-go financing, a building reserve plan (where legal), and bonding have advantages as well as disadvantages as methods of financing capital outlays. Less used but feasible approaches for acquiring needed revenues include bonding authorities, refunding bonds, and switching to year-round operation.

Most of the states are gradually increasing the amounts of money they provide to assist local districts in providing adequate school buildings. The bonding process is fairly complicated, and school districts that handle construction in this way should use the services of a bonding attorney.

School building funds allocated by state to local districts should be disbursed on an equalization basis, just as operating funds are. Property taxes should not bear the entire cost of financing school facilities. Increasing the amount the state pays for financing such facilities, of course, puts the burden of taxes on forms of wealth other than real property.

ASSIGNMENT PROJECTS

1. Some districts in the United States are faced with the problem of eliminating buildings at the same time that others are in dire need of building additional ones. Determine the type of school building problem in the city or county in which you live and what methods are being used by the school boards to solve their building problems.
2. Summarize the arguments for and against local school districts being required to finance their own school construction, regardless of their taxable wealth.
3. Outline a plan for greater state financial support for the construction of local school district buildings.
4. A few states now provide most of the funds for new school construction. Find out what kinds of problems accompany such an arrangement and the methods used to overcome these problems.
5. Determine what criteria a state should use to equalize capital-outlay expenditures in districts. How should it be decided where new buildings are to be built? When buildings are needed? What kinds of capital equipment should be provided? When capital equipment should be replaced? When school districts are "equal" in terms of capital expenditures?
6. Year-round schools, extended days, and double shifts are methods of utilizing school buildings more fully. Discuss the pros and cons of each plan.
7. Several buildings in your district were built over 50 years ago and are now outdated and crowded. Citizens in your district say these buildings were adequate when they were students, so why should they have to pay for new buildings? What approaches would you take to convince the voters that new buildings are needed?
8. Select a local district and ascertain the capital needs of the district, including new construction and remodeling.

SELECTED READINGS

Campbell, Roald F., Luvern L. Cunningham, Raphael O. Nystrand, and Michael D. Usdan. *The Organization and Control of American Schools.* 6th ed. Columbus, Ohio: Merrill, 1990.

Candoli, I. Carl, Walter G. Hack, and John R. Ray. *School Business Administration: A Planning Approach.* 4th ed. Newton, Mass.: Allyn and Bacon, 1992.

Codification of Governmental Accounting and Financial Reporting Standards. Stamford, Conn.: Governmental Accounting Standards Board and Government Accounting Research Foundation of the Government Finance Officers Association, 1985.

Guide for Planning Educational Facilities. Columbus, Ohio: Council of Educational Facility Planners, International, 1985.

Hawkins, Harold L., and H. Edward Lilley. *Guide for School Facility Appraisal.* Columbus, Ohio: Council of Educational Facility Planners, International, 1986.

Hough, Wesley C. *Municipal Bond Registration Requirements.* Washington, D.C.: Government Finance Research Center, 1983.

Naisbett, John. *Megatrends.* New York: Warner Books, 1982.

Webb, L. Dean, and Van D. Mueller. *Managing Limited Resources: New Demands on Public School Management. Fifth Annual Yearbook of the American Education Finance Association.* Cambridge, Mass.: Ballinger, 1984.

ENDNOTES

1. Walter G. Hack, "School District Bond Issues: Implications for Reform in Financing Capital Outlay," *Journal of Education Finance,* Fall 1976, p. 156.

2. William E. Camp and Richard G. Salmon, "Public School Bonding Corporations Financing Public Elementary and Secondary School Facilities," *Journal of Education Finance,* Spring 1985, p. 495.

3. Ibid., pp. 496-497.

4. Richard Salmon and William Wilkerson, "Financing Public School Facilities," in *Managing Limited Resources: New Demands on Public School Management, Fifth Annual Yearbook of the American Education Finance Association,* ed. L. Dean Webb and Van D. Mueller (Cambridge, Mass.: Ballinger, 1984), p. 123.

5. Glen I. Earthman, "Problems and Alternatives in Housing Students: What a School Business Administrator Should Know," *Journal of Educational Finance,* Fall 1984, p. 171.

6. Stephen J. Knezevich and John Guy Fowlkes, *Business Management of Local School Systems* (New York: Harper & Row, 1960), p. 215.

7. "Preparing a Bond Offering," *The Bond Buyer,* 1962, p. 9.

8. David C. Thompson, William E. Camp, Jerry G. Horn, and G. Kent Stewart, *State Involvement in Capital Outlay Financing: Policy Implications for the Future* (Manhattan, Kans.: Center of Extended Services and Studies, Kansas State University, 1991), p. 4.

9. W. Monfort Barr and W. R. Wilkerson, "State Participation in Financing Local School Facilities," in *Trends in Financing Public Education* (Washington, D.C.: National Education Association, 1965), p. 225.

10. Roe L. Johns and Edgar L. Morphet, *The Economics and Financing of Education,* 2nd ed. (Englewood Cliffs, N.J.: Prentice Hall, 1969), pp. 386-387.

11. Allen C. Ornstein and Robert C. Cienkus, "The Nation's School Repair Bill," *Building Education,* June 1990, p. A4.

12. David S. Honeyman, "School Facilities and State Mechanisms that Support School Construction: A Report from the Fifty States," *Journal of Education Finance,* Fall 1990, p. 248.

13. Lonnie Harp, "School Construction Issues Play Key Role in Equity Debate," *Education Week,* Vol. 10, No. 26, March 20, 1991, p. 12.

14. *Pauley* v. *Bailey,* 324 S.E. 2d 128 (W. Va. 1984).

15. Ibid.

16. Honeyman, p. 270.

17. Ibid.

18. W. Monfort Barr and R. J. Garvue, "Financing Public School Capital Outlays," in *The Theory and Practice of School Finance* (Chicago: Rand McNally, 1967), pp. 276–77.

19. Honeyman, p. 289.

Chapter *12*

Administering the School Budget

Clearly, an education budget is more than the sum of its fiscal parts. In many cases, the annual budget is the best statement of values a school system makes. The expenditure plan reveals exactly how many dollars are allocated to competing programs, while the revenue plan indicates the extent to which local and state tax revenues are earmarked for public education.
—*HARRY J. HARTLEY, 1989*

The innovations that are currently receiving such emphasis in curricular and administrative aspects of education have their counterparts in school finance theories and practices, including budgeting and accounting. Present budgetary practices are the result of a long evolutionary development, which has recently been accelerating rather than becoming stabilized or decelerating. The traditional principles and practices of budgeting, which seemed to be well established and proven, are now being supplanted or supplemented by more sophisticated systems of interpreting the educational program of the school.

EVOLUTION OF BUDGETARY PRACTICES

Historians report that budgetary practices originated in and received their greatest early development in England. The British government was using budgeting procedures two centuries before their use by the United States government and was practicing full-fledged budgeting by 1822. As developed in England, budgeting involved budget preparation by the executive branch of government, approval of the budget by the legislative branch (with amendments when deemed necessary or appropriate), authorization of tax levies by the legislative branch to meet the expected expenditures, and administration by the executive branch. Johns and Morphet noted the importance of these developments in budgetary theory:

This may seem like a very simple and natural arrangement. But it took hundreds of years for the people to wrest from ruling monarchs the authority to levy taxes and to determine governmental expenditures. . . . The budget is not just a document containing a list of receipts and expenditures but it is a process by which the people in a democracy exercise their constitutional right to govern themselves.[1]

Budgeting Developed Slowly in America

In the early history of this country, the presence of seemingly boundless wealth thwarted the development of sound budgetary practices in government. Petty jealousies between members of Congress and the executive branch also contributed in large measure to the slow metamorphosis of budgeting practices. The first law providing for a national budget was passed in 1921; it set the pattern for the present budgetary procedures of the federal government.[2]

Budgetary practices became common in business and industry before local boards of education accepted them generally. Until the end of the first quarter of the twentieth century, public school budgetary practices were unrefined and not standardized to any appreciable degree. As in the case of many other innovative practices, urban school systems developed budgetary patterns and routines before rural schools did. Gradually the various states enacted laws that established guidelines and specifics required of all districts in the receiving and disbursing of school funds. The extent of these requirements and the degree of detail of accounting have increased until such practices have become relatively standardized for similar kinds of districts within each state.

Financial Problems Encourage Budgeting Practices

Institutions have established sound budgetary practices following the occurrence of serious financial problems. As long as revenues are plentiful, institutions—state, local, and national—are relatively slow in accepting the challenge of establishing and following budgetary practices. On the other hand, when expenditures increase proportionately faster than income, then school districts, businesses, or even households seek possible solutions from a more strict accounting for funds received and spent—in other words, elementary budgeting practices.

THE BUDGET

Because everyone uses the word budget in government, business, industry, education, and even the home, it is presumed to be commonly understood. Technically, however, *budget* may mean different things to different people. Certainly, the purposes for which budgets are prepared and the degree of adherence to budgetary detail and administration vary considerably among the people and agencies that use them.

Definition

Perhaps each person using the term *budget* has his or her own definition of what it means. Although accepted definitions are numerous, all assume that budgeting involves at least four elements: (1) planning, (2) receiving funds, (3) spending funds, and (4) evaluating results—all performed within the limits of a predetermined time. Thus, budgeting is planning, receiving, and spending funds over a particular period, usually a year for school districts. The evaluative aspects cover examining previous budgets in order to build better budgets for succeeding periods.

Roe defined the educational budget "as the translation of educational needs into a financial plan which is interpreted to the public in such a way that when formally adopted it expresses the kind of educational program the community is willing to support, financially and morally, for a one-year period."[3] Other examples of acceptable definitions of budgeting are the following:

A budget may be defined as a specific plan for implementing organizational objectives, policies and programs for a given period of time. It embodies (1) descriptions of organizational activities and services requisite to attainment of organizational goals, (2) estimates of expenditures and their allocations, and (3) forecasts of fiscal resources available to support the plan.[4]

A public sector budget is a set of data that records proposed or adopted allocative decisions in terms of goals to be accomplished (program plan), resources available (revenue plan), and anticipated services and materials to be acquired (expenditure plan) during a specified period of time (fiscal period).[5]

Few people question the importance of budgeting in the public schools, the branches of government, business, industry, or any activity that involves receiving and expending large sums of money. Its importance in school districts increases as its function develops from purely mechanical and mathematical accounting to appraisal and translation of the educational program into meaningful terms. In the words of Condoli et al., some of the benefits of budgeting are:

1. It establishes a plan of action for the future.

2. It requires an appraisal of past activities in relation to planned activities.

3. It necessitates the formulation of work plans.

4. It necessitates expenditures and estimating revenues.

5. It requires orderly planning and coordination throughout the organization.

6. It establishes a system of management controls.

7. It serves as a public information system.[6]

Some view the continuous process of developing the educational budget as a way of raising the "level of living" and of expressing "broad social policy."[7]

Purposes of Budgetary Practices

The school district budget serves a number of important functions:

1. It projects the proposed school program and educational plan of the district for the next fiscal period.

2. It shows the sources of funds, anticipated expenditures, and allocation of authority for administering budgetary items.

3. It serves to inform the public about the educational program of the school.

4. It provides a guide for evaluating a year's program and a means of comparing school services with those that have been offered in other years.

5. It provides the motivation for careful planning, for establishing systems of control, and for wise and effective expenditure of funds.

6. It points out the relationship of the state, federal, and local units of government in supporting education.

Budgetary administration varies with state laws and with administrative interpretation. To some it may be the master to be followed with strictness and complete propriety. To others it is a guide that need not be followed blindly; its arithmetic must not take precedence over the effects on the educational program that school administrators propose for the benefit of students.

The Budget's Three Dimensions

Traditionally, since its first use by De Young, the school district budget has been represented by an equilateral triangle: The base is the educational program, with one side the cost of the program necessary to produce that program, and the other side the revenue plan. In theory, the educational plan is determined first. It is then converted into cost terms, and finally the determination of the sources of required revenues is made. The rationale for such a sequence is that our educational programs are to be planned for the peculiar needs of the pupils, without letting the available funds be the master or limiting factor in determining the bounds of the educational program.

In the past, affluent school districts were able to follow sound principles and accepted procedures in preparing the budget. Where revenue limitations were not too severe the process worked well. In districts with restricted revenue, budget building was sometimes reversed in sequence of preparation; the revenue was determined and then school officials decided what kinds of programs and services could be purchased for the amount of the expected revenue. This procedure often resulted in selection of programs and services that were inexpensive rather than those that represented the real needs of the pupils. Such planners resemble the prospective consumer who, in the restaurant or the variety store, reads the menu or price list from right to left. He or she may purchase goods or services that do not meet his or her dietary or other needs simply because they are less expensive than those that would be appropriate.

Determining the Educational Program

The educational program is directly related to the purposes and objectives of the school. Unfortunately, the aims and objectives of educational institutions are not always clear or well defined. This makes determination of programs and services very difficult. The superintendent is faced with a myriad of problem questions. What services of the school should be increased next year? Should the school provide more guidance services, or should it put more emphasis on equipping teachers with better facilities and instructional media? Should more emphasis be put on expensive programs such as driver education, or should the social science offerings be increased? Should the school provide for kindergartens and special education classes? To what extent should the pupils participate in paying the costs of education with incidental fees and charges? These and countless other questions must be answered in preparing the proposed educational program to be sponsored by each school district.

The superintendent, regardless of the complexity of school problems, must work with the staff, the school board, and parents in the community to determine the proposed educational objectives and program for the subsequent fiscal year and for several years ahead. Superintendents who suggest to their boards of education that, since there is a potential increase of 5 percent in school revenue, each area of the budget will automatically be increased by that amount are making at least three errors. (1) They are presuming that the previous budget was perfect and that therefore, since costs have increased, each part of it must be increased by the same amount. (2) They are ignoring the need for evaluating the past year's budget and examining and resolving such imbalances as it may have had. (3) They are denying those with an interest in the school— teachers, staff members, school board members, pupils, and the general public—their right and responsibility of continuous evaluation of the public school program.

Superintendents working with boards of education are responsible for involving people in determining educational policies and objectives. They should use all their public relations know-how to get committees or representatives of the PTA, the press, radio, television, and other groups to participate in such policy-making. Final decisions regarding proposed program changes and innovations must rest with the board of education, acting with the advice and recommendations of the superintendent.

Preparing the Budget Document

For budgetary purposes, the educational plan is valueless until converted into dollar costs. Under the direction of the superintendent, those who will be responsible for specific parts of the educational plan determine the needs of these programs. Sound budgeting theory dictates that teachers and other school personnel should be given forms and figures indicating budget allotments and expenditures for one or more past years, with blanks for estimates of next year's needs. As years pass, the budget histories that are established become useful in providing fiscal information for succeeding years.

With increasing frequency, districts are using another aspect of budget building by school personnel. In addition to having teachers and others suggest what they *need* for the following year, many progressive districts ask teachers also to submit requests for those supplies and facilities required for an optimum or superior program, or even for an alternative program. The administration is, in effect, asking school personnel to indicate by their *wants* or *desires* what, if granted, would provide the best possible program that each individual can envision at that moment. Teachers who in past years may not have received the supplies and equipment they requested may not be too anxious to make the extra effort to determine what they could use effectively, if such were to be available. However, regardless of the final disposition of the individual's requests according to needs or desires, it is a worthwhile experience in itself for each school employee to determine how much money should be allocated and for what it should be spent to provide the best possible educational program. Such a problem as determining the kind and frequency of use of instructional media under an ideal budget arrangement will cause the teacher to evaluate carefully the many alternatives available in the teaching process. Besides, there is always the possibility that the requested optimum program may be accepted and implemented in the final budget document.

Unfortunately, the extent of involvement of teachers and other staff members in determining the educational program and allocating resources to attain the school's objectives is minimal in practice. For various reasons, many school administrators use the previous year's budget as the sole basis for the budget for the next year. In this way, inequities and imbalances tend to become perpetuated. Some administrators find that district office determination of budget needs is not only easier and less frustrating but more acceptable to many teachers and staff members, who treat the business of budgeting with apathy or indifference.

> This concept views the development of the budget as strictly a responsibility of management. No staff help is asked for or desired. The central office gives the impression that budgeting is a very complex process, and that only the "chosen few" are sufficiently sophisticated to participate. The prevailing philosophy seems to be that if fewer people know about the budget, there will be less static and fewer questions. Often, value judgments are made without proper evaluation and with no options offered to those affected.

This tight-ship approach is symptomatic of authoritarian systems and has hastened the coming of our present era of negotiations, citizen involvement, and student awareness. While still in existence, it is dying out and will not be an effective concept in the future.[8]

In the districts that follow the staff participation method of budgetary preparation, the principal of each of the various attendance areas combines the budget requests of all staff members working under his or her direction, checks them for omissions, duplications, and errors, and then submits them (usually in combined form) to the school district office, where they are summarized and combined into totals for the district. From these reports and from similar requests from district employees, a tentative budget document is prepared.

The tentative budget is presented to the board of education for its study and recommendations for changes. The board is free to make whatever changes it desires within the limits of the statutes governing such practices in the state. The tentative budget is then accepted, summaries are prepared, and the board of education and the superintendent prepare for a budget hearing.

The budget does not stand by itself. It is related to many other records involved in the school district's business affairs, such as salary schedules, insurance policies, and inventories, and is influenced by them. Many of these schedules should accompany the budget document as it is presented to the board for study and adoption. They aid greatly in interpreting the message that the budget conveys. Ovsiew and Castetter made an excellent and inclusive list of such materials:

> Suggested materials to accompany the budget: asterisked items suggest materials that should be included in the budget document.
> * Letter of transmittal
> * Statement of introduction, especially relating to the school philosophy
> * Justifications
> • Curriculum review, by unit, divisions, and departments
> • Audited statements of funds
> • Bonding schedule
> * Recapitulations of sections of the budget
> * Salary schedules
> * Statistical summary of salary program, showing experience, training, and classifications
> • Statistical summary of other pertinent data, such as
>   • Enrollment, showing trends and projections
>   • Numerical adequacy of staff
>   • Average daily attendance
>   • Pupil-teacher ratio in instruction
>   • Per pupil costs by budget categories
>   • Enrollment by curriculum in the high school
> • State-aid provisions, indicating changes

- Insurance in force
- Transportation schedules
- Property tax experience, including relationship to assessments, market values, percent of collection, and millage limits
- Nonproperty tax experience, by type levied and by potential
- Cost experience, by trends in prices of selected items
- Retirement and social security schedules
* Expenditure and revenue items for two to three previous years
- Policy statements mandating expenditures
- Unmet needs report
- Items mandated by new laws or official directives
- Inventory report
- Budget transfers during previous year
- Summary of germane committee reports
- Comparative costs data with selected school district[9]

The Budget Hearing

Superintendents have long since discovered that there is little interest in budget hearings if no effort is made to summarize and interpret the massive lists of figures and minute details of the budget document. In preparing for a hearing, the superintendent must exercise ingenuity in devising an interesting and informative way of presenting the pertinent facts about the budget so that they can be easily understood by lay citizens. The use of audiovisual materials—videotapes, charts, slides, films, transparencies, and the like—helps greatly in elucidating the points that are of most interest and concern to school patrons.

Not all states have laws that require a formal hearing before adoption of the annual school district budget. In those that do, the board and the administrative staff present and explain the tentative budget, listen to the suggestions and criticisms of school patrons, and make any necessary justifications of questioned items or policies. Final approval of the budget usually rests with the school board in fiscally independent districts. In fiscally dependent districts, a city or county board usually must pass on the total budget levy authorized by the school board, relating it to the tentative budgets of other agencies of government under its general jurisdiction. In such districts, the city or county board usually has the power to require a reduction of the budget levy if necessary, but detailed alterations are left to the board of education, within the accepted total levy approved.

General Provisions of the Budget

Budgets should provide for classification of receipts and expenditures in line with the accounting system that the state and the local school district require. For the most part, these classifications should be in line with those recommended in *Financial Accounting*.[10] The budget should provide for separation of general expenditure funds from bond and debt-service funds. The current-expenditures budget should provide for emergencies by means of a contingency fund. Provision should be made, where possible, for a cash surplus at the beginning of the fiscal period to minimize the need for borrowing money until local tax money or state allocations are received.

School administrators often find it advantageous to provide a comparison of new budget items with similar considerations of the past year or two. There is much to be said in favor of a written explanation and justification of some budget items. Unexplained arithmetical figures in the budget may mean little to the uninformed person, who sees them without perspective or rationale. This is particularly true when unusual changes are being made for specific items. Critics of unexplained items or changes often become supporters of them when they understand the reasons behind them.

Some administrators and students of budgetary practice urge the establishment of priorities in the spending plan of the school district. Such priorities can only be established after much study of the relative value of alternative parts of the school program. The practical advantages of this procedure become obvious when revenues are less than expected or when costs exceed expectations.

ADMINISTRATION OF THE BUDGET

Once the budget is formally adopted, it becomes effective on the first day of the new fiscal period. The superintendent (by law in some states and by assignment in others) is the administrative officer charged with carrying out the programs that the budget authorizes. Unfortunately, some school districts try to differentiate between the strictly educational responsibilities of the superintendent and the fiscal policies, which are supervised by a clerk or business administrator who is responsible directly to the board of education. The dilemma that such an arrangement creates is antithetical to the purposes of the school. A dual head to a school system, with one administrator in charge of the instructional program and the other guarding the treasury, can work satisfactorily only under ideal conditions, and these seldom exist. The board of education should recognize that the superintendent as its executive officer must be in charge of the entire school operation. The official in charge of the business functions of the school, regardless of title, must be directly responsible to the superintendent. Only with such an arrangement can the board hold the superintendent accountable for the educational program of the school district.

Expending Money

Once the budget is formally adopted, the various line items and amounts are posted to the official accounting forms and funds of the district. The new budget then becomes a daily guide for the expenditure of school funds. Work plans and expenditure policies must be established so that the money can be expended for the purposes for which it was intended without undue red tape or unnecessary inconvenience. The purpose of the budget is not to save money; it is to help spend it wisely and expeditiously when needed. All school employees need to know the policies and specific procedures to be followed in carrying out the budgetary plan. It should not be hoped or planned that complicated or time-wasting procedures will discourage proper expenditure of the necessary funds to operate any aspects of the school program that have been approved.

Evaluation of the Budget

No person, least of all the school administrator, expects a perfect budget. He or she knows that careful planning and evaluation may reduce but never completely eliminate the need for making changes in the current budget. The board of education can do this when necessary, operating within the legal requirements of such adjustments. Of course, if the budget is changed at will with impunity, it becomes a meaningless document, of questionable value to the school district.

The superintendent is responsible for seeing that the budget is more than just an accounting system built and administered around a legal requirement to make guesses or estimates about receipts and expenditures. He or she has the obligation to demonstrate that the budget is a well-conceived monetary summary of the educational plan of the school district for a specific time. He or she must be able to demonstrate that it is constructed around the specific purposes or objectives of the school and the plans, services, personnel, and systems to be used in achieving those objectives.

Each succeeding budget should be an improvement over the previous one in terms of utility and effectiveness. It should indicate steady progress toward achieving its main processes and purposes, such as more significant involvement of school personnel and citizens in its preparation, more concerted effort to avoid program imbalance, more conferring and more effective rationale to justify budgetary items, greater effort toward continuous planning, and greater emphasis on program budgeting, with the provision for alternative programs to meet specific objectives.

One of the important lessons school administrators learn is that the budget is the business of all the people in the district, not just the official concern of the superintendent and the school board. This concept has been a long time in receiving wide acceptance. School patrons cannot be expected to support financial claims against them without some degree of understanding of purpose. In reality, budget critics often become budget defenders when they understand the objectives the school is attempting to achieve and the financial limitations under which it operates.

The superintendent is responsible for keeping the board of education informed about the operation and the effectiveness of the budget. He or she usually issues financial reports to the board on a regular basis, showing total expenditures to date, balances in the chief accounts, and anticipated problems in keeping within main budget item limitations. He or she determines the extent to which the budget has been effective, what improvements should be made in the next budget, what imbalances have been created between programs that are overfinanced compared with those that are underfinanced, and other necessary subjective and objective evaluations of budget performance. He or she takes special note and reports from time to time to the board concerning the ever-present problems of protecting the school's funds against dishonest, unethical, or careless handling by school personnel. Experience has shown that any precautions or guidelines used to protect public funds, as well as to protect the reputation of the people using them, will be effort well spent.

The Budget Calendar

School administrators realize that maximally effective budget building must be a continuous process. They recognize a need to follow a fairly specific budget preparation calendar. The details to be followed and the actual time to be assigned to budget preparation depend on the size of the school district, the number of employees involved in budget preparation, and the degree of difficulty encountered in obtaining three-sided balance in the budget triangle. Regardless of these factors, however, budget building should start as soon as the current budget is put into operation.

The fiscal year in most school districts starts on July 1 (in order to confine it to a single academic school year). On the day the current year's budget begins, the superintendent starts planning for the next year. The details involved in the preparation of a new budget will not be the same in all districts, since the legal requirements and the number of staff members responsible for budget planning will not always be the same.

The budget calendar should be organized to include certain minimum requirements. Fixed dates, or at least suggested dates, should be predetermined for the completion of certain actions, such as when new program requests must be recommended, when required supplies and instructional materials must be reported, when the initial and tentative budget document will be presented to the board of education, and when and where budget planning and budget hearings will be held. Although the school district must follow whatever budget preparation requirements are written in the state code, other performance dates and deadlines are usually advisory and need not be followed to the letter if it seems in the best interest of the school district to deviate from them. In any event, the superintendent makes a serious mistake if he or she procrastinates on budgetary preparation to the point where approaching deadlines interfere with conscientious budget-building practices.

Condoli et al. outline a budget calendar, with elements to be considered on a monthly basis throughout the fiscal year:

Month 1   Budget year begins

Month 3   Quarterly revision—to incorporate accurate revenue and enrollment figures (present budget)

Month 4	Population (enrollment) projections
	Staff needs projections
	Program changes and addition projections
	Facilities needs projection
Month 5	Staff requisitions—supplies
	Capital outlay preliminary requests
Month 6	Budget revisions (present budget)
	Central staff sessions on needs
	Maintenance and operations requests
Month 7	Rough draft of needs budget
Month 8	Meet with staffs and principals to establish priorities
	Citizen committees' reports and reviews
	Central staff and board of education budget sessions
Month 9	Budget revision (present budget)
Month 10	Working budget draft
	Meet with staff and community groups to revise working budget
Month 11	Final draft of working budget
Month 12	Budget hearings and adoption of working budget[11]

A NEW LOOK AT BUDGET ADMINISTRATION

The development of theory in educational administration, with an emphasis on the study of administrative behavior, was accompanied by the beginning of what has become known as *systems analysis* (or the *systems approach*), a way of looking at the functions involved in administration. According to the AASA Commission on Administrative Technology, the beginnings of the systems approach can be traced to the first efforts to introduce science into the management of organizations; some crude efforts occurred at the beginning of this century.[12]

During the early 1950s, many of the leaders in educational administration became vitally interested in developing basic theories involved in the practice of their profession. New kinds of textbooks were written, and theory classes in school administration began to appear in the curricula of the graduate programs at many of the progressive colleges and universities. The rationale for this departure from the past was that research and practice in educational administration were too heavily involved with empiricism. The front-line thinkers in the field noted, rather apologetically and almost unbelievingly, that the discipline up to that point had almost completely ignored theory in the study and practice of school administration. In the 1960s with the advancement of technology and the thrust for accountability, education administrators joined the movement to develop a *systems analysis* approach to planning the school program and linking it to developing the budget. Basically, it was a planning-programming-budgeting design.

The systems approach and systems analysis, in various contexts, became increasingly popular and prestigious as terms and practices, but their definitions remained elusive and subjective. Hartley emphasized the problem of terminology and definition concerning the systems approach:

> Systems approaches to planning are not blessed with clear terminology. Different writers and policy makers use terms interchangeably. In addition to general systems theory and such economic concepts as input-output and cost-benefit analyses, several other analytical techniques from management science deserve mention. One writer found forty different code names and acronyms for management controls or approaches such as PERT (Program Evaluation and Review Technique) and OR (Operations Research).[13]

> *Systems analysis* is a broad and general term. It is difficult to define in terms of specifics. For example, one author refers to it as "providing a framework that promotes commonalities in approach . . . [and] encourages interdisciplinary dialogues and combats the myopic fractionalization of contemporary scholarship." Another writer describes it as "orderly analysis of the differentiated component elements and processes within an organization; the relation of each element and process to the other, and all to the missions of the organization; and the perception of the organization as unified, possessing dynamic qualities, and having defined boundaries."

Planning-Programming-Budgeting Systems

In 1961 the United States Department of Defense introduced and applied some aspects of systems analysis to certain difficult problems, with the purpose of facilitating a much more precise evaluation of the outcome of programs. The success of the process prompted other government departments to institute similar planning techniques. The concept was the planning-programming-budgeting system (commonly referred to as PPBS).

A planning-programming-budgeting system is an integrated system devised to provide administrators and other school staff members with better and more objective information for planning educational programs and making choices among the alternative ways for spending funds to achieve the school's educational objectives. Some advocates of the system who felt that *evaluation* was not stressed sufficiently added an E to the acronym, making it PPBES. The Association of School Business Officials was not yet satisfied with the designation and substituted ERMD (educational resource management division), which it felt was more descriptive of this approach to budgetary planning.

The planning-programming-budgeting system is a way of extending the planning period and duration of a program budget, often for five or more years. Its chief thrust is in the direction of replacing broad, traditional objectives with specific, measurable ones. It involves a cycle in planning that includes: (1) establishing objective goals, (2) determining the financial cost of alternative plans for reaching the objectives, (3) evaluating the results, (4) improving the objectives, and (5) adding to and improving the alternative plans to reach the revised objectives.

PPBS is another indication of the need for greater accountability in education. It takes into account the fact that taxpayers are no longer willing to accept increased expenditures unless there is measurable evidence of an increase in the quality of the product. In economic terms, they are asking for a closer relation between input and output. The PPBS concept is a device for distributing limited resources in the public sector to provide the greatest possible returns in services.

Zero-Base Budgeting

Just as many serious reform efforts were made in the 1970s to improve school finance formulas to meet the standards of *Serrano* and other court rulings; so were efforts made to improve budgeting practices in school districts. To the casual observer it would seem that budgeting is a simple process of calculating the costs of operating a projected educational program and then applying the legal provisions of state, local, and federal government laws and restrictions to determine the sources of revenue and the amounts obtainable to meet the anticipated expenditures. Such hit-and-miss procedures were common in the budgeting practices of school districts years ago. They involved little or no direct relationship between the objectives of the school program and the expenditures. Seldom were alternatives considered or found necessary. There was little consideration given to systematic analysis of the budget, and long-range budgeting practices were yet to be developed.

In addition to PPBS, a budgetary plan known as zero-base budgeting (ZBB) has been developed. Although the idea of planning a budget from zero has existed for more than a century, it was little used until the 1970s, when Peter A. Phyrr began writing about it. The idea soon gained a degree of popularity, particularly in Texas, Georgia, and New Mexico. The concept received widespread attention when Jimmy Carter, running for the U.S. presidency, proclaimed that he would use ZBB techniques in developing the federal budget. The one cardinal principle for ZBB is that nothing is sacred. Every program, if it is to receive continued funding, must be justified during each budget development.[14] There is no standard or universally accepted definition of ZBB. The following two definitions represent the general and the specific approaches:

> Perhaps the essence of zero-base budgeting is simply that an agency provides a defense of its budget request that makes no reference to the level of previous appropriations.[15]

Zero-base planning and budgeting involves decision making from the lowest levels of management to the top. Managers are required to analyze each budget item—whether already existing or newly proposed—so that the starting point for the development of the budget is zero.[16]

ZBB is a rational budgeting approach. It is more of a decision-making process than a complete resource allocation system. It works bottom-up from basic organizational activities, rather than top-down from organizational goals and objectives. Developed in industry and adapted for use in the public sector, ZBB emphasizes identifying, ranking, and choosing alternatives.[17] There are several advantages of this type of budgeting, including involvement of staff members, the requirement of annual evaluation of all programs, accurate determination of programs, and the development of priorities with alternatives. The critics of the zero-base system point to the great amount of paperwork involved, the need for more administrative time in the preparation of the budget, and the feeling that the system is too complicated and thus too impractical for small school districts.

Site-Based Budgeting

Site-based budgeting (SBB) is a concept of developing a district budget through the involvement of teachers, community, and administrators at the school level. Gaining support in the 1980s, the process provides an opportunity for the school staff to assist in building a budget that will have an impact on the final decisions made by the board of education. It is a decentralized system of providing revenues for instructional supplies, materials, equipment, texts, and library books and, in some districts, is extended to salaries for teachers, aides, and custodians. Some schools using SBB techniques analyze student needs in relation to teaching resources and may have the latitude to purchase the services of two teacher aides in place of one certified teacher. Such a degree of decision-making power is not always possible because of union or association influences, but it does demonstrate the flexibility possible in a site-based budget process.

To be effective, SBB requires that principals and staff be able to match student needs with available resources. It is not simply a matter of providing a principal with an amount of money based on the number of pupils in the building, to be spent in three or four categories at the school level rather than at the district level. The employees in the building must be a part of the planning and must recognize cultural, ethnic, and socioeconomic factors that may influence student needs and then establish priorities and budget to meet those needs.

District office administration assumes a different role in the preparation of site-based budgets; central administrators become facilitators to the staff and community at the school level. Budgeting for administration, capital outlays, and maintenance costs remains a district responsibility, because of the need for large expenditures on particular projects. A new roof on an older building, for example, may take a large share of the district's total maintenance budget in one year. Lausberg summarizes the responsibility:

The purpose of site-based management is to give the principal and instruction staff more control over budget, personnel, and organization at the school level. The concept's objectives are: greater involvement in decision making, less imposition of state or district level rules which restrict creativity or school level choices, and the development of innovative instructional methods which will ultimately improve educational results and public acceptance of school performance.

Site-based management often gives authority to principals to move funds within a total school allocation among line items in the budget.

The role of the central office, whether it be in instruction, personnel, or business, shifts to one of balancing district-wide standards with local decision making, and providing training and support to school-based decision makers. It means sharing responsibility for many services formerly centrally controlled by the business office or other central office departments.[18]

Essentially, proponents of site-based management contend that schools will be improved because it:

- Enables site participants to exert substantial influence on school policy decisions,
- Enhances employee morale and motivation,
- Strengthens the quality of schoolwide planning processes,
- Fosters the development of characteristics associated with effective schools, and
- Improves the academic achievement of students.[19]

Strategic Planning

Patterned after a technique used in business and industry, educators are utilizing a process of planning that has an influence on the school budget. Strategic planning is an approach to setting district goals for a three- to five-year period. Involvement includes a broad segment of the community who is brought together for intensive training and decision making that may cover two to five days. A mission statement is designed, belief statements may be outlined, and goals or vision statements are defined for the district. Action teams may be organized to refine the goals and prescribe strategies for achieving them. Finally, the board of education is required to adopt the plan to complete the process.

Planning is an integral part of the budget sequence. As with other approaches, the goals and outlined action recommendations usually exceed potential revenues, and priorities need to be determined. Too often, the budget covers the basic program and many action plans are put on "hold."

Hartley summarizes budget procedures from the past three decades and projects the approach schools will follow in the 1990s:

[E]ach of the past three decades witnessed the emergence of a major budget innovation in the public sector: planning-programming-budgeting system (PPBS) in the 1960s, zero-base budgeting (ZBB) in the 1970s, and school-site budgeting (SSB) in the 1980s.

As we develop fiscal year 1990 budget requests, no single budget format dominates and no fiscal innovation lies ahead. Many superintendents are wisely incorporating the best elements of recent budget concepts: budgeting by individual budget that is more responsive to local needs and does not highlight a particular acronym or fad.

The leadership challenge is to develop the best possible budget process and document that will convey to the board and community what is needed and why.[20]

SUMMARY

Historians report that budgetary practices originated and underwent early development in England. In the United States, budgeting became common in business and industry before its use in the public schools. The first law providing for a national budget was passed in 1921; the practice has improved steadily since that time.

The term *budget* has many definitions. The process of budgeting involves planning, receiving and spending funds, and evaluating results in a specified time frame—usually one year. Its purpose is to define the district's educational plan, determine the source of funds, and specify how revenues are to be expended. The budget document provides a guide for evaluating the school program and a way of keeping the public informed about the activities of the school.

The superintendent of schools should administer the budget, and the school board has legal authority for its formal adoption. The budgeting process should be continuous and provide for citizen review and appraisal. In preparing the budget, the superintendent should work with the entire school staff in order to provide an instrument that reflects the goals and objectives of the district.

The systems approach to budgeting has gained some recognition in the field of education. Various program budgeting procedures are being used by schools. Planning-programming-budgeting systems (PPBS) is one such method that provides school personnel with better and more objective information for planning programs; it offers alternative ways for spending funds to achieve the school's educational objectives.

The systems approach to budgeting is another indication that the public is seeking greater accountability for school personnel. Its main disadvantage is the difficulty and the amount of time required to establish such a system in small districts, where the number of qualified staff members to operate the programs effectively is limited.

During the 1970s a budgetary plan known as zero-base budgeting (ZBB) emerged. This method requires justification of every program each time the budgeting process is redone. Its chief advantages are the involvement of nearly all staff members, the requirement for an annual evaluation, and the development of priorities with alternatives.

Site-based budget planning (SBB) involves teachers, community, and principals at the local school level. In a decentralized way, it provides funds for supplies, materials, equipment, texts, and library books and sometimes salaries for teachers, aides, and custodians. Principals need to redefine their roles as they assume a leadership position in coordinating efforts of the staff and community in assessing students, establishing priorities, and developing a budget designed to meet the students' needs.

Strategic planning is a technique that has an influence on the school budget. As with other approaches, the goals and outlined action recommendations often exceed potential revenues, making it necessary to prioritize, then putting some action plans on "hold."

ASSIGNMENT PROJECTS

1. Interview the business manager of a school district and report on the budgetary changes that have taken place in the last few years. Is an accounting system required by the state? What effect has the use of computers had upon school district accounting and budgeting practices?
2. Determine the state requirements for local school district budgeting in your state.
3. Compare the budgetary responsibilities of a school superintendent in a small school district with those of a superintendent in a large school district.
4. Write a paper suggesting ways for school superintendents and boards of education to inform school patrons about budgetary practices.
5. Interview teachers and other school personnel about their involvement in the budgetary process. What information do they give regarding needs and desires for next year? Do they want to be more involved? Less involved? Do they understand how priorities are set and budget decisions made?
6. Prepare a presentation for a new superintendent and newly elected school board about budgetary practices. Outline their responsibilities. How should other school personnel and patrons be involved?
7. Prepare a paper describing the pros and cons in determining a school district budget when the district is committed to a site-based management approach.

SELECTED READINGS

Aliota, Robert F., and J. A. Jungherr. *Operational PPBS for Education.* New York: Harper & Row, 1971.
Campbell, Roald F., Luvern L. Cunningham, Raphael O. Nystrand, and Michael D. Usdan. *The Organization and Control of American Schools.* 6th ed. Columbus, Ohio: Merrill, 1990.

Candoli, I. Carl. *School District Administration: Strategic Planning for Site Based Management.* Lancaster, Pa.: Technomics Publishing, 1990.

Hartman, William T. *School District Budgeting.* Englewood Cliffs, N. J.: Prentice Hall, 1988.

Tanner, C. Kenneth, and Earl J. Williams. *Educational Planning and Decision Making.* Lexington, Mass.: Heath Lexington Books, 1981.

ENDNOTES

1. Roe L. Johns and Edgar L. Morphet, *The Economics and Financing of Education* (Englewood Cliffs, N. J.: Prentice Hall, 1969), p. 441.

2. Ibid., p. 442.

3. William H. Roe, *School Business Management* (New York: McGraw-Hill, 1961), p. 81.

4. Leon Ovsiew et al., "Budgeting," in *Theory and Practice of School Finance,* eds. Warren E. Gauerke and Jack R. Childress (Chicago: Rand McNally, 1967), p. 209.

5. Charles H. Sedenburg, "Budgeting," in *Managing Limited Resources: New Demands on Public School Management, Fifth Annual Yearbook of the American Education Finance Association,* eds. L. Dean Webb and Van D. Mueller (Cambridge, Mass.: Ballinger, 1984), p. 60.

6. I. Carl Candoli, Walter G. Hack, and John R. Ray. *School Business Administration: A Planning Approach,* 4th ed. (Newton, Mass.: Allyn and Bacon, 1992), p. 112.

7. I. Carl Condoli, Walter G. Hack, John R. Ray, and Dewey H. Stoller, *School Business Administration: A Planning Approach,* 3rd ed. (Newton, Mass.: Allyn and Bacon, 1984), p. 128.

8. Condoli et al., *School Business Administration.* (1992), p. 113.

9. Leon Ovsiew and William B. Castetter, *Budgeting for Better Schools* (Englewood Cliffs, N.J.: Prentice Hall, 1960), p. 52.

10. Charles T. Roberts and Alan R. Lichtenberger, *Financial Accounting* (Washington, D.C.: U.S. Office of Education, U.S. Department of Health, Education, and Welfare, 1973).

11. Condoli et al., *School Business Administration,* 1992, p. 137.

12. *Administrative Technology and the School Executive* (Washington, D.C.: AASA Commission on Administrative Technology, 1969), pp. 17–18.

13. Harry J. Hartley, *Educational Planning-Programming-Budgeting* (Englewood Cliffs, N.J.: Prentice Hall, 1968), p. 36.

14. David E. Weischadle, "Why You'll Be Hearing More About" 'Zero-Base Budgeting,' and What You Should Know About It," *American School Board Journal,* September 1977, pp. 33–34.

15. Leonard Merewitz, *The Budget's New Clothes: A Critique of Planning, Programming, Budgeting and Benefit-Cost Analysis* (Chicago: Markham, 1971), p. 61.

16. Paul J. Stonich, *Zero-Base Planning and Budgeting* (Homewood, Ill.: Dow Jones-Irwin, 1977), p. 37.

17. Peter A. Phyrr, "Zero-Base Budgeting: Peter Phyrr Defends His Brainchild," *MBA Magazine,* April 1977, p. 25.

18. Clement H. Lausberg, "Site-Based Management: Crisis or Opportunity," *School Business Affairs,* April 1990, p. 11.

19. Betty Malen, Rodney T. Ogawa, and Jennifer Kranz, "Evidence Says Site-Based Management Hindered by Many Factors," *The School Administrator,* February 1990, p. 32.

20. Harry J. Hartley, "Budgeting for the 1990s," *The School Administrator,* April 1989, p. 31.

Chapter *13*

Accounting and Auditing

The functions of financial accounting include the analysis and classification of transactions, the recording of the effects of the transactions, the storage and accumulation of data and documents, the summarization of data into reports, and the interpretation of those reports.   —*DONALD L. WALTERS, 1991*

Schools are maintained for the purpose of providing a high-quality educational program. This means that they are operated to spend money—but it must be spent for the right purposes. Getting maximum benefits for the money expended, rather than saving money, is the function of the business administration of a school district. Certain key words and expressions are associated with this responsibility, such as *economy, judicious spending, honesty, protection of property,* and *protection of individuals.*

In addition to the responsibility the school has for spending funds wisely to provide high-quality education, it has the challenge of protecting school funds and property and the reputation of those involved in disbursing school monies. There is little to question or to criticize when there are accurate and verified financial records of a school's operations. On the other hand, shoddy or inadequate records can serve to impugn the actions of those in charge, even where there has been no dishonest intent.

Everyone accepts in principle that the business of education, which is the largest and most important in the nation, should use the best possible system of collecting, expending, and accounting for the large sums of public money required. Yet the history of accounting for such funds, especially at the site-level unit of organization, has not been a particularly outstanding one. Far too many examples of shoddy practices and even malfeasance have been brought to light. Such malpractices have done much to cause states and local school districts to require better accounting systems with stronger guidelines and appropriate legal requirements for operating school business.

THE SCHOOL ACCOUNTING SYSTEM

Efficiency and effectiveness in school financial practice require a sound system of accounting for income and expenditures. Permanent records of all financial transactions are an integral part of a system of reporting the reception and disposition of public funds. The legality, quality, and effectiveness of the school board's stewardship of all funds are documented and supported by accounting records. Questions of propriety in the handling of public funds can be cleared up by the records that are kept of the monies at the disposal of a school district. Thus, a system of accounting, which was once something of a luxury in some small school systems, is now a practical necessity in all schools.

Purposes

One of the main purposes of an accounting system for a business in the private economy is to determine its fiscal condition. Determining whether a company has made a profit or a loss, and how much, is fundamental to good business operations. Without such information, determination of dividends or profits or losses to stockholders cannot be made. Since schools are in the public sector, however, they have no concern with the profit motive. Their goal is to provide valuable services for their clientele. For what purposes, then, does the school utilize accounting principles? What values will it receive by establishing a modern accounting system? In brief, a school district employs an efficient accounting system in order to:

1. Protect public funds from the possibility of loss due to carelessness, expenditure for the wrong purpose, theft, embezzlement, or the malfeasant actions of school officers.

2. Provide a systematic way to relate expenditures to the attainment of educational objectives through the operation of a budget and related reports and processes.

3. Provide an objective method of appraising the performance of school personnel in attaining the school's objectives.

4. Meet the legal requirements of the state and other governmental units for reporting basic information for comparisons, reports, and reviews.

5. Provide local school patrons with important information concerning the fiscal and academic activities and needs of the district.

The Governmental Accounting Standards Board emphasizes:

Financial reporting is not an end in itself but is intended to provide information useful for many purposes. Financial reporting helps fulfill government's duty to be publicly accountable. Financial reporting also helps to satisfy the needs of users who have limited authority, ability, or resources to obtain information and who therefore rely on the reports as an important source of information. For that purpose, financial reporting objectives should consider the needs of users and decisions they make.[1]

Principles

The business of school administration is to receive, spend, and account for taxpayers' dollars for education in the most effective and efficient way, in order to produce maximum educational benefits at minimum cost. Clearly, financial management of the schools is a means to an end, but that does not minimize its importance. Schools cannot achieve their instructional goals without the wise expenditure of public monies. Prudent disposition of funds requires that responsible school personnel adhere to generally accepted principles of school accounting.

School accounting practices and principles have evolved during the history of school operation in this country. The modern accounting system in a typical large school district today bears little relation to the unstandardized system used in school districts of an earlier era.

The National Committee on Governmental Accounting developed a number of standard principles and procedures for governmental accounting that have general application to schools.

1. Ensure compatibility with legal requirements.
2. Use the double-entry and general-ledger accounting system.
3. Use uniform terms and standard classifications.
4. Use as few different funds as possible, within legal and accounting requirements.
5. Make "a clear segregation . . . between accounts related to current assets and liabilities and those relating to fixed assets and liabilities."
6. Use the budgetary control principles.
7. Use the accrual basis of accounting.

The Government Accounting Standards Board states:

> Governmental accounting systems should be organized and operated on a fund basis. A fund is defined as a fiscal and accounting entity with a self-balancing set of accounts recording cash and other financial resources, together with all related liabilities and residual equities or balances, and changes therein, which are segregated for the purpose of carrying on specific activities or attaining certain objectives in accordance with special regulations, restrictions, or limitations.[2]

In spite of recommended principles and attempts to standardize practices, variations appear in every school accounting system. Administrators use those accounting procedures that will help most in implementing and accounting for the school's program. There are, however, certain general principles that may be applied to form the basis for an adequate and effective accounting system in every school.

   1. *Accuracy*. There is little value in an accounting system that is not accurate. Audits are useful in discovering and reporting errors, but they are a very poor substitute for original accuracy. More than an absolute minimum of errors not only make financial reports ineffective or useless but may jeopardize the reputation of the administration or ruin the positive image that the school business administrator may otherwise have created.

   2. *Completeness and currency*. Incomplete records of transactions and accounting records that are out of date provide little help to the superintendent when following a budget, explaining a fiscal transaction, or defending future budgetary allocations or expenditures. Any information that the administrator or the school board needs should always be readily available. The actual fiscal condition of the school district should be known at all times. Regular reports of income, expenditures, encumbrances, unencumbered balances, and other useful kinds of information should be made periodically.

   3. *Simplicity.* School accounting practices and procedures are intended to provide information to administrators, school boards, the state, and local citizens. They are valuable if understood and worthless if not. Simplicity is therefore a necessity in school accounting practices. Their purpose is to explain to a relatively unsophisticated clientele what the school has done, how much it cost, where the money came from, and what the fiscal condition of the district is at any particular time. There is no intent to deceive or confuse anyone by extremely complicated accounting systems or professional jargon in explaining the district's expenditures or other transactions.

   4. *Uniformity.* Comparisons of costs between school districts are misleading unless the items being compared are uniform and to some degree standardized. Account classifications and funding practices must be the same in all types of districts if comparisons are to be valid and useful. State reports sent to the Department of Education are presumed to be made with sufficient uniformity to make them useful for such purposes.

STANDARD ACCOUNTING PRACTICES

In spite of much effort, little success was achieved in standardizing terminology and procedures in school accounting practices until recent years. The United States Office of Education exerted a leading role in establishing recommended practices in school accounting. Handbooks in 1940, 1948, and 1957 led the way in promoting uniformity in reporting school financial transactions. The 1957 handbook was particularly important in this regard. It was "the product of the cooperative efforts of five nationwide education associations and the Office of Education over a period of more than two years. Hundreds of individuals constituting a broad cross section of American education shared in its development."[3] The committee preparing the handbook selected items that provided information based on four criteria: (1) importance to a local district in the operation of its school system; (2) importance to local school districts throughout the country; (3) need for financial comparisons among local school districts; and (4) information that can be maintained as a record with reasonable effort.

The U.S. Office of Education suggested that universal use of the standard accounts and terminology of the 1957 handbook would:

1. Help ensure appropriate initial recording of financial data.
2. Improve the accounting for school funds.
3. Improve school budgeting.
4. Establish a sound basis for cost accounting.
5. Improve the accuracy of local, state, and national summaries.
6. Facilitate comparisons of financial information among communities and among states.
7. Enable local and state educational authorities to obtain more suitable information for policy determination.
8. Improve the accuracy of educational research.
9. Facilitate and improve reliable reporting to the public on the condition and progress of education.

The 1957 handbook recommended the use of three chief receipt accounts: Revenue Receipts, Nonrevenue Receipts, and Incoming Transfer Accounts. It also suggested the use of fourteen important expenditure accounts: Administration, Instruction, Attendance Services, Health Services, Pupil Transportation Services, Operation of Plant, Maintenance of Plant, Fixed Charges, Food Services, Student Body Activities, Community Services, Capital Outlay, Debt Services, and Outgoing Transfer Accounts.

The 1957 handbook was revised in 1973 and again in 1980 and 1990 under the title *Financial Accounting for Local and State School Systems*. The most recent edition lists the revenue and expenditure classifications. They are:

Classification of revenue and other fund sources	Classification of expenditures
1000 Revenue from local sources	100 Regular Program, Elem/Secondary
2000 Revenue from intermediate sources	200 Special Programs
3000 Revenue from state sources	300 Vocational Programs
4000 Revenue from federal sources	400 Other Instructional Programs, Elem/Secondary
5000 Revenue from other sources	500 Nonpublic School Programs
	600 Adult/Continuing Education Programs
	700 Community/Junior College Education Programs
	800 Community Services Programs
	900 Enterprise Programs
	000 Undistributed Expenditures

Many governmental agencies, including state departments of education and local districts, have relied on the Governmental Accounting Standards Board's (GASB) *Codification of Governmental Accounting and Financial Reporting Standards*[4] as a guide to accounting practices. Unlike *Financial Accounting for Local and State School Systems* (1990 edition), account codes and budget categories are not specified. Most states require local education agencies to use uniform budgeting and accounting procedures and expect conformity with generally accepted accounting principles. The account code structure is designed to serve as an efficient coding facility and basic management tool and to establish a common language for reporting the financial activities of a school district.

The Government Accounting Standards Board is a private organization administered by the Financial Accounting Foundation, which oversees the operations of standard setting in the private and public sector.[5] An excellent overview of the historical development of GASB and its authoritative document, *Codification of Governmental Accounting and Financial Reporting Standards as of May 31, 1990*, is included in *Miller Comprehensive Governmental GAAP Guide 1991*, by Bailey.[6]

Many states have developed their budgeting, accounting, and auditing procedures by blending principles from the GASB guide and the account code structure from the 1990 revised handbook with updates and modifications to suit particular local needs. In this regard, the following quote is important for boards of education to consider when determining accounting methods:

> The establishment of generally accepted accounting principles for state and local governments is complicated by a factor not present in the promulgation of accounting principles for business enterprises. Some state and local laws do not recognize the GASB or FASB pronouncements as the basis for preparing their governmental financial statements. For example, a governmental unit through its charter or constitution may require that a reporting entity prepare its budget and financial statements on a cash basis. Although the governmental unit will probably maintain its accounting records on a non-GAAP basis for legal compliance purposes, it must adopt a supplementary accounting system that will enable it to report on a GAAP basis.[7]

THE USE OF CLEARING ACCOUNTS

School accounting systems provide for clearing accounts (revolving funds), in order to avoid distorting receipts and expenditures when there is a double handling of money. The practice involves receiving money from the operation of some activity (student-body activity or food services, for example) and then spending it for the same activity at a future time. If "Receipts" is credited when the money is received and "Expenditures" is credited when the money is spent, both accounts have been increased beyond their true state; the books do not then show either account as it actually is. For example, if a school district spends $500 to set up an account for a particular purpose and then is repaid the $500, it is as if nothing has happened as far as "Receipts" and "Expenditures" are concerned. Neither account should be increased by $500, but the transaction should be shown through a clearing account. If, however, the activity does not repay the $500, such amount must be charged to the appropriate expenditure account. Clearing accounts make it possible and convenient to report the complete story of transactions involving the double handling of money without involving the "Receipts" and "Expenditures" accounts.

Transactions under clearing accounts include: (1) activities financed wholly or in part by revenue produced by the activity, (2) prepayments or advancements, (3) abatements, (4) exchanges of one asset or liability for another asset or liability, (5) interfund transfers, (6) current loans, and (7) insurance adjustments.

ENCUMBRANCE ACCOUNTING

Encumbrance accounting is important to any budgetary system. "An encumbrance represents a commitment related to unperformed contracts for goods and services. . . . The issuance of a purchase order or the signing of a contract would create an encumbrance. The encumbrance account does not represent an expenditure for the period, only a commitment to expend resources."[8] As soon as some action involving future payments of money is made, the proper account should be encumbered by that amount. Without such an up-to-date record, the administrator may not always remember when the cash balance of a particular account has already been committed to another purpose. Encumbrance accounting serves the purpose of keeping the administrator informed concerning expenditure commitments. It is a necessary part of the accounting system of every school district. Proper use of this accounting device will not only help to keep the accounts in balance, but may save the administrator from the embarrassment that accompanies a second expenditure of money from an account that has already been depleted by a previous obligation.

The GASB provides the following summary for accounting and reporting encumbrances:

a. Encumbrance accounting should be used to the extent necessary to assure effective budgetary control and accountability and to facilitate effective cash planning and control.

b. Encumbrances outstanding at year-end represent the estimated amount of the expenditures ultimately to result if unperformed contracts in process at year-end are completed. Encumbrances outstanding at year-end do not constitute expenditures or liabilities.

c. If performance on an executory contract is complete, or virtually complete, an expenditure and liability should be recognized rather than an encumbrance.

d. Where appropriations lapse at year-end, even if encumbered, the governmental unit may intend either to honor the contracts in progress at year-end or cancel them. If the governmental unit intends to honor them, (1) encumbrances outstanding at year-end should be disclosed in the notes to the financial statements or by reservation of fund balance, and (2) the subsequent year's appropriations should provide authority to complete these transactions.

e. Where appropriations do not lapse at year-end, or only unencumbered appropriations lapse, encumbrances outstanding at year-end should be reported as reservations of fund balance for subsequent year expenditures based on the encumbered appropriation authority carried over.[9]

Encumbrance accounting is so important that some states require it of all school districts.

COST ACCOUNTING

Cost accounting has been an important element in business institutions for a long time. Although it is used to some degree in most larger school districts, the practice has never reached great popularity in smaller ones. The argument that it is not needed in schools because the profit motive is lacking holds little weight, for all schools are faced with the necessity of getting the greatest possible benefit out of the least possible expenditure.

Cost accounting provides the necessary information to answer a number of pertinent questions concerning various aspects of the school program. What are the relative costs of various programs—the athletic program as compared with the physical education program? What is the cost (loss in state allocations of money) due to nonattendance of pupils? How do the costs of elementary education compare with those of secondary education? Speculation concerning the comparative costs of programs is of little value, but judgments based upon the expenditures may produce the evidence necessary to evaluate them more objectively.

The business of education requires sound judgement in decision making. Fortunate indeed are school administrators whose accounting system provides the information necessary to allow them and the school board to make decisions on the basis of adequate, reliable, and relevant facts and figures from a cost accounting system. No other basis can be considered as valid.

Cost accounting has two primary values. (1) It provides information for in-school choices and decisions in the expenditure of funds. (2) Costs for the same services can be compared with those of other schools. Too often, school personnel have seen the importance of this factor but have failed to recognize that the potential in-school values of cost accounting exceed those that might come from comparisons with other school systems.

ACCRUAL ACCOUNTING

The accrual basis is the superior method of accounting for the economic resources of the local education agency. "It results in accounting measurement based on the substance of transactions and events, rather than merely when cash is received or disbursed and thus enhances their relevance, neutrality, timeliness, completeness, and comparability."[10] The essential elements include: (1) deferral of expenditures and amortization of deferred costs, (2) deferral of revenues until they are earned, (3) capitalization of certain expenditures and the subsequent depreciation of the capitalized costs, and (4) accrual of revenues that have been earned and expenses that have been incurred.[11]

Some of the advantages of accrual basis accounting include:

- providing a comprehensive measurement of financial position and results of operations;
- providing accountability for individual assets within the accounting system at the earliest appropriate date;
- providing comparability from period to period; and
- reducing management's ability to control cash flows in such a way as to produce financial statements that will seem to present financial position and results of operations in either a more optimistic or more pessimistic context depending upon management's particular preference at the end of any given fiscal year.[12]

COMPUTERIZED ACCOUNTING SYSTEMS

Most large school districts have entered the computer age by purchasing sophisticated equipment that provides many services beyond business management. Software packages now provide the user with word processing, electronic spreadsheets, electronic filing capabilities, electronic mail, on-line subscription services, pupil accounting, inventory records, and many other administrative tools for convenience and assistance in decision making.

There was a concern for a few years that the costs of computer equipment and related software would make it impossible for small school districts to join the technological revolution. However, continual development of better equipment and software and the highly competitive market have lowered costs until even the smallest district can benefit from data processing equipment in managing its business affairs. Many states make available regional or central mainframe computers that local districts can tie into by purchasing relatively little equipment and leasing telephone lines to the main computer. Some districts share expenses in purchasing a system, and in some cases districts have leased time from private services.

Microcomputers can be purchased for minimal expense, with accompanying software designed to meet most state regulations and reporting requirements. Such equipment will soon pay for itself through reduction of labor costs and improved efficiency in operations. The complex, often confusing, time-consuming tasks associated with business affairs can now be handled in even the smallest district through the use of computers.

When a district is ready to purchase a computer system, an analysis of need should be made, and the hardware and software that best fit those needs should be purchased. The vendor should provide in-service training for all personnel who will use the equipment or request information and reports. Maintenance of equipment is a factor. Special consideration should be given to service contract costs, service availability, and program compatibility. Kory emphasizes that districts must plan when determining their information systems:

> Districts should prepare for these investments by developing an overall architectural plan for their information systems. This is a long-term capital activity, just like any other infrastructure investment. As such, this plan should anticipate both future technological trends and district management objectives.
>
> It is critically important that the time horizon in such a plan be long enough to ensure accurate analysis, to support effective decisions and to create realistic expectations. For large districts this investment will seem enormous compared to any such systems investment in the past. The implementation cycle will, at a minimum, be several years.[13]

RECEIVING AND DEPOSITING FUNDS

The school accounting function begins with the receipt of funds from the county treasurer or other tax agency that collects local property taxes and from the state agency that allocates funds to local districts. There must be agreement between the instruments showing receipt of funds and the amount of such monies received.

The typical school board has control of its own budget and has custody of its funds. Local property taxes are usually collected by a county tax collector, who transfers the rightful share to the school board treasurer(s) in the county. The school board treasurer deposits tax warrants, state allocations, and all other school district monies in the bank or banks that the school board has designated as its depository.

The school board uses the same criteria for the selection of a depository for its funds as an individual would use when establishing a personal account. Many boards find it advantageous to accept bids from various banks when a selection for services is being made. Quality of service, financial standing, convenience to the board, interest rates, and the integrity of bank officials are some of the most important factors to be considered when selecting a bank.

EXPENDING SCHOOL FUNDS

General authorization for the expenditure of funds comes from the budget and the minutes of the board of education meetings. Under the direction of the superintendent, charges and obligations are made against the district accounts as provided by these two documents. Some boards of education authorize charges against the district by sole action of the superintendent but with full accountability to the board, but others require either preapproval or ratification at a board meeting of all expenditures or encumbrances above a predetermined amount.

Invoices received by the district office are checked for accuracy, approved by the responsible official, and then directed to the business office for payment. Other documents that legalize the payment of monies from the school treasury include such items as contracts, time cards, and legal claims by government (social security payments, for example). All original documents must show evidence of proper authorization and satisfactory acceptance of services rendered or goods received before they can be authorized for payment.

All original documents that serve as supporting evidence of money received or expended must be filed as official records of fiscal transactions. They become the supporting records from which audits can be made. Usually the requisition, purchase order, and invoice or voucher for a particular transaction are clipped together and filed, forming a complete record of the events that authorized that particular expenditure. The original documents—receipts, contracts, invoices, checks and warrants, deposit slips, requisitions, purchase orders, payrolls, and similar documents—provide the information necessary for entries in the records maintained in the accounting system.

FINANCIAL REPORTS

The board of education and the general public are kept informed concerning the fiscal operations of a school district by various kinds of financial and statistical reports made by the business office. Typically, these include monthly reports of receipts, expenditures and encumbrances, and balances in all main budgetary accounts. The monthly report forms the basis for future commitments of funds. It allows the board to anticipate further encumbrances and points the way to budgetary control practices that avoid overexpenditures or underexpenditures in specific accounts or funds.

An annual financial report is sometimes required by law, in the form of a newspaper report to the public. It includes a record of the district's fiscal operations for the previous school year. The amount of detail included is often subject to controversy, because of its high cost. A statistical summary serves a useful purpose in keeping the public informed, but it is doubtful that the complete detail of the district's fiscal transactions is worth the cost of its publication.

Other reports are made as deemed important and relevant by the superintendent or the school board. Reports including charts, graphs, pictures, and other visual devices have proven to be popular and effective in telling the financial story of the district. Many superintendents consider such reports to be one of the very best public relations devices at their disposal.

State reports, fiscal as well as statistical, are a requirement for most school districts. The value of such reports can hardly be overemphasized. They form the basis for legislative action and for information that various state agencies and groups use to debate the cause of education. The states submit a summary of these reports and other information to the U.S. Department of Education, which combines them and thereby provides comparative financial information that is available to all the school districts of the nation.

AUDITING

When protection of property and money is being considered (as well as protection of the reputation of the employees involved), the administrator and the board of education turn to the audit for support. Auditing is usually the culminating act in the business of protecting the assets of the school district; it is used in some form and to some extent by all school districts.

An audit is a systematic process or procedure for verifying the financial operations of a school district to determine whether or not property and funds have been or are being used in a legal and efficient way. It provides a service that no business—least of all an institution receiving and expending public funds—can afford not to use on a more or less regular basis.

Purposes

The purposes of auditing are the same now as they always have been, but the emphasis has changed dramatically. Discovery of fraud and detection of errors were once the main functions of auditing, but it has other, more important functions today, as indicated in the following statement by Welsch and Anthony:

> Its purpose is to lend credibility to the financial reports; that is, to assure that they are dependable. Primarily this function involves an examination of the financial reports prepared by the management in order to assure that they

are in conformance with generally accepted accounting concepts and standards. In carrying out this function the independent CPA examines the underlying transactions, including the collection, classification, and assembly of the financial data incorporated in the financial reports. In performing these tasks, established professional standards must be maintained and the information reported must conform to "generally accepted accounting principles" appropriate for the entity involved. Additionally, the CPA is responsible for verifying that the financial reports "fairly present" the resource inflows and outflows and the financial position of the entity.[14]

In spite of the foregoing, it seems likely that the average citizen, perhaps even the average school administrator, views the audit as simply a means of discovering financial shortages or misuses of public funds. That, however, is becoming less and less its main value to the school district. Only a very small percentage of school audits disclose any acts of dishonesty in handling school money. On the other hand, every audit does result in some protection to the honest school officials who have been responsible for the fiscal management of the district. In addition, the audit shows the degree or extent of observance of state and district laws and policies, shows the financial condition of the district and the adequacy or inadequacy of accounting procedures, provides suggestions to improve the system, and gives an official review of the operations of the school system for the period of the audit. These are the values that make the audit worth its cost. State legislatures are wise to require school district audits at periodic intervals.

Kinds of Audits

Audits or appraisals of school finance practices and records are of several kinds, but their purposes are the same—to satisfy state and local district requirements, to protect school funds, and to help establish public confidence in the operation of the schools. All types of audits form a basis for more efficient management of school monies and at the same time protect the school and its employees from what might otherwise be legitimate criticism of the school's handling of public funds.

The most common kinds of school audits in general use are internal, state, and external. These may be subdivided in turn according to when the audit is conducted and its degree of completeness.

Internal Audits

Internal (continuous) audits are conducted by technically qualified personnel already employed by the school district. They may be preaudits, current audits, or even postaudits. Postaudits usually are used in years when districts, in the absence of legal requirements, do not authorize an external audit. Internal audits function as an integral part of a control system that some districts use to assure school patrons of proper and careful management of school monies. By themselves, internal audits cannot guarantee such management, and they are in no sense a justifiable alternative to the more professional external audits that are required at regular intervals by the various states.

State Audits

It has been pointed out that states are paying a high percentage of the cost of public education. It is also known that school funds in reality are state funds. It follows, then, that the states have a direct interest in the management of local school district funds and therefore have a right, as well as a responsibility, to know how school finances are managed. Accordingly, the states require periodic audits of local district funds to ensure that the law is being observed in their utilization. The nature and extent of the audit vary considerably from one state to another. Those states that have many districts with limited resources and those that have many other institutions requiring state audits usually restrict the extent of state-required audits. Some states concern themselves only with local district observances of state laws governing the expenditure of school monies. A few states require such an audit only every three or four years. Many states solve this problem by requiring that independent auditors perform this function on a yearly or other regular basis.

External Audits

External audits are conducted by qualified agencies or individuals (usually certified public accountants). They are usually of the postaudit variety and may or may not be complete audits. The typical district does not require a complete external audit every year because of the cost factor, but this varies with the district's policy and the state's requirement.

External auditing practices follow state laws established for such purposes, as well as certain other generally accepted accounting procedures. Complete year-end audits usually include the following actions:

1. A study of the minutes of the meetings of the board of education. These records are the official authorization for all transactions that occur in the operation of the schools. The financial records of the school must be reviewed in terms of their agreement with the school board minutes and the legal requirements and regulations provided in state laws.

2. Verification of all receipts from all sources—revenue, nonrevenue, and transfer funds. This action includes a check on the allocation of receipts to the current-expenditure fund, to capital outlay, and to debt service accounts.

3. Verification of expenditures—requisitions, purchase orders, vouchers, and checks issued.

4. Review of the entries in the journal, ledgers, payrolls, and similar books of entry and disbursement.

5. Reconciliation of bank statements, accounts, and investments.

6. A review of all subsidiary records, deeds, supporting documents, inventories, insurance policies, trusts, sinking funds, and numerous other records related to the operation of the school.

7. Although some districts tend to disregard the audit for the student activity and other internal accounts, these should be a part of every external postaudit. No school official should accept internal audits as meeting the audit requirements for such accounts (reasoning that they are not under the direct control of the board of education). There has been a tendency in the past to minimize or disregard the importance of spending taxpayer's money for such audits. In the average school district, these accounts are more likely to be in need of review and audit than the regular district-level accounts.

Thus, it is evident that a complete audit means exactly what the name suggests. In the words of Knezevich and Fowlkes, it is a "detailed study of the system of internal control of all books and accounts, including subsidiary records and supporting documents, to determine the legality, mathematical accuracy, complete accountability, and application of accounting principles."[15]

There are other kinds of audits in addition to the complete audit. For example, special audits (considering some particular phase or part of the school operation) are used when suspicion of error or fraud may be involved. Such an audit may be for other than a full fiscal year and may sometimes cover parts of more than one fiscal period.

The kinds of audits that school districts use are sometimes differentiated according to when they are to be made. For example, preaudits occur before the transactions actually occur, continuous audits occur during the length of the complete fiscal period, and postaudits occur after the fiscal period has elapsed.

The preaudit is an informal system to prevent unauthorized, illegal, or questionable use of school funds. It is an administrative procedure to protect the school from spending money for the wrong purpose or from the wrong account. In practice, it becomes a system of administrative control to assure school officials that embarrassing, unwise, or even illegal transactions are prevented. A certain amount of preauditing takes place in every school's operation, where care is taken to prevent unwise expenditures of money. The officials of the school may not think of their informal preventive or protective measures as being preaudits, but they are, nonetheless.

The continuous audit is much like the preaudit, but carried through the entire fiscal period. Large districts may have a more formal organization, with a controller or other official to perform this function. It is important that this function be conducted for the good of the educational program. It should not become a position with the negative connotation of "watchdog of the treasury."

Selecting an Auditor

Boards of education may sometimes wish to employ the auditor who bids lowest. Other factors are usually much more important in the selection: the accountant's competence, reputation, experience with similar assignments, availability, and ability to get the job done in a reasonable time. Competitive bidding for the assignment should never be used. Such a process is analogous to competitive bidding for the position of teacher or school superintendent.

Occasionally, problems arise between the auditing agency and the school district. In no sense is the auditor being placed in a position of evaluating the judgment of the board of education in the use of school monies. It should be made clear to auditors before they accept the assignment that their function is to verify what has happened in the school operation and report the findings to the board—not to the individual who has been in charge of fiscal operations. As technical experts, auditors provide fact-finding and advisory services only. They should have a free hand in performing their services, and the records of the school district and the informational services of the school employees should be at their disposal. These matters seldom are cause for difficulty if they are understood before the beginning of the audit.

It is very important that the board of education and the auditor agree on the extent of the audit to be made and establish some reasonable relation between this assignment and the estimated cost. A complete audit on a per diem cost basis might go well beyond the need of the school district or its ability to pay.

Audit Reports

If, as generally assumed, it is important to require audits of a school's fiscal operations, it is equally important that formal reports of such studies should be made to the school board. Typically, such reports should include:

1. A letter of transmittal, including the general contractual agreement, the procedures followed, and other general information.

2. A specific statement of the scope of the audit and any limitations it may include.

3. A statement of the general and specific findings of the audit, along with the implications of such.

4. A list of recommendations for any improvements, additions, or deletions in the accounting system, together with the rationale for such recommendations.

5. A schedule of tables, figures, and summaries of pertinent information concerning school operations, including inventories, insurance policies, deeds, and the like.

6. Comparisons of school operations with those of other years, including receipts, expenditures, special accounts, and related information.

Administrators and Audits

No wise administrator advises the board of education to avoid or postpone periodic audits of all school district fiscal operations. The cost is little when compared with the input it may provide for improving and evaluating school business operations. No professional educator should leave a position or accept a new one where he or she is responsible for the management of school funds until some kind of formal audit, preferably by a certified public accountant, has been performed. The reputation of a school administrator, and to a lesser degree a teacher, is inextricably related to how the public views the management of public funds. An audit protects the prudent and detects the imprudent. It is therefore a necessity, not a luxury. A comprehensive audit by a qualified agency is the public's best possible assurance of the honest and efficient operation of school fiscal affairs.

PROTECTING SCHOOL FUNDS

A school does not ordinarily impose on itself the rigid legal and system-oriented rules for receiving and expending money that banks and many other businesses usually use. Unfortunately, some administrators and teachers have had little or no training in business and have not placed the necessary emphasis on this aspect of the educational program. No individual can afford to handle public funds without strict compliance with fundamental and sound business practices—regardless of the amount of funds under his or her jurisdiction. Strict observance of basic accounting principles and the bonding of all school employees who manage school funds are absolute necessities in all schools.

Surety Bonds

The chief purpose of bonding school officials is sometimes misunderstood. Bonding is not done, as some suppose, because of questions about the integrity of the officials concerned. Rather, bonds are placed on officials because of the nature of the office itself. Bonding protects the school district against fraud or loss, but it also provides motivation to the official to be businesslike in handling the funds under his or her jurisdiction. Surety bonds are of three main types: fidelity, public official, and contract. There are many varieties and special forms of each of these.

Management of Cash Receipts

The receiving and disbursing of school district funds offer few problems with regard to the money that goes through the normal fiscal cycle. Receipts for income, board authorization for the payment of verified invoices and other obligations, two signatures on checks for all expenditures, regular internal and external audits, and periodic reports to the board of education are evidence of the careful and legal management of school district funds.

But there is less agreement on some methods of handling cash receipts—lunch money, fees, store sales receipts, student activity funds, and many others. School officials should establish guidelines, policies, and procedures to protect these incidental funds as well as the reputations of those who handle them.

Personal integrity is important, but so are records. The accounting system for such funds should follow acceptable guidelines, such as a centralized account for all student activity funds, receipts issued for all monies received, early deposit of cash receipts (with only minimal amounts of cash left in the school safe at any time), an unlocked-safe policy when protecting small amounts of money of less value than the safe door, all payments made by two-signature checks issued only after proper authorization, accurate and complete records of all transactions, supervision of all accounting systems by a faculty member or administrator, continuous internal auditing by qualified personnel, and regular external audits.

SUMMARY

Since schools perform their functions by receiving and expending public money, it is a major responsibility of school personnel to ensure that the money is spent wisely and that accurate and complete financial records are kept. School accounting records and principles have improved greatly since their early introduction into the schools.

There are benefits to be gained by school districts that follow the standardized accounting practices recommended by the U.S. Department of Education (formerly the Office of Education). These practices are refined and changed periodically with the issuance of updated handbooks.

More recently, governmental agencies, including state departments of education and local districts, have relied on the Governmental Accounting Standards Board as a guide. Many states have developed their budgeting principles from the GASB guide and the structure from the 1990 revised *Financial Accounting for Local and State School Systems.*

Encumbrance accounting and the use of computers are examples of important improvements in financial accounting systems in recent years. Their use, particularly in large districts, has simplified the process of financial recordkeeping.

Auditing of accounts by an outside agency is a necessary function for all school districts. Audits serve many purposes—one is to determine whether or not the financial operations were proper, legal, and in agreement with the district's accepted accounting practices. Audits also assist the district in determining the presence of fraud. It is unreasonable for a district to eliminate audits because of their cost. Every school administrator should insist on a preaudit of the district books when assuming office and a postaudit when leaving.

ASSIGNMENT PROJECTS

1. Determine the requirements for accounting and auditing of school district financial accounts in your state.
2. Prepare arguments to justify annual auditing of school district accounts by a professional agency.

3. Interview a school district business manager to determine what improvements have been made in accounting and auditing practices in the last few years.

4. Report on incidents of misuse of funds that might have been avoided if proper accounting and auditing practices had been followed.

5. Report on the uses of computers and accounting software packages in school district business practices. What changes are expected in the next five years?

6. Interview the business personnel of a school district whose computer is tied to a central mainframe, a school district linked to other school districts in a computer network, and a school district that uses stand-alone computer equipment. Why was each computer configuration chosen? What are its advantages and disadvantages? What kinds of reports are generated? Who uses them? Who is trained to operate the equipment?

7. Determine how computers can assist in the auditing function. How are school districts protecting themselves against computer fraud? What type of computerized audit trails can be programmed for use in school district business offices?

SELECTED READINGS

Budget Accounting and Auditing Handbook 1979, Updated 1991. Salt Lake City, Utah: State Board of Education, 1991.

Bureau of the Census. *Statistical Abstract of the United States 1991* (published annually). Washington, D.C.: U.S. Government Printing Office, 1992.

Campbell, Roald F., Luvern L. Cunningham, Raphael O. Nystrand, and Michael D. Usdan. *The Organization and Control of American Schools.* 6th ed. Columbus, Ohio: Merrill, 1990.

Chorafas, Dimitris N. *The Handbook of Data Communications and Computer Networks.* Princeton, N.J.: Petrocelli Books, 1985.

Kroenke, David. *Management Information Systems.* Santa Cruz, Calif.: Mitchell Publishing Company, 1989.

Lillie, David L., Wallace H. Hannum, and Gray B. Stuck. *Computers and Effective Instruction.* New York: Longman, 1989.

Richards, Craig E. *Microcomputer Applications for Strategic Management in Education: A Case Study Approach.* New York: Longman, 1989.

Silver, Gerald A., and Myrna L. Silver. *Data Communications for Business.* Boston: Boyd and Fraser, 1987.

Trainer, Timothy N., and Diane Kransewick. *Computers.* Santa Cruz, Calif.: Mitchell Publishing Company, 1987.

ENDNOTES

1. *Codification of Governmental Accounting and Financial Reporting Standards* (Norwalk, Conn.: Governmental Accounting Standards Board, May 1990), p. 4.

2. Ibid., p. 33.

3. *Financial Accounting for Local and State School Systems* (Washington, D.C.: U.S. Office of Education, U.S. Department of Health, Education, and Welfare, 1957).

4. *Codification of Governmental Accounting and Financial Reporting Standards.*

5. Rita Hartung Cheng and Robert B. Yahr, "The Basics of School District Accounting: How They'll Change in the 1990s," *School Business Affairs,* (October, 1990), pp. 11, 12.

6. Larry P. Bailey, *Miller Comprehensive Governmental GAAP Guide 1991* (Harcourt Brace Jovanovich, New York: 1991).

7. Ibid., Section 1.04.

8. Ibid., Section 20.09.

9. *Codification of Governmental Accounting and Financial Reporting Standards,* p. 81.

10. Ibid., p. 3.

11. Bailey, Section 3.02.

12. *Financial Accounting for Local and State School Systems,* p. 3.

13. Ross Kory, "School District Information Systems: Infrastructure of the 90's," *School Business Affairs,* May 1991, p. 22.

14. Glenn A. Welsch and Robert W. Anthony, *Fundamentals of Financial Accounting,* revised ed. (Homewood, Ill.: Richard D. Irwin, 1977), pp. 14, 741.

15. Stephen J. Knezevich and John Guy Fowlkes, *Business Management of Local School Systems* (New York: Harper & Row, 1960), p. 144.

Chapter 14

Property, Risk Management, and Insurance

In the management of risks . . . school districts should follow the basic concepts of the inherent duty and standards of care. . . . Foreseeability . . . is inherent in our jobs. —DENNIS R. DUNKLEE, 1991

Instructional and administrative personnel would be severely handicapped and their contributions to the educational program greatly minimized in the absence or short supply of appropriate materials and equipment. This is particularly true in the modern school, with its emphasis on instructional media and educational technology. The days of providing teachers with only limited supplies of absolute necessities were not difficult ones for the school purchaser—who often was also a teacher. But purchasing, storing, and distributing the vast array of machines and materials needed by the school staff today is another matter. Instructional devices, aids, office supplies and equipment, custodial materials and machines, and even the large amount of gadgetry used in food service preparation and in instructional materials centers have revolutionalized education and brought management problems to school district business offices.

The costs of such devices have increased in relation to the change from such essentials as chalk, paper, pencils, textbooks, and a few maps and charts to the list today, which includes radios, recorders, television sets, projectors, computers, globes, charts, mockups, models, adding machines, cameras, duplicating machines, and numerous other items. It is doubtful that the average school patron, who seldom visits a school, is aware of the technological revolution that has taken place in education during the past quarter of a century. Unfortunately, this may cause criticism of the costs of instructional materials and machines. Certainly, the patron will not be fully aware of their tremendous value to the school program.

THE BUSINESS OFFICE

The school business office is often spoken about as if such an "office" always existed in a school system. Very often indeed there is no such place as an entity by itself; the office referred to is usually only a part of the all-inclusive function of superintendent of schools. The superintendent in most small school systems is, in effect, the business manager, the purchasing agent, and perhaps even the accountant for the district. In some instances, the role may also include being the high school principal and even a part-time teacher. But the purposes to be served by a business office and the problems encountered in school business management are much the same in all districts.

The superintendent of schools is directly responsible to the school board for the educational program in all its aspects. In small districts, duties include most of the functions of the business manager, sometimes with little clerical assistance. In medium-sized districts, an assistant superintendent or an official clerk may be assigned as the business manager. In the larger districts, the office has a staff of assistants, clerks, and office workers who perform the business functions of the school, often under the direction of an assistant superintendent.

DELEGATING RESPONSIBILITY

In today's complex school community, regardless of its size, the superintendent's chief responsibility is to provide educational leadership. No chief officer can possibly perform all of the generally accepted functions of the superintendency alone; some of the duties of the office must be delegated to others. Since the business aspects of the school are clearly secondary to the educational aspects, the superintendent should delegate some of the former duties to capable employees but retain direct leadership responsibility for the academic program. In delegating responsibilities to members of the staff, superintendents should remember that their major responsibility is that of educational leaders, not office clerks or purchasing agents, although the responsibility for supervising the work of all departments of the school operation remains with the superintendency.

Having selected managers to assist in performing the business affairs of the school district, superintendents are then free to devote their time and ability to improving the educational program. They cannot, however, escape responsibility for the conduct of the business affairs of the district. They must know what is being done, and they must remain qualified to advise and to confer with those who perform the functions of the business office. There is no school district large enough, wealthy enough, or with a large enough district office to justify the superintendent's ignoring fiscal and material resources management.

Knezevich and Fowlkes emphasized the point in the following:

> But delegation of authority does not in any way justify ignorance of the principles of the functions and duties delegated. The chief administrator does not get rid of his responsibilities by this action, for the chief executive is held accountable for the acts of assistants. Top management has the further responsibility to consult with and review the progress and efforts of assistants. . . . It can be concluded that the principles of sound business management must be known by the large-system superintendent upon whom falls the burden of performing many of the details of business management.[1]

THE BUSINESS MANAGER

Occasionally, a newly appointed superintendent of schools discovers that the board of education has an employee, a treasurer, a clerk, a purchasing agent, or a business manager who is directly responsible to the board, not to the superintendent. As a sort of "watchdog of the treasury," he or she is responsible for the money and the superintendent is responsible for the educational program—a dichotomy in school administration. Although some districts in this country and in Canada make claims for the virtues of such an organizational pattern, few candidates for the superintendency would take a serious look at such a position. The objective of the school system is not to save money; it is rather to spend it wisely for the goods and services a good educational program needs. The person in charge of the school must be in charge of the financial program, subject only to the board of education and the state code. All employees of the district must be responsible to the superintendent of schools, and he or she in turn must be accountable to the board.

Knezevich and Fowlkes raise their emphatic objection to the separate arrangement:

> Authority in school business affairs was one of the last responsibilities to be entrusted to professional school administrators. . . . The vestigial remains of board execution of business affairs and the reluctant delegation of authority in this area are still apparent in many school systems. One vestige of such board executive activity is the secretary or treasurer to the board of education. The secretary or treasurer to the board enjoys special status and his position often makes him coordinate with the general superintendent. The functions performed by such individuals include such activities as operation of business affairs, preparation of board agendas, and recording and keeping the minutes of board meetings. . . . If the superintendent of schools is the *chief* executive officer of the school system is there a need for an independent board of education secretary or treasurer? The answer is *no.*[2]

In fairness to boards of education, it should be pointed out that tradition was often the reason for dual responsibility to the board for the operation of the schools. Over time, this arrangement has changed in most districts as right attitudes and working relationships have evolved. H. Ronald Smith, President of the Registered School Business Officials, characterized the situation:

> Backing (the superintendent) up with the staff and expertise necessary to quickly respond to problems is one of my important duties. . . . Some business administrators have a problem putting this "back up" function in a proper perspective. . . . [T]hese "back up" duties can get a little tedious at best and frustrating at worst . . . [but] by cooperating with our own superintendents, we can enhance the educational programs offered in our schools. As school business administrators, we can definitely make a difference. Let's all be sure it's a positive difference.[3]

FUNCTIONS OF THE BUSINESS OFFICE

The functions of the business office increase as the size and demands of the school district increase. Some writers have designated the so-called business management assignment of this office "fiscal and material resources management" in an effort to describe its function more comprehensively and accurately.

Regardless of the size of the school district, there are certain services that must be provided as a part of its business administration function. Some of the most important of these are: providing supplies and equipment; operating and maintaining the school plant—cleaning, lighting, heating, and repairing; transporting pupils—purchasing and maintaining school buses and providing bus services; and providing school food services—employing and supervising personnel and purchasing food supplies. Frederick W. Hill writes:

> School business administration is not an end in itself. It exists for the sole purpose of facilitating the educational program of a school and school district. It should operate to support the teacher in the classroom, the principal in the school, the school board and central administration as each strives to fulfill its responsibilities toward the accomplishment of the educational mission. . . . The best school business official is one who understands the primary goals of education and who works closely with others in promoting the best education the community can afford.[4]

SUPPLIES AND EQUIPMENT

Increasing pressures on school administrators for economical use of the school tax dollar and mounting demands for additional quality and quantity in educational programs make it essential that school administrators take a critical look at their entire fiscal operation. The objective of producing high-quality education at minimum cost has never been emphasized more than at present. The movement for accountability, the main thrust of systems analysis, and the negative reaction of taxpayers all point to the need to operate schools more efficiently without reducing their quality. Since salaries of personnel account for a major share of the total cost of education, and since cost cannot be reduced without decreasing the number of personnel employed, the superintendent must turn to economical purchasing and the efficient use of school supplies and equipment to try to effect savings and avert waste.

Financial accounting systems treat supplies differently from equipment. Procurement of supplies represents a charge against the current operating expenditures of the district, but equipment (except replacement equipment) is a capital-outlay expenditure. It is therefore important to distinguish between the two terms.

A supply item is any article or material that meets any one or more of the following conditions:

1. It is consumed in use.
2. It loses its original shape or appearance with use.
3. It is expendable; that is, if the article is damaged or some of its parts are lost or worn out, it is usually more feasible to replace it with an entirely new unit than to repair it.
4. It is an inexpensive item; even if it has characteristics of equipment, its small cost makes it inadvisable to capitalize the item.
5. It loses its identity through incorporation into a different or more complex unit or substance.

An equipment item is a movable or fixed unit of furniture or furnishing, an instrument, a machine, an apparatus, or a set of articles that meets all of the following conditions:

1. It retains its original shape and appearance with use.
2. It is nonexpendable; that is, if the article is damaged or some of its parts are lost or worn out, it is usually more feasible to repair it than to replace it with an entirely new unit.
3. It represents an investment of money that makes it feasible and advisable to capitalize the item.
4. It does not lose its identity through incorporation into a different or more complex unit or substance.[5]

The differentiation between supplies and equipment is sometimes very difficult to make. In the interest of consistency, schools and many other institutions sometimes use a fixed standard of cost as the arbitrary determinant of the classification of the materials used in the operation. Thus, a material costing $100 per single unit might be classified as a supply, while one costing more than that would be called equipment. Standardization and consistency in whatever distinction is made is important if cost comparisons are to be made from year to year or from one district to another.

PURCHASING

Accountability in education might well start with the procurement of school materials. It is among the first of the school's business operations to be studied and improved when the pressure of public opinion is directed toward economizing school business operations. The increased size of schools and the recent influx of devices, machines, and gadgets necessary to implement innovative programs have combined to multiply the problems involved in purchasing supplies and equipment for a modern school program.

Purchasing supplies and equipment is not just a simple process of ordering something from a vendor, although some people may view it as such. Involved in the complicated process of purchasing are such problems as determining what is needed and in what quantity and quality, synchronization of the time of need and the time of delivery, providing the quality of the product needed without overspending the amount budgeted, storing what is required without keeping too much money invested in inventories, keeping unsuccessful bidders happy, and satisfying school personnel when recommended brands of items are not purchased, deliveries are late, or some other reason prevents delivery of essential materials or equipment.

Great as the purchaser's problems are, planning and efficiency of operation will solve most of them. Written policies concerning the use of requisitions, purchase orders, and statements of standards or specifications are mandatory for efficient procurement and use of materials.

The problems involved and the procedures used in purchasing materials for schools differ somewhat from those usually encountered in business and industry. Businesses tend to specialize to some degree in certain kinds of products; schools require a great variety of items spread over many areas. In private business, and to some degree in industry, procurement of necessary supplies and equipment is usually restricted within limited fields of a highly specialized nature. The materials required are usually selected, designed, or developed by technical staffs and passed on to the procurement officers. In general, school purchasing agents do not have the benefit of such specialized aids; they must devise their own methods of evaluating the characteristics of the many items that appear on their requisition lists. In so doing, they must satisfy the needs of teachers at all levels of education and in many special departments.

In all purchasing, economy, speed, and accuracy are important. The measure of efficient purchasing in any organization is having a particular item in the right place at the right time, at a fair price. If this ideal is to be realized, a procurement program must be established to provide adequate supplies and equipment that meet the immediate and long-range needs of the local school program.

Much has been written in textbooks and periodicals to help school administrators in establishing workable and efficient purchasing departments and improving those already in existence. According to the California Association of Public School Business Officials, regardless of differences in the size of school districts or the character of materials procured or the sources from which they are obtained, some sound principles of purchasing procedures are commonly recognized. Purchasing practices in a school district should:

1. Accomplish a definite objective in the shortest possible time and in the easiest manner consistent with accuracy and efficiency.

2. Provide simplicity to speed operations and reduce possibilities of error.

3. Establish procedures that are definite and understandable to obviate friction, duplication, and confusion.

4. Fix responsibility for each step of performance.

5. Establish procedures that are sufficiently elastic to allow for expansion as the district grows.

6. Provide a system of procurement that is inexpensive and consistent with the job to be done.

7. Ensure that the system is adequate to perform the task for which it was created.

Policies Governing Purchasing

Effective school purchasing requires a systematic purchasing organization, operated by established procedure. The first step in establishing such an organization is for the board of education to adopt written policies concerning purchasing. Such policies are extremely valuable, not only to the board, school staff, and pupils, but also to the patrons of the school. They bring clarity and understanding to school operations. Carefully considered and well-written policies are the basis for all board functions. They legalize actions and relieve employees of the responsibility for making policy decisions under the pressure of time or expediency. They help interpret institutional purposes and facilitate speed and accuracy in translating policy into action. They clarify the relationships among school board, superintendent, and staff in the matter of providing materials for the school program. Ferguson suggests that if four aspects of purchasing are handled properly, the overall school program will be improved. They relate to: (1) the staffing of the purchasing department, (2) professional objectivity in vendor relationships, (3) patrons' interest in education, and (4) user input and feedback.[6]

To supplement the policies that the school board has adopted, the superintendent of schools or the assistant superintendent in charge of the business office should establish procurement regulations that will serve as detailed guides for staff members. If the purchasing policies of a school district are to achieve the desired level of effectiveness, they must be known and understood by everyone affected by them. The most effective means of communication possible must be used to make the information available to staff personnel and to vendors and interested patrons in the community.

Those in charge of purchasing at the district level must be aware of codes and purchasing regulations that may be established at the state level and apply to all state government entities, including school districts. Some state purchasing requirements may supersede local policies, and districts may be held responsible to abide by the state-adopted procurement code.

Standardization

Many of the supplies that a school district uses can be of a standard size and quality without loss in effectiveness. Where such standardization is possible, the use of standard lists has certain advantages. Unit costs can be reduced through buying larger quantities and through competitive bidding by vendors. Even when the personnel concerned help determine the standards and specifications of materials to be used, sometimes there will be justifiable reasons for buying special supplies or supplies with nonstandard specifications. Important as standards are in procuring supplies and equipment, no worthwhile school program should suffer unduly because of inability to use standardized materials.

Among other benefits, standardization:

1. Allows lower costs from bids on large quantities of one item.
2. Reduces and facilitates repairs and replacements.
3. Reduces inventories, thereby reducing storage costs, and at the same time increases the amount of school funds available for other purposes.
4. Speeds delivery of materials or equipment.
5. Reduces the number of materials and equipment for which specifications must be written.
6. Reduces the work of the purchasing department, including that of business office recordkeeping.

One of the problems involved in determining standards of quality (and therefore of price) is determining what quality in a product is required to achieve a particular function for a particular period. This is the same problem that the purchaser meets when buying an automobile for personal use. He or she must decide whether a second-hand car of a certain quality will provide the proper amount and quality of service for the duration of known needs, or whether additional investment in a new car will prove to be more economical in the long run. The school district purchasing agent facing the same problem may often be tempted to procure the least expensive item, in order to allow for purchases of other items. All too often this results in employee dissatisfaction, poor performance, high repair costs, early replacement, and an unwise and uneconomical expenditure of school funds.

In determining the standard of quality, the purchaser should consider:

1. Length of term for which the product is to be used;
2. The comparative service that each potential choice is known to have given;
3. Prestige factors involved, if any;
4. The extent of safety hazards involved, if any;
5. The availability of the products under consideration;
6. Initial cost and upkeep costs; and
7. Disposal problems and costs.

Specifications for materials to be purchased often require much time and effort in preparation. When possible, districts take advantage of the standard specifications already prepared by private companies or by the Federal Bureau of Standards. The use of brand-name products will save the time of the business office in soliciting quotations and in ordering the product. It also provides some foreknowledge of the quality of the product being purchased. It has one important disadvantage: the user is often required to use one brand-name product when experience and personal bias would strongly suggest the purchase of a different one, often at little or no additional increase in cost.

Quantity Purchasing

School districts usually try to buy in large quantities to save on original cost and to reduce office work and delivery problems. This kind of purchasing policy requires a knowledge of needs and assures the business office of budgetary control in all supply and equipment accounts. At the same time, the practice could result in tying up the funds of the district in unnecessary inventories and requiring large areas of district facilities for storage. It may also occasion early purchase of certain materials that later become undesirable because of changes in teacher preferences or because better materials are invented or discovered. This may result in having to use supplies or items of equipment that are outmoded, obsolete, or not as effective as newer items. There is no standard rule for the purchaser to follow in deciding between quantity orders and more frequent orders. Experience with the products, as well as with the desires and working policies of school staff members, is necessary to determine the best policy for each district in quantity purchasing.

Bidding

Most states, local districts, or both have rules and regulations concerning the need for competitive bids for the purchase of school supplies and equipment. Ordinarily, purchases or contracts for services for more than a stipulated amount or cost must be by bid. Here again, determining the maximum amount that does not require a bid is difficult. If the amount is low, little saving is possible— advertising for and receiving bids is expensive to the district and also to the vendor. Low maximums also tie the hands of the purchasing agent, who may otherwise have the opportunity of making frequent small purchases at a saving. On the other hand, placing the maximum too high encourages the district to purchase required materials without the formality and the savings of competitive bidding.

Bidding requires advertising, establishing specifications, obtaining sealed bids to supply the materials at a certain price, and determination of the successful bidder by the board of education. Bids are let to the bidder under a general policy of "lowest-best bid." This is not always the lowest bid in terms of unit cost. Other factors to be considered are quality of product, quality of service, ability of the vendor to provide the product, service, or both (usually covered by a performance bond), time when delivery can be made, and reputation and fiscal responsibility of the vendor.

Often states have bid contracts for particular equipment that school districts may find beneficial. With the state's ability to buy in large quantities, savings can be generated for smaller districts especially. Small rural districts may find it advantageous to form a consortium for obtaining bids on certain high-priced items.

SUPPLY MANAGEMENT

Once the supplies have been ordered and received, the neophyte purchasing agent may think the problem is solved. But the problems of receiving, storing, and distributing supplies loom large in the average school district. Supplies or inventory have little value unless they are available when needed. The main functions involved in receiving supplies are checking purchase orders against the goods received, noting the differences if any, calling any errors to the attention of the vendors, certifying delivery, and authorizing payment. This work requires a careful and well-trained person. Irresponsibility in the receiving of supplies may cost the district money through errors in shipment or difficulties with vending companies. One of the advantages to be gained by receiving all purchases at the district or a central receiving warehouse is that it eliminates the careless checking that often occurs when many individuals perform this service.

Supply Storage

In large school districts, the problem of supply storage is often a serious one. The district must decide between a central storage facility and several site-level facilities. The advantages of these two methods tend to balance out. Central storage provides for better district control and accountability and reduces the number of employees involved in storing and distributing supplies. The decentralized system assures more school unit control and guarantees the availability of materials whenever needed, but less experienced employees are involved in their handling.

As pointed out before, the primary concern is for the fiscal implications of the school's operation. The details of storage, distribution, and use of school supplies are therefore beyond the purview of this brief treatment. However, it is within the purpose of this work to suggest certain policies and procedures that do affect the costs of education. The following list of six requirements for an effective storage system seems pertinent:

1. All supplies must be stored in spaces that are free of destructive factors such as excessive heat or cold, moisture, vermin and insects, and fire hazards.
2. All storage areas must be accessible for both incoming and outgoing supplies.
3. All supplies must be so stored as to be readily available when needed.
4. All storage materials must be administered under the rule that old stock is used first.
5. A current inventory should be kept for each storage area.
6. Responsibility for proper operation of storage areas must be specifically assigned and clearly understood by all involved.

Distribution of Supplies and Equipment

Each school district has its own special system for the distribution of supplies and equipment. The essential characteristics of any system involve use of requisitions, records of distribution, and stock or inventory records.

The policy involved in the distribution of school supplies in the modern school is much different from the traditional policy of an earlier era. No longer are supplies stored in the darkest corner of the basement under lock and key, available only on certain days or at certain hours, and distributed on the basis of a permanent short-supply philosophy. The modern approach encourages a policy of putting supplies where they can be seen and obtained with the least possible inconvenience by the teacher or other staff members. Modern administrative policy recognizes the value of materials in helping the staff achieve the purposes of the school. It is economically foolish to employ a teacher at a good salary and then deny that person a chance to succeed by limiting the supplies, devices, and other aids so essential to the educational program. The old fear that open shelves of readily accessible supplies would encourage waste has proved to be groundless. Today's teachers use more supplies and greater varieties of them, but there is little evidence of their misuse.

RISK MANAGEMENT

The concept of risk management has changed drastically in the past few years as litigation has put the onus on boards of education, administrators, and teachers as responsible parties for accidents that occur in the classroom and on the playground. As a result, many districts are taking positive steps to alleviate problems before they occur by assigning *risk management* responsibilities to a staff member. "The term 'risk management' did not come into use until the 1960s. However, the practice of risk management dates back to 4000 B.C. with the practice of Bottomry. Bottomry was the method used for spreading risk in maritime adventures through loans that were repayable at exorbitant interest rates for successful ventures."[7] In education, past history has been simply that of alerting schools of possible danger areas and providing some workshops related to health and accident hazards.

Business and industry have led the way in demonstrating the value of taking an aggressive approach in preventing accidents in the workplace and have found it financially beneficial to hire a person specifically assigned to risk management responsibilities. The public sector, including school districts, has become much more involved and it appears the future will require more and more services through a risk management office. Constantino provides evidence that school districts might have an even greater need than other public entities:

> A school board needs to evaluate the relationship between risk management and the high cost of risk. Even if a town employs a risk manager, school district risk management differs from municipalities in its liability exposure. A municipality is primarily dealing with adults—school districts deal with young, immature adults. School districts face a tidal wave of new and expanding exposures to loss, not the least of which is the liability of public officials and public bodies such as school boards.[8]

These predictions for the future indicate that more and more services will come from the risk management office:

> Risk management in the year 2000 and beyond will require a holistic approach to the management of risk. The days of risk managers solely purchasing insurance, filing claims and reviewing contractor's certificates of issuance will be a distant memory.[9]

> Risk managers are unique. There is no other position within a public entity requiring an individual to communicate continuously among all levels of management.[10]

> I believe that the role of the risk manager of the year 2000 will be that of engineer, financial analyst, politician/lobbyist and human resource manager. In light of key issues in the year 2000, entities won't rely on risk managers as "insurance technicians" so much.[11]

In Utah, the Office of Risk Management is charged by statute with the responsibility of establishing a risk control program for state agencies and participating school districts. The office identifies the following as its purpose:

Risk control is the art of anticipation and action and is an inherent management responsibility. It is embedded in the risk management process and has
to do with identifying risk of loss and then eliminating, reducing or avoiding
risk in the most appropriate way in each circumstance. It encompasses safety
programs, inspections and training, but goes beyond traditional concepts of
"safety" to include management issues such as policies and procedures,
programming and contracts. It should be as broad and pervasive as risk of
loss is. Among the main objectives of our risk control program are these:
1) to save lives, 2) to eliminate human suffering, 3) to avoid disruption of the
services you provide and 4) to reduce the cost of losses and thereby meet the
public trust you have for the resources you control.[12]

Constantino emphasizes the need to assign the risk management task to a
trained employee:

Without a professional employee with the expertise to develop and maintain
safety and loss control activities, the loss experience for school districts can
be significant, and insurance carriers handling public business have been
finding it less and less desirable to write coverage under these circumstances. The discipline of risk management gives each school district a tool
that will enable them TO NOT ONLY work with the future but also to cope
with it. Boards of education need to know this.[13]

Increasing Safety Hazards

The purpose of the school is to provide its pupils with high-quality education
of the variety and quantity that will improve their behavior and competence
as law-abiding and self-supporting citizens. But that purpose is not all-inclusive;
the school's first responsibility involves maintaining the safety and protecting the health and well-being of all who attend. Education has relatively little
value to the seriously injured pupil or to the one whose physical or mental health
has been jeopardized through negligence on the part of anyone in the school
community.

Too often in the past, school employees have given only limited attention to
protecting the safety and maintaining the health of their pupils. These activities,
they reasoned, were the responsibility of other government agencies and of the
home. They often found their own academic or administrative responsibilities
too time-consuming to permit significant involvement in the primary safety and
health concerns of students.

The potential and the real hazards to the health and safety of pupils in the
school complex are greater than is commonly believed. As schools have become
larger, many of the dangers to its members have increased. From automobile-
motorcycle-bicycle hazards outside the school itself, to the playground heavily
stocked with potentially dangerous equipment, to the overcrowded classrooms,

gymnasiums, and laboratories, the dangers to life and limb manifest themselves on every hand. As a result, the importance of eliminating safety hazards, protecting the health of pupils, and providing adequate insurance, using risk management principles, is much greater today than ever before in the history of education.

The usual method of guaranteeing protection for the educational community is to transfer risk to an insurance carrier. There is an emphasis now on reducing the probability of loss by eliminating safety hazards.

Most schools are not negligent in providing pupils with a safe and hazard-free environment, but a few are. Every school, regardless of its safety record in the past, should constantly be reviewing and improving its policies and procedures to protect the safety and well-being of all members of the school community.

Principals need to protect themselves from lawsuits through a systematic approach of determining how safe the school facilities are for students and staff. A survey of the buildings and grounds on a frequent basis is essential. Establishment of a safety committee, including a teacher, parent, school nurse, a representative from the fire department, and the school administrator, has proven a successful approach in taking inventory of safety needs in some districts. Use of a self-evaluation safety checklist has also proven helpful in identifying hazardous problems in the school setting. Often, such surveys reveal areas of concern that may be costly to modify or repair. However, the risk management approach of prevention may prove to be the least costly in the long run. In addition to the desire to protect schoolchildren, school staff members should remind themselves that courts will look very critically on an institution whose members, required to be present by edict of the state, have not been given the greatest possible personal protection while in attendance.

Members of the community must be protected as well. In a bizarre case involving a 19-year-old youth who was technically a burglar, the importance of reducing safety hazards in a timely manner was clearly demonstrated. As reported in *Time* magazine:

> A burglar supposedly fell through the skylight of a school, sued and was awarded $260,000 plus $1,500 a month. The full story, it seems, is that a 19-year-old man and three friends tried to take a floodlight off the roof of a California high school as a lark; he fell through the skylight and suffered loss of the use of all four limbs, plus severe brain damage. The skylight had been painted the same color as the roof and was indistinguishable at night; the school district knew that it was dangerous because someone else had been killed falling through a similar skylight at another school six months earlier, and *had scheduled the skylight for repainting*.[14]

Most schools do a great deal to protect the safety of people, but there are other risks against which the board must protect itself. There is always the danger that buildings and property may be damaged, altered, or destroyed, or that some of their vital parts may be stolen, in spite of the best protection the school can provide. In addition, school personnel may become involved in tort action in the courts. Boards of education and school administrators must therefore know and observe state laws concerning safety precautions as well as exercise their best judgment in providing insurance protection as it relates to all aspects of the school program.

Insurance Defined

Insurance is a method of providing for cooperative sharing of the risk of financial or other loss in the event of some unfortunate incident. School districts are concerned primarily with insurance protection against loss of life, acts of criminals, the alteration or destruction of school property or damage thereto, the liability of school personnel for tort action, and the personal welfare of school employees.

Insurance has been called a necessary expenditure to provide for benefits in case of an incident or emergency that the purchaser hopes will never occur. The risk taker (school or individual) purchases insurance from a professional risk bearer (the insurance company) as financial security in the event that some undesirable event occurs. No person looks forward to the burning of a home or a schoolhouse so that insurance will be collected. The insured is merely trying to soften the financial blow of a catastrophe in the hope that the loss will not be permanently damaging.

School Board Responsibility

The school board's responsibility for operating schools carries with it stated and implied powers for the protection of public funds and property. It is taken for granted that schools and their pupils must be given reasonable protection from interruption and loss from emergencies, disasters, or other less serious events. The legal responsibility for such protection rests solely with the board of education in each school district, except in states where such protection is provided at the state level. This is an important obligation that the board can ill afford to ignore or minimize. At stake are several needs: protection of the state's and local district's large investment in school buildings and property; financial protection for individuals in the event of injury, tort action, or death; and public protection against interruptions in the normal school process in the event of emergencies.

Just as prudent individuals protect themselves against financial loss from fire in homes or places of business, so a responsible board of education will protect a community from the same risks with its school buildings. This is best accomplished by buying insurance in amounts commensurate with the size of the investment the district has in such properties.

Unfortunately, it is often no longer possible to buy such insurance at a reasonable cost. Many school districts view the provision of adequate insurance as a crisis. Insurance premium rates have skyrocketed, juries award claimants large amounts of money, and some school districts and municipalities are simply unable to pay extraordinarily high insurance premiums.

Basic Principles

Since it would usually be unwise economically for a school district to provide insurance to protect it from all the possible risks such an enterprise might face, school boards are often faced with the problem of selecting those items or assets for which they are most obligated to provide insurance protection. There are a number of basic safety measures that school boards can use to help cover many of the areas of low risk, to supplement the insurance program considered necessary for high-risk facilities and operations. These would include loss prevention through good building design, safety programs, regular inspections of buildings, the provision of adequate fire-fighting equipment, and the accumulation of reserves to pay for any losses sustained.

As thousands of school boards have dealt with their insurance problems over a long period, certain basic rules or principles have evolved:

1. A well-organized and conscientiously administered safety and loss-prevention program is not only inexpensive but also very effective in reducing injuries and property losses through accidents. Such a program is needed for humanitarian reasons, and it is also the best and least costly kind of insurance.

2. The board of education has a moral and legal responsibility to provide protection for its employees, its students, and its patrons against ordinary accidents that often occur within the jurisdiction of the school. Once a discretionary power of the board, the provision for a well-conceived insurance plan is now a mandatory duty of every board of education, acting within the legal framework and guidelines provided in each state.

3. The board of education has a moral (and sometimes a legal) obligation to formulate in writing its policies and regulations concerning the safety and protection of all those in the school community.

4. The insurance program of a school should be the result of careful study of risks involved, past experiences in the district, and the recommendations of consultants. The field of insurance is so broad and complex that school administrators cannot hope to advise their boards concerning such needs solely on the basis of their own knowledge and experience.

5. The insurance program should not be static and unchangeable but should reflect changing needs and risks. To continue an insurance program year after year without evaluation and change or adjustment is a practice that only the inexperienced, the careless, or the uninformed pursue.

MAIN TYPES OF INSURANCE

Insurance on almost any risk can be purchased if cost is of no concern to the purchaser. Thus, insurance may be available for almost anything and everything the school board may want to insure. The establishment of insurance priorities is therefore highly important to the board. The following is a list of some of the most common kinds of insurance that a typical school board would want to consider. No priority is intended, for that would vary from one school to another.

1. *Fire.* Insurance on the building and its contents against loss from damage by fire; common to all school districts; may use coinsurance, blanket insurance, specific or specific-schedule insurance, or self-insurance.

2. *Extended coverage.* Insurance that is added to fire insurance policies to cover miscellaneous risks, usually windstorm or tornado, smoke, loss by vehicular or aircraft damage to buildings, hailstorm, or riot damage; often difficult to obtain and expensive in riot-prone areas.

3. *Glass.* Insurance against loss of windows or door glass; usually too expensive for buildings with extensive window areas. Some schools are experimenting with plastic windows that are unbreakable in order to reduce high insurance costs.

4. *Boiler.* Insurance for protection against property damage, injury, and death due to boiler or pressure-tank explosions; a *must* for high-pressure boilers but not so necessary for the low-pressure ones now being used in many schools.

5. *Floater.* Insurance to protect all valuables and equipment used by the school; originally was inland marine insurance, which protected property in transit from one location to another.

6. *Crime.* Protection against loss by burglary, robbery, or theft.

7. *Automobile; bus.* Protection against damage or destruction and liability for damage and injury to others caused by district-owned automobiles or buses.

8. *Liability.* Protection against bodily injury or damage caused by accidents due to the negligence of employees or those sustained on school-owned property; also protection to the school board in states that have waived the immunity rule for school boards.

9. *Workmen's compensation.* State protection from loss to the employee because of injury or death resulting from employment.

10. *Surety bonds.* Protection for the school district against loss or damage through dishonesty of employees.

11. *Accident.* Protection for pupils for injury sustained in the activities of the school.

Fire Insurance

Financial protection of the large investment that every school district has in buildings, equipment, and other property is an absolute necessity. The serious predicament of the small school with inadequate insurance that loses its only building to fire is not pleasant to contemplate. If such an event should occur, no amount of explanation based on the board's opinion that insurance costs were beyond its budgetary provisions would satisfy the local citizenry, replace the school building, or in any way provide for the future school program. Thus, fire insurance is a necessity in order to protect the capital assets of a school district.

Rates Are Increasing

The ability of a school board to purchase fire insurance on public school buildings can no longer be taken for granted. Increases in vandalism have had an effect on the willingness of insurance companies to insure schools. "Schools, once wooed by insurance companies, are now either flatly rejected or asked to pay higher premiums and to accept increased deductibles." The fact that some insurance companies may have overreacted does not alter the possibility that social problems of the day may have a deleterious effect on schools' efforts to protect the assets required for their operation. The penalties—difficulty in getting adequate property insurance and being forced to pay high rates for coverage—fall on districts with a record of few claims just as they do on districts with a record of many high claims.

The current problem of securing insurance coverage is greatest in urban areas. Some city school systems have been forced to close their doors for a short time after policies were cancelled or their renewal refused. Some of the larger cities use self-insurance; smaller city school districts are almost forced to count on greater state or federal financial assistance to help solve this problem.

Determining Insurance Needs

Neither overinsurance nor underinsurance represents an economical expenditure of funds for a school district. Overinsurance is a financial waste, for the district can never collect more than the actual loss of a building. On the other hand, insurance companies never pay more than the value of the insurance policy, regardless of a greater amount of loss. It is therefore in the interests of the school district that fire insurance policies be maintained at the right level at all times.

Determining the insurable values of buildings involves original cost (excluding the cost of the site, architectural fees, foundations, and other noninsurables), depreciation, and replacement costs. The insurable value is the replacement cost (minus noninsurables) minus the value of depreciation for the number of years the building has been in existence.

It is essential that school boards know the insurable value of their buildings at the time they are insured. The savings that a board may presume to make by determining its own values for original purchase of insurance may be lost when fire insurance adjusters determine the value of claims on fire loss. The value of using qualified appraisers and professional services in determining insurance needs is obvious.

Fire insurance rates are determined in terms of the risks involved. The type of construction of the building, adequacy of the fire department and its water supply, kind and age of equipment, distance from the fire department to the school, and fire alarm systems are all determinants of the rates school districts must pay for insurance. Buildings that are not fire-resistant require higher rates than those that are fire-resistant. Rates are lower for buildings that are near adequate and modern fire departments. Rates are also lower for insurance issued for longer periods; the typical term of an insurance policy for school buildings is either three or five years.

Coinsurance

School districts have generally favored a system of coinsurance for protection against fire losses. Coinsurance involves a sharing of the risk between the school district and the insuring company. "The coinsurance concept was developed as a result of investigation which showed that the aggregate sum of partial losses paid by insurance organizations exceeded the aggregate sum of total losses."

Coinsurance policies are usually written with either 80 percent or 90 percent coverage. This means two things. (1) If the school district maintains its required coverage (the 80 or 90 percent of insurable value it chose), the rate will be less than if it allows its coverage to be less than the agreed-on percentage. (2) If full coverage of the 80 or 90 percent is maintained, the insurance company will sustain the total amount of fire loss up to the value of the insurance; but if full coverage is not maintained, the district will share proportionately in every fire loss regardless of how large or how small it may be. As an example, suppose two districts each have school buildings of the same insurable value; one insures at 80 percent coinsurance, and the other at 90 percent. Table 14-1 illustrates the operation of the insurance program in the event of fire loss.

The table shows that it is important for the district to have the correct amount of fire insurance as determined by its coinsurance agreement. Too little insurance causes the district to share in fire losses of any amount. The amount of insurance carried, written as the numerator of a fraction, and the amount required under the coinsurance agreement, which is written as the denominator, represent the fraction of any fire loss that the insurance company will pay. The district must stand the rest of the loss itself. Coinsurance uses lower rates as an incentive for districts to carry the maximum amount of insurance that it has agreed to carry. Since any amount less than that agreed on makes the district liable for some fraction of any fire loss, districts are motivated to keep their coverage at the maximum. Since most school building fires do not result in complete loss of the building, less than maximum insurance coverage would never fully protect the district for any of its fire losses.

In light of the table, it becomes evident that a district must keep accurate and up-to-date records of property values and insurance coverage. Regular appraisal of property by qualified professionals is an absolute necessity. Appraisal services are often available through state agencies or insurance companies, usually at low cost to the school. Certain organizations, such as the National Board of Fire Underwriters, perform useful services that are now available to schools in the improvement of the fire insurance policies and standards necessary to protect public property.

TABLE 14-1 Calculating Losses with Coinsurance Policies

	District A (80 percent)	District B (90 percent)
Insurable value of building	$3,000,000	$3,000,000
(Replacement cost minus depreciation)		
Required insurance coverage	2,400,000	2,700,000
Recoverable amount (with full coverage)		
Complete loss of building	2,400,000	2,700,000
Fire loss of $300,000	300,000	300,000
Fire loss of $6,000	6,000	6,000
Recoverable amount (with $1,800,000 insurance)		
Ratio of actual coverage to the amount of required insurance	3:4	2:3
Complete loss of building	$1,800,000	$1,800,000
Fire loss of $300,000	225,000	200,000
Fire loss of $6,000	4,500	4,000

EXTENDED COVERAGE

All the real and imaginary risks to buildings are not covered by ordinary fire insurance policies. For example, the risks of damage from riot, explosion, windstorm, tornado, hail, smoke, or aircraft are not ordinarily covered in such policies. Extended coverage policies, however, provide such insurance, at some additional cost. Just what kinds of insurance the district should carry and in what amounts are judgments each school board must decide for itself. Ideally such decisions are made only after careful study of the experience, over time, of comparable districts in comparable locations and with the recommendations of the administrative staff (made only after consulting professionals in school building insurance).

No school board, regardless of its revenue-producing ability, can afford to protect the school district from all possible hazards or risks. The cost would be prohibitive and would represent a degree of misuse of public funds. The insurance carried by a district should be determined on a "degree of risk" basis. For example, a school building near an airport represents a different degree of risk than one located in open country not covered by commercial airlines. Again, fire-resistant (sometimes erroneously referred to as fireproof) buildings in open country represent a much different risk from frame construction buildings in the same location. The responsibility of the school board is to protect itself and its clientele as best it can, keeping in mind the cost as compared with the risk involved in each unit insured. Good rules of thumb for the board would be to provide adequate insurance on all high risks, establish priorities and exercise sound judgment on all average risks, and eliminate or minimize insurance on low-risk insurables.

STOCK VERSUS MUTUAL INSURANCE

In planning the insurance program for a school district, there arises the question of the advisability of dealing with mutual companies as compared with stock companies (Table 14-2). A stock company is organized as a corporation that issues capital stock to be purchased by investors. Such stock becomes a guarantee that the company will be able to pay losses even when the premiums paid by insured participants are not large enough to cover them. On the other hand, mutual companies, since they do not issue capital stock, must depend on insurance premiums for the payment of losses.

SELF-INSURANCE

Insurance costs are determined by many factors, including the probability of loss as determined by experience with large numbers of similar risks under similar circumstances. Thus, the danger of loss of several buildings in a school district may be slight, particularly if they are scattered at random within the district. Under such conditions, a very large school district with a large number of buildings and with adequate financial resources may decide to provide

TABLE 14-2 Characteristics of Stock and Mutual Companies

Characteristics	Stock companies	Mutual companies
Capital stock	Issued to investors	Not issued
Ownership	Stockholders	Policyholders
Losses are paid from	Premiums (and when necessary from capital stock)	Premiums (and some companies assess policyholders for this purpose when necessary)
Risk rests primarily with	Stockholders	Policyholders
Profits go to	Stockholders	Policyholders[a]
Insurance rates	Usually higher in order to pay dividends to stockholders	Usually lower; sometimes subject to assessment to cover high losses
Legally available	In all states	In most states— especially if non-assessable

[a]Considered only as a refund of excessive premium charges; sometimes retained by the company to protect against future losses.

"self-insurance" for its buildings and other insurance needs. The board may reason that the risk of loss of one or more buildings is offset by the large sum necessary to pay the insurance premiums over time. It may then proceed in one of three ways: (1) with no insurance—losses to be paid out of tax revenues or from special bond issues; (2) with the provision of insurance only on property with the greatest risk of loss and no insurance on the rest; or (3) with the provision for reserve funds (instead of premium payments), from which future losses will be paid.

The use of self-insurance in protecting schools in the event of insurance loss is obviously controversial. The argument at one extreme is that such a procedure offers no protection whatever; the argument at the other extreme is that some districts could and should insure themselves. Consequently, state law and the judgment of the board of education must provide the answer to whether or not to self-insure.

Self-insurance can be effected in large districts more easily than in small ones. The key for small districts is establishing self-insurance programs by "pooling" with others—locally, regionally, statewide, and perhaps even in multistate contracts. In states where joint power agencies are established, pooling resources and spreading the risk is an option to be considered when insurance rates are prohibitive. Joint power agencies or some other legal mechanism can be established to facilitate pooling resources and sharing risk.

To establish a budget for self-insurance, consider an analysis of the five preceding years. Assume that the claims average $5 per average daily membership (ADM), and an insurance carrier increased rates to $10 per ADM in a time of insurance crisis. A district might place $5 into a self-insurance fund and watch the market carefully for changes. If and when the crisis passes and insurance rates decrease below the $5 average, the district should consider purchasing the coverage and investing the difference in a major protection account.

District personnel should scrutinize the size of the claims the pooling districts have accrued in the preceding five years. If the majority of claims have been small, that provides a good history by which to budget future potential claim dollars. If most have exceeded $50,000, a major protection plan with deductible options might be considered. Self-insurers should maintain the flexibility to have a totally self-insured program, a commercially provided one, or a combination of self-insurance and commercial insurance.

While self-insuring has advantages in insurance crises, it may not be cost-effective in a soft insurance market. Careful monitoring of insurance rates is essential for prudent management of insurance needs.

LIABILITY INSURANCE

With the demise of archaic immunity laws regarding school board liability for tort action in several states, providing liability insurance becomes a relevant consideration. May school funds be legally expended for liability insurance to protect school boards for the torts of its employees in common-law states? The question still produces more than a little controversy, but there is no such paradox in the states that have abrogated that rule. The law and a sense of fairness to pupils require that all those who have a responsibility for pupils' safety, welfare, and education be insured. In the common-law states that adhere to the immunity principle, this means liability insurance on school employees at district expense. To the gradually increasing number of states that have cast aside the immunity rule, by court edict or state statute or both, this means liability insurance on school employees *and* school boards at public expense.

Regardless of whether the law mandates or simply approves school district liability insurance on itself or its employees, school boards have moved to provide whatever liability insurance coverage is necessary to protect all those with legal liability. This is a necessary part of the cost of education—one that experienced boards of education will not refuse to approve.

REGULATION OF INSURANCE

It is necessary that the broad field of insurance be regulated by some agency of government to protect all parties concerned. Without regulation, the cost of insurance could be placed at almost any point at the same time that some companies could default in their insurance payments to the parties who had suffered losses.

Most states control insurance companies through the office of a state commissioner. Through that office, insurance companies are approved to sell insurance if they meet the state rules and regulations that apply. The possibility of deception or fraud is decreased under this form of state regulation. School boards need to become familiar with the general pattern in their state for control of this important service. Among many other benefits to be obtained by the school board from such regulatory procedures, there is the value that comes from obtaining a reliable rating of all insurance companies licensed to operate within the state.

SUMMARY

Every school district is faced with the problem of procuring, storing, and distributing supplies and equipment in the most efficient and economical manner possible. As school budgets are reduced in the face of adverse economic conditions, the need for effective management of fiscal and material resources increases. Regardless of the size of the school district, the chief school administrator is responsible for assuring that maximum benefits are provided by the expenditure of each dollar in every aspect of the school program. The person or persons who supervise and administer the supplies and equipment program of any school district should be capable and well-trained. Even though this operation is secondary to the instructional program, it demands care and wisdom on the part of all those who are responsible for its administration.

Some school districts are finding it advantageous to assign a staff member to a risk management position, a concept that is gaining greater acceptance in the public sector. As a preventive measure, boards of education and principals of local schools should survey the facilities on a systematic basis to be assured that hazardous areas for students and staff do not exist.

As the risks of operating schools increase, the need for evaluating and improving the insurance program increases. It is easy to overinsure or underinsure the property and potential loss and liability from a myriad of causes. In procuring insurance, the school board should be certain that its program is providing coverage at reasonable cost for risks that often exist and that it does not provide high-cost insurance for risks that seldom exist. Regardless of the insurance provided, the program should be under constant evaluation by knowledgeable insurance advisers in order to provide the necessary coverage at minimum cost, using sound risk management principles.

In times of insurance crisis, self-insurance may be the answer. In an inflationary period, school boards may find that a district that was properly insured is now underinsured. Neglecting to carry adequate insurance on school supplies and inventories is a common oversight of many school districts. In very large districts, but not in small ones, self-insurance can sometimes be substituted for a formal insurance program.

ASSIGNMENT PROJECTS

1. Determine the major school district insurance requirements in your state.
2. Interview the school administrator in charge of the insurance program in the district in which you reside to determine the major difficulties involved in obtaining a satisfactory insurance program in the district.
3. Determine the major changes that have taken place in school district insurance needs, particularly in the area of liability for lack of supervision of students, failure of students to learn, tort actions, etc.
4. Develop a rationale for and against self-insurance for a school district.
5. List the arguments for and against state insurance of all school buildings within that state.
6. Determine what approach a local district and the state are using for risk management procedures. Is there evidence that employing a risk manager is fiscally sound?
7. Suggest a plan for the orderly procurement, storage, and distribution of school supplies and equipment for a medium-size school district.

SELECTED READINGS

Campbell, Roald F., Luvern L. Cunningham, Raphael O. Nystrand, and Michael D. Usdan. *The Organization and Control of American Schools.* 6th ed. Columbus, Ohio: Merrill, 1990.

Hadden, Susan G. *Risk Analysis, Instructions and Public Policy.* Port Washington, N.Y.: Associated Faculty Press, 1984.

Mehr, R. I., and E. Cammack. *Principles of Insurance.* 7th ed. Homewood, Ill.: Richard D. Irwin, 1980.

Rejda, George E. *Principles of Insurance.* Glenview, Ill.: Scott, Foresman, 1986.

Schael, L. D., and C. W. Haley. *Introduction to Financial Management.* 2nd ed. New York: McGraw-Hill, 1980.

Webb, L. Dean, and Van D. Mueller. *Managing Limited Resources: New Demands on Public School Management. Fifth Annual Yearbook of the American Education Finance Association.* Cambridge, Mass.: Ballinger, 1984.

Williams, C. Arthur, Jr., and Richard M. Heins. *Risk Management and Insurance.* 5th ed. New York: McGraw-Hill, 1985.

ENDNOTES

1. Stephen J. Knezevich and John Guy Fowlkes, *Business Management of Local School Systems* (New York: Harper & Row, 1960), p. 4.

2. Ibid., p. 14.

3. H. Ronald Smith, "From Your President: Business Administrators Play on Education Team, Too—School Business Affairs," *Professional Journal of the Association of School Business Officials,* June 1986, p. 6.

4. Frederick Hill, as quoted by Smith, "From Your President."

5. Charles T. Roberts and Allan R. Lichtenberger, *Financial Accounting* (Washington, D.C.: U.S. Department of Health, Education, and Welfare, 1973), pp. 93, 108.

6. Joyce E. Ferguson, "The Purchasing Administrator," *School Business Affairs,* August 1985, pp. 20–22.

7. Rita T. Constantino, "School Boards Need to Know This . . . ," *Public Risk,* July/August 1990, p. 7.

8. Ibid.

9. Daniel J. Cullen, "Risk Management Holistically Speaking," *Public Risk,* September/October 1991, p. 7

10. W. Taud and Hoopingarner, "Carving a Niche," *Public Risk,* September/October 1991, p. 8.

11. Mary Lou Emmert, "90's Trend to Continue," *Public Risk,* September/October 1991, p. 5.

12. "Risk Management for School Principals," Utah School Boards Association, Utah State Office of Risk Management, 1991 unpublished, Section 4, p. 1.

13. Rita T. Constantino, "School Boards Need to Know This . . . ," *Public Risk*, July/August 1990, p. 8.

14. "Sorry, Your Policy is Cancelled," *Time,* March 24, 1986, p. 23.

Chapter 15

Personnel Administration and School Finance

Boards and superintendents can get the most out of the limited funds they are allotted by addressing the largest price of their budget: personnel.
—NATHAN CHESLER, 1991

In industry and other fields the term *personnel* refers to those employed in a particular undertaking, but the educational field has adapted it to include all the people in a school—the staff and also the students. Thus, education refers to "employed personnel" and "student personnel."

This chapter is concerned only with the administration of the services of school-employed personnel. It deals largely with the effect salary schedules and fringe benefits have on the rising costs of education. It is not particularly concerned with the methods used to determine those costs. The importance of negotiations and collective bargaining in setting salaries, wages, and fringe benefits is recognized but is not discussed here, because it is not relevant to the subject at hand. It matters little to the administrator of a school district budget whether a particular percent of salary increase or the cost of a certain fringe benefit occurred as a result of negotiation, because of the work of a teacher salary committee, or by any other process.

PROBLEMS IN SCHOOL PERSONNEL ADMINISTRATION

Many difficult problems face the administrator and the board of education in the administration of personnel services; most of them are directly concerned with the expenditure of money. (1) The best possible salary schedule in terms of teacher and other staff requirements, as well as the funds that are available, must be determined. This problem involves determining the size of the beginning salary as compared with the maximum, the number and size of increments in each classification, and evaluation of experience in other districts. (2) Administrators must determine what other factors should be used to place teachers on the salary schedule, such as merit pay, career ladders, and extra pay for extra service. (3) The policies and procedures to be followed in moving from one salary schedule to another must be set.

Since 75 to 80 percent of the expenditure for public education is usually spent in providing financial rewards for the services of school personnel, the subject of personnel administration is of prime importance in any study of financing education. No school can attain its goals unless it has a corps of competent teachers and other staff members. At the same time, no school can attract and keep the qualified personnel so necessary for its purposes unless sufficient funds are available to provide adequate salaries and fringe benefits.

Perennial Nature

Some of the problems involved in personnel administration are of long standing, and their "solutions" have often been found each year in some measure of socioeconomic crisis. The perennial problems of salary increases and the determination of the extent and nature of fringe benefits have resulted in increasing confrontation between teachers and local boards of education.

Personnel administration in the public schools has lagged behind the policies and practices that business and industry generally use. Satisfactory personnel policies, including recognition of the worth and contribution of school personnel to the social as well as the economic well-being of the community, have been minimal or even nonexistent in many public school systems. Although business and industry have recognized for a long time that their success largely depends on qualified and satisfied employees, many schools have not shown evidence of realizing this relation.

The success of any endeavor that involves human beings, whether it be business, industry, or education, is determined by the quality of the people who perform the tasks needed to achieve the mission and purposes of the organization. The extent to which the educational enterprise is successful depends primarily on the personnel engaged therein, the conditions in which they work, and the efficiency and effectiveness with which they discharge individual and group responsibilities. Funding is essential, the nature of the program significant, and leadership imperative, but the effort of the people responsible for the growth and development of the children in the schools is paramount.

Changing Personnel Relations

Recent years have seen extensive and dramatic changes in school personnel administration. Educators, long known for their complacency and subordination to the will of school boards and the general public, have risen to assert themselves. No longer content to accept willingly what school boards offer as compensation for services, teachers and their professional organizations are demanding a larger part of the tax dollar in higher salaries, better working conditions, and increased fringe benefits.

It requires no figures and very little imagination to predict that professional negotiations by teachers will result in higher salaries, greater fringe benefits, and even better working conditions for them. There is no desire here to enter into debates concerning their need or justification. Neither is there any disposition to contest or to defend the apparently changing ethics of the teaching profession. The perspective herein is simply stated: "Using . . . collective bargaining . . . organized teachers have secured contractual gains . . . that . . . increase the cost of education."[1]

Expanding Role of Personnel Administration

As the school complex has expanded in size, the need for improving school personnel services has also increased. Likewise, as the number of teachers in a school or community has increased, the voice of the profession has been magnified. School boards continue to face concerns related to the selection and recruitment, orientation, assignment, and payment of instructional and other personnel; to these have been added the relatively new concerns involving professional negotiations and all their ramifications. The calmness and matter-of-factness that characterized school personnel administration to the middle of the century have been replaced by uncertainty and seriousness that borders on confrontation between school boards and teachers.

Castetter referred to six factors that justify the expanding role of personnel administration in the public schools:

- To be effective, organizations must continually adapt to current internal and external conditions.
- The paramount rationale for establishment and continuation of organizations of all types is that their *purposes* can be achieved only through the *unified efforts of people.*
- Goal-directed behavior of personnel can be influenced positively by human-centered approaches to managing systems designed to educate children and youth.
- Human resource planning is a major component of total organizational planning.
- Designing ways to strengthen relationships between organizational purposes and the behavior of its members is an omnipresent task of management.
- The personnel (or human resources) function has evolved into a *premier* force for enhancing a school system's capability to improve its effectiveness and efficiency.[2]

TEACHER SALARIES

One of the central tasks of educational administration is to allocate funds, facilities, personnel, and information in such a way that the improvement in educational achievement between entering and leaving students is maximized. To that end, the general purpose of the compensation process is to allocate resources for salaries, wages, benefits, and rewards in a manner that will attract and retain a school staff.[3]

Since the chief function of the school is to provide those who attend with human services in the form of high-quality academic instruction, the biggest cost of public education is salaries to instructional personnel. Thus, the problems of school finance are directly related to the problems encountered in personnel administration.

Providing increases in teacher salaries and satisfactory fringe benefits is not a new problem to the field of school administration. Teachers have been among the last of the occupational groups to obtain financial compensation commensurate with their training and experience. Salary increases and generally improving fiscal policies of the last few years have, however, brought some hope for a satisfactory outcome.

Salary Schedules

Salary schedules for teachers are a product of the second quarter of this century. Only a few of the progressive city school systems were using such schedules to any great extent prior to the 1920s. The bargaining policies involving higher salaries for high school teachers than for elementary teachers with the same qualifications, and many other now outmoded practices, preceded the formal salary schedule.

As salary schedules developed, they gradually became the single-salary variety (equal pay for personnel with the same qualifications and experience, without regard to sex, grade level to be taught, number of dependents, or other previously used factors). Experiments with merit pay and dependency provisions in salary schedules seldom satisfied the teachers involved, the school boards, or the general public. At the same time, defense of the single-salary schedule became no easier. Mere passage of time, without evidence of teacher improvement, has always been difficult to defend as the sole criterion for salary increases.

Merit Provisions in Salary Schedules

Merit pay has received attention nationwide because of the call for educational reform and more accountability. Legislators, reflecting the attitude of the public, are expressing the opinion that salaries for teachers and administrators should be based on performance. Some career ladder programs have attempted to meet the criticism by tying performance to increased compensation.

The arguments have changed little in the last half-century; the salaries of teachers should be determined by merit or the contribution teachers make to the education of boys and girls. Some say, however, that such merit cannot be measured objectively. As Shannon states:

> Merit pay continues to bask in the spotlight of political initiatives intended to advance education excellence and reform across the U.S. School policy-makers—sensitive to this burgeoning political reality at the local, state, and federal levels—are mulling possible ways merit pay can be made to work and be made attractive to teachers.
>
> School board members know the main stumbling block to installing merit pay for teachers is trust—or, more specifically, teachers' *lack* of trust that their school administrators will implement such a plan fairly. . . . [4]

Consequently, the subject is under constant review.

Extra Duty Salary Supplements

The practice of adding salary supplements for additional services of teachers is becoming common. It began with small stipends for coaching some of the major sports, football and basketball in particular. The original rationale centered around the many extra out-of-school hours required in many athletic programs. From that beginning, the practice has spread to many other fields of activity. There are at least three significant objections to this practice. (1) It often creates problems between those who receive such supplements and those who do not. (2) It is difficult to find a teaching area in which supplements could not be justified if the teacher is making a maximum effort to develop it. (3) The practice tends to erase some of the characteristics that education must possess if it is to be a real profession; teachers under this system tend to think in terms of the time required to perform a particular function rather than in terms of units or elements of service.

Salary supplements for extra duties represent one means of avoiding the evils of the lockstep single-salary schedule. Justified or not, the practice represents an attempt to determine salaries on the basis of services rendered. Its deficiencies come from the fact that it is generally a quantity rather than a quality measurement.

Salary Scheduling Problems

The teacher is a public employee and as such suffers from the fact that salaries paid out of public funds are usually not competitive with those paid in the private sector, where the profit motive prevails. Government employees at all levels are victims of the same unwritten law of economics. The salaries paid in the public sector are controlled by boards of education that are sworn to protect the public treasury; in the private sector the individual operator or the board of directors of a business is free to pay whatever is required in the competitive complex in which they operate. Also, the latter can usually measure quite objectively the amount of production of the worker, but the controlling board of education has real difficulty in measuring the increased production of services resulting from the work of higher-paid teachers.

Salary schedules, regardless of their base or structure, must be minimal in nature. Even the poorest teacher, the teacher with the fewest dependents, or the teacher most lacking training or experience must be paid an adequate salary if his or her services are engaged. Provisions for extra pay for extra service, merit pay, career ladder, or any other special consideration must be additions to this minimum schedule.

TRENDS IN SALARY SCHEDULING

The business of salary scheduling is not static, for innovations are constantly being introduced into the process. Such additions and improvements usually add to the increasing costs of education but decrease the unfairness and inequities that have so often characterized salary schedules in the past. Some of the most important trends in salary scheduling include:

1. Retention of the single-salary schedule as a minimum or base scale, with virtual elimination of individual bargaining for salary purposes.

2. Serious consideration given to salaries based on measures of teacher effectiveness, such as career ladder or merit pay programs.

3. Greater emphasis on and wider acceptance of index salary schedules that will facilitate the salary determination for a differentiated staff and at the same time give more favorable salary consideration to career teachers at or near the top of the salary scale.

4. More attention to salary supplements for the extra services rendered by some teachers—particularly in supervision of extra class activities; this seems likely to lead to continuing controversy.

5. More recognition of the cost-of-living factor in determining salaries at all levels, with greater concern for the demands of teachers for generally higher salaries.

6. More attention to the benefits to be derived from longer-term contracts for those teachers who desire them; 10-, 11-, or 12-month contracts will likely be offered to many more of the instructional staff than at present.

7. Increased annual salary increments at all levels, with various increments to reach the maximum salary in most catagories.

8. Salary schedules that will continue to be written in such a way as to encourage additional academic and professional education for teachers.

9. More progress in adopting salary schedules by which the career teacher will be able to double a beginning salary in about ten or twelve years.

FRINGE BENEFITS

School districts were generally slow in accepting the functional value of fringe benefits to teachers and other school employees. Business and industry led the way in inaugurating such benefits as retirement plans, tenure, sick-leave privileges, and insurance benefits. For the most part, these are benefits that have entered the educational scene in the last half-century, most of them since World War II, which acted as a catalyst for fringe benefits. Because wages were frozen during the war, benefits were used to compensate workers. In today's competitive market, fringe benefits have become an important part of the reward system of publicly as well as privately employed personnel (Table 15-1).

Some of the important aspects of these fringe benefits as they apply to education are the following:

1. School boards, like private employers, have discovered that fringe benefits rank next to attractive salaries and good working conditions as motivators of efficiency and maximum productivity.

2. Fringe benefits serve a double purpose. (1) They provide needed personal benefits that teachers often would not provide for themselves. (2) They do not involve the increases in income taxes that would accompany payment for the same benefits by the teachers themselves from increased salaries.

3. Fringe benefits help to increase job satisfaction and thus reduce disruptive changes resulting from faculty resignations and consequent replacements.

4. Some of the matching employer costs of retirement, insurance, and other fringe benefits are now being absorbed as state rather than district expenditures, thus making such benefits available to the personnel of financially weak districts as well as all others.

The costs of fringe benefits are increasing significantly. They have reached such proportions that in some states and school districts salary increases are limited in order to pay the various benefits. Social Security contributions, as of Fall 1991, were 15.3% of salary (7.65 percent by employer, 7.65 percent by employee). Leave benefits are becoming more expensive and costs for medical insurance have skyrocketed. Estimates for fringe benefit costs to districts can range from 35 to 40 percent of salaries.

TEACHERS AND SCHOOL FINANCE

It is no secret that teachers as a group have not been particularly concerned or informed about the rudiments of school finance. Stories of teacher naiveté in this field have seldom been exaggerated or magnified. A few teachers received their initiation to the subject when their local or state professional organizations

TABLE 15-1   A Summary of Fringe Benefits

Program	Frequency	General provisions
Retirement	In every state	A guaranteed amount (depending on length of service and contributions) on retirement; disability and death benefits; some programs include withdrawal privileges (with interest) of employee contribution for those who leave the system before retirement; some plans provide for investments in stocks and mutual funds that will offset any losses due to inflation.
Social Security	Nationwide	Joint contributions; members pay part and the state pays part; available to certified and usually to full-time noncertified employees. Federal program, which supplements state retirement; survivor benefits for on-the-job workers; death benefits; guaranteed monthly income on retirement if 62 or over; employee takes benefits with him as he moves from one state to another.
Sick leave	In nearly all districts	Full salary while employee is ill—up to a stipulated number of days, which are usually cumulative to some established maximum number. Required in some states; some districts pay teachers for unused sick leave days accumulated; may not be available to noncertified employees.
Personal leaves	In many districts	For emergencies other than illness; usually not more than 1 to 5 days per year; the circumstances of each request are usually considered on their own merits, rather than according to a universal policy; not usually available to noncertificated personnel.
Leaves of absence	Becoming more widely accepted	Usually provides for extended leaves without salary for study or professional improvement, disability, political activity, travel, or maternity reasons. Some districts provide some compensation for sabbatical or improvement leaves for certificated employees; seldom available to noncertificated personnel.
Bereavement leave	In some districts	When a close relative dies, days are allowed to attend the funeral, arrange affairs, and travel distances.
Insurance	Widespread	Employer provides benefits without increasing employee's salary, thereby savings the income tax due; usually provides

(Continued)

TABLE 15-1 (*Continued*)

Program	Frequency	General provisions
		group insurance: health and accident, hospitalization, dental, long-term disability, and life. Many districts now provide liability insurance for tort action on all school employees.
Workman's compensation	Nationwide	Provides various options of benefits for injury and disability of all school employees; usually required by the states as protection for the risks of employment; mandatory in some states, optional in some, and not available in one or two others.
Tax shelters	Nationwide	Federally granted privilege to public school teachers to invest part of their earnings in an annuity payable at a later time; delays federal income tax on these earnings until the benefits are received; since the retired teacher will probably be in a lower tax bracket, there will be tax savings. Some other flexible tax benefits available.
Severance pay	In very few districts	Employee usually gets the value of his or her unused sick leave and other unused leave pay; a very recent and infrequently used fringe benefit; not usually available to noncertificated personnel.
Income tax deductions	Nationwide	Provides income tax deductions (federal) for certain necessary and approved expenses of public school teachers while studying and otherwise improving their professional training required for retaining their present position of employment, as required by the school district or the state; not available for the purpose of position advancement.

appointed them to teacher-salary committees, but the problem of financing education was of little interest to most classroom teachers.

The pendulum is slowly beginning to swing in the opposite direction. By choice, teachers are insisting on a stronger voice in decision making, particularly as it affects reward for service. Increased salaries, more substantial fringe benefits, and better working conditions have accompanied the discovery of muscle resulting from collective bargaining, professional negotiations, and other techniques. The teaching profession appears to be surprised and uncertain about the responsibilities accompanying such power.

Salaries and other benefits are not spontaneously generated. They must come from somewhere, and the normal budgets of most school systems are already overburdened. Teachers, who formerly viewed the fiscal affairs of schools as a foreign language to be learned only by administrators and boards of education, now find themselves among those who have an interest in seeking additional sources of school revenue. Further progress in providing for the still-rising costs of education is virtually impossible without the united efforts and sympathetic understanding of all large segments of United States society, including the vast numbers of professional teachers who stand to receive important benefits in future years.

Only recently has the typical teacher begun to realize the potential benefits of understanding and skill in the field of school finance. Also, state legislative bodies have recently deemed it necessary to turn to the profession for assistance in finding new sources of revenue for schools. Only informed and interested people can respond successfully to this new challenge.

Thus, it seems that present-day personnel administration has reached the point where teachers must develop some acumen in school finance if the objective of teacher rights and participation is to be more than a mere platitude. Teachers, teacher organizations, and administrators face the task of providing the means and the motivation to raise the level of teacher knowledge so as to help find valid answers to the problems of financing education.

A number of avenues are open for fulfilling this need: required courses in the basics of school finance, in-service training projects, workshops, civic study groups, practical assignments to the members of negotiating teams, and many others. Teachers must understand that their participation in negotiations and salary disputes gives them a duty to understand the implications and the problems of higher salaries and benefits. They are citizens, too. Just as it is impossible for school boards to draw additional dollars out of depleted budgets, so it is impossible for an uninformed group to arrive at consensus on teacher salary demands. A beginning point can be established if the teachers themselves, particularly the career-directed ones, assume responsibility for learning the ABCs of school finance.

THE CHANGING ASSIGNMENTS OF TEACHERS

In recent years, innovations of various kinds have changed the traditional pattern of teacher assignments. Computer instruction, flexible scheduling, large-group instruction, team teaching, closed circuit television, individualized and continuous-progress instruction, and similar programs have accelerated the differentiation of staff assignments. The improved use of qualified teaching personnel, with emphasis on specialization and expertise in instructional techniques, has necessitated greater intensity of training, with concomitant increases in salaries. Many of the chores that have hitherto fallen to the teacher can now be assigned to aides, clerks, or less well-prepared teachers, and the more difficult and technical aspects of education left to the well-trained and experienced professional teacher.

The Impact of Technology

Today's teacher finds many kinds of instructional aids available. In addition to relief from the clerical aspects of the business, mechanical aids and devices enrich the program and minimize its monotony. Projection machines, video recording equipment, educational television, automatic data processing equipment, and the like are no longer looked on as threats to the job security of the teacher. Rather, they are accepted for what they are—potential supplements to upgrade and reinforce the instructional program. Audiovisual materials are no longer considered luxuries for the most affluent school districts; they are now part of the ongoing instructional program in every progressive school.

It is hard to generalize about the implications of widespread adoption of educational technology, but the use of computers as a learning resource is certainly increasing:

> [O]ne-fourth of all American workers have a microcomputer sitting on their desks. . . . [T]here is a general purpose microcomputer in more than one-fourth of all American homes. More then half of the purchasers indicate that the equipment is purchased for work-related purposes, and nearly half indicate that it is to help educate their children. The total number of micro-computers in American homes is 10 times the number used for instructional purposes in schools. American business and industry will install nearly twice as many microcomputers for its own use in 1991 as the total number of microcomputers currently being used in our schools.[5]

Moursund indicates that further evidence of the technological revolution has a great influence on school district budgets:

> A computer is a tool designed to aid knowledge workers, and every student is a knowledge worker. Eventually our schools should provide every student with easy and routine access to computer related technology, both as an aid to learning and as an aid to solving a wide range of problems. Every school and school district should have a long-range plan for accomplishing this task. This plan should be developed by the combined efforts of all key stakeholders—parents, teachers, school administrators, local business people, and so on.[6]

In their centennial issue, *Instructor* states:

> [N]ow a school isn't complete without a network of microcomputers and printers. With videodisc and CD-ROM technology you can access specific

video images or information immediately to support something you're teaching. Modems have broadened schools' computer use allowing access to information from thousands of other sources, as well as making it possible for schools to communicate with each other via the telephone and computer.[7]

Teacher Turnover

Retention of teaching personnel in public school work has always been a big problem. Large classes, relatively low salaries, lack of socioeconomic status, apathy of students, and little opportunity for advancement have combined to discourage many teachers and cause them to leave the profession. School districts have tried to stop this loss with greater rewards for service, employment of aides and teaching assistants, better leave policies, smaller classes and lighter work loads, and other such benefits, but high teacher turnover persists. Teachers are among the most mobile of all professional workers. They tend to change positions often, always seeking but seemingly never finding the kinds of positions that they are willing to call permanent.

What are the ramifications of the problems of assignment and retention of teacher personnel from the financial point of view? What will be the net cost of paying higher salaries for the best professional teachers and lower salaries for various grades of assistants? What will be the fiscal result of the use of the vast array of automatic data processing machines and devices that are now becoming part of the instructional program? What is the dollar effect of the extensive recruitment and in-service programs necessary to replace the large numbers of dissatisfied and itinerant teachers? The answers to these and related questions are of great concern in considering the problems of financing the schools of the future.

ADMINISTRATIVE AND SUPERVISORY SALARIES

Much of the information already discussed concerning teacher salaries, schedules, and fringe benefits applies equally well to administrative and supervisory staff members. Professionally, all certified personnel have much the same kinds of problems. Certainly they are all striving for the same goal—the education of boys and girls. There are some differences in how rewards for services are determined for administrative and supervisory personnel, however. The main ones are:

1. The salary of the chief administrator, the superintendent of schools, is most often decided by bargaining, ostensibly on the basis of training and past record; the extent of competition for the position may also have something to do with the salary offered to the successful candidate.

2. Salaries of the administrative and supervisory staff do not fit the teacher salary schedule. Such employees receive higher salaries, for several reasons:

(1) their certification requirements are higher; (2) their positions require knowledge and skills in more fields; (3) they have responsibility for the actions of more people; and (4) they serve for a longer period of time each year (eleven or twelve months, compared to nine or ten for teachers).

3. In the minority of school districts in which administrative and supervisory salaries are related directly to teacher salaries, there are two common ways of determining them: (1) on the basis of a stipulated number of dollars above the salary for teachers with the same training and experience; or (2) on the basis of a predetermined ratio involving such salaries.

4. Some districts determine the salaries on the basis of the teacher salary schedule plus additional amounts per teacher or per pupil, or both, in the school.

5. Administrative and supervisory positions generally lack tenure and do not provide stated annual increments for service. Local school boards, particularly in rural communities, tend to hold such salaries down for at least two reasons: (1) they may not be fully aware of the special training required or the contribution that these staff members make to the educational program; and (2) many board members have never had direct experience of their own with incomes of the size of those of administrative and supervisory employees; they tend to establish salaries having some relation to their own degree of affluence.

NONCERTIFICATED PERSONNEL SALARIES

Over the years, school administrators and boards of education have emphasized the importance of developing attractive salary schedules and providing good working conditions for certificated personnel, but they have often neglected similar conditions for noncertificated employees. The principal reason seems to be that since the purpose of the school is to provide instruction, and almost 80 percent of the current expenditures budget goes for instructional and administrative salaries, this is where emphasis should be placed. Then, too, the qualifications of noncertificated personnel vary greatly.

An important difference is that all instructional or certificated personnel serve under contract for one or more years—service that usually results in tenure after a probationary period. No such arrangement exists for most noncertificated employees. They tend to serve "at the pleasure of the board," with no written contract and no guarantee of salary increments based only on the passage of time. Resignations and replacements are commonplace, and they do not usually involve serious questions of ethics for either the school board or the employees.

Fortunately, the conditions in this area of personnel administration are improving. Large school districts, with their need for many such employees, increased job requirements, the unionization of nearly all of these workers, and the gradual abdication of school boards from nominating power for all school employees are some of the most important reasons for improved conditions in the employment, utilization, and retention of noncertificated personnel. These factors, along with inflation and higher taxes, have forced school districts to raise salaries to a much higher level, thereby adding still another large increase to the costs of public education.

PAYROLL POLICIES AND PROCEDURES

The largest single classification of current expenditures involves payment of salaries to employees. All but one or two of the principal expenditure accounts in a school district's accounting system include provisions for the payment of salaries to employees. Only fixed charges and student-body activities would ordinarily not include salaries for personnel and under some circumstances even these may have salary money chargeable to them. Collectively, more than 80 percent of the current expenditures of a typical school district are for salaries of employees.

The size and importance of a school's payroll dictates that sound principles and procedures of payroll accounting be followed. Most of these would apply to all payroll accounting, but there are some differences. Generally accepted policies and procedures to be followed include the following as a minimum:

1. Arrangements should be made and businesslike procedures followed to guarantee payment of salaries at a specified, regular, and acceptable time. No excuses are acceptable to employees when a payroll division is unreliable and uncertain in delivering salary payments. Only emergency factors beyond the control of the business office can be justified as legitimate reasons for delay or inconvenience in paying salaries.

2. Receiving the salary payment should be made as convenient as possible to the employee. The onus for delivery should rest with the school district's business office, regardless of its size, not with the individual payee. The days of requiring school employees to go in person to the school board office or the clerk's home to receive a salary check, or just to wait for the convenience of the payroll division, are only a dim memory in most districts. Even when the district is temporarily short of funds, there is provision in the law for short-term borrowing on tax anticipation notes so that a school district may operate on a businesslike basis, just as any other institution is required to do.

3. All school employees should possess written copies of rules and policies concerning payroll procedures. The rules and policies should have been established by joint suggestion and approval of representatives of the employed personnel of the district, working with representatives of the board of education. Among other things, each school employee should have easy access to the following:

a. A current salary schedule, with full explanation of increments and special provisions, if any.

b. A statement of policy related to payroll procedures as they apply to the teacher on sick leave or on leave for other reasons. The policy should state how the teacher's salary is affected when a substitute is employed and any other conditions that are directly related to leave privileges.

c. A written explanation of how all deductions required by law are calculated—federal withholding taxes, state withholding taxes, social security, and others. The employee should be able to determine whether the amounts for such deductions are correct.

d. A statement of policy concerning willingness of the district (and the conditions to be met) to withhold other deductions at the request of a school employee or a professional organization—membership dues in professional organizations, individual or group insurance premiums, and others.

e. An explanation of the options available to school employees as they relate to payroll dates for 9-month, 10-month, or yearly contracts. It is particularly important to clarify the school's policy concerning options that teachers on 9-month contracts may have concerning the summer salary payments.

f. A statement in writing concerning the procedure to be followed by an employee in the event of salary dispute or misunderstanding.

4. A well-understood procedure should be followed in reporting to the payroll division relevant information on all individual employees before the regular paying period—days of sick leave, other leave, salary changes, and dates of beginning and ending employment in the case of employees not under contract.

SUMMARY

Since the salaries and benefits provided for school personnel require nearly 80 percent of the average school's revenues, it is obvious that personnel administration is a very important aspect of public school finance. The rapid rise of negotiations with teacher organizations and unions has helped make teacher salaries more competitive with salaries in the private sector.

The extension of state- and district-financed fringe benefits for school personnel in the last half-century has done much to increase the job satisfaction of teachers. School districts must continue to provide such benefits and do what they can to keep the cost of such benefits manageable.

Teachers as well as school patrons would do well to become better acquainted with the problems states and school districts face in financing an adequate and equitable school program. When solving the difficult problem of procuring adequate funds and spending them wisely to provide the best possible education, there is no substitute for an informed public. Along with the numerous other groups that comprise society, teachers should provide enlightened understanding in this matter. The time when school finance problems were legitimately the responsibility of one or two small segments of society has long since passed.

ASSIGNMENT PROJECTS

1. Summarize the fringe benefits that are provided for school personnel in your school district. Determine their cost to the district as a percent of the total salaries paid to teachers.

2. Analyze the personnel administrative procedures in your school district and make recommendations to improve present practices.

3. Secure teacher salary schedules from several school districts in your state and compare their similarities and differences.

4. From the literature, determine current trends regarding merit pay for teachers and list the arguments for and against establishing such a practice in a district.

5. Interview several teachers at a local high school and determine their opinions concerning extra pay for supplemental duties.

6. Determine how administrative, supervisory, and classified personnel salaries are ascertained in your district and in surrounding districts.

7. Prepare a defense for the argument that teachers are overpaid because they only work nine months, have all major holidays off, including two weeks at Christmas, and only work from 8:00 A.M. to 3:00 P.M.

8. Research various career ladder proposals in the states and relate these plans to the salaries, benefits, status, and professionalism of teaching as a career.

SELECTED READINGS

Campbell, Roald F., Luvern L. Cunningham, Raphael O. Nystrand, and Michael D. Usdan. *The Organization and Control of American Schools*. 6th ed. Columbus, Ohio: Merrill, 1990.

Castetter, William B. *The Personnel Function in Educational Administration*. 3rd ed. New York: Macmillan, 1981.

Flippo, Edwin B. *Personnel Management*, 6th ed. New York: McGraw-Hill, 1984.

Rothwell, William H., and H. C. Kazanas. *Strategic Human Resources Planning and Management*. Englewood Cliffs, N.J.: Prentice Hall, 1988.

Taylor, Susan. *Public Employee Retirement Systems: The Structure and Politics of Teacher Pensions*. Ithaca, N.Y.: New York State School of Industrial and Labor Relations, Cornell University, 1986.

ENDNOTES

1. William B. Castetter, *The Personnel Function in Educational Administration*, 4th ed. (New York: Macmillan, 1986), pp. 137, 638.

2. Ibid., p. 5.

3. Ibid., p. 427.

4. Thomas A. Shannon, "Understand the Promise and Pitfalls of a School Merit Pay Commission," *The American School Board Journal*, November 1985, pp. 33–34.

5. Dave Moursund, "Editor's Message," *The Computing Teacher*, February 1991, p. 6.

6. Ibid.

7. "1981–1991," *Instructor*, January 1991, p. 61.

Chapter 16

The Road Ahead in School Finance

It is perhaps time to begin a new chapter and attempt to record the movements of the day for all posterity—to determine how the present drive for excellence encompasses the hopes and dreams of the crusaders against an ignorance which manifests itself in unequal opportunity, in dashed hopes, in wasted lives, and in careless disregard for our most valuable resource: children. In this vein we might exclaim, march onward crusaders! For we have, as poet Robert Frost observed, "miles to go before we sleep . . . miles to go before we sleep."
— *DEBORAH A. VERSTEGEN, 1992*

The achievement of equitable and adequate financing of education is a never-ending quest. Further progress is especially needed in the reformation of school finance systems. The basic finance patterns that undergird the public school systems in the states are a combination of historic procedures, products of the post-*Serrano* movement of the 1970s, the call for educational reforms in the 1980s with the ensuing struggle to fund them, and the revisiting of the equity issue in court cases in the 1990s. "Every man has himself to conquer," and each decade of school finance likewise presents its own problems for educators to solve in order to fund education properly in a climate of constant change. Even now, after extensive revision and improvement, some state finance programs are not consistent with prevailing educational finance theory. In addition, several economic and political factions are making funding even more complex. Some theorists call for more liberal (in the political sense) procedures, and others recommend more conservative approaches. Some propose further support for nonpublic schools; others challenge the validity of such support. Since *Mueller* v. *Allen* (1983) allowed payment of educational expenses (including tuition) as a state income tax deduction, disputation over private education remains unremitting. Minnesota also instituted a modified voucher plan, allowing eleventh and twelfth graders to use a voucher to attend a public or private university and broadened the concept to allow high school students to attend parochial schools through contracts with local districts. Colorado legislated a "second chance voucher," which allowed underachieving high school students a voucher to attend the school that would best meet their needs.

The courts and legislatures have been active; most of the state school finance systems challenged in the courts were declared constitutional or acceptable, but some have been pronounced unconstitutional. Significant cases in point include *Helena* in Montana (1989), *Rose* in Kentucky (1989), *Edgewood* in Texas (1989), *Abbott* in New Jersey (1990), and *The Coalition* in Oregon (1991). The current trend appears to be toward greater state support in financing education.

In some states obsolete and unfair methods of obtaining and allocating funds still discriminate against poorer school districts, and the revenues of some systems are still inadequate or inequitably distributed. The effect of Proposition 13 in California, Proposition $2^{1}/_{2}$ in Massachusetts, and similar initiatives in other states still linger and dim the prospects of adequately funding education.

Many scholars call for complicated funding formulas that confuse state legislators. Other scholars call for nearly full state funding, saying that education is a state responsibility and that financial support should come from that source but that local control should be maintained. A relatively uncomplicated approach utilizes local property taxes as the basis of a minimum support program that requires all taxpayers throughout the state to be assessed a uniform levy. Whatever amount the local tax does not raise toward the minimum is supplemented by the state through other tax revenues. Money allocated on a weighted-pupil formula adds to the equity of the program. Local initiative is provided by allowing some reasonable board or locally voted leeway.

There has been extensive progress in recent years in providing more equitable financing of education for children in the United States. Local property taxation, state nonequalizing grants, equalization programs with greater state participation and responsibility, district power equalization programs, lotteries, and funding education reform have provided progress in school finance that has been little short of phenomenal. During the history of the United States, state after state has moved from high-cost and largely private school education for a few to free and reasonably equitable public education for all its citizens, with reasonably equitable burdens for its taxpayers. This has been done for the most part without destroying the tradition of local control. People have been able to retain at least limited responsibility and control over the institutions that bring education to their children.

In the wake of *Serrano* v. *Priest* (1971), equity for school children and equity for taxpayers became goals to which scores of states and millions of people gave much more than lip service. The principles of school finance for which such educational leaders as Cubberley, Mort, and Fowlkes had fought now seemed realizable. These goals appeared to be within reach if sought with enthusiasm and persistence. A long list of states enacted noteworthy school finance reforms very quickly after the decision in *Serrano*. As early as 1973, Florida, Utah, Kansas, California, Maine, and Minnesota had enacted major school finance reform legislation. Full state funding, district power equalization, weighted-pupil units, and other improvements appeared in legislative enactments—all to the benefit of the school-age population involved.

With the Supreme Court's decision in *San Antonio School District* v. *Rodriguez* (1973), equalization efforts slowed, but the need for reform in school finance plans was still apparent. Many states continued to revamp their finance laws and policies to reflect the contemporary needs of school districts. Groups of interested and knowledgeable citizens outside the realm of professional education began to apply their skills and their prejudices to improving the financing of education. The educators, particularly school administrators, who have traditionally been the guardians of school finance systems and their manipulation and improvement, now feel their influence diluted by the emergence of outside groups of lawyers, economists, political scientists, and legislators. Each group sees the problem and its solution from a different perspective. Consequently, compromises are the order of the day, and no one group can dictate the direction of change. The important point, however, is that extensive improvements have been made and greater progress is envisioned for the near future. Certainly, at no other time in United States history have so many divergent groups worked with such enthusiasm, tenacity, and apparent success to improve the quality of the educational financing system of the various states.

The federal government's role has vacillated between nearly dissolving the Department of Education and embracing the "A Nation at Risk" report that made education the number one priority in many states. The percentage of federal dollars supporting education has decreased. The overwhelming national debt, which tripled from $.9 trillion to $3 trillion by 1991, and to which was added $269 billion at the beginning of fiscal year 1992, has caused some to call for reduced government spending. Yet advocates of more federal support for education, including some of the pioneers of the reform movements of the 1980s, stress that it is time for the federal government to become more involved in financing educational programs that have national significance. World events play a role in federal involvement with education. With the collapse of the Communist regimes in Eastern Europe, and changes in the Soviet Union, some advocate a "peace bonus," which could shift resources from defense to education. That effort was tempered by Desert Shield and Desert Storm, which certain people used to articulate that defense was still essential in a troubled world.

THE UNPREDICTABLE FUTURE OF PUBLIC SCHOOL FINANCE

The future of school finance programs is not predictable. Before projections can be made with any degree of certainty, numerous philosophical questions must be answered in light of current conditions. In view of the retrenchment of federal programs, how will the states make up for the loss in federal monies? Will states cut back educational programs in the face of diminishing revenues, or will they find ways of providing adequate funds to sustain their current programs at desirable or optimum levels? Who should be educated at public expense? To what grade level should free education be provided? What should be the responsibility of each of the three levels of government to provide funds for public education? Should the states continue to increase their share of the revenue mix even if it results in loss of local control of education? Is inadequacy in funding a matter of lack of ability to pay, or is the problem the taxpayers' lack of willingness to pay? These, along with many other related questions, now face the public school systems of this country. The crucial problems that the schools face are not always clearly evident, and the dilemma of finding sufficient revenues to finance public education will continue to plague many states.

But schools and education are considered by citizens of the United States to be of high priority and importance. Progress and improvement usually occur over time, in spite of temporary setbacks. There is no valid reason to believe that this will not continue.

SOME CHARACTERISTICS OF EDUCATIONAL STRUCTURE

Certain important elements must serve as the basis for all educational structures and solutions to the financial problems of the day. Education rests on several basic assumptions that receive general but not universal support. Some are more readily accepted than others. Some rest on firm and long-accepted opinion and practice, but others seem destined to undergo periodic change. Some of the principles that this text has also accepted include the following:

1. The perpetuation of the American form of government is dependent upon an informed citizenry, and that can only be attained by the operation of free public schools.

2. Education is a state function because of interpretation of the Tenth Amendment to the U.S. Constitution; financing it is also a state responsibility, for the same reason.

3. State responsibility for education includes the right of the state to require compulsory attendance of those it deems wise to educate.

4. Education enhances the economic development of a country and is an investment in human capital.

5. Education helps protect individual freedom.

6. Education is no longer regarded as a privilege for those who can afford it.

7. Public funds cannot be used to establish or to aid operation of nonpublic schools unless such aid meets the three-pronged test established by the Supreme Court in *Lemon* v. *Kurtzman* (1971).

8. Public funds cannot be used to prevent desegregation or integration of minority groups.

9. School finance programs that provide equal dollars per student lack equity and fairness; weighted-pupil units are a fairer measure of need.

10. A state's or nation's efforts to support education are more important for social and economic progress than the extent of natural resources found within its boundaries.

11. All but a few citizens should pay taxes for the services of government especially education; some may miss one or more forms of taxation, but few should miss all forms.

12. The ability-to-pay principle of taxation and the benefit principle are both justifiable in providing funds for education.

13. Education is not just a necessary "evil" sponsored and financed by government; it is an investment in future generations.

14. Providing adequate funds for education will give a district or a school the opportunity to produce (but will not guarantee) a good educational program; inadequate funds, however, will guarantee a poor program.

SCHOOL FINANCE GOALS

In the years ahead, school finance programs will undoubtedly change, but in what direction? It is hoped that reform will continue in the direction of providing greater equity of revenues to school districts on the basis of real need and greater equity in sharing the costs on the basis of better measures of ability to pay. School finance programs in the future should:

1. Support education at high enough levels to provide programs appropriate to the unique needs and personal differences of children.

2. Provide a high degree of equity and equality of educational opportunity for all children.

3. Provide greater state financial support of education but at the same time leave much of its control in the hands of local school boards.

4. Clarify the role of each of the three levels of government in financing education and determine the proportionate share of cost that each should pay.

5. Motivate minority children to attend twelve years of schooling in the same proportions as white children.

6. Provide school finance laws that recognize not only the problems and inequities in small schools but also those in large city districts.

7. Eliminate the amount of adult and child illiteracy that continues to exist, particularly among minority groups, in spite of our free educational system.

8. Apply appropriate legal answers to the controversial problem of allocating public funds for the operation of nonpublic schools.

9. Make major improvements in the assessment and administration of the property tax until better ways of financing education can be substituted for this form of tax.

10. Provide less restrictive procedures for local districts to pay for capital improvements and provide additional state support. This involves equitable practices in securing funds for capital outlays, with less reliance on property tax.

11. Eliminate fiscal dependence on other governmental bodies for those districts that still must operate under this handicap.

12. Provide financial support on an equitable basis for extension of the school year well beyond the nine months now used in most school districts.

13. Provide free education to adults who did not obtain it in their younger years but who now seek it for cultural, social, or economic reasons.

14. Extend the years of formal education downward to include nursery school education for three- and four-year-olds—particularly those from homes where these important years of growth and development are misspent or wasted.

15. Solve the problem of teacher-board negotiations in such a way that all additional funds provided by legislative bodies to improve local school district educational programs are not funnelled into salaries, to the detriment of other important parts of the school program.

16. Develop a way to educate people who are denied a full life by a lack of education and vocational skills.

THE CHALLENGE

The decade of the 1990s is fraught with challenges for local boards of education and administrators who must determine the direction for education. There is greater involvement than ever before from forces that are influencing local decisions and in one way or another will affect the financing structure. The turn of the century looms as the magical target date for elementary and secondary schools to have a "new face." Pressures for change have emerged from:

- *AMERICA 2000*: national goals proposed by the president and adopted by the nation's governors.
- Business and industry: willing to provide some revenue through partnerships but demanding a voice in curriculum development and requiring accountability in return.
- Choice: programs that allow parents and students more opportunity for educational options.
- Diminishing local control: some scholars emphasizing that the present system is obsolete.
- The courts: requiring some states to restructure school finance formulas to provide clearer equity for students, including capital-outlay budgets.
- Parent and teacher involvement: decision making through site-based management programs.

- New American Schools Development Corporation: providing $1 million to one school in each congressional district to develop models for other schools to emulate.
- National Standards for Teaching as a Profession: proposed by the Carnegie Task Force on Teaching as a Profession.
- Strategic Planning or Other Goal-Setting Plans: often done at the state level outlining unrealistic goals for education with little involvement from the local level.

These pressures are exacerbated as they are meshed with other more evasive forces that educational leaders must consider in determining the education structure during the next decade. This includes projecting the future in the areas of:

- *Demographics*
  —Echo baby boom: could equal the baby boom of the 1960s.
  —Population shift: some states losing enrollment and others gaining it.
  —Growth in urban areas: with its attendant problems.
  —Family makeup: dramatic alterations in the typical family, more children by teenaged mothers, and more single-parent families.
  —Minorities: major growth of numbers in the public schools.
- *Inflation/deflation*: either has an impact on school budgets.
- *Interest rates*: districts often depend on interest money for additional revenue to stretch tight maintenance and operation budgets. Interest rates affect bonding in capital-outlay budgets.
- *Tax limitation measures*: more demand to control taxes and more limitations in some states.
- *Federal deficit*: has reached such epic proportions that interest payments on the national debt and deficit financing are the largest federal outlays.
- *Risk management*: analyzing preventative measures of risk often require unexpected expenditures.
- *Fringe benefits*: significant increases in health and accident insurance premiums, social security, and retirement benefits.

Educators in past generations may debate that these issues are no more critical than those they experienced. This may be true in some respects. However, the challenges listed above facing future education leaders would indicate that some of the finest minds and most capable persons are needed to meet the demands of educating the youth of this nation. Any list of unsolved problems in financing education could be extended to any length, but there is little value in doing so. The point is that in spite of progress and reform of considerable proportions there is much to be done to improve the financing of education in this country. No reasonable person expects that this will be achieved or that all the problems involved will ever be solved, for the solution of one difficulty often creates others. But educators, legislators, and parents have the responsibility and the challenge to work toward these and other desirable goals. The price may be high, but the rewards are great, in terms of the welfare, the education, and the future of millions of children.

SUMMARY

School finance reform in the 1990s, and into the twenty-first century will undoubtedly be affected by economic conditions, inflation or deflation, taxation policies, legislation, philosophies, and court action. Progress will continue to be enhanced by the actions of numerous states supporting improvements. The new laws that are enacted will continue to bring greater equity and excellence to the financing of education, in the interest of the children who are being educated, but also with greater equity and fairness to the taxpayers who pay the costs.

School finance reform is an ongoing process that is necessary in the operation of public schools. Just as in the past, mistakes made in the name of reform and progress will often be followed by reversals. Over time, innovations and changes will continue to keep public school education in the forefront of the achievements of the United States.

ASSIGNMENT PROJECTS

1. Determine to what extent states have adopted restrictive taxation laws. What have been the general results of such legislation in terms of curriculum curtailment and substitution of other taxes to make up for property tax reductions?
2. What are the areas of greatest school finance needs in your state, and what are the biggest obstacles in meeting those needs?
3. Outline the specific characteristics and provisions of a school finance system that would provide maximum equity for the school children and the taxpayers of your state.
4. Present information to show what the probable direction of school finance reform will be in the next decade, particularly in your own state.

SELECTED READINGS

Black, Theodore M. *Straight Talk about American Education.* New York: Harcourt Brace Jovanovich, 1982.

Boyer, Ernest. *High School: A Report on Secondary Education in America.* New York: Harper Colophon Books, 1983.

Candoli, I. Carl. *School District Administration: Strategic Planning for Site Based Management.* Lancaster, PA: Technomics Publishing, 1990.

Chubb, J. E., and T. M. Moe. *Politics, Markets, and America's Schools.* Washington, D.C.: Brookings Institution, 1990.

Committee on Science, Engineering and Public Policy. *High Schools and the Changing Workplace: The Employer's View.* Washington, D.C.: National Academy of Sciences, 1984.

Goodlad, John I. *A Place Called School: Prospects for the Future.* New York: McGraw-Hill, 1984.

Hodgkinson, Harold L. *All One System: Demographics of Education, Kindergarten through Graduate School.* Washington, D.C.: Institute for Educational Leadership, Inc., 1985.

Mueller, Van D., and Mary P. McKeown. *The Fiscal, Legal, and Political Aspects of State Reform of Elementary and Secondary Education. Sixth Annual Yearbook of the American Education Finance Association.* Cambridge, Mass.: Ballinger, 1985.

National Commission on Excellence in Education. *A Nation At Risk: The Imperative for Educational Reform.* Washington, D.C.: U.S. Government Printing Office, 1983.

Appendix

Some Important Federal Programs

The following outline summarizes some important federal activities that have contributed to American education in the last two centuries. The list is not intended to be complete; the total number of such programs is not known, and their total impact on education can never be measured. They are listed here in terms of general purpose rather than in a strictly chronological order. Discussion of most programs is brief, and objective evaluation has not been attempted.

FEDERAL EDUCATIONAL ACTIVITIES

1. Ordinance of 1785 (land grants)
   1.1 Provided:"There shall be reserved the Lot No. 16 of every township for the maintenance of public schools, within said township."
   1.2 A result of New England colony policy of granting lands to endow education.
2. The Northwest Ordinance of 1787 (land grants)
   2.1 Based on the Bill of Rights for Education—"Religion, morality and knowledge being necessary to good government and the happiness of mankind, schools and the means of education shall forever be encouraged."
   2.2 Became effective when Ohio became a state in 1802, with the provision that Section 16 of every township should be "granted to the inhabitants of such township for the use of schools." In 1803,

Congress provided that control of such land shall "be vested in the legislature of that state." This policy was followed from 1802 to 1848; twelve states received such a grant.

2.3 When the Oregon Territory was established in 1848, Congress provided for Sections 16 and 36 to be given for education to states newly entering the Union; fourteen states received such a grant.

2.4 Utah (1896), Arizona (1911), and New Mexico (1911) received Sections 2, 16, 32, and 36 for education.

2.5 Results: strengthened the position of the states as responsible agents for education; was a real factor in helping the states build their public school systems; a few states managed their lands and funds wisely, whereas others were guilty of gross mismanagement.

2.6 A good example of general federal aid to education without federal control; guidelines may have been unwisely omitted—they would have reduced mismanagement.

3. Other land and money grants (1802 to 1850)

3.1 Grants of funds in lieu of land grants in Indian territory.

3.2 Land grants under the Internal Improvement Act of 1841.

3.3 Saline land grants (beginning in 1802).

3.4 Grants of 5 percent of the funds received by the federal government from the sale of public lands in the states.

3.5 Payments to the states of 25 percent of income from national forests and 37.5 percent received from the extraction of nonmetallic minerals for the benefit of roads and public schools.

3.6 Allocation of surplus federal revenues to the states (1836).

4. Morrill Acts (establishment of agricultural colleges)

4.1 Morrill Act (1862) provided federal land grants of 30,000 acres of land for each senator and representative in Congress for establishment of a college or colleges "where the leading object shall be, without excluding other scientific and classical studies, and including military tactics, to teach such branches of learning as are related to agriculture and the mechanic arts—in order to promote the liberal and practical education of the industrial classes in the several pursuits and professions of life."

4.11 Received much opposition at first; viewed as encroachment by the federal government.

4.12 Began the policy of federal restrictions and controls; the first categorical aid law.

4.13 A significant decision by government that made possible a national system of higher education.

4.2 Second Morrill Act (1890)

4.21 Strengthened the original act by providing funds to each state "to be applied only to instruction in agriculture, the mechanic arts, the English language and the various branches of mathematical, physical, natural, and economic science."

4.3 All states benefited from the Morrill Acts; 69 land grant colleges were established in the 48 states and 3 territories.

4.4 Control over these colleges has been negligible; their curricula have been liberalized well beyond their original emphasis on agriculture and engineering.

5. Acts supplementing the activities of the land grant colleges
    5.1 The Hatch Act (1887) provided for each land-grant college the establishment of experiment stations for the purpose of conducting research in agriculture.
    5.2 The Hatch Act, along with the Adams Act (1906), the Purnell Act (1925), the Bankhead-Jones Act (1935), the Research and Marketing Act (1946), and others, contributed greatly to experimentation in agriculture, with the result that the United States became the most productive of all nations.

6. Vocational education acts
    6.1 The Smith-Lever Act (1914) provided for extension services by home demonstration agents, by 4-H leaders, and by county agricultural agents, and for services and professional training of such teachers.
    6.2 The Smith-Hughes Act (1917) provided about $7,000,000 annually in funds for pre-college-age vocational education; annual appropriations provided for vocational education in agriculture, home economics, and trades and industry.
        6.21 The first special-purpose grants made to public schools by Congress.
        6.22 Strongly influenced public education toward its vocational programs.
        6.23 The act was broadened by the George-Reed Act (1929), the George-Ellzey Act (1935), the George-Deen Act (1937), the George-Barden Act (1946), and the Vocational Education Act (1963; amended in 1968).
    6.3 George-Deen Act added $12 million annually to the same purposes as the Smith-Hughes Act and added distributive education.
    6.4 George-Barden Act increased funds for vocational education: its Title II provided federal funds for practical nursing education; it provided for many federal restrictions and controls.
    6.5 National Defense Education Act (1958); Title VIII amended the George-Barden Act, adding a new Title III authorizing $15 million annually for area vocational schools (for five years).
    6.6 Vocational Education Act (1963): regarded by many as a milestone in vocational education history; provided grants-in-aid to the states increasing from $60 million in 1964 to $225 million in 1967 and each subsequent year; one-third to be spent for the construction of area vocational schools or operating programs for out-of-school youths.
    6.7 Education amendments (Title II—1976)

      6.71 New programs in vocational education—to provide youth part-time employment, improve innovative vocational programs, conduct dropout programs for youth in areas of high unemployment, to eliminate sex stereotyping in vocational curriculum areas.

      6.72 To provide discretionary funds to support projects designed to improve the nation's vocational education programs. To provide special grants for Indian tribes and organizations, opportunities for full-time study by vocational education teachers; encourages persons to become teachers of vocational education and provides for emergency remodeling and renovating of vocational facilities.

7. School lunch programs (1935—)

    7.1 In 1935, the newly established Federal Surplus Commodities Corporation provided for surplus foods to be distributed to schools for lunches for pupils.

      7.11 Expanded in 1940 to include milk.

      7.12 Later the Department of Agriculture began to make cash payments to reimburse part of the food costs of school lunches.

    7.2 The School Lunch Act (1946) (as amended by PLs 95-166, 95-627, and 97-35)—" . . . as a measure of national security, to safeguard the health and well-being of the nation's children and to encourage the domestic consumption of nutritious agricultural commodities and other food by assisting the states through grants-in-aid and other means."

      7.21 Distribution was to be on an equalization basis.

      7.22 Required state matching funds on a progressively increasing ratio.

      7.23 Available to both public and nonpublic schools.

      7.24 Amended in 1962 and 1963 to direct more federal funds to areas of low wealth.

      7.25 Participating schools were required to (1) serve lunches that meet prescribed nutritional standards, (2) use foods declared by the Department of Agriculture to be in abundance, (3) provide free lunches for children unable to pay for them, and (4) maintain adequate records for federal auditing purposes.

    7.3 National School Lunch and Child Nutrition Amendments (1977)

      7.31 Provides cash grants and donations for breakfasts for school children, a special milk program, grants to schools in low-income areas for the procurement of equipment, funds to assist states in operating summer month programs, funds for special school projects, and grants for development of comprehensive nutrition information and education projects.

8. Relief and emergency programs

    8.1 Civilian Conservation Corps (CCC) (1933–1943): an act designed to relieve unemployed youth by "restoration of the country's depleted natural resources and the advancement of an orderly program of useful public works."

8.11 Work relief for men 17–22 years of age.

8.12 Helped restore depleted natural resources.

8.13 Provided camps where enrollees were housed and provided for low wages while they built dams, bridges, picnic areas, and did other useful work.

8.14 Carried on organized educational activities that became a kind of parallel school system rivaling state school systems in some respects.

8.2 National Youth Administration (NYA) (1935–1944): Established by executive order of the president.

8.21 Organized to provide work relief for unemployed youth 16–25 years of age.

8.22 Provided part-time employment in practical activities.

8.23 Enabled some secondary school and college students to continue their education; many others learned occupational skills.

8.3 The Federal Emergency Relief Administration (1933)

8.31 Superseded by the Works Progress Administration in 1939.

8.32 One of the many "pump-priming" activities of the federal government designed to get money in circulation and bring economic relief to people during the Depression.

8.33 Conducted programs in school building construction and maintenance, adult education, vocational rehabilitation, and in many other areas.

8.4 Public Works Administration (PWA) (1933)

8.41 Made grants for public building construction on a 30 percent of cost basis; later 45 percent.

8.42 Made loans for school construction.

8.5 These emergency programs were inaugurated as relief measures during the Depression of the 1930s. Stimulation of the economy was the main consideration; educational programs and benefits were secondary in importance.

8.6 Youth Employment and Demonstrative Project Act (1977)

8.61 Amended the Comprehensive Employment and Training Act of 1973. Designed to establish a program with significant long-term impact on youth employment and career opportunities.

8.7 Emergency School Aid Act (See Section 15).

9. Programs in the war on poverty

9.1 Area Redevelopment Act (1961)

9.11 Aimed at areas of poverty.

9.12 Established programs to alleviate conditions of unemployment by providing for orderly referral of unemployed people who could benefit from occupational training.

9.2 Manpower Development and Training Act (1962)

9.21 "The purpose of this act is to require the federal government to appraise the manpower requirements and resources of the Nation, and to develop and apply the information and methods needed to deal with the problems of unemployment resulting from automation and technological changes and other types of persistent unemployment."

9.22 Aid for vocational education to help solve economic problems.

9.3 Economic Opportunity Act (1964)

9.31 "To eliminate the paradox of poverty and pools of long-term joblessness in the midst of plenty in the nation by opening to everyone opportunity for education and training, the opportunity to work, and the opportunity to live in decency and dignity."

9.32 Provided vocational education and training in the Job Corps; focused on the special needs of a small minority of youths who because of educational deficiency are at a competitive disadvantage in the labor market.

9.4 Head Start (Title V, Economic Opportunity Act of 1967, as amended by PLs 93-644, 95-568, and 97-35, 1982)
The program was designed to assist economically disadvantaged preschool children with a range of developmental services.

9.5 Follow Through (sections 661–669—PL 97-35, Omnibus Budget Reconciliation Act of 1981)
Designed to assist in the development of economically disadvantaged children in kindergarten through third grade and to continue working for educational gains achieved in Head Start Programs or other high-quality preschool programs.

9.6 Comprehensive Employment and Training Act (1973)

9.61 Title I provides job training and employment opportunities for economically disadvantaged, unemployed, and underemployed.

9.62 Title II provides for public service employment in areas of high unemployment.

9.7 Emergency Jobs and Unemployment Act (1974)—Title VI designed to help establish job opportunities for low-income unemployed.

9.8 Teacher Corps (Education Amendments, 1976)—to establish a program for education opportunities for children in low-income areas.

10. High-quality education programs

10.1 The National Science Foundation (1950)

10.11 The Foundation was created "to promote the progress of science; to advance the national health, prosperity and welfare; to secure the national defense; and for other purposes."

10.12 Provided no direct funds for school districts or state departments of education.

10.13 Provided for payments to colleges and universities, and to nonprofit research and professional organizations.

10.14 Its programs were established to help increase the number of science and mathematics teachers and provide new instructional materials for public schools.

10.2 National Defense Education Act (1958)

10.21 Purposes: to strengthen national defense by increasing the supply of competent teachers; provided financial assistance to public schools to improve instruction in mathematics, science, and foreign languages; encouraged states to improve guidance programs; provided funds for research in the use of instructional media.

10.22 Its provisions were extended in 1963 to include other areas and functions.

10.3 The Cooperative Research Program (1954)

10.31 Program was established in the U.S Office of Education to contract with higher education institutions to conduct research, surveys, and studies in education.

10.32 Funds allotted were very limited; results were good in shaping and defining educational research.

10.4 National Endowment for the Arts and the Humanities Act (1965) and as amended—P.L. 91-346

10.41 Funds made available to develop aesthetic awareness of the arts, and to strengthen teaching and learning of the humanities.

10.5 Environmental Education Act (91-516) as amended by the Education Amendments (1974) supports research and demonstration through pilot projects with environmental quality and ecological balance.

10.6 Educational amendments (1978)

10.61 Preschool Partnership Program—to provide a more successful transition of Head Start students in regular school programs.

10.62 Health Education—a program to prepare students to "maintain physical health and well-being and prevent illnesses and diseases."

10.63 Biomedical sciences—encourages economically disadvantaged students to pursue a career in biomedical science.

10.7 Elementary and Secondary Education Act (1965)

10.71 Considered a "breakthrough" in the controversy over federal aid.

10.72 Authorized more than $1 billion for education.

10.73 Contained "titles" authorizing educational programs for educationally deprived children of low-income families, improvement of school libraries and instructional material centers, stimulation of educational research, and improvement of state departments of education.

10.74 Designed to help bring economic and social equality to blacks, the poor, the underprivileged, and the educationally disadvantaged.

10.75 Elementary and Secondary Education Act (1965) as amended (1978). Title I—to extend and improve compensatory education in state-supported schools.

10.76 Education and Consolidation and Improvement Act (ECIA–PL 97-35)(1982), Hawkins-Stafford School Improvement Amendments of 1988.

10.77 Chapter 1 superseded Title I of original Elementary and Secondary Education Act of 1965 and subsequent amendments. Very little change from that legislation, but does allow local education agencies more leeway.

10.78 Chapter 2 established a single block grant for the states, incorporating some 30 categorical programs from older legislation.

10.79 Reauthorized programs operated directly by the state educational agency, including Migrant Education, Neglected and Delinquent Children, etc.

11. Programs of direct federal responsibility

11.1 The Citizenship Act of 1924

11.11 Accelerated the shift of Indian education from predominantly church-operated schools to federally operated schools.

11.2 The Johnson-O'Malley Act (1934)

11.21 Authorized contracts with the states for the education of Indians.

11.3 A variety of educational programs, principally vocational, for adult Indians.

11.4 Federal programs for veterans include:

11.41 The Vocational Rehabilitation Program of 1943 for disabled veterans emphasized the need for vocational advisory services and vocational rehabilitation training.

11.42 The G.I. Bill of Rights (Servicemen's Readjustment Act of 1944)—to encourage the education of war veterans. The bill resulted in benefits to thousands of World War II and other war veterans.

11.43 War Orphans Educational Assistance Act of 1956

11.44 Veterans' Readjustment Assistance Act of 1952

11.5 Indian Self-Determination and Education Assistance Act (1974)

11.51 Allows Indian organizations to operate their own programs under contractual agreement with the government.

11.52 Provides for vocational training and employment for Indians.

11.6 Indian Elementary and Secondary School Assistance Act (P.L. 81-874)

11.61 Assist with special educational needs of Indian students.

11.62 To plan, develop, and implement supplemental programs and program centers to increase Indian student educational opportunities.

11.63 To improve educational opportunities for Indian adults.

12. Federal programs in lieu of taxes

12.1 The federal government uses three different methods to determine how much it should pay local school districts or other local units of government in lieu of funds lost by the taxexempt status of federal property.

12.11 Payments based on the value of the federal property multiplied by the local tax rate (for some types of tax-exempt property).

12.12 Payments from public lands include 12.5 percent of revenue from grazing fees in national grazing districts, 50 percent of grazing fees on other federal lands, and 37.5 percent of revenues collected from mineral rights on federal lands.

12.13 The use of Public Laws 815 and 874. Here federal payments are related to the number of public school children that are added to the school district because of federal programs. Public Law 815 provides funds for the construction of school facilities; 874 provides operating funds in eligible impacted areas; the future of these two laws is uncertain.

13. Special emphasis programs

13.1 Special Projects Act—Education Amendments (1974 and 1978)

13.11 Career Education—to demonstrate teaching career education.

13.12 Metric Education—to encourage teaching of the metric system.

13.13 Gifted and Talented Children Program—funds for planning for teaching the gifted.

13.14 Community Education—to expand and improve community education.

13.15 Women's Educational Equity Program—to eliminate sex inequities in policies and practices in education.

13.16 Elementary and Secondary School Arts Education—to promote integration of the arts into public schools.

13.2 Basic Skills Improvement Education Amendments (1978)—funds for planning and evaluating programs dealing with basic skills.

13.3 Improvement in Local Educational Practices—Title IV-C Education Amendments—1978. To help meet needs of local education agencies.

13.4 Bilingual Education Act (90-247) (amended by PL 95-561)—to promote programs utilizing bilingual concepts in teaching children with limited English-speaking ability.

13.5 Indo-Chinese Refugee Children Assistance Act (1976)—to assist in educating students from Viet Nam, Cambodia, and Laos.

13.6 School Finance Study (1978). Funds for a national study of school finance.

13.7 Aid for Neglected and Delinquent Children (ESEA, 1965, as amended by PLs 95-561 and 97-35, 1982)

Provides aid for state agencies that are responsible for providing special education programs for children in institutions for the neglected and delinquent or in adult correctional institutions.

13.8 Migrant Education (ESEA 1965, as amended by PLs 95-561 and 97-35, 1982)—a program designated to meet special educational needs of migrant children of agriculture workers and fishermen.

14. Education of the handicapped

14.1 Education of the Handicapped Act, Title VI (P.L. 91-230). Provides for free services, instructional media, preschool programs, auxiliary services, increases in the numbers of teaching personnel who teach the handicapped.

14.2 Education of the handicapped (as amended by P.L. 95-49).

    14.21 Funds for development of demonstration projects, research programs including physical education and recreation.

    14.22 Funds for programs for postsecondary or adult programs for the handicapped.

15. Desegregation programs

15.1 Education Amendments (1972–1974)—to assist in decreasing isolation of minority groups, support innovative programs for improving academic programs of minority children, enhance intercultural and interethnic understanding, to provide support of special programs such as art and mathematics.

15.2 Civil Rights Act (1964)—to assist school systems and school personnel in resolving problems related to educational desegregation.

15.3 Emergency School Aid Act—and as amended by Educational Amendments (1976). A program for the development of magnet schools and planning neutral sites in cooperation with universities and businesses.

The foregoing examples of federal activities in education illustrate the diversity and the extent of such programs. The list could easily be extended, but to no useful purpose. The average reader will no doubt approve highly of some but question the contribution of others to American education. Some will criticize the imbalance that many of these federal activities have tended to create in the public schools, and others will accept them in lieu of more appropriate general federal aid to education. A list of all federal programs is contained in the *Federal Domestic Assistance Catalogue,* published annually by the United States government.

Index